D0757183

Also by Pierre Birnbaum

❧

The Idea of France

Jewish Destinies:
Citizenship, State, and Community
in Modern France

Anti-Semitism in France:
A History from 1789 to the Present

States and Collective Action:
The European Experience

The Heights of Power:
An Essay on the Power Elite in France

The Jews of the Republic: A Political History of
State Jews in France from Gambetta to Vichy

The Anti-Semitic Moment

The

Anti-Semitic

Moment

A Tour of France in 1898

PIERRE BIRNBAUM

Translated by Jane Marie Todd

The University of Chicago Press

Chicago & London

The University of Chicago Press, Chicago 60637
Copyright © 1998 by Librairie Arthème Fayard
Translation copyright © 2003 by Jane Marie Todd
All rights reserved.
Published by arrangement with Hill and Wang,
a division of Farrar, Straus and Giroux, LLC
University of Chicago Press edition 2011
Printed in the United States of America

20 19 18 17 16 15 14 13 12 11   1 2 3 4 5

ISBN: 978-0-226-05206-9 (paper)
ISBN: 0-226-05206-0 (paper)

Library of Congress Cataloging-in-Publication Data

Birnbaum, Pierre.
[Moment antisémite. English. 2011]
The anti-semitic moment : a tour of France in 1898 / Pierre Birnbaum;
translated by Jane Marie Todd.   p. cm.
Includes bibliographical references and index.
ISBN-13: 978-0-226-05206-9 (pbk. : alk. paper)
ISBN-10: 0-226-05206-0 (pbk. : alk. paper) 1. Antisemitism—
France—History—19th century. 2. France—Ethnic relations.
3. Jews—France—Social conditions—19th century. 4. France—
History—Third Republic, 1870–1940. 5. France—Politics and
government—1870–1940. I. Todd, Jane Marie, 1957– II. Title.
DS146.F8B5613 2011
305.892'404409034—dc22
2010041423

♾ This paper meets the requirements of
ANSI/NISO Z39.48-1992 (Permanence of Paper).

To my father

Contents

ENGLAND

London

NETHERLANDS

Rhine R.

Brussels

BELGIUM

GERMANY

English Channel

Dieppe

LUX!

Cherbourg

Le Havre

Rouen

Seine R.

Caen

Paris

Nancy

Épinal

Rhine R.

Brest

Saint-Malo

Orléans

Vesoul

Lorient

Rennes

Loire R.

Dijon

Besançon

Vannes

Angers

Tours

FRANCE

SWITZERLAND

Saint-Nazaire

Nantes

Atlantic Ocean

La Roche-sur-Yon

Montluçon

Moulins

Rhône R.

La Rochelle

Guéret

Clermont-Ferrand

Lyon

ITALY

Limoges

Saint Étienne

Périgueux

Brive-la-Gaillarde

Le Puy

Bordeaux

Garonne R.

Bay of Biscay

Cahors

Rodez

Carpentras

Digne

Nîmes

Pau

Tarbes

Toulouse

Montpellier

Avignon

Béziers

Marseilles

Carcassonne

Perpignan

SPAIN

Mediterranean Sea

0 Miles   100   200

0 Kilometers   200

© 2002 Jeffrey L. Ward

The Anti-Semitic Moment

Introduction

In January 1898 Emile Zola published "J'accuse," a denunciation of the civil and military authorities who had convicted a captain in the French Army, Alfred Dreyfus, of treason. What followed was the "anti-Semitic moment," a pogrom without fatalities that nevertheless threatened to topple France. It was a return to a time of imprecations and violence. A country on the threshold of modernity experienced the unexpected shock of a new religious war reminiscent of the Crusades. This time it was waged in the name of extreme nationalism, a convenient banner behind which Catholics, Boulangists,* reactionaries, and even republicans fell in line. The defenders of Dreyfus and the Jews were quite alone. For once the "war of the two Frances," which has regularly punctuated the history of that nation, magically evaporated. Cries of "France for the French!" "Down with Zola!" and "Death to the Jews!" rose from one camp, and "The Republic for the republicans!" "Long live the army!" and "Down with the Jews!" from the other. For

---

*Boulangists: followers of Georges Boulanger, a French general and politician who, in January 1889, nearly brought about a coup d'état.—trans.

a time the Enlightenment almost disappeared from the French hexagon.

It looked as if the anti-Semitic moment would sweep everything away, break down barriers, unite enemies. Hatred of the Jews drew from every possible source: the traditional anti-Judaism of the Catholic world; the renewed denunciation of usury, now transformed into a rejection of Semitic capitalism; the visceral fear of conspiracy and treason; a reactivated fear of the "Prussians"; and fantasies of racial degeneration. France was well placed for a game of fabrication and finger-pointing: in the cities and in sleepy towns, an anti-Semitic revolt erupted. Though fed by ancient undercurrents, it was resolutely modern in its expression.

This anti-Semitic moment was subsequently erased from historical consciousness, eclipsed by the Dreyfus affair itself or, later, by the Vichy regime; it lay dormant, deep in unmined archives. A great deal is known about the Dreyfus affair: the power of propaganda, the inventiveness of artists and writers, the frenzy of the press, the passion of the politicians, and the extent of the prejudice, which existed even within the institutions of the republican government. But virtually nothing is known about the streets, the demonstrations, the parades, the marches, the racket, or the burned effigies during the affair. Nothing is known about the vociferous and out-of-control mobs, their screams, their slogans, their songs, or about the intermittent attacks on merchants who were Jewish or taken for Jewish, or about the rage to destroy their shops or break down the doors of synagogues.

Just when it looked as if everything were collapsing, when citizens were being cornered and the state and its leaders were doing nothing to help, the state apparatus suddenly mounted a resistance and held fast, and the worst outcome was avoided. The institution of the state did not give way. No one would make fools of the prefectural corps, the police, and the gendarmerie, who maintained public order and suffered blows to protect the Jews and the civil peace. Even when firearms went off and caused panic, and when blades of all sorts appeared from the rioters' pockets, police officers and gendarmes tirelessly cleared the streets, made mass arrests, and protected shops, office buildings, and synagogues.

The type of account I am about to give has never before been attempted. It is a new kind of tour of France, a random wandering from one department seat to another. I have put my faith in an unbridled microhistory that departs from conventional methods and leaves room for improvisation. This tour of anti-Semitic France turns its back on meticulous research methods, on the desire to explain, on the goal of providing the carefully selected evidentiary proof, on quantifying and demonstrating how the variables were constructed, and on reaching definitive conclusions. In 1898, just before the dawn of a new century, French society and French mores were in a state of confusion. This alone warrants that we pause, without worrying about the eternal distinction between "limestone" and "granite" evidence, without paying heed to cultural or social divisions, supposedly the only factors to produce meaning, and without lingering over each region's long traditions to discover a decisive guiding thread. The confusion that has blurred reference points had a source. From the time "J'accuse" was published until Zola's trials, in February and April 1898, from the legislative elections of May 1898 until the last days of December, and, to varying degrees, up to the trial in Rennes, French society, both openly and covertly, abandoned itself in great measure to a multiform anti-Semitism. Of course, even today people will sometimes proclaim that anti-Semitism was not at the heart of the Dreyfus affair, that it was a secondary factor. As in the case of the Vichy regime, there is a danger of "Judeocentrism," but there is also a risk of underestimating the anti-Jewish sentiment. I will not settle the matter here through multivariate analyses, carefully compiled statistics, or unassailable geographical charts.

Rather, by randomly exploring the archives, by moving from place to place, drawn to one thing or another, I shall build my account on everything and on nothing. As I plunge into the local and immerse myself in the daily life of the provinces to listen in on the Dreyfus affair, I shall depend a great deal on intuition, on the desire to reimagine one province or another, one city or another, in the grip of the affair. It is up to readers to decide whether this archival fishing expedition is productive.

I hope that readers will at least give me the benefit of the doubt, that they will imagine in turn the apprentice "historian of the local" in his endless travels, his lonely days and nights brightened by the daily harvest of departmental archives, at the mercy of everyone's goodwill. I hope that readers, confronted with so much disorder, so many liberties taken with the rules of research as it should be conducted, will forgive my somewhat vagabond "taste for the local archives." It will quickly become clear that, in addition to the risks of reaching the saturation point, of being overly repetitive—something that can have no demonstrative value—and of becoming dangerously absorbed in the material itself, I faced another formidable difficulty as I dived headlong into the local, namely, that of resorting too often to quotation. And clearly, "that captivated restitution is insufficient."[1]

All the same, it was worth the gamble, if only to stake out a territory to better explore later by the rules. It was particularly worthwhile since the only book dealing with the anti-Semitic moment in France, Stephen Wilson's remarkable but already old study,[2] relies solely on the filtered and slanted archives centralized in Paris. But they are merely the tip of the iceberg and hence wholly inadequate. I took a preliminary look at that material, but my goal was to anchor the anti-Semitic moment in the local,[3] by slowly moving through two geographical circles that I constructed for the occasion. They differ in their circumference, but both revolve around the center of France.

I can hardly express the pleasure I felt in discovering the infinite treasures of the local archives—too rapidly mined, to be sure—from Périgueux to Nancy; from Rouen to Tarbes; from Bourges to Marseilles; from Angers to Dijon to Le Puy-en-Velay; from Toulouse to La Rochelle; from Caen to Guéret, Montpellier, and Lyon; from Orléans to Bordeaux; from Quimper to Clermont-Ferrand and Bar-le-Duc; from Limoges to Rennes; from Rodez to La Roche-sur-Yon; from Nantes to Pau, Avignon, Tulle, and Nîmes.[4] I barely know how to tell of the joy I experienced in uncovering vast local archives tucked away, forgotten, even in the office of the Paris prefecture; of my amazement when I saw these neat rows of virtually untouched folders. In these local documents daily life can be decoded, a life that presses on and adapts, indifferent to the events.

Do not dwell too much on the weaknesses of this approach compared with the usual methods: it may finally bring to life the protagonists in that forgotten anti-Semitic moment.

C h a p t e r   O n e

Is Paris Burning?

On January 14, 1898, an anonymous police informant sent this alarming report to the Paris prefecture:

> What is about to happen in Paris is a much more dangerous riot: it will have a definite goal, the looting of Jewish shops. Everyone is sick at what has happened; they are stupefied that no one has managed to shut up the German Jewish hirelings, and a movement is manifestly under way. The students? You know about them. The people in the outlying districts? Perhaps I'll tell you about them.
>
> Yesterday I was in Montmartre and Clignancourt listening to the conversations in cafés, at bar counters, and in the streets: the exasperation is universal. These good people, moved by understandable feelings, will be joined by a mob of vagrants who have nothing to lose, fanatical young people, anarchists, enemies of the Jews. I myself know ten employees of Jewish companies who seek only revenge.
>
> Paris is going to see what Algiers and Oran have seen, and what Vienna, Austria, saw a few months ago. When a street movement

has a precise goal, and that is the case here, it is dangerous and will take a long time to quiet. The bourgeois Frenchman by blood will not defend the money-grubbing Jews.[1]

Could it be? The violence of Karl Lueger's Vienna, which thrilled the young Hitler, transposed to Paris? The Algiers and Oran massacres repeated in the City of Light?* Unbelievable. This police report must be erroneous, and its author an inveterate lover of tall tales. Nothing could have suggested such a catastrophic scenario in Paris, where fog would suddenly give way to rain, giving an almost unreal character to the rue du Cherche-Midi, where the war council was meeting. The acquittal of Major Ferdinand Esterhazy on January 11 was well received: it seemed to mark a definitive end to the Dreyfus affair, to forever eliminate the idea of a review of the case. Dreyfus, the deportee to Devil's Island, was truly the traitor. Esterhazy was the embodiment of innocence itself, and with his ringing rehabilitation, the army had recovered all its glory. To be sure, since the early morning of January 10, law enforcement forces had been exercising increased vigilance on the boulevard Saint-Michel and were keeping close watch on the brasseries and cafés of the Latin Quarter. They feared an outburst of joy on the part of students despite the icy rain, an outburst that might have had unforeseeable consequences.

The scene of the acquittal was reported in all the newspapers. From *Le Jour*: "never have we seen a more beautiful, a more grandiose spectacle." *La Libre Parole* described Esterhazy's liberation: "The shouting increases. Shouts of enthusiasm. Shouts of furor. Men weep for joy. A lame man can be seen dancing. In the blink of an eye, that street, previously so calm, is invaded by several thousand people. Cheers for the army are combined with insults hurled at the Jews. From every side, you hear: 'Bandits! Scoundrels! Pigs!' Any Yid who, to his misfortune, might pass by, would be lynched without fail. Canes wave, fists clench. Long live the army! Down with the Jews!"[2] *L'Echo de Paris* rejoiced at "that re-

---

*Algiers and Oran massacres: deadly anti-Jewish riots erupted in Oran in May 1897 and in Algiers in January 1898. They were aimed at abrogating the Crémieux decree, which in 1870 had given French citizenship to the Jewish residents of Algeria and to Jews in metropolitan France.—trans.

lief for the national conscience . . . It is profoundly satisfying for the patriots . . . It was a great error on the part of the Jewish world to have appeared to make common cause with Dreyfus." In *L'Autorité* the anti-Dreyfusard editor and writer Paul de Cassagnac maintained that "the acquittal of Major Esterhazy surprised no one, not even the Jewish gang that went all out for his conviction."

Edouard Drumont, editor of the fiercely anti-Semitic *La Libre Parole*, was triumphant: with this judgment, "the Yids and their accomplices are wallowing in the mud, the filth, the torrent of shit they unleashed and with which they claimed to splatter the army." The same newspaper turned to threats: "To try the Esterhazy trick again would be imprudent, because Populo is not patient and might briskly shut up the sinister Dreyfusian Hebrew face by turning a few lampposts into gallows. We've seen that in Paris in the past, on place de Grève, when the Jews got out of hand." Courageously, the prominent politician Georges Clemenceau denounced the judgment and ended his article in *L'Aurore* with the words, "Truth will find its way. Justice will have its day."

The morning after Esterhazy's acquittal, at the other end of Paris on the place Blanche, across from the Moulin Rouge, the artists of Montmartre, followed by a crowd of working men and women, burned an effigy representing the captain's brother, Mathieu Dreyfus, to celebrate the event. A gallows was set up, and the straw effigy was suspended from a rope. At that moment a long shout erupted: "Let's burn Dreyfus!" And as the flames were rising, the crowd responded by chanting: "The dirty Jews! The dirty Jews! The dirty Jews!" Meanwhile, according to *La Libre Parole*, "the Hebrews of the neighborhood in their shops must have thought their last hour had come."[3]

A day later, on January 13, the bomb that was Zola's "J'accuse" detonated and sent shock waves through Paris and the provinces. Its publication was a turning point in the affair. The police, sensing the probability of demonstrations in spite of the silence still reigning in the streets of Paris, reinforced their monitoring on January 13 and 14, in the Latin Quarter as well as on the boulevard Montmartre, the rue Laffitte, and the rue du Croissant, where the main offices of the major newspapers were located.

The police noted the comings and goings of small groups of students, who crossed the Seine and tried to reach *L'Aurore*, shouting,

"Long live Rochefort!* Down with the Jews!" They closely followed the feverish gatherings of students on the place de la Sorbonne and collected information in the cafés of the Latin Quarter on the demonstrations planned for the next day. When Professor Izoulet's course let out at the Collège de France, his students went to protest in front of *L'Aurore*. During the entire day of January 14, the police pushed back students, only to have them return via adjacent streets. At the Taverne du Panthéon and in many cafés on the rue Soufflot, the students denounced Zola's article and feverishly composed lampoons against the Jews. Several hundred walked out of the law school and went down the boulevard Saint-Michel, shouting, "Down with Zola! Death to the Jews!" while people who had appeared at their windows applauded.

In the afternoon a procession, which some estimated at two thousand students, went up the boulevard Saint-Michel, turned onto the rue Soufflot, and then the rue Cujas, and arrived at the rue des Ecoles, where it ran into a police roadblock. *La Petite République* made fun of the "Catholic and anti-Semitic students, those little gentlemen creating an uproar," while *L'Intransigeant*, *Le Jour*, and *La Libre Parole* congratulated them. When classes let out, the high school students formed another procession that went through the Latin Quarter. Both groups attempted to reach the Théâtre-Français, still shouting, "Out with Scheurer!† Out with Zola! Down with the Jews!" At nightfall about a hundred students, pursued by the police, reached the pont Neuf and attempted to cross the Seine at the pont des Saints-Pères; dispersed by the forces of law and order, they took the quay toward the pont Royal, which they crossed, went through the rue des Tuileries and the rue des Pyramides and past the Opéra, then took the boulevard des Italiens and the boulevard Montmartre, repeating the same slogans along the way. Other students took the rue de Clichy and headed toward the rue de Bruxelles, where Zola lived, before disappearing.[4]

The next day, the fifteenth, the same scenes recurred. A very long report from the police superintendent retraces in detail the different incidents that erupted in the various neighborhoods of Paris. Again, it was

*Rochefort: Henri Rochefort, anti-Semitic journalist; Boulangist leader and editor of *L'Intransigeant*.—trans.
†Scheurer: Auguste Scheurer-Kestner, vice president of the Senate and a Dreyfusard.—trans.

the students from the law school who took the initiative: in the early afternoon, three hundred of them assembled on the place du Panthéon,
danced around a bonfire, climbed through the windows into the closed
law school, ran back out, and—joined by students from the school of
physics, chemistry, and natural history—took the rue Victor-Cousin,
then the boulevard Saint-Michel. They ran into police roadblocks on
the rue Racine and the rue de l'Ecole-de-Médecine, attempted to reach
the rue Médicis, went by the Luxembourg Gardens, back down the rue
d'Assas, and through the rue de Rennes. They then reached the boulevard Saint-Germain, took the rue du Four, then the rue de Sèvres, went
by the Bon Marché, took the rues Vaneau and de Bellechasse, turned
around at the rue de Varenne, and came to the boulevard des Invalides.
Having passed over to the Right Bank, they crossed the Champs-Elysées
and marched up the avenue de Marigny, where they were stopped by the
police. There they took the opportunity to shout, "Death to the Jews!"
in front of the Rothschild mansion, turned off near the rue Royale, entered the Tuileries Gardens through the gate on the place de la Concorde, and crossed the pont des Saints-Pères. Their journey resumed
through the Latin Quarter and finally ended on the boulevard Saint-
Michel. As a police officer reported, "their numbers were constantly
swelling and their excitement increased with their numbers." How many
were there? Between two and three hundred, or between five and fifteen
hundred, depending on the time of day.

Their tour of Paris resumed, particularly since police officers were
now giving chase. The students limited their march to the rue de Richelieu and the Grands Boulevards, which they followed to the place de la
République: "The customers in the neighboring cafés, hearing the
shouts of 'Out with Zola! Death to the Jews!' joined them and considerably swelled their numbers." As the police superintendent observed,
"the demonstrators proved to be more aggressive than they were the day
before yesterday. So it was that, on the avenue des Champs-Elysées, they
insulted several people out walking, followed by chauffeur-driven carriages, calling them 'dirty Jews!' " *La Libre Parole* reveled in that ardor:
"Like scalded rats, the Jews no longer know which way to turn . . . On
every street corner came the sharp cry: 'Down with the Jews!' "

Late in the evening the students could be found on the boulevard
Saint-Germain but also on the rue Soufflot or, on the other bank of the

Seine, the rue de Turenne, the rue des Filles-du-Calvaire, and the rue de Bretagne, then the rue Réaumur and finally the rue Montmartre, where students from Condorcet high school joined them. That night a meeting was held at Tivoli Hall, during which the anarchists Louise Michel and Sébastien Faure denounced anti-Semitism as "a pretext by means of which the monarchist Catholics might put the Republic in mortal danger, provided the people are dupes to that clever diversion." When the meeting let out, there were confrontations on the boulevards. At about midnight Paris finally recovered its calm.[5]

On January 16, in the neighborhood of the place Vendôme, an imposing ceremony took place in honor of the retirement of General Saussier, the governor of Paris. An enormous crowd assembled on the rue de Castiglione, the rue de la Paix, and the rue de Rivoli, extending to the Tuileries. Behind the military band, in close ranks, paraded the veterans of the Crimean and Mexican Wars, the veterans of Gravelotte in 1870–71,* the Alsace-Lorraine societies, and the Veterans of Land and Sea Armies, all of whom advanced behind their flags. The ceremony took place in peace but after the crowd dispersed, cries of "Out with Zola! Long live the army! Down with the Jews!" could again be heard on the rue de Rivoli. *La Libre Parole*, exaggerating the event as was its habit, maintained there were "twenty thousand people who booed Zola and the Jews . . . Everywhere in Paris the implacable rallying cry rose up: 'Death to the Jews!' " A large group, estimated by several police reports at two thousand students, formed in front of the statue of Joan of Arc and, via the rue Sainte-Anne, the rue des Petits-Champs, and then the rue Montmartre, attempted to reach the rue de Bruxelles, where Zola lived, shouting, "Down with the Jews! Death to the Jews!" They finally came to the boulevard Haussmann, number 184, the home of the Dreyfuses. They tried to break in, knocking down the building superintendent, but suddenly found themselves face to face with intrepid police officers who barred the way to the stairwells, "elbowing their way through, and who were almost roughed up." The group then left through the faubourg Saint-Honoré.

Another, smaller group of students went up toward the Bastille,

---

*Gravelotte: the scene of one of the most important battles of the Franco-Prussian War. —trans.

while yet another, with more than a thousand demonstrators, took the rue Rambuteau, the rue Vert-Bois, the rue Volta, and the passage du Pont-aux-Biches to reach the boulevard de Sébastopol. They ran into the police on the corner of the rue de Turbigo, then headed toward the Latin Quarter. The processions were composed not only of college students but also, as *Le Journal* noted, of "heterogeneous elements, apprentices, schoolboys, salaried workers, kitchen boys, etc." Stones were thrown at stores whose owners were thought to be Jewish. On the rue du Cardinal-Lemoine, the crowd was led, according to a police report, by one person "carrying a frying pan, another a laundry basket, and several others, sticks." According to *Le Journal*, it arrived "outside the shop of an antiques dealer whose name seemed to indicate an Israelite origin. As soon as they stopped, they closed ranks and bombarded the shopkeeper's window with everything they could pick up."[6] Then they headed toward the Panthéon via the rue Clovis, tirelessly repeating: "Out with Zola! Death to the Jews!"

On the seventeenth the unrest further increased in intensity. At about noon close to a hundred students from the Beaux-Arts went up the rue Bonaparte and, intercepted by the police, took refuge in the café des Deux-Magots. At about two-thirty p.m., when school let out, the students from Louis-le-Grand and Henri-IV high schools entered the rue Soufflot, shouting, "Out with Zola! Death to the Yids!" After they were dispersed, they returned to the Panthéon and took the rue Valette, where the students from the Sainte-Barbe secondary school joined them, then headed toward the rue de l'Ecole-de-Médecine and invaded the boulevard Saint-Michel. They shouted "Out with Zola!" ran into the police roadblock on the rue des Ecoles, headed toward the place Maubert, and crossed the pont de la Tournelle in force. Passing by stores whose owners were Jewish, they threatened in particular a man named Lévi, who ran a store on the rue Vieille-du-Temple. They then threw stones before being dispersed by the police and scattering, "to the applause of residents who had come to their windows."

Almost at the same time, another large group of students was chanting the same slogans on the rue Soufflot and the boulevard Saint-Michel, some of them threatening a young woman on the rue Gay-Lussac. They shouted at her: "You won't get through if you don't shout 'Down with the Jews! Down with Zola!' " At the other end of

Paris, about a hundred students from Jean-Baptiste-Say came out of the high school and, passing by the shop of a certain Jacob on the place d'Auteuil, shouted: "Out with Zola! Death to the Jews!" At about five p.m. young people coming from the Rollin secondary school reached the Grands Boulevards via the rue Laffitte and the rue Drouot before being dispersed; at the same moment close to three hundred students went down the rue Soufflot, took the rue Monsieur-le-Prince, and the boulevard Saint-Michel, then ran into the police at the Médicis intersection. At about six o'clock, three hundred more reached the Opéra, joined with several other groups, and assembled on the rue Montmartre. "The crowd was becoming overexcited." It shouted, "Death to the Jews!" The cavalry intervened.

At about seven o'clock, a group of pharmacy students, "followed by young apprentices coming out of the workshops," formed on the place de la Sorbonne and dispersed via the rue Victor-Cousin. Some distance away, on the boulevard Magenta, the police charged another column of demonstrators. According to the reporter at *La Libre Parole,* "the eliminated students were replaced by workers, shopkeepers, employees who were going home at the end of their day, but who, hearing the shouts of 'Down with the Jews!' felt something atavistic vibrate within them and followed close behind the demonstrators, shouting the same slogans."

Things became more serious when the nationalist and anti-Semitic leaders organized a political meeting at Tivoli Hall on January 17. For several days a poster plastered the capital, inviting Parisians to assemble to protest the "machinations of international Jewry* and its accomplices intended to dishonor France . . . We are making an appeal to all French people with love for their country in their hearts to protest against . . . the insulters of the army who want to turn France over to a handful of Jews who have grown rich on the spoils of all." That appeal was signed by both Edouard Drumont and Henri Rochefort, and by leading figures of anti-Semitism such as Jules Guérin, Edouard Dubuc, Théodore Denis, Lucien Millevoye, and Albert Monniot. It was also signed by the Blanquist-Boulangist-turned-anti-Semite† Ernest Roche; by the dyed-in-the-wool Boulangist Charles Le Senne; and by anti-

*Jewry: *juiverie.* The term is pejorative.—trans.
†Blanquist: follower of the revolutionary socialist Louis-Auguste Blanqui.—trans.

Semitic Boulangists such as Albert Chiché and Marcel Habert. Habert had become one of Paul Déroulède's faithful* along with Albert Gauthier de Clagny, who also signed that text. Nationalist, anti-Semitic, and republican Boulangists who had rallied behind Paul Déroulède, such as Maurice Barrès, signed; as did nationalist and anti-Semitic socialists, such as Clovis Hugues and Alphonse Humbert; anti-Semitic royalists, such as the vicomte Paul de Hugues and Roger Lambelin; and Bonapartists, such as Gustave Cuneo d'Ornano and Paul Chassaigne-Goyon. Another signatory was a Boulangist ex-royalist who had become a key figure of traditional Catholicism, Albert de Mun. Finally, almost all the members of Parliament and of the Paris municipal council signed. In spite of their profound disagreements with one another, all these people coexisted without difficulty on the basis of an explicit anti-Semitism.

L'Intransigeant, probably too enthusiastically, estimated that eight thousand people were waiting inside Tivoli Hall. The police stretched itself to the limit to face the anticipated disturbances. In addition to the mobilizing municipal forces, the prefecture asked the Republican Guard for a hundred guards on horseback and four hundred on foot, plus a reserve force of a hundred on horseback and two hundred on foot. Since it was a cold night, six braziers operating on coke were set up to warm the troops massed in the barracks of Prince-Eugène. After a discussion with the prefect and an exchange of letters, the decision was made to leave them there "until peace has returned."

Everywhere squads of watchmen alternated with squads of Republican Guards on horseback; police cordons blocked all the roads. In the prevailing thick fog, as *La Petite République* observed, "from the place de la République to the quai de Valmy, there was a vast and tumultuous sea of humanity . . . a company of municipal guards came to take its place along the wall of Tivoli. The view of the rifles frightened the courageous members of the Catholic and anti-Semitic circles, and a good number of them briskly returned to the boulevard . . . The entire neighborhood was militarily occupied." In the hall Jules Guérin, the journalist Georges Thiébaud, and Edouard Dubuc took over the operations and proclaimed Drumont and Rochefort honorary chairmen. Everywhere cries of "Long live the army! Death to the Jews! Out with Zola!" reverber-

*Paul Déroulède: a Boulangist and head of the Ligue des Patriotes.—trans.

ated. The students sang and brandished flags bearing pictures of Dreyfus wearing a Prussian helmet. Guérin gave a long speech accusing the
Jews of dominating the country; Thiébaud followed but could not
speak because of the enormous din. He nevertheless managed to have
the following resolution passed: "The Parisian population, represented
at the Tivoli Vauxhall and mingling without distinction of class and
opinion in an enormous feeling of patriotic solidarity, sends, with all its
soul, a fraternal salute to the national army, whose honor has been violated by the Jews and their allies."

From everywhere shouts of "Death to the Jews! France for the
French!" rose up, now combined with a few cries of "Long live Zola!
Down with the priests!" shouted by anarchists, whom the nationalist
press considered "the servants of Jewry." A general melee followed:
people fought with canes, flags, and fists. Many were wounded. As *Le Figaro* noted, from one corner of the room could be heard: "'Out the
door, dirty Jew!' Immediately it was like a whirlwind surrounding, tight-
ening around the unfortunate man, who may not even have been Protestant, let alone Jewish. He was pounded by fists. The whirlwind threw
him out into the street."

When the meeting broke up at about ten-fifteen p.m., a number of
demonstrations erupted. As *Le Journal* reported, "the earth shook under
the hooves of a platoon of guards on horseback. They pushed a mass of
demonstrators back toward the canal, and the demonstrators hastened
to flee by the only path open to them." One group headed toward the
place de la République; another arrived at the place de la Bastille. Some
took the direction of the rue Saint-Antoine, others made their way to
the Latin Quarter, while still others went to the Jewish quarter. There
they first attacked the Hemmann house at number 13, trying to force
the door, then the Jewish bookstore at number 11, shattering the windowpanes. As a police report noted, "the pork butcher established at
number 9, also being of the Jewish religion, locked himself in his shop
at the approach of the demonstrators; they insulted him and made
death threats. But the agents from the city council in the fourth arrondissement, who hurried right over, dispersed them." From every side
columns of nationalists surged forward. At about midnight more than a
thousand of them again turned down the rue Réaumur, a flag leading
the way, and shouted, "Long live Rochefort! Death to the Jews!" They

then returned to the Latin Quarter, while "the people awakened by the din began to shout in unison. In the midst of these ovations from the populace, students stood in the streets, orators climbed onto the tables of cafés and harangued their comrades. The commotion was indescribable" (*Le Nouvelliste de Lyon*, January 19).

At about twenty minutes to one a.m., a group of approximately 150 people, "most appearing to be vagabonds," again crossed the pont Saint-Michel before being dispersed on the rue Gay-Lussac at the corner of the rue Saint-Jacques. At the same moment other groups were still causing a row in front of *La Libre Parole* and on the rue Laffitte, repeating the same slogans late into the Parisian night. An enormous crowd loitered until one a.m. on the place de l'Opéra; the peace officers, aided by gendarmes on horseback, charged and finally dispersed these unrepentant nationalists. *Le Nouvelliste de Lyon* reported the scene: "Without notice, the Republican Guard charged the demonstrators at a brisk trot into the fog. Some were struck, knocked down, wounded. The guards charged onto the sidewalk. The pavement was slick. Two horses fell and unseated their riders." *Le Jour* also described this final scene: "In the fog, the guards on horseback could be seen deploying the entire width of the avenue to the command: 'Forward! Battle order! At a gallop!' The riders set off. Cries of pain could be heard: many demonstrators had been thrown to the ground and even trampled by the dust-covered horses."

In the early afternoon of the eighteenth, about a hundred people met in front of *La Libre Parole* on the rue Montmartre and shouted, "Long live Drumont! Death to the Jews!" before fleeing via the passage Jouffroy. A little later a new group formed and became a column at the corner of the rue de Richelieu and the boulevard des Italiens. At about five p.m. approximately five hundred students left the law school via the rue Soufflot: many "vagrants" accompanied them. All at once "they entered a hatmaker's shop on the boulevard Saint-Michel, where they bought berets to distinguish themselves from their companions, the young vagabonds." They now constituted a troop of one thousand people. Attempting to reach the pont du Carrousel, they ran into police roadblocks every time; they then headed toward the pont des Arts, where they confronted police officers, shouting, "To the Bastille! We shall get through! Out with Zola! Death to the Jews! Death to the pigs! Death to the cops!" They then returned to the Latin Quarter.

A little later about two hundred students coming from the rue de Rennes arrived at the boulevard Saint-Germain, chanting, "Zola is a big asshole! The older he gets, the stupider he becomes!" At the same moment, about five hundred students came through the boulevard Saint-Marcel and the boulevard de l'Hôpital and forced their way to the pont d'Austerlitz. They got to the Bastille and a little later broke the windows of a haberdasher's located at 10, boulevard Beaumarchais and run by a Madame Schwab. They went on to the boulevard Poissonnière, where they ran into the police, passed through neighboring streets, and gathered outside the Crédit Lyonnais, about fifteen hundred strong, before being dispersed by charging police on the place de l'Opéra.

At about six p.m., another group of close to six hundred attempted to cross the Seine at the pont des Arts, while on boulevard Haussmann 150 students from the Ecole des Hautes Etudes Commerciales began drumming in front of Mathieu Dreyfus's home. Also at about six approximately two hundred students from Jean-Baptiste-Say high school decided to demonstrate once again, but the police, to avoid incidents like those of the previous day in front of Jacob's store, dispersed them quickly near the gare d'Auteuil. At the same time, about a hundred students from Turgot school gathered around Ecole Centrale, chanting: "Out with Zola!" Early in the evening students at the school of design paraded along the boulevard Saint-Michel. At the same moment, bombs were discovered outside the home of Alfred Dreyfus's father-in-law, David Hadamard, and outside the home of a financier, Spilmann. The previous day Spilmann had found attached to his door a piece of white paper, on which was written in enormous letters, "To Death to the Jew Tomorrow You Be Blown Up [*sic*]."

A little later, at the café de la Petite-Bourse on the rue de Richelieu, an anti-Semitic meeting was held, run by Jules Guérin. He alleged that the Jews were relying on an organization created by Adolphe Crémieux in 1860, the Alliance Israélite Universelle, to undermine the foundations of a strong France. "The Jews have produced nothing, either from the literary perspective or from the scientific perspective," another participant maintained. One speaker accused the Alliance Israélite Universelle of procuring resources for all Jews, which helped them dominate the French. Guérin railed against the previous day's skirmishes at Tivoli Hall and refused to pay the damages: "In the future," he promised (as noted in a police report), "there will be some fifty burly police chiefs; butcher boys and cowherds from La Villette, along with their dogs, will take over the policing operations of the hall . . . These chiefs will surround the troublemakers and throw them out . . . Every individual who has wounded one of their friends will be knocked senseless if he is encountered in the street and recognized. That was Morès's* old tactic, and it produced good results."

These measures were decided upon in planning a demonstration to be held a few days later on January 23 in the hall of Mille Colonnes, on the rue de la Gaîté, where the demonstrators would wear a tricolor ribbon in their buttonholes. As a preventive self-defense measure, one participant "asked that hostages be taken from among the Jews." Later, past midnight, as if by way of provocation, about fifteen students came out of the café Valette and went up the boulevard Saint-Michel shouting. Then silence finally fell over the streets of Paris.

On the nineteenth the city caught its breath. Apart from a certain agitation perceptible in the early afternoon on the Grands Boulevards, there were no incidents until about four-thirty, when students crossed the Seine bridges "armed with heavy canes." Others mounted an assault on the top decks of cars on the Batignolles-Clichy-Odéon line, shouting and brandishing canes. Ten minutes later, in front of Louis-le-Grand high school, a meeting was held that united three hundred students with demonstrators from the outside. Together, in a group that different police reports estimated at six hundred or even a thousand, they left for the rue Soufflot, entered the boulevard Saint-Michel, went along the rue Monsieur-le-Prince, and reached the Odéon and then the rue de Seine before being dispersed by the police near the rue Saint-Benoît and the rue Jacob.

On January 20 *La Libre Parole*, reporting on that demonstration, wrote:

Five hundred students reached rue Saint-Benoît. Store signs were minutely inspected by the head of the line, and no Jewish shop was spared. We then witnessed this curious spectacle: enormous half-circles formed outside the stores operating under the names

*Morès: the marquis de Morès was a violent anti-Semite and founder of Morès et Ses Amis (Morès and His Friends), a model for the anti-Semitic leagues.—trans.

"Meyer" or "Lévy." And the demonstrators began to sing every note of the scale: "Out with the Jews! Out with the Jews! Down with the traitors!" All evening long, the streets of Paris continued to reverberate furiously with the shouts of hatred against Israel. A few days from now, the Jews won't be laughing anymore.

The law students, joined by three hundred pharmacy students, three hundred chemistry students, and nearly two hundred students from the Boulle school, joined the fray. At about five p.m. demonstrators left the rue Bonaparte, went to the boulevard Saint-Germain, and wound through the rue Saint-Benoît pursued by the police. At the same moment about three hundred demonstrators were loitering outside the Collège de France.

Throughout the Latin Quarter, from rue des Fossés-Saint-Bernard to boulevard Saint-Michel, groups shouted their slogans. On the Right Bank at about six o'clock more than five hundred students, taking the boulevard de Sébastopol, headed toward the Grands Boulevards but were intercepted by police officers at the corner of the rue du Bourg-l'Abbé and the rue de Turbigo. The police estimated that at that moment the demonstrators numbered nearly a thousand. Four hundred nationalists then turned onto the place de la République.

At about seven o'clock on the boulevard Montmartre, someone shouted, "Long live Zola!" and was immediately pursued by about fifty demonstrators chanting, "Out with the Yid!" They hounded him through several streets until he managed to take refuge in a café, where more than two hundred angry individuals surrounded him for a long time. Late into the evening, until about eleven-thirty, the demonstrators repeatedly clashed with the police in the neighborhood of the Grands Boulevards, and the police reacted vigorously.[7]

The police kept meticulous accounts of the demonstrations. From January 15 to 20, they made a complete list of the eighty individuals arrested and then released. Among them were more than thirty university and high school students (in law, medicine, letters, and dentistry). There was also a wood sculptor, four mechanics, two pavers, a bread baker, a tin potter, and an inlayer. Also arrested were two butcher boys, four day laborers, six store clerks, a tinsmith, an electrician, a tailor, a farmer, a mill owner, two cabinetmakers, a joiner, and a florist. There was a well borer, two electricians, five printers, a bronze fitter, a carpenter of carriages, and a leather worker. Add to that list a delivery boy, a house painter, two street hawkers, a goldsmith, a coachman and a delivery man, four plumbers, and a coil winder. There was a wine merchant's assistant, an artistic painter, a baker, a gardener, a cobbler, a cardboard manufacturer, a pipe maker, a fitter, and a heating engineer. Finally, there was a cutter-stamper, a roofer, two masons, a house painter, a color applier, four jeweler-clockmakers, a cartwright-blacksmith, a bookbinder, a truck driver, a pastry chef, and two waiters. Most, but not all, of those arrested were from Paris originally and were in their teens or early twenties.[8]

The socialists were as yet not prominent in the streets of Paris and rarely engaged their forces in a battle that seemed to concern them only remotely. The socialist singer J.-B. Clément, the author of "Chant des cerises" (Cherry Song), wrote in *La Petite République* (January 20):

What century are we living in, then?
Loyola is back from the dead!
You hear nothing but ting-a-ling-ling
From all the bestowers of holy water.
Will the people and King Moneybags
Take to the streets?
France has reverted back
To the wars of religion.

What do they matter to us,
Dreyfus, Esterhazy, and the lot?
It's all the same law, it's all the same plague,
And they are not one of us.
General Galliffets* when the occasion permits,
Out of hatred for the populace,
They would shoot us all en masse
What does their religion matter to us?

---

*Galliffets: General Gaston de Galliffet participated in the repression of the Paris Commune in 1871.—trans.

What matter to us, my friends,
The merciful god of the capitalists,
Whether they're circumcised more or less,
*They're all equally Panamaists.**
They all have love for their millions,
Whether they're Jewish or Catholic,
It's really the same arithmetic
And the same religion.[9]

The day of the twenty-first was astonishingly calm. In the early afternoon a few students wearing berets drifted from one bank of the Seine to the other. Some demonstrators moved along the boulevard Haussmann, and a few students from Jean-Baptiste-Say high school, as was by now their habit, shouted slogans. A few dozen students demonstrated after nightfall around the fountain of Châtelet. *Le Gaulois* observed on January 22 that several arrests were made of "shabbily dressed people wearing caps, several of them carrying knives and brass knuckles. All live in the outskirts of the city and are vagrants . . . The students considerably curtailed their movements in order not to compromise themselves in unsavory activities, for which they feel repugnance." On the same day, *La Presse* expressed a similar view: "There had come from the remote districts, the outlying neighborhoods, a multitude of sickly-looking vagrants who have not worked in a long time. A few of them had ferruled knives, skeleton keys, and pliers in their pockets. They had come from Gentilly, Montmartre, Plaisance, Saint-Denis. Our students will therefore do well to be even more wary of the illicit mob that follows their demonstrations. This morning the berets, a rallying sign, made their appearance in classrooms where a contained but powerful fever and agitation were palpable." Once again many arrests were made.

---

*Panamaists: The company formed by Ferdinand de Lesseps to build the Panama Canal went bankrupt in 1888, whereupon it was discovered that in its attempt to avoid financial ruin, the company had bribed several cabinet ministers, 150 members of Parliament, and virtually every major French newspaper. The three financial promoters who had handled the bribery were Jewish. This discovery gave rise to a wave of anti-Semitism and undermined faith in the Third Republic. See William L. Shirer, *The Collapse of the Third Republic: An Inquiry into the Fall of France in 1940* (New York: Da Capo Press, 1994), p. 48n.—trans.

Private gatherings of anti-Semitic groups met late into the night. Fiery speeches were heard, but their audiences were extremely small. On the other side, revolutionary organizations attracted Allemanist* militants, who attacked Henri Rochefort and the clericals. One speaker maintained that "the Jew Dreyfus and the uhlan [German cavalryman] Esterhazy do not worry [him] at all. The duty of the socialists is to unmask the campaign of the clericals, who are attempting to lead the people astray by inciting religious wars, as in the Middle Ages." Finally, as the police's daily general report observed, "all day long, Paris maintained its habitual physiognomy of peaceful days."

On the twenty-second as well, Paris appeared peaceful, the calm before the storm. On Sunday the twenty-third, by contrast, the city reached the boiling point. The nationalists decided to hit hard. The political meeting at Mille Colonnes on the rue de la Gaîté, planned for two-thirty p.m., was to ignite the mobilization. The authorities were very conscious of the potential danger of the demonstration and took exceptional measures to ensure order. Anything could happen. An anonymous informant sent the following report to the prefect: "One hundred and fifty butchers from La Villette will attend the meeting . . . It will be very large, since a frenetic propaganda effort has been conducted in recent days . . . They are counting on twenty-five to thirty thousand people . . . The demonstrators, or rather the organizers, fear the peace officers and municipal guards. As for the troops, they would like to make contact with them, because the troops are convinced that the police would make common cause with them. That also increases their audacity and means they will go to extremes."

Enormous posters covered the walls of Paris, proclaiming:

NATIONAL DEMONSTRATION!

CITIZENS. IN SPITE OF THE PROTEST THROUGHOUT THE

COUNTRY, THE ORGANIZERS OF TREASON, THE ACCOMPLICES OF

*Allemanists: followers of the revolutionary socialist Jean Allemane.—trans.

COSMOPOLITAN JEWRY ARE CLAIMING TO CONTINUE THEIR ANTI-
FRENCH MANEUVERS. THE PARISIAN POPULATION, WHICH HAS
ALREADY RESPONDED TO OUR APPEAL . . . WILL AGAIN OFFER
THEIR PARTICIPATION. WE ARE ACTING IN THE NAME OF NO
POLITICAL PARTY; FROM THE BEGINNING, WE HAVE APPEALED TO
ALL THOSE WHO HAVE LOVE FOR THEIR COUNTRY IN THEIR
HEARTS. WE HAVE ONLY ONE GOAL, TO DEFEND FRANCE,
ALREADY SORELY TESTED BY THE SCANDALS AND INCURSIONS OF
JEWISH FINANCIERS AND THEIR SYMPATHIZERS . . . BY ALL THE
ENEMIES WITHIN WHOM WE WERE IMPRUDENT ENOUGH TO
WELCOME TO OUR COUNTRY.

At noon four squadrons of the first regiment of cuirassiers were ap-
portioned to every corner of Paris, to the barracks of Château-d'Eau,
inside the walls of the Pépinière barracks, in the Tuileries Gardens, and
on the rue de Presbourg, between the avenue d'Iéna and the avenue
Marceau, to keep watch. Four other squadrons from the second regiment were held in reserve at the military school, ready to march. The
twenty-eighth regiment of dragoons were ready to move from Vincennes
to Paris at a moment's notice. All troops were confined to their quarters;
no leaves were granted; and harsh disciplinary measures were imposed to
make sure that no soldier would mingle with the crowd of demonstrators. Because the posts occupied by the Republican Guards would be
taken over by other troops to free up the total force, and because the
guards in charge of theaters and balls would be reduced by half, 880 ex-
tra foot soldiers and 350 cavalrymen were to be made available. Finally,
350 peace officers and 50 Republican Guards surrounded the hall on
horseback. The capital was in a state of siege.

"Paris," according to *L'Intransigeant*, "has transformed itself into a vast
entrenched camp." *Le Figaro*, like *L'Eclair*, *Le Petit Parisien*, *L'Aurore*, and even
La Libre Parole published striking descriptions. More than two thousand
people entered the Mille Colonnes hall, where the tasks of law enforcement, as planned, were assumed by butcher boys, most of them in work
clothes, wearing a tricolor armband. According to *L'Aurore*, "Catholic
students guarded the entrance . . . About fifty young jingoists, armed

with lead-tipped canes, were ready to club suspects." Nationalists Jules Guérin and Georges Thiébaud, along with the anarchist Paul Brunet, led the demonstration. Thiébaud passed a motion that "outlawed those who make peace with universal Jewry" and concluded with a ringing "Long live the old, free republican France, standing purified." When Thiébaud distinguished "those who wish to demolish the Jewish Bastille from those who want to consolidate it," Brunet interrupted him, arguing that "not all Bastilles are Jewish." After several more interruptions, Thiébaud left the hall. Fights broke out, pitting the thousands of nationalists against the few anarchists who had managed to breach the wall.

When the meeting ended just before three, the crowd, finding the rue de la Gaîté barred by peace officers from the sixth, thirteenth, fourteenth, and twentieth arrondissements and by Republican Guards on horseback, withdrew via the avenue du Maine and the boulevard Edgar-Quinet. In the disorder police reports accumulated, detailing incidents that had erupted throughout the afternoon. One group took the rue Froidevaux and arrived at the place Denfert-Rochereau and the boulevard du Montparnasse, the rue Vavin, and the Luxembourg Gardens. On the place du Châtelet, there was a report of an omnibus at gare Saint-Lazare–place Saint-Michel, its upper deck full of cane-wielding students, from which hung signs reading "Out with Zola! Death to the Jews! Death to the Yids! Long live the army!" Many groups of more than three hundred each passed one another on the bridges, heading toward the Latin Quarter or the rue Montmartre, led by the speakers from the meeting at Mille Colonnes. All of them chanted, "Death to the Jews! Out with Zola!" There was another group farther along, near the rue Saint-Denis, the rue d'Hauteville, and the rue des Messageries, and in the Poissonnière district. A fairly large crowd outside the gates of the Tuileries Gardens, which some police reports estimated at ten thousand, was barely managed by more than four thousand police officers.

In spite of the demonstrations, few people were apprehended: a sales representative, a day laborer, three butcher boys, three hatmakers, a cooper, and a few unemployed people.

But the climax of nationalist mobilization led nowhere. Indeed, it seemed as if the entire protest might come unraveled. Although the prefecture planned to have another hundred guards on horseback patrolling the streets of Paris on Monday the twenty-fourth, peace reigned. *Le Jour* described "those patrols of municipal guards on horseback and of dragoons, each about twenty men strong and commanded by officers who crisscross Paris in every direction," but there was not a single shout, not one threatening parade—dead calm. It was the same on the twenty-fifth, with only a report that a few students in berets had been received at *La Libre Parole*. The police superintendent of the first arrondissement was astonished: "All is calm in my arrondissement, and no guard has heard threats uttered against Israelite houses."

On the twenty-sixth the boulevard Saint-Michel remained empty, as did the Latin Quarter and the Grands Boulevards: the demonstrators seemed to have vanished. Police were reinforced when rumors of another demonstration spread, but they turned out to be unfounded. On the twenty-seventh false rumors were circulated again. Students milled restlessly around Zola's residence, while others passed rue Montmartre again and again; but no noise was heard, everything was calm. On the twenty-eighth, the unrest increased slightly: three hundred students from Jean-Baptiste-Say high school got together on the rue La Fontaine and repeated the slogans that some people thought had already been forgotten. A little later 150 students made their way along the rue Montmartre and shouted, "Down with the Jews! Out with Zola!" Tracts were handed out, inviting passersby to a demonstration planned for the next day.

On the twenty-ninth strict surveillance was set up on the place de la Concorde, where the demonstration was to take place. The police arrested the college and high school students who had come, staving off any demonstration. Other students, who were loitering behind the church of the Madeleine, decided to leave. At the Petit Casino, about a hundred students again caused an uproar, shouting slogans, but then dispersed. At the close of that wild January, the police reports were virtually blank. An ill-placed humor prevailed, illustrated by this insert published by *L'Echo de Belleville* on January 31:

Brawls and songs. In Paris, there is singing, shoving, booing, demonstrating. We cannot resist the pleasure of reproducing one of the little songs, the most characteristic one, by our friend J. Cailly, the devil-may-care songster of the Parisian anti-Semitic groups:

*   *   *

And if ever, good citizens,
Our ministers should chicken out,
It's up to us, no straw men we,
It's up to us to replace the fuzz
We'll send Scheurer, Mathieu,
Reinach,* and maddening old Zola,
To join the dear and tender lad
Who's bored as sh——heck alone in his cage.[10]

The respite proved short-lived. When Zola's trial opened on February 7, the police again showed their vigilance, since new rumblings of an anti-Semitic demonstration had been heard.[11] On February 8 the litany of hatred seemed to be starting up again. The Palais de Justice was in a state of siege: on the pont Neuf, the pont Saint-Michel, and the pont au Change, on the place Dauphine, and in all the surrounding areas, nearly seven hundred gendarmes and police officers erected roadblocks to contain the angry crowd. Despite the increasing rain, the crowd thronged, sprawled onto the quai des Grands-Augustins, and impatiently awaited the arrival of the protagonists—Zola, Rochefort, Esterhazy, and the generals of the staff. Their shouts of "Down with Zola! Down with the Jews!" grew louder when Lieutenant Colonel Georges Picquart† appeared. The crowd attempted to break through the police cordons to attack the "traitors who sold out to the Jews." Whenever a general crossed the place Dauphine to get to the Palais, cheers came from the windows, along with cries of "Long live the general! Death to the Yids! Down with the Jews!" The residents of the place Dauphine rented spots at the good intersections for a fortune, and some people even stood at places with the best view from two in the morning on, to cash them in for the highest price the next day. In the late afternoon, when people were expecting the court to recess, "a sea of heads [could] be perceived" (*Le Petit Soleil*).

When court recessed, "anti-Semitic fanatics," as *Le Figaro* called them, attempted to seize Zola. The generous Paul de Cassagnac maintained in

---

*Joseph Reinach: Jewish politician and Dreyfusard leader.—trans.
†Lieutenant Colonel Georges Picquart: officer who discovered evidence that the spy passing information to the Germans was not Dreyfus but Esterhazy.—trans.

L'Autorité that "to go a thousand against one, even against Judas, even against Zola, is admissible only among the savages," but he nevertheless believed that the violence against Zola and the Jews, of which he did not approve, "attests to the vitality of another faith that some have wanted to destroy, faith in the fatherland." *Le Figaro, Le Jour, La Fronde, La Libre Parole, L'Intransigeant, La Petite République,* and *Gil Blas* all devoted several full pages to the event.

La Libre Parole judged with satisfaction that "popular exasperation is growing by proportions that, day by day, seem very troubling for Israel . . . It is no longer mockery and jokes that come out of that crowd but rather cries of vociferous hatred, fists raised high when Jews pass." And Drumont's newspaper added, "The Yids are not entirely wrong to be scared, since the Dreyfus-Zola affair is ending very badly for them." *Le Gaulois* explained that "it is the idea of a Saint Bartholomew's Day massacre of the Jews that has passed like a bolt of lightning through the minds of the French people."

That same Saturday, the morning of February 8, a disturbing letter reached the prefecture. The informant wrote: "I have just met a person living in the Saint-Antoine district who informed me that someone is openly seeking recruits in small cafés to loot the Jewish stores this evening." Violent incidents erupted. In the late afternoon, when classes let out, more than a hundred students from Charlemagne high school headed toward the rue des Rosiers and broke windows at the home of Rabbi Friedmann. Maxime Fontable, an eighteen-year-old grocer, was arrested after he shouted, "Death to the Jews!" while assaulting a shop. A little while later someone attacked the store Au Bûcheron on the rue du Roi-de-Sicile. Still later about ten people heading down the boulevard Saint-Michel, then rushing toward the rue des Ecoles, provocatively shouted, "Long live Zola! Down with the army!" Students gave chase and were preparing to rough up the demonstrators when officers separated them.

On the ninth an enormous crowd invaded the quai de la Mégisserie, from the pont Neuf to the entrance to the Palais de Justice. Guards on horseback intervened, and the police worried: "Unless there's a good downpour to help law enforcement clear place Dauphine," wrote one officer, "we'll have a hard time." Reports estimated that more than ten thousand people had assembled and that the crowd was very "tumultuous"; that it was composed of anti-Semitic and Catholic groups, joined by "shady characters" recruited from among the liquor merchants and amply remunerated. In a humorous vein, *La Fronde* wrote:

> Our balcony overlooks a very picturesque little street . . . Since the Zola trial, when "the good people of Paris" began inundating the quays, the bridges, and the streets around the Palais de Justice, we have been bathing in an almost rural tranquillity. There are no longer any pimps around here, and even the prostitutes went with them, shouting: "Into the water, Zola! Death to the Jews!" The prostitutes who remain, not having any more customers, take advantage of their solitude to launder undershirts and socks, with which they deck their windows and the yard.

Not far away police dispersed five hundred demonstrators who were preparing to throw someone who had shouted, "Long live Zola!" into the water. At the other end of Paris, groups were also forming outside Zola's house, and upon his return from the Palais, cries of "Yid! Bastard! Rotter!" could be heard. At nightfall three hundred people bearing torches paraded on the rue Montmartre, shouted slogans in support of the army, headed toward *La Libre Parole*, and they were dispersed by the police.

On the tenth incidents multiplied throughout Paris. A large police force protected the Palais de Justice and pushed back those in the crowds who proved too aggressive to the quai des Orfèvres or the place Dauphine. At about five p.m. more than five hundred people were loitering outside the home of Rothschild, a silk merchant, shouting, "Death to the Jews!" They invaded the store, overcoming his efforts at resistance. Officers intervened and arrested Edmond Demare, eighteen years old, a sculptor; Jules Rendu, twenty, a roofer; Arthur Denard, seventeen, a painter; Jean Baudoin, eighteen, a business employee; and Paul Chevallier, eighteen, a tailor. The rioters, with the police in pursuit, escaped via the rue de la Cossonnerie; one group headed toward the rue Meslay and the rue Béranger, then the rue de Turenne, still shouting the same slogans. At about six o'clock, four hundred demonstrators stood on the place du Châtelet, shouted slogans against Zola and the Jews, and left again via the rue de Rivoli. A half hour later five hundred students in berets passed through Les Halles and gathered outside *La Libre Parole* before being dispersed by the police. When Zola returned home, cries went up: "Down with Zola! Into the water! Death!"

On the eleventh the anti-Semitic incidents reached an intensity that may have never been equaled in the capital. At about five o'clock, as *La Petite République* reported, "approximately fifteen hundred demonstrators, young schoolboys and students from the religious schools, gathered on the quai de la Mégisserie facing the place Dauphine, and lit enormous fires." They shouted, "Out with Zola! Death to the Jews!" then ran through Les Halles, soon constituting a small army of four hundred. Upon reaching the rue Montmartre, they were greeted by the applause of travelers in the upper deck of the omnibuses and by passersby. The army, now nine hundred strong, beat on doors of Jewish businesses, brandished canes, and again attempted to invade the Rothschild house.

An hour later the police caught sight of "about fifteen students with long hair, soft hats, and large coats timidly crying, 'Long live Zola' before suffering the invectives of passersby." It was, as always, the anti-Dreyfusards who were in the best position. At about seven close to two hundred young people crossed the place de la Bastille and passed through the Saint-Antoine district. Upon reaching the furniture store of Hergott Brothers and Jacob, at numbers 16 and 32, they shouted, "Out with Zola! Down with the Jews!" and broke the store windows. Though they made every effort to get inside, they did not succeed. Next they attacked the marble plaque at the Schmit company, the largest cabinetmaking business in Paris, then the facade of the Tilliez store on the rue Jean-Macé. As the police explained, however, "Schmit is a Christian. Tilliez as well."

At the same moment, not far from there, about three hundred demonstrators broke the windows of the Kahn pastry shop. On the rue des Blancs-Manteaux they attacked a haberdasher's shop, then headed toward the rue des Tournelles, where they broke the windowpanes in the synagogue. The Paris prefecture received numerous reports concerning that incident, which was considered particularly serious because the demonstrators had also destroyed the glass in the main door and two side doors. The synagogue's watchman, a man named Haarcher, went to the police station in the fourth arrondissement and asked for protection.

The anti-Semitic brutality continued despite all efforts to stop it. At close to nine p.m. a huge crowd threw stones through the windowpanes

of Salomon, Schill, Dreyfus, and Company, and two revolver shots were
fired from a streetcar: the bullets struck the wall of the building. On the
rue Notre-Dame-de-Nazareth, an "anarchist" was arrested while he was
inciting the crowd to loot stores whose owners were Jewish.

At about ten p.m. close to six hundred demonstrators "of all categories," coming from the Bastille, attacked the windows of the jersey
factory of the Bernheim Brothers on the boulevard Voltaire. They destroyed hundreds of windowpanes with stones, wounding one worker,
Amélie Moquet. The owners of that factory demanded police protection. As a police report noted, "the Bernheim brothers are Israelites.
The gang made death threats, provoking the Bernheims, threatening to
burn them. The Bernheim family, whom I saw this morning, are in a
state of panic, which is easy to understand, and they demand protection." The *Archives Israélites* of February 17 vigorously protested: "Last
Friday evening, these good little young people reared at the Church's
knee, whose souls have been molded by educators in cassocks, without
provocation demolished the windowpanes of the synagogue on the rue
des Tournelles and attacked commercial establishments belonging to Israelites, shouting out things to the effect 'Death to the Jews!' "

The Bernheims mentioned they might lay off their fifteen hundred
workers if they did not get protection—a particularly troubling pros-
pect given that, as police reports indicated, many businesses had already
been forced to reduce their staffs as a result of the unrest, particularly
those in the construction and garment industries. "Homeworkers are
short of work in the districts of Belleville, Charonne, and Bagnolet."

The national press gave a great deal of play to the Bernheim affair,
which was so serious and threatening that it had to be referred to the
state authorities. They seemed to share the concern of Joseph Reinach,
who wrote: "Paris and France have lost the habit of rioting. These riots
displayed the brutality of unbridled beasts."[12]

According to *Le Siècle*,

the anti-Semites of Paris are imitating the example of their friends
from Algiers. Not content to print insults in their newspapers and
to vociferate in the street, they've now come to blows . . . The gang
goes through like a whirlwind, shouting "Death to the Jews! Death
to the Jews! Death to the Jews!" A few leaders in redingotes bran-

dish top hats, inciting the mob they are driving forward . . . Three or four hundred windowpanes were broken . . . enormous paving stones from a construction yard are strewn across the floors of the workshops . . . If the workshops had not been closed, it would have been a real catastrophe.

In a similar vein, *La France* wrote: "They threw projectiles, fired shots from revolvers, broke storefronts. These are unquestionably the aggravating symptoms of civil war . . . A very serious investigation ought to be opened regarding the looting suffered by the Israelite companies . . . The campaign may turn from anti-Semitic to anticapitalist. From that moment on, our country would risk bankruptcy." *La Paix* was optimistic, writing: "Anti-Semitism, cornered, howls and yowls. All the Jesuit forces come together and deliver the final assault on the Republic . . . Anti-Semitism is a demonstration of clericalism; anti-Semitism must be denounced and combated by all true republicans . . . Let the government do its duty therefore." *Le Voltaire*, on the contrary, no longer had any illusions: "We are very wrong to compare this period to that of May 16*; May 16 was unquestionably better. The professed enemies of the Republic were in power then, whereas today it is the republicans who govern and administer." According to a report that arrived at the prefecture on February 12, a lawyer at the Palais predicted that "it will end in a purge. A riot against the Jews, and a riot by the numbers, is certainly to be feared."

A large number of songs created for the occasion were widely circulated and further charged the atmosphere. For example, "Zola, ferm' ta boîte, t'as assez vendu!" (Zola, Shut Your Trap, You've Done Enough Betraying), by Aristide Bruant, was sung to the tune of "A Ménilmontant":

> So tell us, when will you be done
> Defending the Yiddies, Zola;
> If you don't want us to boot you around
> Shut your trap! . . .

*May 16: The crisis of May 16, 1877, pitted Marshal-President Marie de MacMahon against the Chamber of Deputies over the choice of a premier. MacMahon eventually dissolved the Chamber, but the elections in October of the same year returned a republican majority to the legislative body. MacMahon finally gave in and reluctantly supported a premier acceptable to the Chamber.—trans.

As you well know, old chap,
The Yids are nasty lads,
Your letter is too maladroit,
Shut your trap! . . .

You took your odious Yids
For all too serious dupes.
But they's got a stingy conscience,
Shut your trap!

Since your case has been settled
And you came out the loser,
They're going to tell you: Rabid dog,
You've done enough betraying.

Of the innocence of your traitor
You alone remain convinced;
Deep down you think it's a joke perhaps;
You've done enough betraying![13]

This song, "Levée des cannes" (Lifting of Canes), was sung to the tune of "Le pendu" (The Hanged Man):

[Refrain]

One! (strike your cane)
The Jew is grumbling!
There's the whores!
Brrat! (strike your cane)
The army trumpets
*That four-letter word**
For the Yids!
Zing! (strike your cane)

*"That four-letter word" (mot de Cambronne): according to legend, Napoleon's general Pierre Cambronne, called upon to surrender, uttered the word "Merde!" (Shit). Hence mot de Cambronne refers to that word.—trans.

Two! Three!
Out with Zola! (bis) Out!

He just laid another one at L'Aurore,*
A big boiled egg that's isolated him;
It's not the Gallic cock that's holding forth,
And the people respond: Out with Zola!
After the articles he cackles at us
Nothing to do but shut him up!
Oh! my friends, what a debacle!
For Zola, it's the knock-out blow!†

To be able to take money for your debauchery
Of spitting on our dear flag,
What could you have there under your left breast?
You need twelve bullets in the flesh . . .

We can sing all night long,
And all the next day, without going to bed:
With Zola there's no more material
than at the Richer Company!‡
But that's enough. We have to end.

We're disgusted. Let's leave it at that.
You feel like you're crushing vermin
When you pronounce Zola's name.[14]

Some organizations, such as the Groupe des Etudiants Communistes (Group of Communist Students) circulated brochures denouncing the riots.

The army of frocked bandits is organizing.
    With the money from the union Jesuits, a cargo of cosmopoli-

---

**L'Aurore*: the Dreyfusard newspaper whose name means "dawn."—trans.
†Knock-out blow: *l'assommoir*, an allusion to Zola's novel by that name. *La débâcle* is another of his novels.—trans.
‡Richer Company: a theater company that produced popular entertainment.—trans.

tan rabble has been shipped in from Algeria, spewed out by Algeria, Malta, and Italy so that they can sack Paris. At the head of these lower-than-shits is a brat by the name of Milano who, ashamed of his Italian nationality, goes by "Régis."

That spitwad from Calabria openly proclaims he has come with his retinue to teach the Parisians the art of looting the Jews' shops. We are going to show those nigger-Arab choir boys and their entrepreneur aspergillum wielders that the Boulevard is not Bab-Azun Street and that, at this moment, the people of Paris are more disposed to give lessons than to receive them.

Comrades! Beware the dirty fount water named Guérin, Thiébaud, Pradelle, Milano, and all the anti-Semitic and Roman wop brigade. Comrades! Let's gather all our energy, it's now or never. Far be it from us to be spineless and wavering! Let's block the way to that flaccid riff-raff, the army of thieves and murderers![15]

Nationalist Paris seems to have been so imposing that the battle was completely one-sided. It is true that the anarchists, the Confédération Générale du Travail (General Confederation of Labor), the Fédération des Bourses du Travail (Federation of Labor Services), and the Allemanist Parti Socialiste Ouvrier Révolutionnaire (Revolutionary Workers' Socialist Party) all planned to demonstrate in support of Zola. Furthermore, "a Russian student promised to come with about fifty of his compatriots," and the police were so afraid for Zola's life that they agreed to pay working men ten francs a day to defend Zola when court recessed at the Palais de Justice.

On February 12, however, the tension eased once more. When Zola left his home to go to the Palais early in the morning and when he arrived at the Palais, cries of "Down with Zola! Death to the Jews!" resounded as always. But all things considered, these demonstrations were minor; the city was licking its wounds. The worst outcome had been avoided, and the hardest part was over.

A large police contingent remained in place and mobilized hundreds of cavalrymen, companies of infantry, and thousands of municipal police officers, but accounts of incidents were rare. On the thirteenth, on the rue Montmartre, dozens of students wearing berets sang ribald refrains. Small groups of curiosity-seekers loitered outside Zola's home, while "families looked on through the closed shutters." "The greatest calm" reigned in the different districts of the city: the police surveillance of the rue Montmartre district, the Saint-Antoine district, "the Israelite synagogue of Les Tournelles," and the Bernheim Brothers company all seemed pointless.

On the fourteenth, according to *Le Gaulois*, "on the rue Paris, Paris is breathing. A full fine day off, after the weeks of battle and feverishness . . . What a propitious and good day of rest, under a sky that itself appeared to be in a lull, overcast and very mild. All of Paris came out, not to demonstrate, but to drink up the already almost springlike air. The boulevards swarmed with peacefully cheerful strollers; the café terraces were packed." A police informant warned the prefecture that Guérin, Thiébaud, and Lucien Millevoye (a former deputy and violently anti-Semitic nationalist republican) continued to conduct meetings where "people spoke with a revolting violence: without exaggeration, their speeches could be considered an incitement to civil war and religious war." A few days later, in almost identical terms, another informant warned that they had launched into speeches "that may be considered a true incitement to a Saint Bartholomew's Day massacre, this time against the Jews."

On the nineteenth the Republican Guard, in preparation for the nationalist political meeting that was to take place the next day in the Salle Chayne, readied two hundred men on foot and twenty-five on horseback; this draconian police force ruthlessly screened the six hundred people entering the hall. Jules Guérin, Lucien Millevoye, Georges Thiébaud, and Max Régis, the leading figures of anti-Semitism, galvanized their own troops. Surprisingly, the day unfolded peacefully. A few people in costumes and masks even went to Mardi Gras balls.

On the twentieth the court was close to handing down a verdict in the Zola trial. At about four p.m. almost 250 students wearing berets walked along the boulevard Montmartre and proclaimed their hostility to Zola. Led by about a hundred students wearing white smocks and equipped with canes, they marched toward the place de la République in rows of eight. They distributed the song "Youpins, Mouscaille, et Cie" (Yids, Shit, and Company), signed by the "Union of Cesspool Cleaners":

The element of the Jew is shit,
He revels in it, splashes about.
And anyone who's rubbed against him
Always comes out covered with crap . . .

They would like to get that circumcised fellow
Off of Devil's Island:
Me, I say if he weren't culpable,
They never could've cut off*
His . . . rations. I understand the riff-raff
And the reasoning of its defenders:
He was working in the shit
Of the Union of Cesspool Cleaners.

A gang of wretched scoundrels
Paid by those hideous toads
Makes Prussian money roll
Across all the tables of bistros.
The repulsive little slaves
Of the Yiddies have bad manners
That stink from fifteen paces with the shit
Of the Union of Cesspool Cleaners.

They are demeaning our army,
Wanting to impose their yoke on us;
But our nation, in alarm,
Will return the Yids blow for blow.
To the nation, the ignoble riff-raff
Has shown every dishonor:
We must drown it in its own shit,
That Union of Cesspool Cleaners.[16]

At about five p.m. on the place du Panthéon, the police dispersed a crowd estimated at a thousand, headed by a swaggering Millevoye. On the corner of the rue des Ecoles and the rue Monge, another group led

*Cut off: the French word for "guilty" or "culpable" (*coupable*) can also mean "cuttable."—trans.

by Ernest Roche, a nationalist deputy, also clashed with police. Because Henri Rochefort was supposed to enter the Sainte-Pélagie prison, the Republican Guard had committed itself to supplying 550 guards on foot and 150 guards on horseback to help maintain order. Decorum was disturbed only by a very drunk Louis Rochette who, armed with a loaded revolver carried in his belt, shouted again and again, "Down with Zola! Death to the Jews! Long live Rochefort! Long live Drumont!" Rochette was quickly overpowered.

There is no record of February 21 in the police reports. On the twenty-second students attempted to demonstrate on the boulevards, but their hearts were no longer in it: "The public's only concern was to amuse themselves launching confetti, and they turned a cold shoulder to the demonstrations." The bad weather played a role and dispersed the people strolling on the boulevards. It began to look like commedia dell'arte: at the corner of the rue Drouot, "a group of young people threw confetti at a gentleman and lady who were passing. The gentleman got angry, and immediately these individuals began to shout: 'Down with the Jews!' " Joy was scarce at the Mardi Gras festivities, as the journalist for *L'Avenir du XV*ᵉ reported:

> I attended our battle of confetti on the boulevards, as I do every year. Did you go? Did you, like me, notice the sense of sadness and worry hanging over Paris, stifling any boisterous joy? There were few people, in short, and people who seemed not to be having unabashed fun. Unlike last year, there was none of that exuberant joy of the carefree Parisian amusing himself. Later, the rain played a role. In that case as well, the impression was sad, worried. The rain hit the large glass panes, and it too seemed to cry over the sadness of Paris and to want to stifle a joy so little in harmony with our patriotic sadness. But what I observed with pleasure, and I would even say with emotion, was the ever-growing success of the patriotic song. The troubadour came on the scene with his repertoire of old regimental songs; he was met with a veritable demonstration and had tremendous success. What brave hearts Parisians have! In the street, under small groups of umbrellas held fraternally close to one another, the crowd was listening to the

ironic anti-Zolist songs. In sum, a sad day for Mardi Gras but also a bad day for the Dreyfusard clique.

Finally on the twenty-third the demonstrators made one paltry last stand. Rain mixed with snow was falling. Because of the great fear of violent incidents, law enforcement was present and prepared. In Paris under siege, thousands of peace officers were aided by nearly 950 cuirassiers of the Republican Guard. It was the day that had been anxiously awaited, too anxiously perhaps, but the large crowds were weary and finally gave up the fight. The pont Neuf was barred to pedestrians; a fairly large crowd waited patiently on the quai de la Mégisserie. At the Palais de Justice, the session opened at ten past noon.

The thirty-two permanent jurors had sat for several weeks in an extremely tense atmosphere. One juror, Louis Grognet, was a fifty-one-year-old paint dealer. Eugène Brylinski was a fifty-four-year-old merchant. Alfred Boucreux was a fifty-four-year-old butcher: "His youngest daughter was at a religious boarding school near the church of Notre-Dame, and his eldest daughter had done her studies at the same institution; he is said to be very patriotic and he reads *Le Petit Journal*." Jean-François Bouldoire was a fifty-three-year-old wholesale wine merchant, who "professes radical* republican opinions, reads *Le Petit Parisien* and sometimes *L'Intransigeant*." Pierre Emery was a thirty-four-year-old businessman: "He is a practicing Catholic; his wife goes to mass every day, and he goes to services every Sunday. He does not express hostility toward the Israelites and counts a certain number of them among his clients." Auguste Chalmin was a fifty-five-year-old wholesale wine merchant. Auguste Leblond was a fifty-four-year-old roofing contractor: he "is a member of the Catholic religion, has a cousin who is a priest." The police had similarly complete files on each and every one of the jurors.[17]

Ferdinand Labori, Zola's lawyer, resumed his defense before the jury until four-forty p.m. After a short recess, Georges Clemenceau took the floor and spoke until six-fifteen. The public prosecutor responded with a few words, and the jury deliberated for thirty-five minutes: Zola was

*Radical: under the Third Republic, the term *radical* referred to liberal and secular republicans.—trans.

found guilty of libel and sentenced to one year in prison and fined three thousand francs. As applause broke out, Zola was heard to exclaim: "They're cannibals!" *Les Droits de l'Homme* wrote:

> The cannibals are shouting, intoxicated with joy . . . No, it is not over; not so long as anti-Semitism, which masks the offensive return of the Church, is able to unleash religious war; not so long as one can hold up French citizens of another faith to the hatred and greed of the populace; not so long as unnameable gangs are able to loot and kill to the barbarous cries of "Death to the Jews!" Nothing is over. Not the coalition of the saber and the aspergillum, not the lunatic laws, not the collapsing Chambers, not even the majority of the nation panic-stricken by the newspapers in the Esterhazy syndicate, and, above all, not imbecilic and reprehensible anti-Semitism. By no means is it over. Zola is not alone.

In *L'Aurore* Clemenceau commented on the verdict: "They're dancing around the victim Zola, preparing to scalp him . . . With the republicans of the victorious government under the heel of the general staff, the Church is trumpeting religious war against the Jews, the Protestants, and the atheists . . . Anti-Semitism is truly what's at issue, anyone can see that. If there is no law for Dreyfus, it's because he is Jewish, that's all . . . There's a major movement of anti-Semitic Boulangism under way."

When court let out, the crowd shouted slogans hostile to the author of "J'accuse" one last time. Outside the Palais gates, a diversionary deployment of 150 Republican Guards and 100 police officers made it possible for Zola to leave discreetly via the quai des Orfèvres.[18] As *Le Matin* reported,

> the verdict condemning Zola to the maximum penalty was welcomed by indescribably enthusiastic demonstrations . . . For five minutes, people enthusiastically stamped their feet. All hats waved at the ends of canes, lawyers tossed their caps in the air. Many wept, others embraced one another as if they had just escaped a cataclysm. Then a rhythmic chant, muffled at first, but becoming more pronounced in a tremendous crescendo, rose toward the

vaults of the Palais. Death to the Jews! Death to the Jews! No one thought to boo Zola, whom the jury's verdict had just struck with a harshness that the country as a whole finds well deserved; there was no further cheering of the army; only the sinister chant "Death to the Jews! Death to the Jews!" resounding in the vast gallery.

A true concert of joy welcomed Zola's conviction. Cries of satisfaction rose up in Paris and throughout all of France. The police prefecture received a mountain of repetitive reports describing a population happy with Zola's penalty.[19] In Nantes, Caudéran, Verdun, Guéret, Hendaye, Caen, Poitiers, Lille, Saint-Germain-en-Laye, Cognac, Lunéville, Issoire, Clermont-Ferrand, and Châlons-sur-Marne, it was with the "greatest satisfaction" that the population learned of the news. In Nancy and Saint-Nicolas-du-Port and in Avricourt, "the satisfaction is universal . . . The only defenders of Zola were Israelites and foreigners."

All the reports agreed that Dreyfus's supporters were "exceedingly rare." In Grenoble "satisfaction could be read on every face. This morning Grenoble returned to its accustomed calm and its confidence in the destiny of France." In Gérardmer "the sentence found unanimous approval both in the working class and among patriots inspired by the love of a strong and prosperous France." In Douai, "with the exception of the socialists, the vast majority, not to say the unanimity, of residents, both in the city and in the towns, approve of the court's judgment." In Béziers "more than nine-tenths of the population" approved of the judgment. In Briançon "houses were immediately decked with French and Russian flags as a symbol of joy." In Montauban the police superintendent wrote: "From all sides, everywhere I went, I observed a general, complete satisfaction regarding the end of that real nightmare." Similarly, in Amiens, "in cafés, in clubs, everyone discussed the news and felt relieved of a nightmare that has weighed on people's consciences. Apart from the anarchist element, the population was unanimous in approving the verdict." In Tours, where the population welcomed the verdict "with keen pleasure," a locally printed obituary notice framed in black circulated: "You are requested to shed a tear over the sad end of *Mein Herr* Emilio Zola, dutifully deceased in Paris, bd du Palais, in the courtroom of the Assize Court, on February 23, 1898." A poem followed: "La complainte de Nana" (The Ballad of Nana).*

> *It is said that Dreyfus's syndicate*
> *And his riff-raff*
> *Has put you in such a rotten state,*
> *My poor Pan-face,†*
> *That if you stick your nose outdoors,*
> *Without the police,*
> *Someone would surely do a bad turn*
> *To your yellow face!*
>
> *It is said that you, to cause a stir,*
> *Had yourself circumcised . . .*
> *And then as well that you can be proud*
> *That Berlin admires you.*
> *Well! You know, I won't hide it from you,*
> *I'm only a whore*
> *But palling around with Judases*
> *I find abhorrent . . .*
>
> *If not for the Yid Reinach,*
> *With his greasy face,*
> *Whose fortune comes from a hold-up*
> *Of notorious memory,*
> *Who swore to get a review of the case*
> *Or even do a burglary,*
> *You scoundrel, you wouldn't be*
> *In this mess.*[20]

Zola's defeat represented a victory for an anti-Semitism that went far beyond nationalist circles. The mobilization that stirred Paris and so many other cities in France stemmed from deeply rooted prejudices, as well as from the decisive action of well-established and influential anti-

---

*Nana: the title character in one of Zola's novels.—trans.
†Pan-face (*Pot bouille*): the title of one of Zola's novels.—trans.

Semitic leagues. On January 1, 1898, the first issue of a new journal, *Bulletin Officiel de la Ligue Antisémitique de France* (Official Bulletin of the Anti-Semitic League of France) was published in Paris. Edouard Drumont, who had founded the league in 1888, sent a letter of support. "I wish this bulletin success," he said, adding: "It may happen, it will happen—I want to hope, for the salvation of France, that the anti-Semites will play a major role in public affairs, that their ideas will prevail, that they will deliver this country from the ignominious yoke under which it has fallen."

The journal was edited with an iron hand by Jules Guérin, whom a police report of October 1897 described as follows: "Physically, he's a tall and strong man. He never goes out without an enormous bludgeon on him. He specializes in holding public meetings and street demonstrations. In concert with his brother, he has created a clientele of butcher boys in the slaughterhouses of La Villette, and they escort him, applaud him, and support him with their fists."[21] Whenever Guérin went to meetings that might not be safe, he was accompanied by two colossi: "One of them is named Joseph, is of Herculean strength, and is blindly devoted to Guérin. He is easily recognizable, since he always wears a white smock and carries an enormous umbrella."[22]

Guérin, a particularly determined leader, was extremely violent, close in that respect to the marquis de Morès. It was Guérin who invented the lethal cane that the militants would use at the end of the year. A police report describes the following scene: "Guérin is inside the brasserie La Grande Maxeville. With satisfaction he displays a cane to those around him, 'the new anti-Jew' destined to subdue the sons of Israel. It is an oak cane, like a Basque *matrila*, with a tip resembling an ordinary cane but whose head is made of steel or lead. That cane is very heavy and must be a terrible weapon. In the lining of his overcoat or morning coat, within easy reach, a holster has been sewn." The so-called "anti-Semitic canes," distributed by Guérin to his acolytes and also to political figures, were produced by the arms manufacturer Goyot, exclusively for Guérin's use.[23]

The Ligue Antisémitique, present in every city in France, was particularly well organized into branches in the arrondissements of Paris.[24] As an astonishingly complete police report noted:

The Ligue Antisémitique of France had long since fallen apart, when, about a year ago, after Morès's death, Jules Guérin reconstituted it. That reconstitution was not very strong until the advent of the Zola trial allowed Guérin to revive the league . . . Large donations were made, some anonymous, others openly, such as that by the prince de Croÿ, who paid 300 francs all at once. The leaguists obey Guérin as soldiers obey their colonel. Discipline is absolute. The league is composed of a central committee, Parisian branches, and member branches in the provinces. At the head of each branch are the most determined of the leaguists in the arrondissement and the city. Every leaguist receives an order number, for example, 27388, which serves as his signature in his correspondence with Guérin. The latter knows only these numbers . . . In Paris, seven branches are normally operating . . . Fourth arrondissement: the weakest branch, it has barely fifteen members . . . The organization is a more serious matter than believed because its cadres are solid and well chosen. The troops follow without question.[25]

In the early part of the year, the police had complete lists of Parisian members along with their addresses and sometimes, but infrequently, their professions. There was Marréaux-Delavigne, lawyer; E. Davot, industrialist; Alfred Godfroy, pork butcher; Paul Manteaux, musician; Cousin, industrialist; Talagrand, joiner; Godfroy Senior, pork butcher; Gabriel Pelin, publicist; Rouyer, engineer; Roncin, merchant; Saint-Auban, lawyer; Legrand, industrialist; F. Paris, lawyer; Gentil, wine retailer; Collignon, publicist; Lobien, journalist; Marseilles, merchant; C. Bastien, photographer; Quentin, merchant; Ribot, property manager. They represent twenty of the total 350 members listed.[26]

Standing beside the Ligue Antisémitique was the Jeunesse Antisémitique et Nationaliste (Anti-Semitic and Nationalist Youth), which also proposed to do battle with "the Jewish race, which in the moral, economic, intellectual, and social realms will cause the downfall of the French race." The national committee organizing the action was composed of Edouard Dubuc, engineer, president; Camille Jarre, lawyer; Charles Sellier, architect; André Jacquemont, lawyer; Alcide Laforest and Henry Lecornay, students of medicine; Edouard Dessein, law student; Montclas, man of letters; Jacques Cailly, industrial draftsman; J. Courtier, lawyer at the court of appeals; Sylvain Sallière, sculptor; and F. de Clerbois, bookkeeper.[27]

In the days that followed the verdict in the Zola trial, the anti-Semitic organizations sent posters, designed to launch further unrest, all over France, some 40 by 28 inches, entitled "The Nation in Danger." In Trouville these posters were found, among other places, on the houses inhabited by Jews; in Grenoble and Nevers, they "were put up by the clerical faction"; in Angers, Reims, Valenciennes, Perpignan, Nantes, Blois, Montpellier, and Mâcon, "they were posted on churches and religious establishments by members of the Catholic club and elicited keen emotion among the Israelite shopkeepers." In Châlons-sur-Mer they "were posted by members of the Catholic club"; and in Nancy more than fifty of them were put up on the walls. The poster read as follows:

FOR MORE THAN TEN YEARS, PATRIOTS LIKE DRUMONT AND

MORÈS HAVE BEEN DENOUNCING *THE JEWISH PERIL.*

THEY UNMASKED THE MONOPOLIES, THE STOCK MARKET

TAMPERING OF A VILE HANDFUL OF HEBREWS SPILLING INTO

FRANCE FROM ALL THE GHETTOS OF GERMANY.

NO ONE WANTED TO HEAR DRUMONT AND MORÈS. ANTI-SEMITES

WERE TREATED LIKE PROPHETS OF DOOM.

WE NOW HAVE THE ACT OF TREASON. JUDAS DREYFUS SOLD OUT

FRANCE FOR A LITTLE MORE THAN THIRTY PIECES OF SILVER.

YOU'D HAVE TO BE BLIND NOW NOT TO SEE THE JEWISH PERIL.

FRENCHMEN! THE NATION IS IN DANGER!

THE JEWS, HAVING RUINED US, DIVIDED US, AND DISHONORED

US, ARE IN THE PROCESS OF TURNING FRANCE ON ITS HEAD FOR

THE GREATEST PROFIT OF UNIVERSAL YIDDISCHRY. SO LET US

UNITE TO TURN JEWISH OMNIPOTENCE ON ITS HEAD. AND WHILE

WE WAIT TO DRIVE THOSE DANGEROUS PARASITES THE JEWS

OUT OF FRANCE, LET US DESTROY THEIR INFLUENCE BY EVERY

MEANS. IT IS BEGINNING TO BE TIME TO RETURN FRANCE
TO THE FRENCH!
DOWN WITH THE SYNDICATE! DOWN WITH THE JEWS AND THE
TRAITORS!
LONG LIVE THE ARMY![28]

The early months of 1898 saw a worsening in the relations between Drumont and Guérin: their rivalry, more obvious every day, led Guérin to create *L'Antijuif*, with the help of money from royalists disappointed by Drumont's republicanism. The police also believed that "a number of Drumont's friends are absolutely Catholic and say that any anti-Semitism not based on Catholicism is destined to fail. Guérin believes the opposite. And that is the starting point that has divided people in their admiration."[29] Guérin was now in a position to become the real architect of the anti-Semitic mobilization. His role in the demonstrations in January and February 1898 was essential. Let me give just a few examples, since it is practically impossible to list all the meetings that the league or its closest allies, such as the members of the Jeunesse Antisémite de France or of Abbé Garnier's Union Nationale.[30] On January 13 the Jeunesse Antisémite held a meeting on the rue de Richelieu, and the royalists gathered on the rue des Archives and the rue des Petits-Champs, demonstrating their conviction that "once the king is in power, he will have the Jews expelled." The same day a lecture by liberal writer Anatole Leroy-Beaulieu was disrupted by shouts of "Down with the Jews!" On the sixteenth a large patriotic demonstration took place and ended in an anti-Semitic demonstration. On the seventeenth Guérin collected his troops and prepared for the major demonstration on the nineteenth. "That demonstration," according to a police report,

> will begin in four or six different points at about the same time . . . Guérin says he needs only about fifty students or young people at each starting point for the demonstration to immediately become large and, given the sympathies of the crowd for those protesting the machinations of those who insult France and the army, to snowball. Many workers will participate, and he hopes to have many butchers from La Villette . . . The anti-Semitic students

are overexcited . . . Guérin says that, for these demonstrations to have real importance, they must be allowed to remain unexpected, sudden, abrupt, which gives an accurate picture of the state of mind that opposes the traitor's defenders.

On the evening of the nineteenth, another, smaller meeting took place on the rue de Richelieu: Guérin organized the next demonstration for Sunday afternoon, because "the workers have the day off, and it will be more successful. The rendezvous point is the Concorde and they will march toward the Champs-Elysées . . . Things have been coordinated with Nantes, Nancy, Lyon, Reims, Brest, Clermont, etc." On the twentieth the Ligue Antisémitique gathered again on the rue de Richelieu, where members drank to the hope for the death of Joseph Reinach and the writer and early Dreyfusard Bernard Lazare. Another meeting of the Union Nationale was held on the rue de la Gaîté, attended by two hundred people. A motion was passed "reprobating the conduct of universal Jewry." On the twenty-first Guérin again gathered together the leaders of his organization on the rue de Richelieu to plan the major demonstration for January 23 at Mille Colonnes. On the twenty-fifth the Union Catholique held a meeting on the rue de Fontarbie, attended by 350 people. On the twenty-ninth the Union Nationale de Vincennes held a meeting that brought together 350 people, during which Ernest Billiet lamented that the workers "do not see that they are under the heel of the Jews who are oppressing them." A motion was passed demanding "the Jews' exclusion from public office." On the thirtieth the Jeunesse Royaliste held a meeting in celebration of the Day of Epiphany that attracted five hundred people. The comte de Lanjuinais, a deputy, told them that "the country has been handed over to the Freemasons and the Jews." The Ligue Antisémitique held meetings almost daily, which were observed by the police and during which Guérin put his troops in battle order. He chose the locations where they would regroup and the tactics they would use: "Above all, he recommends that the demonstrators adopt the tactic of secret agents, which consists of not forming into groups and of appearing not to know one another before the opportune moment."

Like Guérin, Georges Thiébaud and Edouard Dubuc put all their strength into the service of the anti-Semitic cause, going from one city to another to incite unrest. In that sense, during all these agitated weeks, Drumont and his lieutenants, as well as Guérin, worked to establish rival centralized organizations that were all pursuing the same goal. On February 1 the Ligue Antisémitique held a private meeting and the Union Catholique summoned its members to the Saint-Ambroise and Folie-Méricourt neighborhoods. Two hundred people showed up. The Bonapartist Napoléon Magne declared that "the Jewish race is as dangerous to France as Freemasonry." A motion was passed "condemning the Dreyfuses and the whole Jewish gang to public condemnation and urging voters to choose only liberal republican candidates." On the second the Jeunesse Antisémite gathered on the rue de Cluny and sang "Les Tribulations de Boule de Juif" (The Tribulations of Jewball). The same day the Clignancourt branch of the Union Nationale attracted two hundred people, with Abbé Garnier in attendance. On the fourth about sixty people, including Drumont himself, came to listen to Guérin within the context of a new study circle, where Dr. Kimon demonstrated that "the entire strength of the Jewish race's resistance and penetration lies in its religious organization." The Jeunesse Antisémite met on the fifth and again on the seventh. That day the Catholic electoral committee in the fifteenth arrondissement met at Cité Talma and promised to denounce "the Jewish and Freemason sectarians." On the eighth the members of the Ligue de la Jeunesse Royaliste denounced "the campaign conducted by Zola and the Jews." On the ninth, at another meeting, Guérin "was of the opinion that it was possible to fight the Jews, not in a duel for a matter of honor but in order to do away with them in a legal manner." On the tenth three hundred people attended an assembly at the Pascaud gymnasium organized by the Union des Démocrates, during which Charles Le Senne, a deputy, denounced the German Jews. Thiébaud then declared that "the Jews are insulting our army. Day before yesterday there were ten thousand people at the entrance to the Palais de Justice; yesterday there were twenty thousand; today forty thousand; tomorrow there will be one hundred thousand. And if Zola is acquitted, two hundred thousand will rise up to take the law into their own hands." On the eleventh the Cercle d'Etudes Sociales et Antisémitiques (Circle for Social and Anti-Semitic Studies) held its work session and heard a lecture by Guérin. On the twelfth there was a meeting of the Ligue Antisémitique on the rue Lantonnet, with only twelve people present. On the thirteenth the plebiscitary committees of Seine held a meeting on the rue Serpente, run by Baron Legoux and with 250 people in attendance. Dubuc violently attacked the Jews, and people shouted, "Long live the army! Down with Dreyfus!"

On the fourteenth Guérin gathered certain leaders of the league to organize the meeting that was to take place the next day at the town hall of Suresnes. On the fifteenth that demonstration attracted more than a thousand people: Jewish domination was denounced, and Lucien Millevoye claimed that "these men who demand a review of the Dreyfus case did not voice the slightest cry of indignation—nor did the intellectuals and academicians, in fact—in the case of the massacre of Fourmies ordered by the Jew Vel-Durand and carried out by the Jew Isaac."* Alexandre Zevaes took the floor to represent the socialists and attacked "the capitalist power of the Jews and Jew sympathizers." He added that the socialists were fighting "capital, whether it is Jewish, Protestant, or Christian." Georges Thiébaud and Max Régis accused "the Jewish race of wishing to dominate the world," and the group separated, shouting: "Long live the social revolution!" On the sixteenth, seventeenth, and nineteenth, the league held private meetings under Guérin's leadership.

On the twentieth, in Salle Chaynes, the league held a demonstration attended by more than five hundred people, who were screened by Guérin himself after being questioned at the entrance. Guérin, then Régis and Millevoye all accused the Jews of dominating France. Régis told the audience that in Algeria "the Jews have responded to shouts of 'Death to the Jews!' with blows, so that the anti-Semites did not hesitate to sack—not loot—their shops." In a great outburst, Millevoye shouted that he was "ready to defend republican liberties, just like Camille Desmoulins† used to do at the Palais-Royal." On the twenty-second four hundred royalist members of the Jeunesse Royaliste gathered in the hall of the Société d'Horticulture on the rue de Grenelle, protesting

---

*massacre of Fourmies: In 1891, during a May Day demonstration by workers in Fourmies, army troops fired on the crowd, killing nine, including women and children. Although the subprefect, Charles Ferdinand Isaac, was Jewish, the prefect, Henry Vel-Durand, was not. See Pierre Birnbaum, *The Jews of the Republic: A Political History of State Jews in France from Gambetta to Vichy*, trans. Jane Marie Todd (Stanford: Stanford University Press, 1996), chap. 10, esp. p. 166.—trans.

†Camille Desmoulins: a journalist and leader during the French Revolution.—trans.

"the attacks on the army by the cosmopolitan Jews, of whom Zola has made himself the defender." On the twenty-fourth the Jeunesse Antisémite held a meeting where speakers denounced the Jewish peril, and the Union Démocratique summoned 250 anti-Semitic nationalists to listen to Guérin assert that he wanted "the peasants of France to imitate those of Galicia who, one day, burned a Jew with his family. He was a witness to the deed and was sorry that people don't do the same thing today to the Jews, who have done so much harm in France." At the end of the meeting, the following motion was passed: "The voters of Père-Lachaise reprobate the machinations of cosmopolitan Jewry in the Dreyfus affair, to the cry of 'Long live the army! Down with the Jews!'"

On the evening of March 4 a meeting was held at Salle Wagram with seven to eight hundred militants of the Ligue Antisémitique in attendance, tightly controlled by the La Villette butchers. The discussion concerned "the 1898 legislative elections and anti-Semitism." Guérin began by asserting that "there are only two factions left in France: the men who are for France and those who are against it. The anti-Semites are the former because they want to force the shady Jewish dealers, those who bankrupt the worker and build the most scandalous fortunes on the poverty of the proletariat, to make restitution." After him Lucien Millevoye, then Max Régis praised the prowess of the Algerian anti-Semites; they "opened the campaign against Israel and showed they were determined to drive the Jews from France by any means." They demonstrated they were certain that "during the coming legislative elections, the Catholic and French deputies will be in the majority." In the general enthusiasm, a motion was unanimously passed that stated: "Within the framework of the coming elections, in the higher interest of French workers, it is indispensable that the candidates for the legislative elections of May 1898 accept anti-Semitic ideas and commit themselves to defend them energetically before Parliament."

As the May legislative elections drew closer, the various anti-Semitic movements had to set aside minor differences. The month of March was marked by countless nationalist meetings of all sorts. Day after day the Ligue Antisémitique held meetings. For example, on March 26 three hundred people met in Salle Chaynes to protest the arrest of Max Régis; Guérin gave an interminable speech expressing his hope that France would "not always be prey to the Jews, thieves, and cosmopolitans." And in Montmartre on March 30, at the hall of Le Rocher-Suisse, more than two hundred people listened to Edouard Dubuc attack Prefect Louis Lépine "who is at the disposition of the Jews." Also in March the league received considerable assistance from Auguste Chirac, one of the most important nineteenth-century theorists of anti-Semitism. On the eleventh and twelfth, for example, Chirac examined the ethnic origin of the Jewish race and denounced its ascent.

At the same time, the Bonapartists rose up against the Republic and the Jews. Its plebiscitary committee held many meetings, like the one on April 13 on rue de Turbigo, at the end of which people shouted: "Down with Marianne!* Down with the Jews! Long live the emperor!" The royalists did the same: for example, on March 16, they staged a celebration on the rue Sainte-Apolline, during which Charles Vincent, an editor at the *Gazette de France*, gave a lecture on Charles Perrault's fairy tales. According to a police report, "he sought out the origins of the tale called 'Bluebeard,' quoted legends, and said that Bluebeard was the Jew, his wife the aristocrat who wants to know of his misdeeds, and the two brothers who rescue her Generals Pellieux and Boisdeffre,† who arrived in time to save the aristocracy and make it victorious. These two saviors are the precursors of the duc d'Orléans, living in exile in London."

All the competing organizations worked relentlessly to prepare for the coming May legislative elections. The Catholic world was also ready for a fight. In addition to the Union Nationale, the Comité Justice-Egalité, established by the Pères de l'Assomption (Fathers of the Assumption) and aided by the priest correspondents at *La Croix*, methodically organized itself, making a precise list of Catholics, Protestants, and Jews commune by commune. In December 1897 it wrote: "At the elections next year, candidates will have to run while making the sign of the cross. Yes, Christian candidates will appear everywhere. In

---

*"Marianne" was the symbol of republican, revolutionary France.—trans.
†Generals Georges de Pellieux and Raoul de Boisdeffre were involved in the investigation and cover-up of irregularities in the Dreyfus case.—trans.

one place, the candidate will be republican, in another, monarchist; elsewhere, he'll be an imperialist. What will it matter? Everywhere he will have to be Christian and Catholic." In March 1898 *L'Oeuvre Electorale*, in the name of the Catholic board of elections in Paris and of the Comité Justice-Egalité, published two brochures, one to denounce "the Jewish peril," the other to warn about "the Protestant peril." In Paris it also printed two thousand copies of a brochure signed "Lebonsens" (Commonsense) and titled *Elèctions générales 1898: Les sept péchés capitaux de la France* (General Elections 1898: The Seven Deadly Sins of France). It read: "Through their perfidious mutual accord, the Freemasons, the Protestants, and the Jews are truly the Devil's Pitchfork . . . It is therefore obvious that God, Catholicism, and Christian France are their common enemy . . . Let us thus be united in heart and soul in hoping for exclusively liberal and Christian republicans in the coming elections. Instead of playing into the hands of the Devil's Pitchfork through our divisions or abstentions, let us attempt to break its back. Long live God!"

On April 6 that bulletin of the Catholic board of elections lauded the "success of the anti-Semitic movement in Algeria and France, which is spreading like wildfire." On April 20 it attacked Henri Brisson, "friend of the Jews and Freemasons." In its view, "the traitors are Jewish, Freemason, and Protestant sectarians who have infiltrated everywhere and are dishonoring the nation. The traitors are the supporters of the betrayer." It distributed a number of brochures and tracts, including one that declared: "Patriots, today more than ever, our dear France must remain for the French! No more Jews to suck the marrow from the Nation! Down with the Jews! Down with the Freemasons! To Devil's Island, all the antipatriots!" On April 6 the bulletin "expressed the wish that the French voters challenge the schemes of the Dreyfus syndicate in the coming elections by refusing to vote for any candidate who might have connections to Jewry and Freemasonry." On May 12, between the two rounds of the elections, *L'Oeuvre Electorale* exclaimed: "God be praised! The prayers, the offerings of our friends have achieved a first success."[31] In the face of such determination, which brought together heterogeneous movements that all had in common a rejection of the Republic, associated, in their minds, with the Jews and Protestants, a police report dated March 24 warned: "The anti-Semitic unrest is taking on alarming proportions in Paris."

For its part, the Ligue Antisémitique de France launched an urgent appeal for funds:

> Dear fellow citizen and friend. With the approach of the electoral campaign of 1898, at a time when cosmopolitan Jewry is going to concentrate all its efforts against French interests and throw around fistfuls of gold to influence the decisions made by universal suffrage, we come to make an appeal for your generous participation in our propaganda fund . . . We address all French people of good will who are determined to stop the invasion of our country by the Jews and their usual creatures, to help us support the struggle against the enemies of France, the insulters of the army who, in the Dreyfus affair, have shown us what they were capable of doing to carry out to their abominable plans. The resistance against Jewish schemes by the Ligue Antisémitique de France requires resources, which we must expect from French people of good will. The assistance we find will be useful to us as the legislative elections approach, in facilitating our active campaign for our nationalist ideas.[32]

The league prepared for the elections with an unconcealed desire to impose the nationalist candidates on Paris. It also intended to benefit from the widespread indignation at the judgment of the Cour de Cassation* on April 2, 1898, voiding the criminal court's conviction of Zola. The nullification prompted astonishment and outrage. In Epinal "the rural voters in particular" rose up in protest, and many "saw philo-Semitic influences at work." As for Montauban, "there is universal disappointment in this essentially military city, where chauvinisn is nearly universal." In Fécamp and Saint-Dié people were "stupefied"; in Nancy "the disappointment" was perceptible; in Clermond-Ferrand an "impression of distress" was noted. In Paris there was considerable emotion, commensurate with the joy that had welcomed the conviction.[33] It was a political opportunity that the anti-Semitic movement as a whole would not miss.

Beginning the first week of April, the Ligue Antisémitique and its al-

---

*Cour de Cassation: the French supreme court.—trans.

lies (*L'Intransigeant*, Abbé Garnier and his troops, the royalists, and others) organized a large number of public protests.[34] An enormous quantity of propaganda materials was set in place: posters, local newspapers, tracts, lampoons, songs. Systematically, in every ward, the group deployed an intensive nationalist campaign, plastering "This candidate is a supporter of Dreyfus" labels across the posters of opponents. On the street urinals in several neighborhoods, small signs announced: "Frenchmen, a century ago, the Jews possessed nothing in France. Today, they are masters of everything and have stolen half the national fortune. Have you had enough? If you have, everyone shout: 'Down with the Jews! Long live France for the French!'" Every member of the league had bundles of tracts of this kind, which they plastered generously on posters, walls, buildings, and shops. The league and its allies threw all their strength into the electoral fray, closely watched every candidate, organized expeditions to heckle speeches or, on the contrary, to provide hired clappers and law enforcement. In each of the branches, people vied with one another in their passion to support the nationalist candidate.[35]

The course of the May 1898 legislative elections in both Paris and the provinces is largely unknown today. Curiously, although they marked one of the vital stages in the rise of anti-Semitism and attest to the great vitality of a nationalism that threatened to sweep away the Republic, apart from localized exceptions they have generally remained terra incognita.[36] At the time anti-Semitism had made great inroads into people's consciousness.

The socialists achieved good results in Paris and in Seine, thanks to the successes of Alexandre Millerand, René Viviani, Philippe Berthelot, Marcel Sembat, and Edouard Vaillant, but some—Clovis Hugues and Paul Chauvière, for example—openly and repeatedly used anti-Semitic rhetoric. Here the anti-Semitic nationalists did not have the success they anticipated and would have to wait until 1902 to get a foothold in Paris. Nevertheless, some of their most virulent representatives were elected or reelected, such as Lucien Millevoye, Paulin-Méry, and Ernest Roche (former Blanquist turned committed anti-Semitic nationalist). Also elected were men who had run as republicans but did not hide the violence of their anti-Semitism: Paul Bernard and the radical Alphonse

Humbert, for example. Unexpected alliances operated without great difficulty. Rochefort and his newspaper *L'Intransigeant*, Drumont's ally in the nationalist battle, supported the candidacies of Paulin-Méry, Roche, and Bernard without reservation, but they also supported the nationalist socialist Hugues and the socialists Millerand and Viviani! People with the most varied political alliances embraced anti-Semitism. The audience for the nationalist message was thus infinitely broader than its supporters narrowly defined. In addition, a number of its official spokesmen were only barely defeated after a campaign in which they proclaimed loud and clear their hatred for the Jews. Levasseur, for example, supported by *La Libre Parole* and *L'Intransigeant* in the fourth arrondissement, received 6,946 votes in the second round, and his radical-socialist opponent, Chassaing, won with only 8,125. A huge sign made by Levasseur's supporters left no doubt about the tone of their ideological message: "Chassaing and the Jews. In a secret meeting, Chassaing has promised to call for a review of the Dreyfus case in the Chamber. Chassaing has wanted to earn the good will of Israelite voters in the arrondissement. Chassaing wants to be the Jews' candidate. The Jews themselves are rejecting the advances of that double-dealer. Long live the Republic."[37] In other words, the terrible months of January and February had undoubtedly left their mark on the population of Paris and beyond.

Incidents occurred on a daily basis: brief anti-Semitic demonstrations took place in the streets of Paris, and persons thought to be Jewish were once again attacked. The unrest increased as a result of the persistent presence of an illuminated board set up in front of *La Libre Parole*, on which the following inscriptions appeared: "Down with Lépine! Death to the Jews! Down with Rothschild!" Everywhere the members of the Ligue Antisémite galvanized their troops.[38] Shouts of "Yid! Traitor!" echoed in schoolyards during the election meetings.[39] In the sixth arrondissement, Prache, considered a *rallié*,* won in the second round, with 4,856 votes to his radical opponent Leveillé's 4,286. During the campaign the following tract was distributed: "Patriots! Do not vote for Leveillé, who is the candidate of the Freemasons and Jews."

---

*A *rallié*: a Catholic who rallied to support the Republic beginning in 1890.—trans.

Similarly, in the first ward of the seventh arrondissement,* Decombe-jean, who wanted "France for the French," clearly displayed his opinions but received only one vote; he attacked his opponent, Charles Benoist, an Opportunist,† on a huge poster that read: "The Jewish faction is no longer content to live among us like a worm in a piece of fruit, it wants to be the master. To help France and the Republic to regain control of itself, to come out of the feverish state and the illness into which the Jewish faction has cruelly sent them, we need free men." Benoist received only nineteen votes. Both were trounced by the socialist Philippe Berth-elot, who was supported by Rochefort.

In the second ward of the same arrondissement, election posters an-nounced:

THE INVALIDES NEIGHBORHOOD WILL BE FAITHFUL TO ITS

TRADITIONS AND WILL GIVE AN OVERWHELMING MAJORITY TO

THE CANDIDATE WHO EMBODIES LAW AND ORDER.

COSMOPOLITAN JEWRY HAS ATTEMPTED TO DESTROY OUR ARMY.

LET US REPROBATE THE SYNDICATE OF TREASON.

IN THE NAME OF DISCIPLINE, YOU WILL ALL SUPPORT THE

PATRIOTIC CANDIDACY OF PAUL LEROLLE.[40]

Paul Lerolle was far ahead in the first round with 6,896 votes, while his radical opponent received only 4,628. He would be elected without difficulty in the second round. But Lerolle did not belong to the nationalist camp; although he was a monarchist, he (unlike Levasseur, Prache, and others) did not share the ideas of Paulin-Méry and Millevoye. In the first ward of the ninth arrondissement, Georges Berry, the incumbent Opportunist deputy, easily prevailed in the first round with 3,790 votes, crushing his nationalist opponents. Teissonnonnière received only 377 votes despite a frenzied anti-Semitic campaign. "The Jews are inassimilable foreigners," he wrote on an election poster: "They

---

*The deputies representing Paris in Parliament are elected by arrondissement and are allotted on the basis of the number of residents. Each arrondissement has several voting wards.—trans.
†Opportunist: a member of the centrist majority in Parliament. The term is not pejorative. —trans.

obey a moral code and laws that are the opposite of our own. They constitute a state within the state. This must end. Long live France for the French!" Even though Léon Lobien was a monarchist and the president of the Ligue Antisémitique in the ninth arrondissement, he received only 430 votes.[41] In the twelfth arrondissement, second ward, Susini, a socialist, nationalist, revisionist,* and member of the Comité Républicain, punctuated his tracts with exclamations of "France for the French! The Republic for the republicans!" and attacked his opponent Paschal Grousset, a socialist. Susini wrote: "I am Christian and proud of it. Mr. Grousset is, above all, the friend of the Jews and the stateless." He attracted 1,064 votes but not enough to beat Grousset.

In the thirteenth arrondissement, the national camp was victorious, taking both seats. In the first ward, it was Paul Bernard, a radical-socialist, whose merits were vaunted in *Le Jour* (May 12, 1898): "He has taken a stand against Dreyfus and the Jews. And by virtue of that alone, Bernard has all the Dreyfusards against him. We truly want Paul Bernard to be deputy." In the second ward, Paulin-Méry, the incumbent deputy, a socialist-revisionist and frenzied anti-Semite, crushed his opponents in the first round.

The local press also spread boundless hatred of the Jews. *Le Journal du XIII*, "the democratic organ of local interests, a republican newspaper," informed its readership of concerts given in the Parc Montsouris and in the Jardin des Plantes, and of shows scheduled for La Fauvette, writing at the same time: "The Jew wants at all cost to reverse unfavorable public opinion; that wandering race is becoming entirely bound up in the act of treason by one of its own . . . The working people in our arrondissement hate lies and treason." In another article, that newspaper added: "France is becoming more Jewified every day. Three-quarters of French soil is in the hands of the Jews. The Jewish invasion is also mani-festing itself in the absorption of small businesses by the Jewish bazaars." Finally, little stories like the following were published on the front page of *L'Avenir du XIII*.

It is nine o'clock in the morning. Deputy X is feverishly pacing back and forth in his office. Sometimes, while looking at the clock,

---

*Revisionist: here, one who favors the revision of the constitution. The term can also refer to those favoring a review, or "revision," of the Dreyfus case.—trans.

he displays a keen impatience . . . Suddenly, the bell located in the antechamber rings . . . The door opens. A man, meticulously dressed in the manner of doddering old men, comes into the office. By his nose, it can be discerned that his name must be Abraham.

ABRAHAM: Gut day, Misser Deputy, are you vell?

DEPUTY: Okay, but things could be better.

ABRAHAM: I see dat you do not look zo hoppy.

DEPUTY: No, I am shi—out of sorts.

ABRAHAM (*aside*): How distingvished he is, dat von. (*Aloud*): Oh, really, I zoospegted dat.

DEPUTY: ???

ABRAHAM: Yah, politics, you zee, dat's made to bodder peoples.

DEPUTY: That's right, you never know what to do.

ABRAHAM: For to make your foters hoppy?

DEPUTY: Oh, that, I don't give a damn about that. I mean, my voters are not difficult, they are satisfied with very little.

ABRAHAM: Zo vy are you ubzet?

DEPUTY: Don't you understand? I'm low on loot.

ABRAHAM (*stupefied*): Loot?

DEPUTY: You know, moola.

ABRAHAM (*understanding less and less*): Moola?

DEPUTY (*aside*): Ay, what a fool! (*Aloud*): Yes, bread, dough, lettuce, don't you understand the language?

ABRAHAM (*bewildered*): No, I don't know dat.

DEPUTY: (*makes him understand with a significant gesture, sliding his index finger across his thumb*).

ABRAHAM (*whose face suddenly shows understanding*): Barfectly, barfectly, you vant to talk money?

DEPUTY: Naturally, times are hard, and the poor Lefties who catch a thirst from all the bawling don't give a bean to wet their whistles.

ABRAHAM: Vell, here's da deal. You are supporter of dee syndicates?

DEPUTY: Why, of course, necessarily. We need them.

ABRAHAM: Vell, me too, and de proof is dat I am a syndicate member.

DEPUTY: Ah!

ABRAHAM: Yah. I belong to de syndicate of Treyfus, you know, dat unfordunat gaptain dat vaz condemned for a trifle.

DEPUTY: Well, come on, what are you getting at?

ABRAHAM: Vell! Here it is. I offer you a chance to yoin de syndicate.

DEPUTY: But only the bigwigs join it, you know, the moneybags.

ABRAHAM: Bardon, bardon, der is two cadegories, dem that pays and dem dat receives.

DEPUTY: If there's any way for me to be one of the second group, I'm with you.

ABRAHAM: Understoot. You are von of us, dat's bery easy. Start to-morrow in your newspaper wid a heart-felt ardicle for our gut friend Treyfus.

DEPUTY: Bravo. Nothing could be easier. That works perfectly. It's an easy cause to defend: the duty of the socialists is to defend the oppressed. Let us fight the alliance of the saber and the aspergillum. Clericalism is raising its head again, we must crush it, etc. (*He dances and sings. Then, striking the belly of the Jew, who gives a muffled groan:*) Huh, old pal, isn't that right?[42]

In the first ward of the fourteenth arrondissement, Cuverville, listed as an independent democrat, was defeated by Girou, a nationalist socialist. The winner, Girou, who was a committed anti-Semite, was supported without reservations by *L'Intransigeant* and its nationalist friends. Nevertheless, his opponent, Cuverville, did not hide his anti-Semitism. In the second ward of that arrondissement, E. Jamier, listed as a democratic republican patriot, wrote in his platform statement: "Let's hunt down the shady cosmopolitan speculators and the Jewish speculators. France for the French first, and for all the rest afterward, if anything remains: crumbs from the national table are enough for them." He was defeated, receiving only 749 votes.[43]

In the fifteenth arrondissement, *L'Avenir du XV*ᵉ ran the following anecdote under the heading "On the Lighter Side": "On the rue de la Chaussée-d'Antin, a gentleman got into a hackney cab, saying loudly to the driver: 'Twenty-five, rue Jacob.' 'Alas!' said a young pastry chef who was strolling along. 'On the rue Jacob, another Kike.' " On April 30, the eve of the elections, that newspaper put the following on the front page:

Some newspapers have run the news that the Jews intend to throw "a large sum" into the election campaigns to ensure themselves a

majority of deputies in favor of reviewing Dreyfus's case. The Jewish race is audacious . . . The worker must know these things, they
must be repeated to him: as he works constantly to increase the
renown of French industry, as he sweats from sunup to sundown
to toil for his bread, there are men who bear the title of Frenchmen without having any affinity to his race, who enjoy the same
rights he does, and whose aim is to bankrupt the nation physically
and morally . . . Oh, if only our ancestors had seen through the
descendants of Judas, had locked them up in a special neighborhood from sundown till the first gleam of dawn, had imposed a
particular costume on them so that everyone could stay away from
them as they would the center of an infection . . . A hooked nose,
enormous, hairy ears, an accent there's no mistaking, are the stigmata that have replaced the long redingote and the pointed cap of
the past. Like them, they still signify, whatever certain snobbish
and fin de siècle intellectuals might claim, "Mind your purse and
the honor of your race, you are dealing with a Jew."[44]

In the second ward of the fifteenth arrondissement, Rear Admiral
Mathieu received 1,311 votes in the first round, after declaring, in
Vaugirard-Grenelle: "Citizens, these are difficult times. The motto must
be: France for the true Frenchmen and not for those foreigners naturalized yesterday who have no patriotic feelings in their hearts and became
French only out of self-interest. Let us therefore be true Frenchmen.
Our people will return to Christ, who is life." In another declaration
Rear Admiral Mathieu flew into a rage: "Enough Jews, enough rabbis in
our public affairs. We want nothing to do with the clericalism of the triangle,* the annex of Israelite clericalism. Long live France for the
French!"[45] During an election meeting held on the rue des Entrepreneurs in front of five hundred people, he attacked the cosmopolitans
and Jews who destroyed the army, and ended with "God and country!"[46] He was nevertheless defeated by Chauvière (4,041 votes), a Blanquist socialist, whose strong anti-Semitic tendencies were known, and by
Chérioux, a radical-socialist officially supported by *L'Intransigeant.*

*Clericalism of the triangle: an allusion to Freemasonry.—trans.

In the first ward of the sixteenth arrondissement, Marius Touradre announced his candidacy as an anti-Semitic socialist before six hundred people: "He announces his candidacy to do battle with the Jews, who are squeezing the working class."[47] In the second ward of the same arrondissement, Millevoye easily defeated his opponents. During a lecture held on the rue Pergolèse before more than eight hundred people, he mercilessly denounced "cosmopolitan Jewry and the traitors to France who have allied themselves with Zola."[48] In the first round, he attracted 2,441 votes, and in the second 3,178. His unsuccessful rival, the liberal economist Paul Leroy-Beaulieu, received 1,378 votes in the first round and 2,082 in the second. Millevoye denounced on his posters the cosmopolitan Dreyfusards, the "Jews who buy votes," and attacked Leroy-Beaulieu, "that so-called republican openly supported by the international plutocracy and by cosmopolitan Jewry." He was aided in that task by one of his unsuccessful opponents, Charles Fortin, who also attacked Leroy-Beaulieu on his election posters: "Do you want to see the supporters of monopolies, of cosmopolitan high banking, join the Chamber, they who hound the small businessmen and workers with their contempt? Then vote for the philo-Semites, who do not respect our beliefs."[49]

In the seventeenth arrondissement, Charles Le Senne, incumbent deputy and anti-Semitic nationalist, was defeated despite a very active campaign, during which he held meetings where more than twenty-five hundred people assembled in Salle Wagram. *Batignolles-Journal* supported him without reservation, faithfully reporting on all his election meetings, where he attacked Dreyfus and always concluded with a resounding "France for the French!" But to no avail—he was defeated. In the second ward of that arrondissement, Ernest Roche prevailed in the first round with 9,586 votes, against his republican rival, Roger Ballu, who received only 5,870.[50] In the eighteenth arrondissement, the first ward of Montmartre, André Vervoort, supported by *L'Intransigeant* and its friends, conducted a very hard campaign in support of "France for the French" but failed miserably, finding only twelve voters.

In the second ward of the arrondissement, Gérard Legué was soundly beaten by G. Rouanet, a socialist. On huge green posters, Rouanet had declared: "I am a patriot. The ruthless enemy of the stateless, I protest with all my might against the campaigns conducted by cosmopolitan Jewry." On a tract distributed by the Comité Central des Républicains Socialistes Patriotes (Central Committee of the Patriotic Socialist Republicans), it was declared that "Rochefort and the whole republican press that is not in the hands of the Jews recommend Dr. Legué to the patriotic socialist republican voters. Down with Zola! Down with Jew-sympathizing, sectarian clericalism! Long live the national army!" On huge yellow posters, another candidate, Gaston Habrekorn, hurled abuse at Rouanet, "the friend of Dreyfus. Must we all cut our own throats, must our children go without bread, must commerce stop because of a Jew?" Rouanet was elected, but the strength of the nationalist camp was indisputable. In the third ward of that arrondissement, in Goutte-d'Or, confusion also reigned: *L'Auvergnat de Paris* and *L'Intransigeant* and its friends supported Pierre Foursin, who, memorably, won a total of seven votes; G. Delpy attacked D. Lavy, the collectivist candidate, "the friend of Reinach, the hireling of Rothschild," and received three votes; Lavy denounced the "Jewish capitalists" but was barely defeated, receiving 5,761 votes; for his part, Armand Holtz, a radical, who won with 5,946 votes, accused Lavy of having sold out to Zola's gang and, on a large green poster, denounced Lavy as the defender of the Dreyfus Syndicate! Understand that if you can.[51]

In the nineteenth arrondissement, the contest pitted Clovis Hugues, a nationalist socialist supported by *L'Intransigeant* who had frequently made anti-Semitic declarations, against the equally anti-Semitic comte de Sabran-Pontevès, a royalist. Hugues prevailed without difficulty in the second round.[52] The twentieth arrondissement reelected its two socialist deputies. In the first ward, Dejeante prevailed in the second round; the candidate who ran under the anti-Semitic label, Adrien Poccaton, received only 361 votes in the first round, despite the huge yellow posters that read: "Who profits from revolutions? The Jews. The Zola-Dreyfus affair is stunning proof that, in our homeland, they are the vanguard of the foreign invasion. Spewed out by other peoples, always for the same reason, they dream of making our nation a new Judea. Patriots of Belleville, you will not allow it."[53]

The results of each of the two rounds were joyously celebrated by the nationalists as well as by the socialists, who made major inroads. Throughout the evening of May 8, the boulevards were very busy. According to a police report, "the public cheered Drumont's election and applauded Guesde's* defeat in Nord." The next day, true to their habits, young people passed on the place de l'Opéra and chanted their favorite slogan: "Death to the Jews!" On the twenty-second, at about eleven p.m., people were shouting, "Long live the socialist Republic! Long live the Commune!" outside *La Petite République*. An enormous banner covered the windows of *La Libre Parole*, straightforwardly proclaiming: "Down with the Jews!" On the boulevards people booed, chanted, and shouted, "Down with the Jews!" Late into the night about four hundred people were still standing outside *La Libre Parole*, "applauding every time an anti-Jewish election result was announced to them."[54] In the bars people celebrated at length. To revel in the success of Drumont and a number of his friends in Algeria, the branches of the Ligue Antisémitique worked nonstop to throw a party that would befit their hero: beginning on May 21, day after day, people got together to plan all the details of that grandiose event, which was to cap the efforts of the nationalist and anti-Semitic movements in Paris. They planned gatherings, ordered cornflowers and red carnations, and arranged for Bengal lights to be strung along the procession route from the gare de Lyon; they set up close protection for Drumont, fearing an attack by the Jews; they thought up new slogans that would allow them to express hatred for the Jews; and they prepared to put out the flags on the illuminated balconies of *La Libre Parole*. On May 30, the day so anxiously anticipated, a procession of about a thousand people began to march, led by students carrying lanterns. Though brawls erupted near the Bastille, the police managed to cut off the procession just before the place de la République. The crowd, which had swollen considerably, finally reached *La Libre Parole* about midnight. It cheered Drumont and the Algerian deputies, who appeared several times on the balcony. The shouts of "Down with the Jews! Long live Drumont!" lasted about ten minutes.[55]

Always impassioned in battle, the league and its allies, such as Abbé Theodore Garnier's Union Nationale, would remain just as active in the year after the legislative elections. Thus, as the Ligue Antisémitique ex-

*Guesde: the Marxist Jules Guesde.—trans.

pressed it in a brief lampoon, it was able to "support, through a constant propaganda campaign, the parliamentary actions of the anti-Semitic and nationalist legislators, around whom Jewry will try to organize the traditional conspiracy of silence."[56] On May 31 on the rue de Richelieu, Gervaise, a deputy from Nancy, demanded the Jews' expulsion from the army, and Daudé, a deputy from Mende, praised the French peasant who, "instinctively, is the irreconcilable enemy of the Jew."[57]

Before I resume the chronology and proceed to the end of that troubled year, it is important to note that in June 1898 many anti-Semites requested that the names of streets inhabited by Jews be changed or that the streets themselves be destroyed. In that month, nationalist and traditional Paris intended to efface any sign attacking the traditional values of "Old Paris," to cite the title of Drumont's book. Hence residents petitioned to have the names of their streets changed. That was precisely the case for certain residents of the rue des Juifs (Jews' Street). On June 3 Guillé Fils, an importer of coffee, tea, and rum, residing at 20, rue des Juifs, sent a letter to the municipal councilor of the neighborhood to express his hope that, at the session of the council, efforts would be made to change the name of that thoroughfare. The request, approved by the municipal councilor and supported by other tradespeople, occasioned the following report: "M. Guillé's request was certainly spurred by the recent events; as far as we are concerned, we see no disadvantage in reaching a favorable result in this matter." Shortly thereafter, on July 8, a petition signed by numerous residents of the street was transmitted by the municipal council to the administration:

> The undersigned, dwelling on rue des Juifs, are honored to be able to explain to the distinguished members of the municipal council of Paris that, after the anti-Semitic campaign that has been conducted for some time, this name, "rue des Juifs," causes them very considerable commercial harm. During the troubles, several shopkeepers in the neighborhood had their windows broken, and it can be anticipated that, should further demonstrations occur, the ringleaders will proceed to rue des Juifs, a name crying out for anti-Semitic demonstrations.
>
> As a result, the undersigned have the honor of requesting that you,

the distinguished members of the municipal council, may please find another name for their street, for which they will be very grateful.

This text, signed by a barber, four wine merchants, a hardware dealer, a pork butcher, a baker, a laundryman, an oysterman, a grocer, a plumber, and so on, resulted in *rue des Juifs* being changed to *rue Ferdinand-Duval*.[58]

On a number of occasions, nationalist organizations in Paris received the support of deputies from the provinces, such as the legislators Albert Chiché and the hot-headed socialist and extremely virulent anti-Semite Charles Bernard from Bordeaux. Both of them participated in the celebrations of the revisionist socialist patriots, for example, on the rue du Temple and the avenue de Clichy, where many joyful toasts were made to inaugurate a ball. Nearly every day, month by month, meetings took place at various sites in Paris, where people indefinitely repeated the same slogans, read anti-Jewish poetry, compared the Algerian Jew to the Lorrainian Jew, and celebrated "France for the French." So many of these meetings were held between June and October that a full tally cannot be given. Guérin engaged in a stupefying level of activity, his automobile constantly transporting him from Paris to the provinces for propaganda tours.[59] Sometimes these meetings attracted close to five hundred people. For example, on August 19 at the Bouffes Parisiens, a speaker told of the odyssey of Guérin and Morès who, in Verdun, "dressed like cowhands to catch red-handed Jewish butchers delivering unclean meat to the army." Sabran, true to his beliefs, continued the battle for "France for the French." In August and September, other political meetings frequently brought together four or five hundred people and ended in brawls, provoked, with increasing frequency, by the socialists or by Dreyfus's supporters, who were now becoming bolder. In September the Ligue Antisémitique and the Jeunesse Antisémitique delivered copies of the poster "To the Nation" all over France, in response to the eventuality of a review of the Dreyfus case. A review would mean war. "The true murderers of your brothers and sons will turn out to be the promoters of the abominable campaign; know, therefore, how to make the Jews and their accomplices responsible for the blood of France that they will spill . . .

Like our fathers, the heroes of Bouvines, of Rocroy, of Valmy, and of Fleurus,* we will drive the foreign hordes from French territory."[60]

At the same moment, disturbing reports reached the minister of the interior: "It is evident that there is in Paris an actual organization for the surveillance of individual Israelite subjects. It was asserted that, at the desired moment, no Jew could leave the capital, and it was insinuated that care would be taken to destroy all their claims of any kind, to free all their debtors in a single stroke."[61] The league was expanding rapidly at the time, and its militants at the national level were estimated at about eleven thousand; propaganda was constantly improving. The press became more diversified: in addition to *La Libre Parole*, there was *L'Antijuif*, founded by Guérin with the support of Dupuytren, a deputy from Poitiers, which took its inspiration from *La Croix* and tried to put out local editions of the Parisian newspaper. Contacts would be made with the publishing house Hachette to see that all the train stations were supplied.[62] The league established itself on the rue de Rochechouart with offices and a main hall equipped with a piano, a weapons room, and the new newspaper. A fencing master was employed to improve the fighting abilities of the militants.[63] The campaigns to boycott Jewish tradespeople increased in force, and signs were systematically plastered on the walls of Paris: "For the honor and salvation of France, don't buy anything from the Jews."[64] A special effort was made to improve discipline and coordination among the Parisian militants so that they could mobilize quickly; they were provided with new badges, bearing the inscription "France for the French," with an oak leaf and a stalk of wheat. On the reverse side was the personal number known only by Guérin; the militants were supposed to stand ready for action. As a report from an anonymous informant indicated, "if it was decided during the day or at night that a demonstration was to take place, Guérin or his secretary would take a car and go to the homes of the presidents or secretaries of

---

*Bouvines: the battlefield where the French under Philip Augustus defeated Emperor Otto IV, King John of England, and their allies, in 1214; Rocroy: scene of the battle in 1643 in which the French under the Great Condé defeated the Spanish; Valmy: scene of the victory of the French revolutionary army over the combined Austrian-Prussian force in 1792; Fleurus: scene of the battle in 1794 in which the French defeated the Austrians under the prince of Saxe-Coburg.—trans.

the branch to communicate the order. In the branches, delegated couriers would be named to transmit his orders by word of mouth to the members of the league. In that way everyone would be able, within half a day, to assemble in one place without using either the post office or the telegraph office and, as a result, without giving any warning. Guérin announced that, with the complete transformation of the league, efforts would be made even in the provinces and that, in two months' time, a period of concerted activity would begin."[65]

The Ligue Antisémitique also made contacts with the Ligue des Patriotes. The rebirth of the latter league dates from September 1898, when Paul Déroulède explained his position on the key question of anti-Semitism before four thousand people, with another fifteen hundred outside. He said: "We need to find our bearings, we believers of France . . . I ask those who shouted 'Down with the Jews!' to divide the French people not by religion but by opinion. On one side are the Dreyfusards, on the other the French. A Jew who is not a Dreyfusard is two times a Frenchman. A Catholic who is a Dreyfusard is two times a foreigner."[66] Nevertheless, the "naïveté," the "glaring contradiction" between Déroulède and his men becomes obvious in the following police report. Déroulède "was unable to understand the state of mind of his former troops, who had become anti-Jewish; they could follow him in the realm of patriotism but would abandon him on the anti-Jewish question. M. Déroulède will soon realize that."[67] The contacts between the Ligue des Patriotes and the Ligue Antisémitique date precisely from September, when Marcel Habert—Guérin's lieutenant—and Gally came to solicit the help of the Ligue Antisémitique for their major demonstration at the end of the month, on the condition that the cry of "Down with the Jews" be prohibited. As a result, the League Antisémitique preferred to abstain and organized its own anti-Semitic demonstration for the same day on the place de l'Etoile. According to *La Libre Parole* (September 26), "outside the mansions of the big Jews, especially Bamberger at the traffic circle, the column was three thousand demonstrators strong. The crowd, gathered at the intersection, hailed and cheered them." Guérin, wishing to improve relations between the two organizations, addressed an open letter to Déroulède in *L'Antijuif*, writing: "Like you, we love France, the country where we were born, and just as much as you must love it . . . We wish to sleep here under the watch of our descendants, side by side with our ancestors . . . You are a poet, you are a soldier: the machinations of the Jews, men of money, buzzards and vultures, have escaped your attention." Returning to Déroulède's declaration against anti-Semitism, Guérin added: "You have declared that you are not anti-Semitic and that you never will be. We assert the opposite today and tell you: 'A patriot like you must inevitably become anti-Jewish and you will become it.' "[68]

On October 2 a Dreyfusard meeting was planned for Salle Wagram and organized by Francis de Pressensé, director of the municipal theater. During this explosive day, the symbiosis between nationalist and anti-Semitic militants further increased during their joint demonstration against the meeting. Under pressure from Déroulède's troops, anti-Semitic militants, and royalists present on the scene, the hall remained closed—the meeting could not take place. Despite an impressive contingent of law enforcement, brawls erupted on the avenue de Wagram and the place de l'Etoile. The police brutality against the Dreyfusards was unrestrained. The unrest spread from the rue de la Paix to the rue Montmartre, punctuated by the same shouts, tirelessly repeated; ten thousand, perhaps twenty thousand people or more, participated in that near riot. Police charges, on foot or on horseback, followed in quick succession.[69] At the head of the avenue de Wagram, a triumphant Déroulède appeared with his lieutenant, Marcel Habert, and escorted by the fiercely anti-Semitic deputy Lasies, a close friend of Drumont. The crowd cheered him; hats waved in the indescribable mob; and on every side brawls started up between "Frenchmen" and "Dreyfusards," to use the categories of the head of the Ligue des Patriotes. Déroulède descended the avenue des Ternes before ordering people to disperse. On October 3 *La Libre Parole* exclaimed its joy: "Déroulède is at the head of that army. As soon as they see him, our friends shout 'Down with the Jews! Long live the army!' . . . The Jews were driven into all the little streets around the avenue de Wagram. On the corner of the rue Beaujon, more than two thousand demonstrators burned the hats of the Kikes, in order, they said, to purify the air reeking from that riff-raff."[70] On October 7 a meeting was held in Salle Charras, during which Déroulède and Thiébaud spoke in succession. *Le Gaulois* concluded that "the characteristic event of that meeting was the conclusion of an absolute agreement between the friends of MM. Rochefort, Drumont, and Déroulède." That observation led to deep worry on the part of *L'Aurore* (October 9): "A new army is rising up against the Republic: the black-robed army placed under the occult leadership of the Jesuits."

For three weeks a police informant had been warning the prefecture: "M. Déroulède makes frequent visits to *La Libre Parole* . . . [Drumont's] anti-Semites are extraordinary: last night, they spoke of nothing less than of invading the Chamber. They would probably have Déroulède's leaguists with them, along with the members of the Ligue Antisémitique, led by Guérin."[71] An attempted coup d'état was not out of the question. On October 25, on the place de la Concorde, Déroulède officially summoned his troops and participated in a near-insurrection close to Palais-Bourbon as the deputies were beginning a new session of the Chambers. It was masterminded by Drumont, Guérin, Millevoye, and their troops. The people were violent and ardently shouted the usual slogans, "Long live the army!" and "Down with the Jews!" Déroulède was not afraid to strut about for a few minutes to elicit the crowd's cheers. Shortly thereafter the police apprehended Guérin himself for assaulting Superintendent Leproust.[72] On October 30 Déroulède thanked the leaguists and emphasized that "before being a motto of the Ligue Antisémitique, 'France for the French' had long been, and still is, in spite of everything, one of the foremost watchwords of the Ligue des Patriotes."

In December at the Pascaud gymnasium, in front of five hundred people and under the chairmanship of Déroulède, Thiébaud, Millevoye, Paulin-Méry, and Firmin Faure, the major figures of anti-Semitism, engaged in their usual diatribes. The members of the Ligue Antisémitique joined in that meeting with Millevoye. The call for unity was clear: "Ligue des Patriotes: we very vigorously challenge all our friends from the nationalist socialist groups, all the patriots, all the anti-Semites to attend the meeting this evening." As the meeting was letting out, a joint demonstration was attempted near the Ministry of War.[73] Although Déroulède condemned anti-Semitism, he associated his movement extensively with the tactics of the leaders of the leagues and organizations hostile toward the Jews. There was increasing fear of coordinated action. An anonymous report dated November 3 made the tactics explicit: "We are informed by a reliable source that, at this moment, the nationalist and anti-Semitic committees are being brought together into a single group. It is MM. Millevoye and Thiébaud who may be particularly concerned with that question and, in spite of certain difficulties in execution, it is believed that that merger is only days away."[74] As another anonymous report wrote, "tempers are flaring and the conflict may turn serious from one hour to the next." Several anonymous reports from early December revealed that "the leadership committee of the Ligue des Patriotes has just sent a circular to the chairmen of the imperialist committees to invite them to participate in the continuous anti-Jewish demonstrations that the Ligue des Patriotes has decided to hold to defend the army's honor."[75]

However carried away the police informants may have been, undeniable rapprochements seemed to be under way. Consider this report by a police informant, dated December 6: "Truly, those gentlemen [Déroulède, Millevoye, Guérin, and Habert] have displayed antipatriotism, putting themselves at the heads of gangs of terrible rogues, running through the streets of Paris shouting, 'Death to the Jews.' " Consider as well the December 12 demonstration at which the members of the Ligue des Patriotes, the Ligue Antisémitique, and the Jeunesse Royaliste all participated together beside the Bonapartists and the committees from *La Croix* (Comité Justice-Egalité). In a coordinated effort, each group strove to reach the rue du Cherche-Midi for a demonstration. Although the effort failed, it revealed how far the plans for a rapprochement had advanced. As a police officer observed, "although the demonstration remained inconsequential, it nevertheless proves that the elements that once constituted the Boulangist army are again making contact for a joint action."[76]

The year 1898, punctuated by so many anti-Semitic demonstrations, ended with a flourish: a few months after Lieutenant-Colonel Hubert Joseph Henry's suicide on August 31, *La Libre Parole* established a national fund known as the "Henry monument," to aid his widow, a fund that was suspended on January 15, 1899. Anti-Semitism was unquestionably expressed in the many comments that accompanied the donations.[77] On December 17, as had occured in early January, a large group of anti-Semites again wound their way along the boulevard Saint-

Germain, armed with canes and tree branches. According to an informant, they "struck left and right at passersby and at anyone who did not want to join their group, shouting, 'Death to the Jews! Long live the army! Long live Régis!' This reporter himself was hit in the face with a tree branch by a group of anti-Semites on the corner of the rue de Varenne and the boulevard des Invalides, and still bears the marks from it."[78] On December 19 huge posters were put up on the walls of Paris by the increasingly aggressive Ligue Antisémitique: "If our current government were to fail in its sacred duty to protect France, which is threatened by international Jewry, the people would return to the direct exercise of their inalienable rights by declaring the nation in danger and by acting against the enemies within and without. Long live France! Long live the army! Down with the Jews! Down with the traitors!"[79]

The climactic moment, laden with threats that materialized the following year, occurred on December 29. Déroulède sent a letter to the four thousand leaguists assembled at the Saint-Paul riding school, in which he proclaimed his indestructible confidence in his faithful lieutenants Habert and Albert Gauthier de Clagny but also his friendships with Paulin-Méry and Thiébaud. These major anti-Semitic figures, accompanied by Millevoye—names that had already appeared on the poster calling the Parisians to demonstrate against Zola and "international Jewry" at the beginning of the year—now had only to take the floor to inspire enthusiasm in that huge crowd, composed especially of members of the Ligue des Patriotes. Paulin-Méry believed he could point to the rapprochement of the socialists, the anti-Semites, and even the revolutionaries. "Since every party must have a leader," he added, "and since Déroulède is today master of the situation, as Gambetta and Chanzy* once were, it is that man who must be proclaimed leader of the new party." Millevoye followed, ending his peroration with a resounding "Long live the army! Long live France! Long live Déroulède! Long live Drumont! Long live Rochefort!" Thiébaud then had only to launch his war cry, "France for the French!" and to lead the audience in cheering

---

*Léon Gambetta: leading figure in the formation of the Third Republic, president of the Chamber of Deputies, 1879–81, premier of France, 1881–82; Antoine Chanzy: governor of Algeria, 1873–79, senator, 1875, and candidate for presidency of France, 1879.—trans.

Drumont.[80] Everything had been said. At almost the same moment a ceremony was taking place in front of the town hall of Neuilly-Plaisance, in honor of the soldiers who had died in the siege of Paris during the Franco-Prussian War in 1870. Twelve hundred people participated, shouting, "Long live the army! Long live France!" and soon after, "Long live the Republic!" and "Down with the Jews!"[81]

In the areas surrounding Paris as well, anti-Semitic demonstrations had occurred since the early part of the year, in Puteaux in late January, and in Saint-Denis and Choisy-le-Roi in February, where, according to a report in Le Petit Parisien, "numerous conscripts ran through the streets of the locality carrying an effigy representing Zola and shouting 'Down with Zola! Death to the Jews! Long live the army!' " The demonstrators, soon followed by a large portion of the population, then burned the effigy on the place Rouget-de-Lisle to shouts, repeated a thousand times, of "Down with the Syndicate! Death to Dreyfus! Down with the Jews! Long live the Republic!"

During the electoral campaign, from Levallois-Perret to Saint-Denis and from Sceaux to Versailles, a great many candidates openly proclaimed that they were nationalist and anti-Semitic. Several of them were elected, such as Gervais in Sceaux and André Vervoort, one of the most determined leaders of the anti-Semitic campaign. Gervais ran as a radical, but he attracted the entire nationalist camp. Similarly, in Saint-Denis, Stanislas Ferrand, also a radical, benefited from the enthusiastic support of L'Intransigeant and its allies.[82] In Versailles, the nationalist leaders frequently conducted the anti-Semitic meetings: for example, in May, Millevoye and Dubuc spoke at the Salle du Camélia before 450 cheering people. As a police officer laconically reported, "I will not write at length about the speeches of the orators, speeches that all tended to emphasize the scheming of the Jews, the disruptive actions of the Jewish race, a race absolutely unamenable to any French assimilation and which must first be dispossessed by every means possible, and then expelled."[83]

All the variants of leftist and rightist nationalism were found again in Versailles, where Nicoullaud ran with the support of La Libre Parole, declaring in his platform statement: "I am a nationalist and an anti-Semite. I think that, at the current time, the circumstances require that all native French people unite their forces to wrest our country back from the Jews . . . To save a felon Jew from punishment, they do not hesitate to incite an unhealthy unrest." Gauthier de Clagny and the incumbent deputy Marcel Habert, both of whom played an important role in the Ligue des Patriotes, also did not hide their anti-Semitism. Clagny prevailed in the second ward of Versailles, and Habert was reelected in Rambouillet.[84]

Rather than tracing the unrest into the wards outside Paris, let us continue our meandering tour into the French provinces.

Chapter Two

Journey to the Center of France

Any traveler who left the raging capital and headed for the center of France—toward Bourges and Berry, then Clermont-Ferrand—was in for a great surprise. In the countryside the passions raging in the capital seemed a world away; the sound and fury, nonexistent. Orléans remained peaceful. Its population remained level-headed and went about its business. Its newspapers did not slip into simple-minded anti-Semitism. The police reports remained silent; the police superintendents hardly bothered to keep the Ministry of the Interior informed; and, although the prefects' reports from that period have not been preserved, Orléans does not appear in the National Archives' list of places in France where anti-Semitic demonstrations occurred. The contrast between the unrest that affected Paris and the calm that reigned on the banks of the Loire is striking.

Still, an attentive observer would have noticed that the seeming indifference veiled some of the same prejudices. On January 26, as *Le Patriote Orléanais* reported, army conscripts proudly staged an anti-Dreyfus parade.

Boom, boom, boom! With flags flapping in the wind and drums in the lead, the conscripts were off, bedecked in the traditional "livery." Tomorrow they will be soldiers of France and will go bravely to get themselves killed over there, in the trenches of Vosges or the bush of Sedan . . . As they departed, the mothers and sisters wept; the fathers, seeing these strapping boys they had given to the nation, also felt moved . . . Boom, boom, boom! For their part, the boys did not tremble but departed singing refrains that their fathers and grandfathers had sung, naïve songs in which memories mingle with vows to be loyal to the nation . . . Boom, boom, boom! Now they are on the place de l'Etape. The flags are lowered; the boys form a circle; the singlestick players get in position; and the assault begins. What handsome soldiers they will make. . . . The assault is over. The former opponents advance toward each other and extend their hands. Cheers erupt, and then a shout, unanimous, spontaneous, rises up from every breast: "Long live the army! Long live France! Down with Dreyfus! Down with the Jews!" It happened today around two o'clock in Orléans, in front of city hall![1]

Although "in Orléans Zola's conviction did not give rise to any demonstrations in the street . . . in certain boarding houses, officers celebrated the verdict by drinking champagne."[2] On January 13 the front page of *Le Patriote Orléanais*, whose motto was "God and Country," denounced "the tiny minority where the half-French, half-foreign element predominates. It has claimed to impose its ideas, its laws, on France. Hold on—France knows how to resort to extraordinary measures to command respect. There might be limits to the patience of the majority, were it not for the cynicism and audacity on the part of the minority, the Dreyfus syndicate and company." Day after day the newspaper reported various incidents. A prominently placed article entitled "The Designation 'Yid' " recounted in detail the exoneration of the Catholic newspaper *La France Libre* in Lyon. The paper, accused of using the word "Yid," was found not guilty after the public prosecutor maintained it was an expression in current usage that could not "harm the self-esteem of the children of Israel." The prosecutor asserted that he would feel no

more offended if a newspaper called him a "pettifogger."[3] *Le Patriote Orléanais*, in a polemic against *Le Républicain d'Orléans*, accused it of wanting
"to please the Jews."[4] The same week *Le Patriote* combined local news
with anti-Semitic gossip. On January 16, on the same page as reports on
the events of the Dreyfus affair, *Le Patriote Orléanais* offered an "Orléans
chat," called a "true story," that deserves to be quoted at some length.
The newspaper used the metaphor of an "oasis" to indicate that the
French countryside was being threatened:

> Once upon a time in an oasis, there lived— You will say: This is a
> tale you've begun. It may well be so. But a tale can serve to teach
> certain serious things. Thus, once upon a time, in an oasis in the
> desert, there lived a tribe of indigenous people who dwelt in the
> shade of palm trees and subsisted on the fruit of those beautiful
> trees. Peace reigned among all the inhabitants . . . From time to
> time, there were quarrels, but after each quarrel there was reconcili-
> ation. The intermarriages among the various families had, over
> time, produced something like one big family. Everyone was con-
> tent with his fate and lived modestly but sure of his future thanks
> to the fruit of the trees, the few sheaves of wheat produced by the
> land, and the milk of the herds . . .
>
> One evening as the sun was setting on the horizon, turning the
> desert sand crimson with its fire, a stranger appeared at the en-
> trance to the village. He was skinny and tired after a long journey
> on foot. Scantily clad in pitiful rags, leaning painfully on his walk-
> ing stick, his beggar's bag almost empty, his cheeks hollow, his
> members thin, his face pale, he was a fairly good representation of
> Old Man Poverty, who, as the Legend of the Centuries tells us,
> must roam the earth till his last day. Humble and plaintive, the
> new arrival bowed low to the ground, begging for a few days' hos-
> pitality to recover his health and continue on his way. In return, he
> promised to give news of neighboring countries and to reveal a
> thousand wonders, thanks to which the indigenous people would
> easily grow rich. At these words the young men pricked up their
> ears and, after bringing him fruit, implored him to tell his story.
> The old men knit their brows and said nothing . . . "Watch out,"
> said the elders. "You don't know who this vagabond is or who sent

him, or for what purpose he has come to you. We live happily among ourselves, observing the traditions of our ancestors. Let us beware of novelty and of people we do not know." "That's our grandfathers for you," replied the young people . . . The traveler was able to settle in among the tribe. He made himself insignificant, acted obliging toward all, and became a giver of good advice, a master of new things. To the indigenous people, he taught the art of trade. From his beggar's bag, which no one had noticed on his arrival, there appeared gold coins, which seduced the men, and jewels, with which he wheedled the women and girls. Soon no one could make a decision without consulting him first, and his views were always adopted.

One day, he picked up his walking stick. It would be, he said, a short absence. When he came back, he had two companions with him who looked just like him. This time the elders got angry, but the young people insulted them, and the three companions took their place in the oasis. And with them discord settled in. Gradually, by pandering to the pride of one, the vices of another, and the coquetry of the women, our three gentlemen created a considerable faction for themselves within the tribe. They ridiculed the beliefs, the mores, the laws, and the traditions of the tribe; and in keeping with their counsel, everything was turned upside down. These upheavals created two opposing factions that were tearing each other apart. Moreover, the fortunes of the strangers and of their friends incited the jealousy of those who had remained poor. Thanks to these disputes, the strangers reigned as masters. With them gold was the true king of the tribe. They married daughters of the indigenous people, and their children assumed an arrogant and dominating attitude toward the other children. Some fathers wanted to defend their sons—the strangers shut them up, demanding payment of their old debts, which the fathers had believed were forgotten because no one had spoken of them for such a long time.

These conditions festered. But then people noticed how solidly implanted these strangers had become in the oasis. At the first threat of expulsion, they replied that they were without fear . . . In the oasis life was now intolerable. There was nothing but suspicion, arguments, quarrels, and violence: no more community life, no more ringing laughter, no more simple pleasures shared by all. The wealth of some produced envy in the others. But the richest, the most audacious, and the most arrogant were the sons of these strangers, whose arrival had introduced permanent civil war to the oasis.[5]

French society, in its great naïveté, had opened its arms to the Jews, only to have them dissolve local traditions and set in place discord and civil war, to better assure their foreign power. Virtually every day *Le Patriote Orléanais* continued this underhanded offensive. On the twenty-fifth, for example, it printed: "The Jews do not want to believe in the guilt of their co-religionist Dreyfus. The clericals are to blame, they say. The Jews are pursuing the rehabilitation of the traitor by antilegal, antipatriotic, and antisocial means. The clericals are to blame! The Jews are finding the most distinguished Protestants of France to be their allies. And the clericals are to blame!"

In the streets, after the brief demonstration by the conscripts, things settled down and Orléans returned to its usual serenity. But many variations of anti-Semitic discourse were straightforwardly expressed. *Le Patriote Orléanais* was one of the four major newspapers in the region, and the prefect considered it "the unofficial, if not the official, organ of the Church . . . a newspaper of combat above all [that had] an indisputable influence in Catholic circles far above the other organs of the same tendency," given that almost all its correspondents were priests in the department.[6] In fact, it was controlled by priests, including Abbé de Poterat and Abbé Gibier, who both used a network of religious correspondents: Abbé Besson of Montargis, Abbé Barbier, parish priest of Beaugency, Abbé Besauvre, parish priest of La Ferté, and other "assistant priests, all young, intelligent, and passionate," who acted "in a very disciplined manner." This propaganda newspaper relied on the Catholic clubs, on Jeunesse Ouvrière (Working Youth), on young ladies' clubs, and so on. According to the police, "the priest is truly master of his parish. He holds everything in his hands: the army, the bosses, the worker."[7]

In May 1898, while the legislative elections were in full swing, the feast of Joan of Arc, the heroine who had entered Orléans surrounded by soldiers, was celebrated throughout France. *Le Patriote Orléanais* wrote:

> Chime, bells of deliverance! Foot soldiers, artillerymen, grandsons of the heroes of the siege, crossed the bridge to the joyful sounds of brass bands and fell into square formation in front of the basilica. There on the peristyle stood Monsignor Servonnet, archbishop of Bourges; Monsignor Pagis, bishop of Verdun; Monsignor Touchet, bishop of Orléans; and Monsignor Dubourg, bishop of Moulins, surrounded by all the clergy of the city. Just as the troops arrived on the square, chants of the *Magnificat* soared toward the sky; bugles sounded and drums beat; the municipal officials, preceded by a banner of Joan, advanced ahead of the prelates, who came down to meet it. Addressing the prelates, the first deputy of the municipality assured them that the city of Orléans welcomed them joyfully, this year as every year. According to Monsignor Touchet, we are the vanguard nation, and we open the road to all progress with the sword. Stand back, therefore, you stateless persons [i.e., Jews] . . . Let us love France as God made it, and as Joan of Arc understood and wanted it: let us love Christian France. Under this beautiful sun, the sun of Christ, the true sun of the nation, may all the divisions, all the hatred, all the discord be effaced and disappear . . . According to Monsignor Pagis, Joan is a decisive demonstration against the godless, and she is a no less decisive demonstration against the stateless . . . If the sword of France were still a major force among nations, as it once was, would we see that fin-de-siècle power called the dollar, the wad . . . pounce, with equal parts brutality and injustice, on this proud nation, the guardian of faith and of chivalrous bravery? O Lord, for your glory and for the world's honor, may the wad no longer kill the ideal! Now will the stateless persons understand why we need a strong, powerful France respected by the world?[8]

The campaigns of the legislative elections allowed many prejudices to penetrate even the republican camp, which dominated the region. One of the anti-Semitic tracts circulated in Orléans, titled "Voters, Think of the Jewish Peril, I Beg of You," denounced "the veiled, implacable enemy, Jewry, which has sworn to impose its yoke on us and to reduce us to slavery under its domination. The Catholic party is the one and only savior."[9] Certain candidates—for example, in the arrondissement of Gien—explicitly signed their platform statements with a resounding "Long live the Republic! Long live France for the French!"[10] The two incumbent deputies from the arrondissement of Orléans, both of whom belonged to the republican left, refrained from making any clear commitment to support the Dreyfusard camp.[11] Dr. Viger, the incumbent radical who was easily reelected, found himself the only candidate in the second ward. A cautious man, he kept silent about the Dreyfus affair and even went so far as to condemn the campaign of the Dreyfusards. In the first ward, Fernand Rabier, who drew socialist votes, made no mention of the Dreyfus affair and refused to participate in any campaign for a review of the case. Rabier, forced into a run-off after the first round, was reelected in the second, thus confirming the power of anticlericalism in Orléans, which was so supportive of the radical camp that the army took care not to draw attention to its association with Church representatives.[12] Nevertheless, his opponent, the marquis de Saint-Paul, attracted 40 percent of registered voters after conducting a campaign that was not explicitly anti-Semitic but that was openly anti-Dreyfusard. Hence *Le Patriote Orléanais*, with its rampant anti-Semitism, published an appeal to patriots on May 26: "You remember the traitor Dreyfus. You recall the scandalous trial of Zola, supported by the syndicate of treason . . . Do you want to admit that Reinach was right when he boasted that the Chamber would contain more than three hundred deputies favoring a review of Dreyfus's case? No, a thousand times no. The nation comes before politics . . . Vote for Saint-Paul!"[13]

Not far away, on the eve of the second round, the comte de Salaberry, mayor of Fossé, was more explicit: "The honor of the army is violated by the accomplices of that stateless race that swoops down on a nation to pick it clean. In reality, we are under the domination of a trafficking Jewish syndicate. In the magistrature, let there be justice. In the administration, our own interests. In the army, honor and the soldier's life. France for the French! Out with the traitors!"[14]

In May 1898 the archivist Camille Bloch was one of the few people in Orléans to dare to support the captain's innocence openly, and so he became the target of numerous attacks. Another was Dr. Halmagrand, municipal councilor and arrondissement councilor in Orléans-Ouest, who openly declared his support for Zola and asserted he was sure of Captain Dreyfus's innocence. He ran in August 1898 for the Orléans-Ouest seat on the Loiret department council. *Le Patriote Orléanais* attacked him and championed his opponent, Colonel Beaugé, "the army's representative." On the walls of the city appeared a poster signed by "a group of patriots": "Voters, tomorrow you must declare yourselves for or against Dreyfus and Zola . . . Are you for the rehabilitation of the traitor? . . . Vote for M. Halmagrand. Are you for respect for the judicial system? . . . Vote for Colonel Beaugé. Long live the Republic, long live the army!"[15] Colonel Beaugé, the winner with 984 votes to Dr. Halmagrand's 787, was "a valiant soldier, [who] flew high the army's flag, the flag betrayed by Dreyfus and soiled by Zola . . . The voters of Orléans have punished M. Halmagrand, who offended their patriotism. And, above M. Hamalgrand's head, the blame falls on the syndicate of Dreyfus and Zola."[16]

Dr. Halmagrand, although defeated in the local elections, remained faithful to his convictions and in December 1898 founded a local branch of the Ligue des Droits de l'Homme (League of Human Rights) in Orléans. On January 8, 1899, he held a conference at the municipal theater with the director of the League, Francis de Pressensé, the novelist and playwright Octave Mirbeau, and the writer Pierre Quillard. *Le Patriote Orléanais* lashed out recklessly: "You are the defenders of a man, a Jew, Dreyfus, no more and no less . . . We can assert, documents in hand, that you are defending him only because he is Jewish."[17] Even *Le Journal de Loiret* lost its composure: "Certainly, the citizens of Orléans have a calm temperament and their good sense saves them from excesses . . . The speakers will find a cool and wary audience. But the citizens of Orléans are patriots . . . You do not insult the army with impunity in the city of Joan of Arc."[18] Brawls erupted in the theater; outside, a crowd estimated at three thousand went wild. Anti-Dreyfusards broke the windows of M. Hamalgrand's house and demonstrated outside the home of M. Moïse, a secondhand-goods dealer.[19]

Le Patriote Orléanais openly advised its readers to become members of the Ligue de la Patrie Française (League of the French Nation) and added, "The Dreyfusards began the struggle against the citizens of Orléans. The Orléanais are resolved to hold out until the end." Finally, *Le Patriote Orléanais* abandoned all reserve and made more explicit its often-restrained anti-Semitism: "The conduct of nations toward the Jews ought to be to tolerate them but to watch them closely and keep them apart, away from public affairs and the government especially. Let those gentlemen the Jews . . . stop trying to be unbearable tyrants, and appeasement will come on its own."[20]

Conversely, *Le Progrès du Loiret* published an article clearly asserting the captain's innocence—but not until March 4, 1899, did it make this open commitment. Loiret, a level-headed and republican region that did not indulge in the violence taking place in the capital, nevertheless allowed prejudices to be expressed occasionally, and they spread widely. In the 1901 elections, a defeated candidate in the arrondissement of Gien defended the army's honor and harshly attacked "influence, secret and powerful as gold itself," then concluded this diatribe with a shout of "Long live the Republic!" This outburst elicited the anger of *L'Avenir Républicain*, which condemned that "hateful polemic, borrowing the language of those who wish to overthrow the Republic."[21] During this pre–World War I period, republican and anti-Dreyfusard candidates continued to flourish, reinforcing prejudices that were already firmly rooted in the Catholic world.[22]

Let us now continue our slow descent into the heart of France. If we pass by Blois and its surroundings to the west[23] and plunge deeper into central France, we reach Bourges, a city that was built around a grand cathedral. Bourges had been in the eye of the storm in 1848,* but now nothing seemed to touch it. Nevertheless, on January 22, 1898, we find that "a certain number of workers in the military establishments have planned to gather this evening at six o'clock, after they leave the workshops, to go demonstrate in the main streets of the city to shouts of 'Long live the army! Down with the Jews! Down with Zola!' " The police superintendent, a cautious man, ordered that measures be taken to protect the shops belonging to Jewish tradespeople: La Samaritaine, Le Petit Paris, the Crémieux store, and the Bazar Jacques-Coeur.[24]

---

*1848: date of the revolution that overthrew King Louis-Philippe and led to the establishment of the Second Republic.—trans.

A few days later, on January 26, 1898, *Le Journal du Cher* wrote: "Before now, Bourges had not had its anti-Semitic demonstration. As of this evening, it's a fait accompli: a band of conscripts ran through the streets of the city, chanting: 'Down with the Jews! Out with Zola! Long live the army!' In spite of these shouts, order was not disturbed." This item was lost amid the other news, occupying less space in the newspaper column than the description of a cellar ceiling collapsing in a house under construction across from the military hospital—a worker was buried but miraculously escaped.[25]

Le Journal du Cher did not hide its preference, however: it opened a campaign against Captain Dreyfus, inviting its readers to testify against the "criminal machinations" in which the captain had supposedly engaged in 1889–1890, when he was stationed in Bourges. It went so far as to print: "It has already been said that, when Dreyfus was doing his training as second in command of military pyrotechnics in Bourges, he had the cashier at the military club make pouches, which he sewed inside his jacket, similar to the one in which a duplicate of the infamous *bordereau* was found during a search on the island of Ré."[26] The captain's crimes were already piling up: "One afternoon Dreyfus found himself in an unusual situation, absolutely alone in the hall at the club, when the cashier stepped away for a moment. The captain took advantage of that absence to get hold of the cashbook and settle his account."

The newspaper remained faithful to that line of accusation: in July 1899 it even maintained that, while in Bourges, Dreyfus had procured the specifications for a French munition that he then handed over to the Germans: "The time when the secret of the Robin shell became known in Germany coincided with the time when the wretched Dreyfus was finishing his training period in the manufacturing shops of Bourges . . . One day Dreyfus's commanding officer noticed that military papers concerning a new mount had disappeared. The next day Dreyfus tried to slip them into other papers without his captain noticing. But the captain saw everything and sharply reprimanded Dreyfus for taking these secret documents."[27] This passage gives some idea of the force of the prejudices that were expressed in that major local daily and in other newspapers. *La Délivrance du Cher* maintained that Dreyfus "has betrayed a country that was not his own, since all Jews are cosmopolitans . . . We demand that Dreyfus be shot."[28]

On January 23, 1898, the following little story appeared in *Le Petit Berrichon*:

One person who has never been tormented by the Dreyfus affair . . . is the little girl on the rue des Panoyaux! Is her name Jeanne, Jeannette, or Jeanneton? I don't know. Throughout the neighborhood, she is called "Jeannot" and sometimes even "Jeannot-Lapin," on good-humored and cheerfully sunny days. Jeannot is the very essence of the good girl—or the good boy, almost! Born on the second floor, above the rain spout, in a Ménilmontant garret, she grew in spite of it all, like those poor little plants that cling to life and will never die. Her father had been run over by a truck ten years earlier. Her mother made soldier's packs and trousers. Jeannot, for her part, made hats, just the sweetest hats!

Give her anything: a ring of straw, a bit of felt, a scrap of ribbon, a handful of flowers as plebeian as possible. Snip! . . . bing! bam! a stitch here! a snip there! a crease on the right . . . a gather on the left, and in half an hour, Jeannot-Lapin has created a marvelous little thing for you, fresh and tasteful . . . So Jeannot-Lapin leased a very small shop: ten feet of storefront on the rue des Panoyaux! It did not cost very much, and she could display her hats . . . Women stopped by on the arms of their husbands . . . Seven months of paradise. Jeannot sewed and sewed! . . . The hats flew off the shelves! . . . just flew! . . . Mama skimmed the fat from the pot roast . . . In short, they were about to take on a young apprentice when, one day, a stout gentleman entered: fur overcoat, foreign accent, Jewish nose . . .

"Mademoiselle, are you the one making these hats?"

"Yes, sir."

"Well, my pretty girl, when someone has such dainty hands as you have, she does not make little gems of hats on the rue des Panoyaux for the uncivilized folk of Ménilmontant. I am the owner of a large fashion shop in Paris, and I will give you three hundred francs a month if you liquidate this store and come work for me." And Jeannot, suddenly very sad, remembered that she had often seen the nose of that gentleman pressing against the window of her little store . . . Jeannot left her little street in Ménilmontant

. . . Farewell, good little store open at eight o'clock! Farewell to the pleasure of washing her little sidewalk with clear water from the morning stream!

Her stout boss certainly got his three hundred francs' worth, and he didn't give her time to catch her breath . . . Patterns! . . . Always something new! . . . Ideas! And Jeannot made models and more models . . . She felt the inspiration draining from her anemic mind . . . And then . . . everything smelled of Jew here.

In the boss's dining room, the Jew savored his blood sausage, seated across from fat Rebecca, his wife. "Rebecca, pass me the mustard . . . Did you send the latest hat models to Cologne?"

"Yes, and to Vienna . . . A great success . . . They've ordered more."

"So . . . I'll have to go back to the countryside."

"But . . . what about your little girl from Ménilmontant?"

"My little girl? . . . Well, my dear, I managed to extract everything from her in two months . . . I scraped her last idea out of her. There is nothing more to do but to find, and right away, an excuse to fire her before the end of January."[29]

Le Petit Berrichon was inexhaustible on the subject. On January 16, the day after the Esterhazy acquittal, in its editorial signed "The Peasant," it observed that "this was a good day for French patriots, a bad one for the Jewish nation. That people tried to wage battle, but it was too soon for it to definitively establish its ascendancy over the Nation." The same day, "the Little Plowman" warned future voters that they needed to choose "good candidates, men of the land, known, respected, workers, and Christians. Otherwise, watch out for the Panamaists and the Dreyfusards."[30] On January 23 that newspaper claimed that the country was facing a "war to the death between the Jews and the army, or rather, between the Jews and France." On January 30 it argued that "the Jews have pounced on France like a band of voracious buzzards. That is why I say, to all the good people of Cher who have heart, a shred of patriotism, and Christian faith, however little: let us rally round." On February 13 Le Petit Berrichon wrote further: "Plowmen, workers, and tradesmen, the Dreyfus-Zola scandal, systematically exploited by all who hate France, demonstrates that our nation is the victim of a foreign invasion. That invasion is replacing the French race with a race from over the Rhine, dangerous for its international organization, its love of lucre, and its connections to our worst enemies. For twenty years France has been the victim of the Jews from Germany." The newspaper remained true to its convictions: as it reported in detail the miracles occurring in Lourdes,[31] it continued to hope for a similar miracle to deliver France from the grip of the Jews.

There were other signs of a resurgence of anti-Semitic prejudices in the Cher department, part of the historic region of Berry. In public debates, even among people with the best intentions, the stock images reappeared. On February 19, 1898, a meeting was held in Bourges with the socialist candidate for the first ward of Bourges and with Paul Chauvière, the socialist deputy from Paris. Before five hundred people, Chauvière declared, "The current government, by virtue of its cowardice, is driving us toward the victory of the saber and the aspergillum. We are being robbed by the Jews and the Jesuits. Citizens, if revolution is necessary, let us make revolution, but please, let's get it over with and not wait for the saber to get hold of our freedoms." The next day another meeting was held in Mehun-sur-Yèvre with several socialist leaders, including Chauvière and Breton, a candidate in another ward of Bourges. The speakers attacked capitalist domination, denounced clerical schemes, and vigorously defended Zola. They straightforwardly asserted that "whether it is a captain of industry, a large property owner, or a Jewish capitalist such as Rothschild who is exploiting us, we are against them all; their religion is a matter of indifference to us. The anti-Semitic movement is a distraction for public opinion and is really only against the socialists." But when Chauvière took the floor, he presented quite a different version:

> Now then, what is the difference between a Jew and a priest? I have a friend who is Jewish, and every time he comes to see me, he always offers to sell me something. That's the Jewish type. He must always be doing his business, speculating. He sells you everything for 50 percent more than it is worth, but at least he gives you something. The priest, for his part, is always selling you something as well, but he never gives you anything tangible. You don't want to go to hell, he says—give me so much, and you won't go,

I'm the one in charge . . . You see very well that both are of the same value, and we must not attack only the Jews. But that's a minor thing. The real danger of the Semitic point of view is the vice of speculation, which the rich Jews have imported into our country . . . Today the monks, nuns, etc., have come to stay, have gradually increased, and while the Jews are stealing from us, they for their part are seizing our land.[32]

On February 21 Chauvière repeated the same argument in Vierzon, in Quincy, in Folcy, and in other Berry localities, again emphasizing that "the hatred of the Jews is no more justified than the hatred we should have for the Catholic clergy, who are even more thieving, more exploitative." If the clergy and the reactionaries "want to make the proletarians live on peanuts," the Jews are just as voracious. In Mehun-sur-Yèvre, in front of five hundred people, fights broke out, and the socialists were accused of being "subsidized by the Jews." The socialists retorted that, on the contrary, it was their opponent, the candidate Mouchet, whom the police considered a "braggart," "who receives money from the Jews." Among socialists of good will, the defense of Zola and the Jews was not unconditional; it relied on xenophobia and particularly negative judgments of the Jews. A matter-of-fact anti-Semitism persisted even in working-class circles.[33]

With the streets of Bourges, Vierzon, and Sancerre covered with posters proclaiming "Dreyfus is a traitor,"[34] meetings were held in preparation for the May legislative elections. On April 21 the workers in the military facilities in Bourges assembled in Salle Saulnier on the place de la Nation. Nine hundred people crowded in to listen to the speakers, including the prince d'Arenberg, an incumbent deputy, whom the president of the socialist club invited to express his views. Despite some protests the prince declared he was ready to support retirement pay for workers "with all his strength." The police superintendent in attendance judged in his report that "this meeting may have a certain importance, since it may lead to the disappearance of certain reservations that, I am assured, exist against the prince."[35]

The nationalist forces, pushed out or reduced to a subordinate position in the Berry region, were nonetheless active in the heart of France. On September 14, 1899, an invitation was sent out to a large number of people with the aim of creating the Union Patriotique, Plébiscitaire et Antisémite du Cher (Patriotic, Plebiscitary, and Anti-Semitic Union of Cher). A founding meeting took place on the sixteenth under the leadership of E. Martial, director of *Le Journal du Cher*. On the program "Jean Baffier, the master sculptor of Berry, will discuss our national traditions." Demonstrations were quickly organized in Bourges: for example, on October 14, there was one devoted to the Dreyfus affair. The police superintendent nevertheless was skeptical as to the success of the anti-Semitic movement in the area: "This is the third meeting of that league [The Union Patriotique], which has had no more success than the previous ones, and it is already predicted that it will be short-lived. More skillful leaders have undertaken the same task in different times; they have failed, and these ones too will be unable to succeed." According to another member of the police, "the nationalist league of Bourges cannot be sure of any participation from Berry society, except perhaps from the Catholic clubs."[36] In spite of these skeptical reports, in January 1900 the Union Patriotique counted more than two hundred people in Bourges alone who had paid their membership fees. Another branch was created almost immediately in Vierzon. These branches were far from inactive: in February 1900 they held a public demonstration in Bourges under the auspices of Action Française, a nationalist and anti-Semitic group, which more than four hundred people attended. The speakers denounced the catastrophic actions of the Freemasons and the Jews. The atmosphere was heated; the socialists and republicans waited outside for their opponents and, when they came out, greeted them with "a regular hail of potatoes . . . Soon canes and hats were strewn on the ground. It was a mess."[37]

The nationalist forces, although roughed up by the socialists, nevertheless thrived in Cher, drawing on local traditions. In that republican and greatly de-Christianized region, Jean Baffier, the champion of Berry identity, occupied a central place in the rebirth of an ethnic consciousness, which gave a particular coloring to local anti-Semitism. The garrulous Baffier conferred a cultural aura upon the nationalist struggle. In the heart of France, a purely racist anti-Semitism prevailed. The phrase "France for the French" acquired a nostalgic coloration there, a sense of rediscovering one's own traditions, rooted in one's own soil. Baffier identified with Edouard Drumont, who had theorized the nationalist return to the past and who fiercely opposed any form of modernity, seeing it as the source of decadence. Like Drumont, Baffier bitterly fought the political struggle, becoming an important figure in the Ligue de la Patrie Française. The poet and sculptor even ran in the May 1902 elections for the second ward of Saint-Amand. Although he was defeated in the second round by the socialist Mouger, he captured 25.47 percent of the vote on a platform that explicitly stated his convictions. In this platform Baffier boasted of having founded the Société des Gas du Berry (Society of Berry Lads), adding, "I praise the virtue of the old peasant of France, who holds in his hands the source of our nation's life, its prosperity, its glory." On the eve of the second round, he thanked his voters and called on them to

> defend the national Republic against the coalition of internationalist Freemasons and stateless Jews, those exploiters of peoples. Two factions face each other. The first is the cosmopolitans . . . the second, the French people who still have deliberate valor, courageous pride, and analytical good sense, that is, the virtues of the original race . . . It is the latter faction that has been victorious in several regions of France and in Paris. Our great capital, where the French soul still stirs, has freed itself from the foreigner's henchmen . . . We cannot lag behind the Parisians, we nationalist republicans of Berry, descendants of those Gauls who so obstinately stood fast against the Roman invasion and Roman law . . . Long live the nation! Long live the national Republic! Long live Berry! [The text is signed:] Jean Baffier, workman sculptor of Berry, general delegate of the Ligue de la Patrie Française, republican nationalist French worker candidate.[38]

Regionalism particularly affected these lands in the heart of France. At the time Sancerrois, the "Chouan region"* of Berry, still had a solid reputation as a land of sorcery, and its superstitious inhabitants regularly voted on the right.[39] Jean Baffier knew how to awaken these traditions, to give new life to the superstitions, to bring back customs that

---

*The Chouans were royalist insurgents in the Vendée region during the French Revolution (1789–99).—trans.

attested to the permanence of the "Berry race." In his person emerged a strange synthesis of the Republic, trade unionism, nationalism, and racism, but little Catholicism. *Le Réveil de la Gaule* (The Awakening of Gaul), the journal he created as the instrument for Berry nationalism, bore its title because "what we desire is to recover our old spirit as a race, our natural character."

Baffier, born in 1851 into a very poor, rural communitarian world, became a mason in Nevers, where he worked restoring the cathedral. He was inspired by the journeymen of the Middle Ages and presented himself as an artisan, "a peasant of sculpture," a carver rooted in a place, a stranger to the artificial world of Parisian artists, a creator steeped not in cosmopolitanism but in overt Celtism, weaned on Gallic culture, eager to return to Berry and to France as a whole the qualities of virility and strength that were naturally shared by the peasants, the wine growers, and the shepherds who gave life to the regions of now-republican France. Baffier identified with the soldier Nicolas Chauvin, with Jacques Bonhomme,* with the jingoistic and xenophobic soldier-plowman ready to bravely give his life for the nation.

Baffier sent two donations to the Henry monument (the fund created by nationalists for the widow of Hubert Henry, after his suicide in August 1891) and congratulated Drumont: "What success your list is having, and what a current of ideas your fund points to! It is touching that it avenges us a little . . . Between us—you, a great worker, and I, merely a little artisan—there are now resonances that many people could not have suspected even a year ago . . . Two camps are facing off at this moment: the men of the land and the cosmopolitans, the French camp against the Jewish camp." In an angry letter to the Zola committee, he wrote:

> In France, the struggle must be today, and will be tomorrow, between two dominant ideas stemming from two different traditions. On one side, the so-called humanitarian-libertarian cosmopolitans, proceeding from Jewish races and from the Semites of the Mediterranean basin, with their dark and anarchical

---

*Nicolas Chauvin: legendary soldier devoted to Napoleon; Jacques Bonhomme: the nickname for the French peasant under the ancien régime.—trans.

ideology, their extreme materialism, their rapacity, and their mercantile instinct. On the other, the men of the land, with their religion based on the admiration and study of nature, their social science based on equity and justice, their sense of family, respect for the work of our ancestors, the worship of heroes, the feeling of honor, the probity of work. M. Zola and his partners, who are destroying the cult of the native land, the dignity of work, respect for the family and for ancestral traditions, are as much our enemies as Dreyfus, who sold the secrets of national defense . . . Those vipers, bands of sectarian ideologues, scoundrels who entice us with the great principles of liberty, equality, and fraternity . . . asps that inject the most lethal venom into our entrails, toads that stink up our sky and our earth with their poisoned spittle.

Jean Baffier, crafter of the renewal of Berry culture, who permanently marked the urban landscape of Bourges with his numerous sculptures, compared Jewish deputy Alfred Naquet to "a monstrous gargoyle who seems to have come straight off a cathedral facade" and accused the Jews of wanting "to make the country of great cathedrals a bric-à-brac shop, a cosmopolitan bazaar" invaded by "the profiteers and the rasta-couères [vulgar foreigners]."[40] The enemies of France were clearly designated: the Jews threatened the France of Christian culture and French ethnic identity. Baffier offered his enthusiastic support of Drumont's battle and remained faithful to him. In 1902 he wrote:

Even in '78 and '79, I was uneasy about developments, not only in our union halls but in the Republic itself. My workshop was a meeting place for certain big bosses in the republican party. Gauvin, the famous ornamental ironworker and friend of Gambetta, would often meet there with [local republican leader] Louis Combet. One evening I heard certain things said about the actions of the Alliance Israélite Universelle. After Combet left, I asked Gauvin to explain them to me. He snickered. "What you heard," he told me, "means that in twenty years the Jews will do *this* to France." And putting his closed fist under my throat, he twisted his hand as if to wring my neck . . . I believed then and I still believe that, at a certain moment, Gambetta wanted to free himself from Jewish domination . . . it was too late. He could not stem the tide he had created. He was the one who broke down. It is easy to see that our Republic, this Republic that was so beautiful in our dreams and that they confiscated from us, was about to become the property, the prey of cosmopolitans and bankers . . . I raised a first cry of alarm with my brochure *Le Réveil de la Gaule*. I celebrated our beautiful country, our forests, our cities, our thatched cottages, our dolmens, our wine, the bones of the warriors from ancient times that you discover while plowing the soil . . . It was Drumont, that great master, who made me see my own ideas clearly. He gave me a consciousness of myself. Is that not, after all, the most beautiful side of his work, the self-revelation he gave to so many Frenchmen who did not know themselves?[41]

The "Frenchmen of France," Baffier maintained, had to understand that "in our dear Berry, Jewish and Freemasonic omnipotence have gradually destroyed the unity of families, the harmony of guilds. It was to the cry 'Long live the nation!' that in 1792 our fathers defeated at Valmy the foreign armies that had united to lay down the law in France. It is to the cry 'Long live the nation!' that we rise up today to defend our families, our race humiliated by the 'stateless persons' who have settled in our country as in a conquered nation, to pillage our land and reduce us to slavery. For the Republic of the French, for Berry: onward, lads!"[42] Again in 1907 he wrote: "The great noble Celto-Scythian family, wrongly called Aryan, was always for the harmonious development of the territorial zones, with groups of men organized into bodies of nations, in keeping with the holy observance of natural laws . . . By contrast, the perverse Semitic branch aspired only to exploit the land . . . The sole goal of that denatured family was to dominate and subjugate peoples whatever the cost; as an aesthetic doctrine it has the advantage of the lure of luxury, which leads to mercantile industry, to corruption . . . The corrupt spirit of the Semites is manifesting itself in all its forms."[43]

Baffier's sculptures, celebrated locally, served as an instrument in the struggle for regionalism against cosmopolitanism. With these extremely expressive monuments he left an enduring mark on the territory of Berry. His peasants, surrounded by standing stones that evoke ancient rituals; his hamlets dominated by churches lost in the Middle Ages; and his virile

Gauls with brandished swords—all attracted the attention of Edouard Drumont's faithful, such as Gaston Méry, who was delighted to finally find an epic art whose roots were firmly planted in the land and that was not contaminated by foreign influences.[44] In his own heartland dialect, Baffier considered his Gallic stone giants "rough, rough men! And big, big! Fine! Primo! Honest! Strong men who beat up the devil for the love of God" (*des houmes râls, râls! grands, grands! des fins! des primes! des francs! des forts qui battaient le diable pour l'amour de Dieu*). His heroes were "a race good at combat / Valiant of body, pure of heart," lost in the most remote peasant mythology, who rose up against the conspiracies of the internationalist Jews. Baffier also created rustic table settings and furniture true to Berry traditions. At the Paris Salon of 1898, he displayed an enormous fireplace under the title "For the Celtic Tradition," designed according to the "precepts of Aryan religion and the noble tradition of the Celts," and intended to be opposite in every detail to the cosmopolitanism of art nouveau.[45] *Le Journal du Cher* was lavish in its compliments and praised the sculptor's nationalist virtues; he had also revived the choral societies, of Berry lads whose musicians dressed in traditional costumes.

In the charismatic Baffier, the tranquil region of Berry, indifferent to Christian tradition and converted to socialism, found an uncommon nationalist agitator. "The man of the land" who attacked the "Jew-sympathizing bourgeois of Bourges" joined forces with the Drumont of *Mon vieux Paris*, the relentless defender of an old-style city with its streets, covered stalls, and artisans, a city preserved from capitalist modernity. For both Baffier and Drumont—and also for Abbé Hémonet, author of *Nancy juif* (Jewish Nancy)—that modernity had caused the city to succumb to Jewish power and finally to lose its soul. Like Drumont, Baffier led the nationalist struggle: in Cher he personified the Ligue de la Patrie Française and was also, in the fourteenth arrondissement of Paris, secretary of the Plaisance branch. His carefully kept notebooks are a gold mine of inside information about the Ligue de la Patrie Française. Week after week he recorded even the smallest events. The author and politician Maurice Barrès, the important nationalist leader Louis Dausset, and Gaston Méry frequently attended meetings "with musician comrades, who would play tunes inspired by the beautiful natural world of our country."[46] At one meeting Baffier gave the militants a written assignment: "Study how cosmopolitan meddling has insinuated itself among us, and tell how we can shake off the yoke of the foreigner." At another meeting he asked the league militants, "Has the Semitic mind afflicted us with a definitive decadence?" And when he asked the militants to reflect on the idea of the nation, like a conscientious schoolmaster he himself prepared the correct response: "A nation is an expanded family that has developed normally from a territorial zone in harmony with its temperament. What constitutes the French nation is first of all French territory, which has its special conformity, its humus, its flora, its fauna, its mountains and valleys, its flowers and rivers, its streams, its atmosphere . . . A set of customs, practices, and mores constitutes the harmonious law common to all men of the land. All this glorious and precious patrimony is today compromised and threatened with destruction by the corrupt, perverted, chaotic, and mysterious minds of the nomadic Semitic races." In Paris Baffier stayed true to his Berry values: "Our ancestors, who built the most powerful military châteaux, the splendid cathedrals, the sumptuous royal and seigneurial palaces, the gracious homes of artisans, whose architecture was in harmony with our atmosphere and vegetation in France, demonstrate the fertility of our race."[47]

Let us leave Bourges and Berry (and pass by Nevers where, on January 23, the day of the military lottery, when men found out if they were to serve in the army, the conscripts spilled out into the streets of the city to shouts of "Down with the Jews! Out with Zola!" and the Gompel, Weyll, and Dreyfus stores hastily closed their doors)[48] and resume our journey deep into the center of France. Clermont-Ferrand is our next stop. According to a historian of that city, "none of the great political events that shook France before 1914 troubled Clermont . . . The anarchist crisis did not lead to unrest; nor did the Dreyfus affair."[49] In the standard histories, Clermont, solidly republican, remained reserved, silent, and immune to outbursts of violence. In the first half of January 1898, it was not the Dreyfus affair but the mysterious "robbers of the cities" who held everyone's attention in Clermont. These bandits were ruthlessly pillaging the Auvergne region, particularly Clermont itself, boldly breaking into apartments. The police were worn out from tracking down these burglars day after day. On January 18, however, *L'Avenir du Puy-de-Dôme* published the following article:

> The students of Clermont have insisted on associating themselves with the demonstrations that have occurred in Paris and elsewhere, against the ignoble campaign of the Dreyfus syndicate. Without prior agreement, spontaneously, they held a demonstration that, while remaining calm, made a certain stir in the city. The students of the school of sciences passed in front of the hôtel-Dieu, the main hospital, where a group of medical students joined them, then headed toward the place de Jaude and took the rue Neuve, shouting, "Out with Zola! Down with the Jews! Long live the army!" Outside every Jewish store along their way, they stopped, and their shouts became more numerous. Cries of "Down with the Jews" were becoming increasingly frequent. In front of the military club in the building of the Thirteenth Corps, they let out ringing cries of "Long live the army!" The students then returned to the center of town and passed through the rue Saint-Genest, the place Royale, the rue des Gras, the rue Neuve, the place de Jaude, and the boulevard Desaix, energetically expressing their opinion of the Jews. Then they broke up. A considerable crowd of curiosity-seekers, many of whom themselves became demonstrators, followed the students.[50]

The next day, January 19, Clermont's major daily wrote, "The students repeated their demonstration of Monday. About a hundred strong, they gathered at the hôtel-Dieu. A small procession formed. A police sergeant and several officers marched at its head. The shouts resumed in earnest: 'Out with Zola! Long live the army! Down with the Jews! No more Yids!' . . . All along the way, the Clermont students were greeted with a great deal of sympathy."[51] On the twentieth, in contrast, unexpected new shouts were heard in the streets of Clermont: "Long live Zola! Out with Drumont! Down with Rochefort!" To the general astonishment, "a dozen young people appeared—we might even say kids, not more than sixteen years old—who engaged in that strange demonstration . . . They belonged to Jeunesse Socialiste [Socialist

Youth]." On the twenty-first, however, it was learned that some of these "kids" had been cited for disorderly conduct.[52] That small counter-demonstration would not be repeated. Republican Clermont would thereafter see only anti-Semitic outbursts.

Sifting through the local newspapers more carefully, we find evidence of other anti-Semitic demonstrations, even in the small towns. On March 1, 1898, in Lezoux, "the young people joyfully bid farewell to Mardi Gras. Our young people wanted to mingle a patriotic note into their amusements. Astride a donkey, as hideous as possible, were *il signore Zola* and the Jew Dreyfus, facing that animal's rear end. Our two effigies, having been struck many times with a blackjack, were burned across from Town Hall, to the great joy of many witnesses of the spectacle." In Maringues on the same day, a torch ceremony was held: "The youth of Maringues built a straw effigy, which was then dressed up, a Jewish mask put on it, and an Italian cap placed on its head. That 'Zola' was paraded all evening, with more than fifty people forming a procession behind it and booing. At eight p.m. it was burned on the public square amid the torch bonfires. Several hundred people were present at the time."[53] The legislative election campaign gave rise to a number of small and unspectacular but recurrent incidents. On April 26, in Murat and Ségur in the canton of Allanche, after public meetings conducted by rival candidates, cries could be heard: "Down with the Opportunists! Down with the Jews!" On the twenty-seventh, in Ardes and Thiers, during a political meeting, contradictory shouts of "Down with the Jews! Down with Dreyfus!" and "Long live Dreyfus!" echoed in the usually quiet streets. On April 30 in Saint-Nectaire, on May 1 in Boudes, on May 3 in Larodde, and on May 6 in Latour, more public meetings took place with various candidates; brawls erupted, and shouts of "Down with Zola!" "Down with the traitors!" "Down with Dreyfus!" "Long live the army!" and "Down with the Jews!" rose once again.[54]

During the May electoral campaign, many nationalist candidates gave speeches that were utterly unambiguous in their opposition to the Jews. True, the region rested easy—"the vineyards look beautiful, as does the grain, and the harvest must certainly be nothing if not good."[55] For several days people had been preoccupied with the theft of a horse, for which "bohemians" were said to be responsible. All the biweekly reports of the subprefects, however, repeated one leitmotif: "The Dreyfus affair is increasingly stirring up public opinion"; "the Dreyfus affair is on people's minds."[56] Almost all the nationalist candidates, who were not above making anti-Semitic allusions, were defeated in the first round, but the races were close. The nationalist candidates' following was far from negligible, and their slogans had found an audience. It was the same during a cantonal election in June 1899: Molinier-Many, a "republican candidate" in Tauves, wrote in his platform statement, "Like you, I love my country the way a bird loves its nest . . . The Jew Rothschild, who owns racehorses, pays no more fees than the tinsmith in Tauves with a horse that cost him twelve francs . . . For the thirty years we have been in a Republic, the Republic has been only the government of rich financiers, industrialists, Jewish big businessmen, and other cosmopolitans." In October 1900, on the occasion of elections to the general council, Charles Goyon-Robert declared in his platform statement, "I am from Riom, my parents were from Riom; Riom was the birthplace of my father-in-law. I am a property owner in Riom and in the marshlands of Riom. I am a republican with the true liberals who want freedom for others. I am a republican, against the sectarians who, disdaining equality, deny access to public office to independent-minded Frenchmen who refuse to recognize the supremacy of the lodges or of the synagogue." Although he was defeated, he attracted hundreds of votes.[57]

The local press fed the disputes and made no mystery of its own prejudices. *L'Avenir du Puy-du-Dôme* particularly distinguished itself in that respect. Alongside *La Croix d'Auvergne*, it stood out amid a nationalist local press that disseminated its views widely. *Le Républicain du Puy-du-Dôme*, *Le Courrier du Puy-du-Dôme*, and *L'Union Républicaine du Puy-du-Dôme* went head to head with *Le Moniteur*, the only openly Dreyfusard radical republican newspaper, and with *Le Tocsin Populaire*.[58] On January 11, 1898, *L'Avenir du Puy-du-Dôme* gave new strength to an anti-Protestantism that was also very much in vogue at the national level. "The campaign conducted in support of the traitor Dreyfus is the work of a Judeo-Protestant pact," it reported. ". . . What is happening today shows how right we are to battle the Anglicans of Auvergne, of which there are only a paltry handful." On the fifteenth the newspaper attacked the "Jewish and Protestant coteries"; on the twenty-first it again denounced the "Judeo-Protestant syndicate." Even the advertisements adapted: on February 1 the perfumer Hilbert printed an ad declaring, "A bas les suifs!"* to praise the qualities of soap made with coconut oil. Poems sent in by readers were equally edifying, such as this one:

> *Look out! Frenchmen of France,*
> *Look out! They're after our soldiers!*
> *Let us pursue with a cry of revenge*
> *Every traitor, every Judas!*
> *Let us spit on the stigmatized gang*
> *Which, with its hook-fingered hands,*
> *Plays its hand to save Dreyfus.*
> *Pillory the stateless!*
> *Long live France. Pillory*
> *Zola, Picquart, and Labori!†*
> *The Jew has given the nation*
> *The wound of treason,*
> *And, fearing to see it heal*
> *Zola soaks it with poison!*
> *The stranger stamps his feet with glee*
> *But look, he's getting anxious,*
> *In face of that monstrous attack,*
> *France is becoming French again.*
> *France cries: Pillory Zola, Picquart, and Labori!*
> *We will add you to that list,*
> *Club of intellectuals,*
> *Expert rhetoricians, expert dentists,*
> *Reptilian newspapers of Israel.*
> *On our valiant and upright soldiers*
> *The stranger has come to vomit.*
> *Themis‡ pretends to sleep.*
> *Go, traitors of every stripe,*

---

*A bas les suifs: "Down with the tallow," a play on A bas les Juifs, "Down with the Jews."—trans.
†Ferdinand Labori: Zola's attorney at his February 7 trial; later, one of Dreyfus's attorneys. —trans.
‡Themis: the ancient Greek god of justice.—trans.

Go join on the pillory
Zola, Picquart, and Labori.

[Signed:] Patriot.[59]

La Croix d'Auvergne was very active organizing wine growers around Clermont and peasant groups in Limagne and vigorously promoting xenophobic values. "We do not concede that the Jews are French in the same capacity as we are," it wrote on January 26, 1896. "The Jew and the Freemason are the enemy." Similarly, *Le Courrier du Puy-du-Dôme* invoked "the God of Clovis* and Joan to punish Israel as an example to others. Yes, the Jews are threatened; yes, they must face possible expropriation and even reprisals."[60] More surprisingly, the socialist-leaning newspaper *Le Tocsin*, sensitive to the atmosphere of the time, came to write, "Our readers know that we have never looked after the Jews, that we have no reason to look after them and will not look after them, whereas most of the Jesuits who shout 'Death to the Jews!' marry off their daughters to them to restore their family fortunes." It concluded, very logically, "The Drumonts devour Jews and swallow the Good Lord. The Jews devour priests: let them therefore devour one another."[61]

In the vast circle around the central region of the French hexagon, in the prefectures from Moulins to Lyon and Saint-Etienne, from Le Puy-en-Velay to Rodez, from Périgueux to Tulle, Limoges, and Guéret, other rumblings of anti-Semitism could be heard. In Moulins on January 26, 1898, two to three hundred people staged a demonstration "organized, according to the police, by the Catholic syndicate." Preceded by a tricolor flag, the procession passed along the large arteries of the city and cheered the officers outside the military club.[62] Monsignor Dubourg did not mince words in his various pastoral letters, in which he condemned "the sinister race of the stateless," imploring young girls to "pray to the God of Armies for their big brothers." *La Croix de l'Allier* and the Catholic clubs held ever more anti-Dreyfusard and anti-Semitic meet-

---

*Clovis (c. 465–511): the conqueror of Gaul.—trans.

ings on the rue du Progrès in Moulins or on the rue de l'Usine in Montluçon. Near Montluçon several anti-Semitic riots erupted, including one in the small village of Ronnet. People attacked stores assumed to belong to Jews, though their owners sent messages to the newspapers stating otherwise. The legislative elections also elicited unrest. The Allier department was dominated by radicals and socialists, but they carefully avoided calling themselves Dreyfusards. Moderate conservatives as well as radicals delivered diatribes against "stateless persons." Vacher, one of the most virulent candidates, was defeated by his socialist opponent by only thirteen votes. In the wine-producing region of Gannat, Delarue, the radical candidate, denounced the economic power of the Jews, and on numerous occasions during public meetings held in very remote villages such as Saint-Bonnet-de-Rochefort, Ebreuil, and Monteignet, he reassured his listeners that he was "not a friend of the Jews." *Le Journal de Gannat* predicted his victory because he knew how to fight cosmopolitan Jewry. In Lapalisse, Jules Gacon, a radical deputy, attempted to get himself reelected. Even though he denounced the "dirty Jews" in the radical newspaper *L'Indépendant*, his enemies saw him as the spitting image of the Jew, and *La Croix de l'Allier* considered him an element in the Judeo-Masonic plot; nevertheless, they did not succeed in preventing his triumphant reelection in the first round.[63] But afterward the prejudices, far from disappearing, persisted: in the 1902 legislative elections, the right once more stood "against Freemasonry, collectivism, and Jewry" and on that platform still attracted 25 percent of the vote, for example, in Moulins-Est.[64]

Lyon had its first anti-Semitic demonstration on January 16, 1898. Some students from the Catholic schools paraded in the streets shouting, "Long live the army! Down with Zola! Down with the Jews!" before being dispersed by the police at the corner of the rue de la République and the rue Confort. At the same moment, a performance of *L'Africaine* and *The Barber of Seville* was proceeding peacefully at the Grand Théâtre.[65] The local press strove mightily to launch the movement. *La Croix de Lyon et du Rhône* wrote, "What stands out in the prosecution of Zola's case before the assize court of Paris is the triumph of the Jewish tactic . . . People talk about Jewish gold. Something more is needed. That indomitable Jewish tenacity that, for nineteen hundred years, has allowed that people, however dispersed it may be among nations, to maintain its character and nationality, stands out in all its brilliance . . . It is despicable in the extreme, and harm could come to Israel if it displays it with such impudence." *La France Libre*, for its part, attributed "the entire conspiracy supporting the traitor to the Kahal, the shady association of chief rabbis that runs the world through intrigue and corruption."[66] On January 17 about four to five hundred students and passersby soon formed an imposing crowd, which *Le Nouvelliste* estimated (certainly exaggerating) at five thousand—*La France Libre* even advanced the figure of six thousand. They demonstrated outside the offices of the newspaper *Le Peuple* to protest an article that had damned them as "little runts, petty bourgeois idiots, beer drinkers and regulars at public houses, future rapacious process servers, potbellied notaries, and shifty lawyers."[67] They crossed the quai Claude-Bernard, took the pont du Midi, and shouting the usual slogans, headed toward the socialist newspaper. Defending their premises from inside, the typographers and editors countered with stones, pieces of coal, and fragments of broken bottles, shouting, "Down with the Jesuits!" A violent battle followed: canes and fists rained down, windowpanes were shattered, blood flowed. Many were wounded, including several students, before the police intervened. The next day *Le Peuple* condemned "those murderers, those brutes who continually threw paving stones at us weighing more than three kilograms. Lethal! The cowards struck us with canes, ganging up on us ten or twenty to one."[68] The newspaper also published a letter addressed to its editor in chief, Anthelme Simond, who had sharply condemned the students: "On the envelope is this inscription, as stupendous as it is idiotic: 'To Citizen A. Simond, Israelite worker, employee at the newspaper *Le Peuple.*' In the envelope was the following short epistle: 'Sir. Your open letter to the students of Lyon certainly does not deserve the honor of any response whatsoever. We would be curious to know how much the Jews and your antipatriotic friends paid you, so we can have an idea of the price for such rubbish. The students of the university of Lyon.'" Simond responded, "The fact that I am not a 'dirty Jew,' as others assert, in language of rare purity, is one more thing they cannot imagine. To all of them, I have only one simple word to say: cretins!"

The next day, the eighteenth, at the Grand Théâtre, spectators could attend a performance of Umberto Giordano's drama *Andrea Chénier*, which "all of Lyon was rushing to see." In Salle Bellecour "many people attended the performance of the prestidigitator Velle, who performed experiments transmitting thoughts over distances, along with song and piano auditions." At the Catholic university, Abbé Blanc spoke about hypnotic suggestion, "advising people to refrain from any participation in hypnotism because of its illicit and dangerous character." Professor Cazeneuve, from the university's school of medicine, gave a lecture on the ravages of alcohol, "since insanity also feeds on alcoholism." And Professor Gairal, from the Catholic law school, presented a lecture on Joan of Arc and international relations.

The police had to come up with a battle plan for what promised to be a perilous evening. The stations were reinforced. Though they were worn out, all available men were ready for war. The services of Sûreté Générale were activated.* There were numerous patrols; other police officers protected the synagogue, *Le Progrès*, *Le Peuple*, and Jewish stores; the reserve brigades stood ready, as did the horsemen, who were waiting for the order to charge. General Zédé, the military governor of Lyon, told the prefect, "It is not impossible that the troubles that have occurred in Paris and Marseilles will have repercussions in Lyon. I have the honor of letting you know that, to be ready for any eventuality, I gave the order in all the barracks that the so-called fire pickets [soldiers who respond to fire emergencies], suitably reinforced and commanded by officers, should always be in a position to march at the first call. The picket of Fort Lamotte includes two companies of one hundred men; that of the cavalry division, two squadrons with one hundred sabers. Under these conditions we will be ready to respond, at the first call, to your requisitions."[69] On the walls of the city small signs, clumsily composed by hand, were put up:

THIS EVENING AT SIX O'CLOCK, DEPARTURE FROM THE UNIVERSITY

OF THE SECOND LARGE ANTI-SEMITIC PROCESSIONAL.

SACKING OF THE KIKES' STORES. THIS PROCESSIONAL IS FORMED

AT THE INITIATIVE OF STUDENTS IN MEDICINE IN THEIR

THIRD, FOURTH, AND FIFTH YEARS.[70]

---

*Sûreté Générale: a branch of the Ministry of the Interior charged with policing functions.
—trans.

At about eight p.m., as a police report observed, courses let out at the schools of law, medicine, and science (where a botany course was attended by particularly "turbulent" nationalist students). Between five hundred and a thousand people, half of them students, gathered in small groups on the place Bellecour around the statue of Louis XIV and attempted to make their way to *Le Peuple* and the synagogue on the quai de Tilsit, shouting, "Out with Zola! Long live the army! Down with the Jews! Down with the kikes! To the synagogue!" These cries were repeated, according to a police report, "by the students at the Marist* institution, who had come to their windows on the rue de la Charité." That report underscored the presence among the demonstrators of priests and soldiers, and it observed that "many residents of the neighboring houses opened their windows and chimed in with the demonstrators." The police forces intervened and made many arrests. According to *La France Libre*, "two thousand young people cried 'Out with the Jews!', striking their canes between the closed shop windows of a large Jewish store." Dispersed by the police, those two thousand people (or three thousand, according to *L'Express*) headed toward the place Bellecour and confronted the municipal guards, who charged on horseback several times, making "their mounts rear up to break free." The columns formed again: some groups headed toward the rue Sala, while others reached the place Bellecour and turned back toward the synagogue. They shouted anti-Semitic slogans outside the Grand Bazaar in front of the police, who charged at them at a gallop. They clashed with the police protecting the synagogue and for several hours crisscrossed the city in every direction. Many arrests were made. Only around eleven o'clock did Lyon return to calm.[71]

As *Le Peuple* noted ironically, "the demonstrations of the sprinklers of holy water seem to be over . . . That black-robed band is losing its head. The bloody instincts of these worthy inquisitors have just been revealed in all their horror and in all their cowardice . . . Fear grips them; they shout 'Long live the army' and treacherously plunge a dagger into a Jew's chest! The Drumonts, the Rocheforts are cowards, cowards in spades! Hiding behind a desk, they shout, 'Down with the Jews!' . . . If we are

*Marist: a member of the Roman Catholic Society of Mary founded by Jean Claude Colin in 1816.—trans.

not careful, we will be transported back to the centuries of barbarism . . . The white terror* is obsolete."[72] But the nationalist press was virulently anti-Semitic. *La France Libre* accused one of the radical leaders of "walking arm in arm with the Jew Marix. Nothing was left for him but to be the friend of the Yids. We also noticed several anarchists in the demonstration who were escorting Jews strolling along as curiosity-seekers. In the lead was the caretaker of the synagogue, a big devil of a Yid." *Le Nouvelliste* reported that "tempers are flaring at the Dreyfus syndicate and at the Jews. What dominates all these demonstrations is the anti-Semitic note, a symptom of the populist exasperation against the race that dominates us. Definitely Drumont was right: the Jews have become impossible in France."[73]

Those arrested during the demonstrations were arraigned on April 7, 1898. Addressing the judge, one of them made the following declaration: "We do not come to ask for your pardon, because we are not ashamed of our acts. It is up to you to say whether you approve of the conclusions of the public prosecutor in Rennes who recently congratulated students, guilty like us, for their patriotism, or whether, on the contrary, you judge we must be punished, even as M. Zola receives the congratulations of Prussia outside and of Jewry inside." The response was clear: they were all fined the modest sum of one franc, the minimum penalty, and they received the warm congratulations of *La France Libre.* Conversely, *Le Peuple* gave free rein to its anger: "There are forty of them, like the Immortals [the forty members of the Académie Française], and they are trying to become immortal by shouting like savages in the streets . . . A one-franc fine does not bestow the crown of martyrdom. But everything comes to he who waits, and our fiery little patriot will wait all the time necessary . . . Will the magistrate who was so lenient toward those students—to the point of complimenting the learned defense attorney—be as lenient toward the workers who will have to appear before him?"[74]

In Lyon and everywhere else in the region in late January, life resumed

---

*White terror: after the French Revolution, royalists perpetrated two waves of terror: one in southeastern France in the spring and summer of 1795, then again in 1796; and the other throughout the Midi in the summer of 1815, against the Bonapartists and the republicans. White was the color of the royalists.—trans.

its course. People impatiently prepared for the wine growers' festival, the banquets that accompanied it, and the numerous firemen's balls that enlivened it.[75] February 22 was Mardi Gras. One night when the performance at the Théâtre de l'Eldorado was over, about fifty students, under close surveillance by the police, walked along the cours Gambetta and arrived at the pont de la Guillotière, which they crossed, singing the refrain of a song entitled "La Youstia" and mingling with the masquerade ball: "The streets of the central city were very busy, with people in masks crossing back and forth."[76] Week after week *La Croix de Lyon et du Rhône* vented its ire at "the indomitable Jewish race which, since Judas, has had a genius for treason." It rejoiced at Zola's conviction: "Yes, the Jews and their accomplices were wrong to believe that their domination, their gold, their corrupting influence had already destroyed all noble feelings in France. We did not doubt the Catholic part of the country, knowing that a Christian heart never separated the two words *God* and *country*. But the masses, compromised by the bad influence of the Masonic press, have just shown that they too are ardently patriotic." The paper denounced the campaign "in support of the Alsatian Jew. In Lyon that campaign coincided with an unleashing of anticlerical fury . . . By that outburst, that rage against Christ, it is easy to recognize the actions of the eternal enemy of Christ, the influence of Jewish gold." *La France Libre* still believed as well "that Jewry was too deeply wounded by the treason of that wretched Dreyfus. So to reestablish the virginity of the species with hooked noses and fingers, that Yid must be saved and made into a martyr."[77]

On the left as well, the force of prejudice was easy to perceive. *Le Peuple*, for example, at the height of the battle against the nationalists, wrote on January 19:

Who could have said that the day would come when "the traitor Dreyfus" would attach the vengeful ball and chain to the foot of rotting society, which will help bury that society? The Jews were the economic masters. The army existed for them; in front of the strongbox, the great mute kept a strict and silent guard. Then all of a sudden, a singular phenomenon occurred. The effect revolted against its cause. An implacable family struggle began. Gold begrudges the Sword, and the Sword rebels against Gold—they are mutually annihilating each other. And the common people, who succumbed under the crushing load, will soon have nothing more to do than to take the broom and sweep into the sewer the shapeless debris that was once a whole society.[78]

On the twenty-fourth the newspaper held a public meeting in Salle Laroche, headed by Simond, attended by about nine hundred socialist and anarchist militants. Someone read a letter from Paul Bernard, the Paris deputy, who declared that "there is a great danger to the Socialist Party since if the Catholics and the Jews quarrel, it is only with the aim of lulling the proletarians to sleep." A speaker maintained that they must not take the side of Dreyfus or Esterhazy, and a mason proposed that the university building be cast into the Rhône: "He worked to build the monument, he would happily destroy it." A motion, which passed unanimously, declared that "all the socialist schools lump the Jewish and Christian capitalists together and express their profound contempt for the brats led by the Catholic clubs who have attempted to pillage our newspaper."[79] On June 26 the Blanquist revolutionary central committee called a meeting. Bonard and Florent, both socialist deputies, denounced "Jewish scheming." "The Jews and the clericals," they said, "are allied to divide the Socialist Party": applause and then brawls followed. A speaker shouted, "Ours is a great crime. We do not take the side of high Jewry, any more than that of the high Catholic bank. Neither God nor master: long live the revolutionary Commune!" At the same moment, at a meeting held by the Union Nationale Catholique, one of its leaders, Desroches, cried, "Dreyfus was nonetheless a Jew! Which means: a representative of the exploiters of our class and of yours, the socialists. The Jews are exploiters who live and grow rich at the expense of the nation and the working class, and they have become so odious to the French that, to get back their power, they are not afraid to make three hundred thousand Frenchmen perish."[80]

In the meantime, however, the May legislative elections surprised everyone when Lyon elected five socialist deputies at once: two radicals, one Opportunist, two moderate republicans, and one liberal republican completed its political representation. Catholic Lyon was crushed. In despair, *La Croix de Lyon et du Rhône* could not understand how "a department as patriotic as our own" could identify with "five socialists and two radicals, partisans of internationalism and the more or less avowed defenders of Dreyfus."[81] During the campaign there were frequent anti-Semitic outbursts. In the first ward, the contest pitted General Voisin, nominated by the Comite des Républicains Progressistes de Government (Committee of Progressive Government Republicans), and supported—when all else failed—by *Le Nouvelliste*, and the right, against Lanessan, who had been nominated by the Radical Party. On one election poster, Voisin's supporters attacked the "defender of Dreyfus" and "the admirer of Zola" and denounced "the prominent Jews from the first arrondissement who moreover support the Dreyfusard Lanessan." It concluded, "Long live the Republic! Long live General Voisin!" Similarly, this song about Lanessan circulated in the city, sung to the tune of "Ma gigolette, elle est perdue" (My Young Lass Is Lost):

It was a Monday, a stormy day,
In a meeting,
Full of hope, anticipating
He would be elected,
He had not counted on Bessières,
That hardy fighter,
Who made him bite the dust
In front of his voters.

Bessières told him:
"Shameless Dreyfusard,
You shouldn't try anything with the people of Yonne,
You old Communard.
Go back to Paris, to Gascogne,
Return to Canivet,
Go on, get lost or I'll hammer you
On your noggin.

Go away, you Cochin China reject,
You charlatan, you stooge,
Try for a seat you're coveting
Among the dirty Yids,
The anger is rushing to our heads

It's making us sick,
Because for us it's really a disgrace,
Not another word, go."[82]

Although the radical Lanessan barely won in the second round (4,149 votes to 4,127), Voisin had been far ahead in the first round. This means that prejudices in Lyon had far from disappeared. Anti-Semitic demonstrations occasionally resurfaced. For example, when Edouard Drumont came through town on June 5, an anti-Semitic group noisily welcomed him at the gare de Perrache with bouquets of blue cornflowers, because blue was the color of anti-Semitism.[83] At the end of the year, with the formation of the Ligue de Défense Républicaine du Rhône (League of Republican Defense of Rhône), Francis de Pressensé and the socialist leader Jean Jaurès arrived in Lyon, rekindling *Le Nouvelliste*'s hatred of "the Lyonnais Dreyfusards, that is, all the Jews and the revolutionaries."[84]

Lyon was not an isolated case in that respect. During the legislative campaign, election posters tinged with anti-Semitism appeared in Grenoble, a city that, on January 18, 1898, had seen students parading on the place Victor-Hugo and shouting, "Down with Zola! Out with the Jews!" The legislative elections were marked by anti-Semitic unrest: sympathizers of the Union Nationale organized many meetings concerning the elections. Influenced by Abbé Garnier, who was himself traveling, the priests of Saint-Marcellin and Saint-Antoine, as well as Abbé Foulu, gave lectures against secular education, divorce, the Jews, and Zola.[85] Augustin Biessy, a Catholic candidate, devoted his platform statement to condemning "the influence of the Jews over commerce, finance, the army, and domestic and foreign policy. Freemasonry and Jewry are the enemies of France." He was defeated in the second round.

Grenoble's Catholics and supporters of a return to an authoritarian state waged a long-lasting battle against Dreyfus. *L'Impartial de l'Isère* wrote in January 1899, "After the Opportunist and the radical appeared, it was the Jew's turn: sly, hateful, and greedy, extending his hooked fingers over the corpses to be stripped bare. Since the Jew is much stronger than our earlier exploiters, the latter are openly recruited under the banner of the golden calf, come what may." The Ligue Antisémitique de Grenoble was not dissolved until April 1901.[86]

Lyon, however, remained an influential epicenter of nationalist demonstrations. Despite the impressive electoral success of the forces on the left, a profusion of new anti-Semitic committees appeared in Lyon, prolonging the battle against the Jews. In late summer 1899, a Ligue Antisémitique, organized by arrondissement, emerged and for several years stirred unrest in the capital of Gaul, closely allied with the royalist movements and relying on the Jeunesse Antisémitique movement as well. The Jeunesse Antisémitique was created in early 1900 and was soon transformed into the Parti National Antijuif (National Anti-Jewish Party), which remained active until 1904. The newspaper *L'Antijuif de Lyon* disappeared only in 1905.[87]

In Saint-Etienne on January 23, 1898, a demonstration of students from the Saint-Michel religious school ran through the streets shouting, "Down with the Jews! Down with Zola! Long live the army!" On January 22 posters appeared on the walls that read, "In the face of the ignominious acts of the Dreyfus syndicate and the campaign, which cost a fortune to run, against the army and the nation, unite, patriots, and shout: Down with the Jews, the eternal conspirators! Out with Zola, the vile insulter of the army! Imitate your brothers in Paris, Lyon, Marseilles, Nantes, and Toulouse. Combine your efforts with theirs and demonstrate to shouts of: Long live France for the French! Long live the Republic! Long live our beautiful and great army!" The poster was signed by the secretary of the Ligue Catholique et Sociale (Catholic and Social League) and by the secretary of an anti-Semitic group and the Association de la Jeunesse Française (Association of French Youth). To avoid incidents, the prefect of the Loire department ordered the police forces to protect the Jewish-owned stores.

The clubs of the Union Nationale in Saint-Etienne proved to be particularly active in the struggle against the Dreyfusards and hardly missed a chance to hold the usual demonstrations. Former high school students met on the cours Hippolyte-Sauzéa and joined other young people from the Catholic club of Saint-Louis-de-Gonzague, run by Abbé Robert. Leaving the rue du Parvis-Notre-Dame, they went to the rue du Chambon, shouting and singing "The Marseillaise." In the parks the little gang, reinforced by other young people from the school of design, burned "a little banner on which a figure had been drawn. It was unrecognizable, but someone said it was Zola or Dreyfus." The demonstrators, reuniting after the police had dispersed them, went to the Saint-François-Régis store, run by the Jesuit Croizier; then the group, swelling with new arrivals, headed toward the synagogue on the rue d'Arcole, and its members attacked the Jewish stores that were protected by the police. The police superintendent dispatched ninety-five officers to disperse the crowd, which scattered into the neighboring streets, then reformed throughout the night. There were numerous arrests: the presence of "students or former students of the Jesuit fathers or brothers at the Christian schools" was noted.

The Parti Ouvrier Stéphanois (Worker's Party of Saint-Etienne), for its part, held a vast gathering on September 24, 1898, at the Prado to denounce anti-Semitism, but it allowed a municipal councilor who supported Jules Guesde to "declare himself anti-Semitic" and judge that "we will be devoured by the Jew." The anti-Catholic minister Coste, conversely, maintained that "the Dreyfus affair is the eternal conspiracy from the Middle Ages."[88]

The Haute-Loire department, east of Corrèze, seems to have been a haven of peace. There was no trace of street demonstrations in Le Puy and Brioude, not even an insignificant procession of wild conscripts. The region remained calm. The May electoral campaign proceeded without incident; the platform statements and the meetings appeared to know nothing about Dreyfus or the Jews, to such an extent that the "elections 1898" file in the archives is almost empty.[89] The republican candidates earned tallies in the first round that were so high that every opponent dropped out of the race early. The results of these elections testify to the strength of republican ideas.[90]

An attentive reading of the press, however, is perplexing. *Le Républicain de la Haute-Loire*, which vigorously supported the two incumbent republican candidates, Néron-Bancel and Chantelauze, wrote, "Today we see the Protestants and the socialists allying themselves with the Jews, because, before seeing France in need of salvation, they see the Catholic clergy in need of rough treatment." On several occasions the newspaper also denounced the "sons of Israel," and it wrote that Zola's conviction was "the apotheosis of law, justice, and truth."[91] Similarly, *Le Journal d'Yssingeaux*, which supported the reelection of the republican deputy

Néron-Bancel and embraced ideas of progress and tolerance, declared, the day of the verdict in the Zola trial, "That verdict condemns not only Zola but all the enemies of our France. It condemns the Jewish race, which thinks of only one thing—of working the territory of France to satisfy its social hatred. The verdict condemns the Dreyfus syndicate."[92]

For its part *Le Moniteur de Brioude* wrote, "Jews and Protestants are conspiring against France. Dreyfus is only a pretext. We must send them all to Devil's Island." And a month later, it added, "The Jews! We do not often speak about them regarding what concerns us, since the arrondissement of Brioude does not have many of them. But after all, they have slipped into the lucrative posts just about everywhere," dispossessing "true Frenchmen."[93] According to *Le Journal de Brioude*, "the trial stolen by the Jewish syndicate is ending . . . Opportunism lets it happen: for it, the Jewish campaign is an excellent distraction." A few days later it expressed the wish for a vigorous "shakedown to rid us of the machinations of cosmopolitan Jewry."[94]

Nevertheless, Haute-Loire refrained from anti-Semitism and demanded respect for justice and the law in the trials under way, though it argued that Zola was a "raving lunatic." The newspaper of Charles Dupuy, the former prime minister who reigned supreme in the region, reported a minor incident that took place on May 7 in Le Puy: during a final electoral meeting of fifteen hundred people, Dupuy was suddenly interrupted by a listener who shouted, "Down with the Jews!" His reply elicited applause from the audience: "Long live the army and woe to anyone, Jew or otherwise, who sows the seed of doubt against its leaders."[95] That kind of press leads us to wonder whether the republican elected officials who were supported by such newspapers were truly devoid of all prejudice. And what are we to think of their voters, who were also readers?

Extending the arc of our geographical circle to the southwest, we find more outbursts of anti-Semitism. For several nights in a row, the Aveyron city of Rodez suddenly became particularly agitated. On the afternoon of January 26, little pieces of paper were distributed in the streets: "Anti-Jewish demonstration. Wednesday at 8. Processional.

Palais de Justice." In the evening several hundred young people gathered, and though they were rapidly dispersed by the police, they managed to regroup outside the cathedral, then on the place de la Cité, which was "packed with people." The next day, the twenty-seventh, two hundred people marched on the boulevard Gambetta, the place d'Armes, and the place de la Cité. The police, who were very vigilant, intervened and arrested several people, but they were immediately released after being taken to the station house. On the twenty-eighth these events were reproduced on the place de la Cité, where a large crowd repeated the usual cries against Zola and the Jews.

The two major dailies, *Le Journal de l'Aveyron* and *L'Union Catholique*, gave a great deal of coverage to these demonstrations and harshly condemned the police intervention. Both published the following letter, addressed to the mayor of Rodez and signed by a group of residents: "You, who know the character of the residents of Rodez, will understand that such a show of force had only a theoretical interest here and should not raise the slightest objection. We refuse to believe that the shouts of 'Down with the Jews!' could possibly constitute sedition." Moreover, *Le Journal de l'Aveyron* added, "what could there be to fear from Rodez? Israelites are not numerous here; are there any here, in fact?" *L'Union Catholique* concurred: "The population is sickened by the police's conduct in repressing a demonstration that every patriot could only approve." It concluded that "the students of the high school of Rodez are good kids, solid and obstinate citizens of the town. We cannot blame them."

La Gazette de l'Aveyron attacked the director of *Le Courrier de l'Aveyron*, who had been one of the very few bold enough to express regret about these demonstrations: "You would think by that shrill prose that M. Nussbaumer is preparing to be circumcised." *L'Aveyron Républicain* declared ominously: "We do not doubt for a single instant that good intentions motivated the demonstrators; we wonder whether the enemies of our republican institutions might not have hatched some plot around that question." In the local press, A. Marion, a lawyer who was arrested during the demonstration, accused "the Kikes of obeying the Talmud in order to reduce us to slaves. It is for that reason that the Jews have formed a coalition to save a guilty man; that frightening solidarity has brought to light the threatening peril denounced by Drumont."[96]

Most of the local press constantly spread extreme anti-Semitism. *Le Journal de l'Aveyron* announced that "a handful of ignoble Jews" had organized "a diabolical machination"; Picquart had "hired himself out to Israel"; and "all the Jews, from Chief Rabbi Zadoc-Kahn to the caretaker of the synagogue," had undertaken a "terrible, savage, ferocious" struggle against "the French." In his view, the outcome was certain: "the Jews will come out crushed, annihilated, condemned for centuries to be execrated by all Frenchmen and hunted down like wild beasts by that blind Republic, which had been so auspicious for them until now." The editor in chief of *Le Journal de l'Aveyron* wondered, "Do you find, reader, that upstanding France is wrong to shout down the Jews? I do not."[97] *L'Union Catholique*, a major local daily, did not lag behind; on January 4 it exclaimed: the ship of state "is ours, Frenchmen, and not the Jews', not the Freemasons'. Yes, valiant citizens of Aveyron." In the following days, it asked, "Does patriotism consist of serving one's country or of serving the Jews? That is the question, which the voters must truly answer," especially since "Judases do not belong to the French family." That newspaper had no doubt that "things will end badly for the Jews!" And it concluded, "For us, the ideal thing is to wrest France from the Jews by legal and peaceful measures."[98] Although anti-Semitic posters were put up in the main streets of Rodez throughout the year,[99] it was the elections that truly relaunched the anti-Semitic campaign. On January 18 *Le Journal de l'Aveyron* opened fire: "If Lacombe [a deputy and mayor of Rodez] wants to go over to the Jews, fine; but let him go find a ward where the Jews dominate. That is not the case in Aveyron." *L'Union Catholique* fully agreed, arguing on January 16 that "Lacombe is undoubtedly anxious to look after the Jewish and Freemason gang. But we doubt that the citizens of Aveyron, who are Catholic and patriotic, will be satisfied with his behavior." Several days in a row, Lacombe sent long letters to the newspaper to defend himself: "Know that no motive will lead me toward the slightest complacency toward the Jewish gang, which is causing too much of a stir"; and "I have always preached resistance to the invasion of cosmopolitan finance represented by the Jewish element." It was no use: the republican deputy and mayor, attacked on all sides, was defeated in the legislative elections. For the candidates ardently supported by these two dailies, the overall results were very favorable.[100]

Not far away, in Cahors, the students from Gambetta high school protested the Dreyfusard views of one of their teachers, who called the anti-Semitic students in Paris "scoundrels." In the evening, throughout the neighborhood of Badernes, the Cahors students vigorously shouted, "Long live the army! Down with Zola! Down with Dreyfus and the Jews!" Accompanied by residents of the city, they positioned themselves under the offending teacher's windows and attacked him.[101]

In Corrèze the streets were calm, but prejudices were nevertheless expressed. *Le Radical de la Corrèze* warned that the country was headed straight for civil war since the provocations of "Jewish money" and "the scheming of Reinach, Zadoc-Kahn, and all the barons for the advantage of their race" would be answered by all "the champions of the army."[102] In Tulle, for example, a candidate in the legislative elections declared quite simply, "I am anti-Dreyfus. Silence must be imposed on that band of cosmopolitan Jews who for six months have bankrupted the nation, maligned the army, and disrupted the country." He was elected in the second round, receiving 65 percent of the vote. In Brive a poster was put up in support of Dr. Lachaud, reading, "The association of socialist workers of Brive, vigilant guardian of republican institutions, gives the rallying cry: Republicans of the vanguard, let us close ranks! We will vote en masse for Dr. Lachaud. He is a true friend of the people. On your feet then, workers, against capitalist Jewry." Théodore Brosse, candidate of the Comité Républicain Socialiste et Patriote de Brive (Socialist and Patriotic Republican Committee of Brive) hoped that the population of Brive would look to him to crush "Jew-sympathizing cosmopolitan finance."[103] In Ussel, Yves Coudert, mayor of Saint-Pardoux-le-Vieux and a candidate in the election, presented himself on a poster as "an honest working man" who was committed to "eliminating the sinecures of the priests." He declared he was proud to have voted for the construction of the railroad lines between Ussel and Neuvic, and from Bugeat to Faoux-la-Montagne via Tarnac and Peyrelevade. He promised that, were he to be elected, these lines would be extended. He ended with a ringing "Long live the army! Down with the Jews and their friends! Down with the stateless!" His opponent, A. Delmas, an *agrégé* in letters and doctor of letters who could not stand alleged Jewish domination anymore, proclaimed in his platform statement, "My opponents call me an outsider. That allegation is a lie. I am a child of the land." And in *Le Radical de la Corrèze*, he made clear his unshakable anti-Dreyfusard sentiments.[104]

Farther to the west, the press in the department of Dordogne devoted many columns to accounts of the Dreyfus affair and the Zola trial, publishing long excerpts from *La Libre Parole*. It recounted in detail the progress of the anti-Semitic demonstrations in Paris, and it condemned Zola, declaring its certainty in Dreyfus's guilt. Nevertheless it regretted the anti-Semitic violence. "The passions from another age," wrote *L'Avenir de la Dordogne*, "the religious and racial hatred that are swelling up again in the streets," were unacceptable.[105] Locally, the press reported at length various sexual assaults, jewelry thefts, and assaults with scissors, and it devoted long articles to two wolves, "terrible carnivores" that were attacking flocks of sheep.[106] The region appeared safe from anti-Semitic outbursts, especially since royalism and nationalism of all kinds were almost nonexistent.[107] On February 22, however, an anti-Semitic meeting was held in Périgueux with Pradelle, the mayor of Mustapha, Max Régis, and Georges Thiébaud. A squadron of cuirassiers was mobilized, as well as a company of the Republican Guard on foot, guards on horseback, and two hundred peace officers. That show of force indicates the importance of the event, which occurred unexpectedly in Périgueux, a peaceful and republican prefecture of Dordogne. Three hundred people attended the public meeting, where violent speeches against the Jews were given. Brawls erupted.[108] The fit was short-lived, however, and the city and region quickly returned to peace and quiet.

Anyone looking attentively at the speeches and platform statements given during the legislative elections in Périgueux, however, will be greatly surprised to see anti-Semitic prejudices surfacing in that supposedly problem-free region. In the city's second ward, for example, Henri Chavois, the incumbent republican deputy, declared his allegiance to Gambetta and the former French premier and colonialist Jules Ferry and concluded his platform statement with these words: "In the interest of our colonies, I will not hesitate to urge the government to rescind the Crémieux decree, which has unquestionably created, for those of us in Algeria, great difficulties where the Jews are concerned." Receiving only 6,544 votes in the second round of the legislative elections, however, he yielded to Napoléon Magne, an explicitly anti-Semitic Bonapartist, who won with 7,237 votes.[109] A little later to the north, a strident electoral battle took place between Theulier, a republican doctor in Thiviers, and Louis Réjou, editor of *L'Union Nontronnaise*, a newspaper in the canton of Nontron. In January 1898 *L'Union Nontronnaise* warned that "the Jews of Frankfurt are taking up Dreyfus's defense," and that "the Jews are putting money aside in preparation for the coming electoral operations." It denounced "the Jewified Zola" and gave learned analyses of "the Jewish question as a race war."[110] On May 5, the eve of the elections, that newspaper published, on the front page, Réjou's platform statement, which ended this way: "It is only the votes of Jews, of Dreyfuses, of traitors with which I want nothing to do. Long live France! Long live the army! Down with the Jews! Down with the traitors! Down with Dreyfus!" The same issue editorialized, "We are being devoured by the Jews!" Nontron must have had a martial atmosphere, judging from the kind of concerts that could be heard on January 16 ("March of the Zouaves," "The Bold Grenadiers," and "March of the Preobrajevsky Regiment" of the Imperial Guard), on April 24 ("March" from *Aïda*, "The Dragoons of Villars," and "If I Were King"), and May 15 ("Fire," a military allegory; "Carmen"; and "The Smith"); in that locality Réjou defeated Theulier. He almost accomplished the same thing in the arrondissement of Nontron but had to yield to the doctor from Thiviers. Réjou's honorable defeat was hailed both by *Le Journal de Dordogne* and by *La Croix de Périgueux*. Farther to the south, in Bergerac, R. Delpit, candidate in the first ward, attacked Labatut, the incumbent republican deputy, declaring in front of six hundred people in March 1898, "You have placed yourself on the side of Zola and the Jews." Although he was defeated, Delpit received 6,253 votes to Labatut's 9,798. In the second ward, the incumbent republican deputy, Clement, also prevailed, with 7,625 votes, over his opponent, Raymond de Lortal, who received only 4,256. Lortal received that share after declaring in his platform statement, "We have the right to command respect by putting a halt to the odious campaign of a band of cosmopolitan Jews who, not content to exploit us by every means possible, have now insulted our army."[111]

In Sarlat the electoral contest pitted Sarrazin, the incumbent republican deputy, against R. de Boysson, a reactionary major landowner; Molène, a radical republican; and Raymond Gendre, a socialist. Boysson told voters, "If, in your view, business is booming in your commune, vote for my opponents, who have allowed the Jews to grab all the business in France with their enormous stores. But if you can no longer sell your livestock, if you do not have the strength to fight the invasion of the Jews, vote for me." The newspaper *Le Sarladais* campaigned for Molène who, during numerous electoral meetings—for example, in Saint-Cyprien on April 30—expressed the hope that Dreyfus would remain on Devil's Island, eliciting thunderous applause. Opposing them, the socialist Raymond Gendre conducted a lively campaign, declaring, "The people want a Republic of their own, the Republic of workers, of the humble; a Republic rid of the speculators, the money-grubbers, the enemies of the army, of financial and cosmopolitan Jewry, which is eating away at us. Long live the Republic of the People!" He received 5,400 votes in the first round. In the second Molène rallied behind him, publishing his platform statement in *Le Sarladais*, which ended with the paragraph just quoted. Between the two rounds, Boysson, who continued his candidacy, launched an appeal: "Voters! By voting for me, you have demonstrated your profound aversion for the Opportunist regime, which is handing the country over to the Jews. We want to return the ancient freedoms to this sweet country of France. We want to see a sincere and Christian fraternity reign among all French people. Long live France! Down with the Jews!"[112] In the second round, the republican Sarrazin prevailed with 11,089 votes over Gendre, who received 9,754, and Boysson, who drew 4,236.

Finally, in Ribérac, the contest pitted Pourteyron, a doctor and incumbent republican deputy, against Lanauve, a reactionary lawyer who had rallied behind the Republic. He was supported by *Le Journal de Ribérac*. Lanauve's supporters attacked the incumbent deputy in the following terms: "Our business is at the mercy of the Jews, who come from Germany, our sworn enemy. Yes, voters, it is those Germans, who dream of destroying our nation, who send us these Jews to steal our secrets. And to think that, among the deputies of Dordogne, some look after the Jews and refuse to have them condemned when they are guilty. In the Dreyfus-Zola affair, Pourteyron denied the French army the signs of respect it is due." After this campaign Lanauve found himself in the lead in the first round with 5,844 votes, versus 5,432 for the incumbent republican deputy. Pourteyron nevertheless won in the second round. The republicans easily beat their opponents everywhere; but surprisingly the anti-Semitic attacks by candidates of every political leaning in no way prevented them from receiving impressive tallies.

Périgueux seemed to have recovered its calm on December 9, until several distributors of *L'Antijuif* and *La Croix* went through the streets of the city "under the surprised and slightly mocking eye of the good residents of our countryside. Their excitation could not have any grip over the calm good sense and the vast tolerance of the republican population of our regions," predicted *L'Avenir de la Dordogne*, which preferred to devote long reports to poultry thefts and concerts held that day. Unpredictably, the situation turned grave during a meeting held by the indefatigable Guérin and Magne, an anti-Semitic Bonapartist deputy from the second ward of Périgueux. Republicans turned out in force to heckle the speakers, but "the conservative bigwigs of Périgueux and surrounding areas crowded onto the platform." Guérin launched into violent diatribes against Jews, who he said had seized hold of public services, and against "Jew-sympathizing Christians," ending with a traditional and vigorous "France for the French!" Other speakers took the floor with the same message, calling for people to unite against the Jews and attacking godless education. *L'Avenir de la Dordogne* reported, however, that "the mocking audience" was content to let them be, facetiously chanting, "Holy spirit, descend upon us!" It concluded that "the speakers must have understood that their apostolate had done nothing but provoke a distinctly republican demonstration against them."[113] Nevertheless, Périgueux experienced open anti-Semitic turbulence in June 1899, when posters appeared publishing the Cour de Cassation's annullment of Dreyfus's conviction; the following inscription was written by hand in bold letters: "In the name of the Jewish people."[114]

The Haute-Vienne department as a whole went over to socialism in 1898. In its capital, Limoges, republican imagery, adorned fountains and statues, marking that, in this "red city," the Republic was at home. In 1895 the city elected as mayor the socialist Labussière, making itself a socialist municipality; in 1896 the socialists came out ahead almost everywhere else in the municipal elections, too, and Labussière was reelected. The Catholic world constituted the only real opposition: *La Croix de Limoges* fanned anti-Semitic hatred, maintaining that "all those

Jew and Freemason scoundrels are worthless as tits on a boar." The Dreyfus affair stirred up royalist and nationalist unrest. In 1898 the comte Etienne de Montbron, Villelume, and other monarchists from Limousin "arrived from their country châteaux to find allies in the godless city."[115] Along with shop and office workers, they formed an anti-Semitic movement and held meetings where they chanted, "France for the French!" and denounced the Jews. Abbé Masrévéry, assistant priest of Saint-Pierre, was an important local personality who attempted to attract workers to Catholicism; he entered the anti-Semitic ranks with Abbé Cazals, assistant priest of Sainte-Marie, and Abbé Desgranges, parish priest of Condat. At meetings in Limoges, the speakers proclaimed, to repeated applause, that they would wage "relentless war against the Jews and their religion. Death to the Jews!" "We will be happy only when France is rid of that scourge."[116] In April 1900 Abbé Ardant declared, "Everything for God and for France, nothing for the Jews."

But the Dreyfus affair and the Zola trial did not unleash nationalist demonstrations in Limoges; most of the year 1898 passed peacefully in the streets. On October 10, 1898, however, on the place de la République, a lecture organized by Sébastien Faure (who in the end could not be there) and other anarchists led to a certain amount of unrest. In addition, people who came in cars from Périgueux distributed *L'Antijuif.* But that was about all: the Dreyfus file in the archives is virtually empty.[117]

The population of Limoges appeared to want nothing to do with nationalist ideas. Criticism of the role of the army in the Dreyfus affair even merged with criticism of employers, as attested in this astonishing report by a police superintendent: "The workers share the revisionist view. Acerbic criticism in the workshops against all leaders in general. Their favorite theme is to establish a connection between the workshop and the army and to make the hatred and jealousy they profess against the bosses rebound onto the army's leaders. From there it is only one step to wishing the officer would disappear, as they wish the boss would, and the boldest often take that step in their conversation. In this case, it is excessive boasting, but it nevertheless denotes that a dangerous state of mind has developed and deserves the serious attention of supporters of law and order."[118]

Although the superintendent noted that "calm reigns out in the fields," his report reveals that in the "red city" the Dreyfus affair intensified the rejection of the bosses' power, which was conceived as identical to that of the officers; both were perceived as guilty of illegitimate maneuvers. This police report is altogether unique in conveying the state of mind of the working world during the affair. The absence of nationalist populism[119] turned the Limoges workers away from anti-Semitism, of which few traces can be found here. The legislative elections, which ended in the reelection of two radicals, proceeded without any explicitly anti-Semitic positions being expressed. No candidates attacked the Jews or Captain Dreyfus. The local political scene was entirely absorbed in social issues.[120]

Still, *Le Messager du Limousin* wrote, "It must be admitted—by anyone whose ears are not plugged up as tight as a corked champagne bottle— that there is a Jewish question and that it will not be dodged. The Israelites are preparing a terrible future—you would have to be blind not to have some glimpse of it."[121] During his lecture before 250 people on February 20, 1898, the radical J. Tourgnol was questioned by a peasant regarding his feelings about the Jews. He responded, "I think that the Jews are dangerous creatures who respect nothing, who attack what we hold most dear and most sacred, who soil everything with their slobber, who know nothing except money, and have no other God but the Golden Calf. Those stateless people ought to be driven from our home, as was done in the past."[122] This former school principal did not mince words: he denounced the "bigwig voters," proclaimed himself "the father of the little guy," and asserted that he did not aspire to any "fat sinecure." He continually raised resounding cries of "the republic for the Republicans" and on election day waxed lyrical. "Your fathers," Tourgnol wrote on the front page of his newspaper, "the immortal victors of Jemmapes* and Fleurus, the valiant volunteers of the First Republic, enlisted under the flag of 'the nation in danger.' Like your ancestors, citizens, you have come running at our cry of alarm . . . [I am] not a cold fop raised in the lap of luxury. [I am] a worker . . . [I am] a man, against the caste of selfish ideas, against the supporters of expensive bread, and against the Jewish speculators favored by greedy

---

*Jemmapes: battlefield where the French, under General Charles Dumouriez, defeated the Austrians on November 6, 1792.—trans.

minorities and bigwigs. This must end."[123] Tourgnol won easily. In reality, anti-Semitism extended far beyond the nationalist candidacies, even in Haute-Vienne.[124] In the arrondissement of Bellac, the incumbent radical was defeated by the rightist candidate, Gabiat: the latter proclaimed loud and clear that he was the "enemy of the stateless and of that vile sect that is seeking to cast aspersions on our dear and fine army. I want France for the French." In his view, his opponent "has classed himself with those Jews who have spent millions to keep Zola from a deserved conviction. I am a patriot above all." To the great joy of *Le Courrier du Centre*, he won with a very strong voter turnout of 73 percent. He would be reelected in 1900 before being defeated in 1902.[125]

Before we journey onward to Creuse and complete this first circle in the heart of France, let us note that, in the neighboring department of Vienne, in Montmorrillon on January 21, after the military lottery, the conscripts built an effigy on which they wrote, "Death to the Jews!" "Long live the army!"[126] Conversely, in the department of Creuse, it is possible to claim, at first glance, that "conversations dealt less with the convict on Devil's Island than with the hoof-and-mouth disease that was then raging and the prefect's prohibition on fairs."[127] The press was nevertheless almost unanimously anti-Dreyfusard. In Bourganeuf the newspaper *La Jeune Creuse*, read by a number of migrants living in Paris, came out as fiercely anti-Dreyfusard. Desfarges, a former mason who easily won the seat of deputy, declared in his platform statement that he was against "the scheming of the Jewish cosmopolitans and financiers who, through the power of money, have unleashed unrest in the country to save the traitor Dreyfus, who was justly convicted by his peers."[128] Abbé Pichot, one of the rare Dreyfusard priests, had to leave his job at the small seminary of Felletin. Harshly attacked by *L'Avenir du Puy-du-Dôme*, he gave a lecture on "Anti-Semitism and Race Hatred" and, in August 1898, published a brochure entitled *La conscience chrétienne et la question juive* (The Christian Conscience and the Jewish Question), writing, "One day it will be good to have spoken, to have protested, to have broken rank. It is good, even now, to hold a place among the protesters, among the rare friends of Christian charity, of justice for all." When he was condemned by his superior, he protested and emphasized that he "worshipped the French army"; nevertheless, he had to resign his post and leave the region.[129]

Before it became revisionist, even the very respectable *L'Echo de la Creuse* wrote that one cannot "allow a traitor to be rehabilitated because he belongs to a religion that boasts of buying everything with money, which many of his co-religionists have earned in speculation at the expense of French finance." A number of newspapers in the region were openly anti-Semitic, such as *La République de la Creuse*, which, on September 2, 1898, attacked "the ignoble son of Israel . . . With him, the cosmopolitan Jews, without conscience and without a nation, the foul yeast of all nations, are branded." On January 22 *La Jeune Creuse* condemned "gold-plated Jewry" and "enslaving Catholicism" and refused to follow in the "wake of the cosmopolitan plutocrats." And when the law was passed moving the case to the three united chambers of the Cour de Cassation, on February 21, 1899, *L'Abeille* took aim at several local deputies: "You are accused of voting for judges won over to the Dreyfusard cause. We wonder (since the people of Creuse are rather curious) if the bribes you have received or will receive in compensation for your good services to the Jewish cause are or will be lavish."[130] The silence in the center of republican France masked many prejudices, which circulated from one edge of the political chessboard to the other.

Chapter Three

In Barrésian Lorraine

Our arrival in Lorraine opens our second geographical circle. This one will be wider than the first; passing through Marseilles, Montpellier, Toulouse, and Bordeaux, it will allow us to visit La Roche-sur-Yon, Nantes, Brest, Rennes, Caen, and Rouen. On January 27, 1898, *La Croix de l'Est* (a Lorraine newspaper) invited its readers to participate in a writing contest. Participants were to address the chosen subject "concisely, two hundred lines maximum. The editor of the newspaper reserves the right to correct entries and will award the prize more on the content of the ideas than on the form." First prize was to be a statue of Joan of Arc, valued at twenty francs; the second, a color poster by Hugo d'Alési. The subject the newspaper proposed for the consideration of its readers was "The role of the Jews in the countryside. Authentic anecdotes. The means to remedy the abuses." (The program for the competition at the conservatory, given the same day in an adjacent column of the same newspaper, was of a completely different nature: excerpts from Michel-Richard Lalande's *Soupers du roi*, Jean-Philippe Rameau's *Dardanus*, Edouard Lalo's Symphony in G Minor, and Camille Saint-Saëns's *Prélude du Déluge*.)

The writing competition occurred slightly more than a century after another famous writing competition held in 1787 by the Royal Society of Sciences and Arts of Metz, which had been designed to justify the emancipation of the Jews. In spite of his prejudices, the winner, Abbé Grégoire, a Lorrainian priest from Emberménil, a small locality close to Lunéville, offered a resolutely optimistic solution to the integration of the Jews into French society. This time the emphasis, even in the remotest parts of Lorraine, was on the distrust that the Jews allegedly elicited. Both in Paris and in the countryside of Lorraine, where you could frequently run into them, all the Jews could do, it was said, was betray those who trusted them—as "authentic anecdotes" amply proved.

Readers soon submitted their entries, and on February 17 *La Croix de l'Est* wrote, "A fine subject, don't you think, my reader friends, and well designed to excite your verve. Who has not been cheated by a Jew at least once in his life? Thus the compositions have arrived in great numbers at the newspaper office, and our only difficulty lies in choosing . . . We are nonetheless sorry that the anecdotal side was a little neglected . . . But everyone showed evidence of sound observation, without bias, with the calm that befits Catholics, with the strength that comes from legitimacy." That day the newspaper awarded the first prize to "Mélibée," the pseudonym of M.D., who wished to remain anonymous; and the second to Emile Masson from Cirey-sur-Vezouze. It conferred honorable mention on the compositions of J. René from Nancy, and of F—, near Rosières-aux-Salines. On February 18 and 19 *La Croix de l'Est* published the prize-winning essay on the front page. According to the happy winner,

> The Jews have just spent a very bad little spell in the city [Nancy] . . . The countryside said nothing, because it hates a ruckus, and yet the countryside, at least as much as the city, is the place where the Jews' misdeeds are multiplying. The Jew produces nothing. It is as if, in his eyes, handling a plow or an artisan's tool is a dishonorable thing, suitable, at the very most, for the Christian . . . In the fields, there are weeds called parasites that attack the vigorous stalks and suck the nourishment from them, without themselves having roots in the soil. That is the Jew! . . . Someone mentioned a

Jew who had the audacity to tell a good woman that the cow she had sold him a few days earlier had died soon after it arrived at his home; he asked her by way of settlement to discharge him of half the price, which had not yet been paid. Only too happy not to lose the whole thing, the weak-willed woman fell into the trap. But one fine day a neighbor informed her that the animal was peacefully grazing in the meadow of the closest village. That swindle deserved to be handled in criminal court . . . Customers coming in from the fields have the choice between the Jew's shop or the Catholic's; too often they patronize the Jew because his shop seems to have the best things, and especially because you can haggle there from morning till night. What a ludicrous comedy—the buyer is still duped. Let the Jews pick up the plow or the plane like our villagers. That would be equality.

La Croix de l'Est, forging ahead, published other stories, each one spicier than the last.

Listen to the two following anecdotes, both of which took place in the same commune. A man died with no heirs. Someone was supposed to sell his house, but only one person wanted it: the niece of the dead man, who had long lived there with her uncle. A Jew acquainted with the matter—they know everything, those hearty souls—came looking for her and said: "I yam tcharged by someone to bush ferry hart for de sale of de house. Gib me two hundard vrancs, and I vill zay nutting at all." The good girl, without suspicions and without money, signed the promissory note. A few years later, she married a retired teacher, and the day after the wedding, the Yid showed the note to the husband and demanded he be reimbursed.

The head of a large family, an honest and thrifty man, had paid a very high price for a house he bought from a Jew. He was supposed to pay annual installments set out in the contract. Each year he was very prompt in acquitting himself. But alas, shortly before the last payment was due, he realized that it would be impossible for him to make it. He went to find the descendant of Jacob and asked him for an extension, committing himself to pay 5 percent interest. "No," said the circumcised one, "jour note is on de market. If jou do not pay it, dere will be many esspenses." The good man, terror-stricken, told his story to a good Christian, who advanced him the money and thus wrested him from the clawlike fingers of that terrible Yid.[1]

Militantly Catholic Lorraine, galvanized by a Barrésian* nationalist populism that was absolute in its radicalism and solidly rooted in the region, leaped headlong into the anti-Semitic mobilization. In Nancy on January 14, 1898, a military review precipitated the leap. A crowd assembled at the place Caron and the cours Léopold. "The workers hastily took their meals"; the troops arrived; the 227th Brigade presented arms; the soldiers of the 21st put on their dress uniforms; the artillery paraded, as did the Fifth Hussars with a squadron on horseback. General de Monard emerged via the rue de la Pépinière, followed by a large, sparkling general staff. General Forget, who commanded the troops, went to meet him: "The enthusiasm was indescribable. As the bugles sounded and the drums beat in the fields, as the band played 'The Marseillaise,' the true patriots were there applauding him." When the general bestowed crosses on his officers, students who had gathered at the university began to shout, "Down with the Jews! Down with Dreyfus! Down with Salmon!† Down with Zola!" Outside all the gates of the barracks, as the troops were returning, they shouted the same slogans. More than five thousand people spread out into the streets, repeating them. "France is hypnotized by the affair," observed *L'Est Républicain*.[2] Two days later an "imposing demonstration" again passed through the main streets of Nancy, with shouts of "Long live the army! Down with the Jews! Out with Zola!" before dispersing at the place Stanislas. On the seventeenth, three hundred law students, joined by students from the Chemistry Institute and accompanied by a large following, demonstrated in the streets of Nancy to shouts of "Out with Zola! Out with the Jews! Death to the Jews! Down with the Kikes! Long live Drumont!" Someone shouted, "To the synagogue, home of the

---

*Barrésian: following Maurice Barrès (1862–1923), a nationalist politician, journalist, and author of the nationalistic trilogy *Les Bastions de l'Est*.—trans.
†Salmon: a professor at the University of Nancy.—trans.

Yids!" The students set off briskly, hit the entrance gate with canes, and then dispersed at the place Stanislas.[3]

For other residents of Lorraine that day, life lost none of its charm. The Femmes de France ball proceeded at the town hall: "The crowd proved to be splendid and full of life . . . The dances began at about six p.m. As usual, they lasted until about five a.m." Along with that report on the superb evening, *Le Journal de la Meurthe et des Vosges* wrote on the same page, as shouts were still reverberating in the city, "The Jews are tenacious and will do anything to succeed. They had better watch out. Watch out! The reprisals could be terrible."[4] Not far away on that same evening, January 17, "M. Guy Ropartz continues to procure very nice concerts for us. Mlle Mathieu d'Ancy, with her graceful soprano voice, supple and light, gave a remarkable interpretation of the music of [Gabriel-Urbain] Fauré, who had supervised the rehearsals and accompanied the singer himself." "But why are the women's choruses so weak?" protested *La Croix de l'Est*, applauding a performance of the overture to Richard Wagner's *Die Meistersinger*, "music that needs to be heard often to be properly understood and appreciated." On that agitated day, this calm and very civilized review of the concerts at the conservatory was placed next to a paragraph inveighing against "all those Jews who are taking the defense of the odious individual on Devil's Island."[5]

On the eighteenth students from the Anatomy Institute came to the place de l'Académie, shouting, "Out with the Jews! Out with Zola!" On the nineteenth the Union Catholique from the Saint-Epvre parish held a lecture on "the Jewish question." The speaker, M. Gérard, with "stirring eloquence," pointed out "the hatred that every Frenchman of France bears in his heart for every Jew." He presented "a study of the means to be rid of them" and then ended his short speech with these shouts, "which the assembly repeated: 'Long live the Jews in Jerusalem! Long live France for the French!' The entire audience was clearly under the spell of the warm and ringing words, expressing the loftiest and most noble feelings in precise and vigorous language . . . The session was adjourned after the prayer."[6] That same day in Nancy, students distributed a tract in the streets that read, "Not by the fist! Not by the sword! French students refuse to associate with Jews; they are ready to fight against those whom Dreyfus and his friends would like to bring to

France." In that overcharged atmosphere, the prefecture received several anonymous letters. One of them purported to expose a secret meeting between William II of Germany and one of Dreyfus's sons, which supposedly took place in annexed Alsace-Lorraine: "A pact of friendship was established between the son of Dreyfus and William II. Since 'Dreyfus' means 'three feet' or 'triple foot,' he will become stronger than the Triple Alliance, which will make Germany master of France and of all its military secrets." The author added, "I cannot sign my name, because I might be arrested for treason. But if my testimony interests you, you will put this announcement in *Le Messin*, three different times: 'For further information Nancy.' Then I will get a message to a French officer, who will let you know my name."[7]

In Lunéville, also in January, several hundred demonstrators marched to the military club on the place Léopold, shouting, "Down with the Jews! Down with Dreyfus! Long live the army!" They "gathered outside the café Collet, which was frequented by the well-to-do Jews. The demonstration was kindly escorted by the police." The same day in Toul, during the military lottery, a service was held to pray for the soldiers who had died in combat. After the ceremony, people shouted denunciations of "the traitor."[8] On the twenty-first and twenty-second, "the mocking and arrogant attitude of certain Jews" provoked new demonstrations in Lunéville: "patrols of dragoons and cuirassiers covered the streets; the crowd cheered them; the troops and the gendarmerie sought to disperse the groups as gently as possible." "Families strolled along peacefully; from time to time, shouts of 'Long live the army! Down with the Jews!' rose up. Nearly a thousand people demonstrated. Several Jewish residences were guarded by the troops. Fifteen cuirassiers guarded the café Collet . . . At about ten a.m., everyone went home. After three days, the Jews must have the feelings of the population fixed in their minds."[9] The Lunéville police superintendent emphasized in his January 24 report, "It is undeniable that the great majority of the population, ordinarily so peaceful and so undemonstrative, are only too willing to lend a sympathetic ear to the excitations of these heads of columns [the Catholic groups causing the disturbances] . . . In every social stratum of the population and even among the old-time republicans, tempers have flared against the Israelites, especially since the Jewish colony is very large and rich in Lunéville."[10] Anti-Semitic posters were plastered on the walls of the city. On the twenty-fifth in Baccarat, more than two hundred people booed the Jews. The same day in Nancy, the students who had been arrested at the previous demonstrations were sentenced. After imposing a one-franc fine, the judge gave them some fatherly advice: "Your matter is settled, you can go back to class."[11]

Lorraine went through many new developments in 1898, to such an extent that, at the end of that furious year, *L'Est Républicain* wrote, "For more than a year, France has had almost a civil war . . . This is evident in Nancy more than elsewhere because the Israelites are both numerous and powerful here . . . There is no city in France where the situation is so delicate as it is in Nancy."[12] To all appearances Nancy, the capital of Lorraine, remained the epicenter of the anti-Semitic mobilization: throughout 1898 countless demonstrations against the Jews took place there.

The May 1898 legislative elections marked the culmination of the anti-Semitic demonstrations, which became so frequent that they were almost commonplace. This time they occurred particularly within the context of election propaganda meetings. The open race for the anti-Semitic vote was on, and almost everyone exaggerated the extent of the movement in order to benefit from it. On February 13, 1898, the first meeting of the Ligue Antisémitique de France was held at Salle Gauschenot in Nancy, with the attorney Gervaize* presiding; the league's general secretary, Jules Guérin, was in attendance. Before eight hundred people, Gervaize congratulated the students of Nancy for so vigorously confronting "the Jewish race, whose dangerous influence has manifested itself so strongly in this city." During his lengthy speech, he denounced the Jews' hold over French society and their tactic of "doing battle in the dark." Against "the Jewish peril," he said, "the French must unite against the Jew, a stranger to our race." His motion hailing Rochefort and Drumont passed unanimously. The local branch of the Ligue Antisémitique long hesitated in choosing between Maurice Barrès and Ludovic Gervaize as best suited to lead the local battle for the leg-

---

*Ludovic Gervaize: anti-Semitic deputy from Meurthe-et-Moselle, closely associated with Jules Guérin.—trans.

islative elections. On April 3, at Saint-Nicolas, the two men came together in spite of their rivalry, for a meeting devoted solely to the fight against the Jews.[13]

Still, a Homeric struggle tore these two giants of the radical and anti-Semitic right apart. Their confrontation was an important moment. Barrès, a former Boulangist deputy, elected in 1889 with Catholic support, championed a Catholicism identified with a race. He invented a populism and a national socialism fiercely hostile to the Jews and devised the most racist, most provocative terms to condemn Dreyfus solely on the basis of his Jewish origin.

On April 17 a Comité Républicain Socialiste Nationaliste (Republican Nationalist Socialist Committee) was created in Nancy to support Barrès. On the twentieth the Socialist Committee of Meurthe-et-Moselle also declared its support for Barrès, "the defender of the worker, the enemy of the Jews."[14] On the twenty-third, before six hundred people in Salle Gauschenot, as a great number of members of the Catholic clubs were invading the hall, "Citizen Georgel, from the federation of trade unions, took the floor to support Barrès, who is the enemy of the Jews and of Zola." The police superintendent noted that "law enforcement was taken care of by workers wearing red carnations in their lapels." Barrès "demanded that the Jews who are seizing hold of the prefectures, the magistrature, and the ministries be held in check; he hoped for a development in the education and welfare of the working and peasant masses . . . In that way, his socialism follows from nationalism." When "two hecklers supporting the Jews were pummeled and thrown out," the hall screamed, "Down with the Jews!" The floor was then ceded to Gervaize, who "dealt with the Jewish question with even more bitterness than the previous speaker . . . He calls himself an independent republican."[15]

On May 3 Gervaize held another meeting in Salle Gauschenot. "He explained that he was an independent republican, that he was anti-Semitic, that he thus demanded that all Jews be excluded from public affairs, that he wanted France for the French and public office for the French alone. He denigrated the secular laws enacted by a Masonic coterie and by Jewry, demanded freedom for fathers to have their children reared in the religion that suited them, and advocated no tolerance for any foreign workers; for him, agriculture must be protected. Finally, he accused Jewry of establishing different railroad fares to benefit big businessmen at the expense of small ones."[16]

On May 13 Barrès, accompanied by Paul Déroulède, held a series of meetings in Mazerulles, Rosières, Dombasle, and Saint-Nicolas: "Déroulède's words elicited the enthusiasm of the listeners, about three hundred of them in Rosières, and five hundred and fifty in Dombasle." The last meeting of that eventful evening took place in Moncel-sur-Seille: here Déroulède "expressed regret that, in keeping with republican discipline, Gervaize had not withdrawn, especially since Barrès's program shared the issue of anti-Semitism with Gervaize's. The speaker appealed to the patriotic feelings of the voters and declared that, if someone did not quickly find a remedy, the Jew would lead France to its destruction. He finally concluded by elaborating on Barrès's platform, which he said was his own."[17] On May 16 a meeting was held at the Saint-Nicolas brasserie. The room was "packed" with about three hundred people. Barrès, who had already held six meetings that day, declared, "We are nationalists. We want France for the French. We want protection for national workers against foreign workers . . . The invading flood of Jews from Poland, Russia, and Germany must stop." Then Marcel Habert took the floor to support Barrès and demanded that "measures be taken against the Jews to protect the French nation. You must choose the party that defends France and not Dreyfus." He criticized Gervaize, who had "nearly the same platform as Barrès but supports clericalism"; Edouard Drumont, for his part, did not hide his support for Barrès.[18] On May 19 in Malzeville, before five hundred people (including the mayor of that locality), the writer found himself accompanied by Henry Ferrette, an anti-Semitic candidate in Bar-le-Duc (who would win in that ward after a particularly xenophobic campaign and who, once in the Chamber of Deputies, would join a brand-new anti-Semitic group organized by Drumont).[19] Barrès said that, "instead of disavowing Dreyfus, the way all the Catholics disavowed Bazaine,* the Jews formed a syndicate and supported him. At the same time, they revealed themselves as constituting a peril that no one had suspected . . . If the Chamber is unable to find the

---

*Achille Bazaine: marshal of France and commander in chief in the Franco-Prussian War; surrendered to Otto von Bismarck in 1870. He was court-martialed and sentenced to death, but the sentence was commuted to twenty years in prison.—trans.

force of resistance necessary against that peril, universal suffrage must give the government a sign." He ended by shouting, "Long live the Republic! Long live the nation!" "That ending was hailed with many rounds of applause."[20]

The anti-Semitic tension was now at its height. An audience of close to three hundred workers, almost all of them supporters of Barrès, interrupted a meeting held by Lavergne, a workers' socialist. Lavergne was maintaining that "anti-Semitism has no reason for existence among the workers. It is true that the Jews are thieves, but it was the Christians who . . . gave them the right to steal. The clericals use the weapon of anti-Semitism to distract attention." He declared that he "didn't give a damn about La Croix and its supporters, that he preferred [the candidate] Dr. Bernheim, who is Jewish and has always concerned himself with relieving the workers' poverty," over Constans,* who was Catholic and had "the workers in Fourmies shot." "Guilty or not, Dreyfus was one of those men who, under Constans's orders, massacred the common people in Fourmies." Lavergne denounced both Barrès, "the saber," and Gervaize, "the aspergillum." During the same meeting, a worker "said a few words in support of the workers' association and maintained that there were no Jews among the workers . . . A M. Nordon of Malzeville protested and addressed the crowd, saying that he was Jewish and an ironworker. Shouts and boos in great number were heard, drowning him out, and he could not make himself heard. Lavergne tried to quiet the crowd so that the Jew could speak, but he was unsuccessful." The police superintendent also noted that Lavergne "certainly disgusted almost all the listeners with his anarchist and antipatriotic theories."[21]

A Groupe de Patriotes supported Gervaize as the candidate of anti-Jewish protest: "The Jews took our money. Those stateless people wanted to take our honor away from us. One of them betrayed us! Let them keep the money but leave us our honor. Long live France for the French! Long live the Republic! Long live the army! Death to the traitors!" A poster signed by the Comité Ouvrier (Workers' Committee) of Nancy attacked Nicolas, the candidate supported by Le Progrès de l'Est, the only newspaper in the region with (extremely moderate) Dreyfusard leanings: "That good Nicolas was booed by a thousand workers at the

---

*Ernest Constans: minister of the interior.—trans.

public meeting in Nancy, on the twenty-third of last month, and was rejected as unworthy. In Nancy we know him only too well. Do you know that, by voting for him, you would be voting for Dreyfus? Nicolas is the Judas, the Zola, who sold himself to the Jews and is manipulated by them like a puppet."[22] A song was circulated, sung to the tune of "La promise" (The Betrothed) and titled "Mon gros Nicolas" (My Fat Nicolas):

My fat Nicolas,
I have to tell you
Things you may take
For foolishness . . .
But my poor lad,
You know my frankness;
You're a good lawyer.
But that won't do.

They say, Nicolas,
That you're taking loot
From the big syndicate,
Damn, that's not honest,
Or you call yourself Zola,
Jew, opera glass merchant.
All that's not so clear:
You're cornered, my friend.

True, my dear colonel,
The matter isn't pretty;
You gave, so they say,
To the Jews at L'Etincelle
Seven hundred francs in cold hard cash,
Quite a little sum.
Apprentice deputy,
That's not a good start.[23]

On the sidewalks and on the walls, in public meetings of various currents, in nearly all the newspapers, anti-Semitism burst out in torrents.

In that very Catholic region, meetings of the Union Catholique became places where people expressed their rejection of the Jews. In October 1897 an assembly of about a hundred members of the committee of the Saint-Sébastien parish gathered, with several priests in attendance. The presiding officer, Gérard, called himself "republican, and a sincerely Catholic republican; but my republicanism will come into being only when we have a true Republic and not a Republic whose strings are pulled by the Freemasons and the Jews." "Dr. Rémy dealt with the workers' health and elaborated on his article in La Croix about alcoholism. Abbé Goney from Pont-à-Mousson stood up and pronounced a violent indictment of the Jews and Freemasons: 'Bring your friends, your neighbors. Today we are a hundred: at the next meeting, if you like, that figure will be doubled or even tripled.' He made a heated appeal to the workers to unite: by this means they would have the upper hand and the Jews would be annihilated."[24]

On February 5, 1898, a meeting of the Union Catholique at the Saint-Epvre parish drew two hundred people to plan a protest that was to take place the next day at a lecture by Hubbard, deputy and "supporter of the Dreyfus syndicate." "All the Catholic committees are supposed to go . . . M. Bombray, editor at La Croix, will go to answer him, and when he gives a hand signal, all their supporters are supposed to shout 'Down with the Jews! Down with Zola! Down with the Freemasons!' He recommended that the workers do everything possible to attend that lecture. He indicated the position that each parish was to occupy in the hall: the Saint-Epvre parish on the left; the Saint-Sébastien parish on the right; the Saint-Nicolas parish in the center. The Saint-Fiacre parish will be the honor guard, in front."[25]

Shortly thereafter, on March 13, the Saint-Fiacre committee of the Union Catholique held a meeting attended by about a hundred people: "Gérard, a hatmaker, gave a speech against the Jews and demanded they be excluded from politics and the army because, in that way, France would truly be for the French."[26] On April 21 the Union Catholique of the Saint-Georges parish held a meeting in Salle Gauschenot. Gérard told the audience that " 'the Jews are the scourge of France. People must no longer associate with Jews or buy anything from them. Then when they see that they are being marginalized, they will desert France.' He invited the members present to vote for the candidate who supported the abolition of laws on Catholic religious communities; that candidate is a fervent Catholic. He is our friend Gervaize."[27] On September 25 the minor nationalist leader Max Lancry "arrived at the Nancy train station, where he was welcomed by Bombray and others; they went to church and, after mass, to a 'democratic banquet'; the presiding officer thanked Lancry for being kind enough to replace Abbé Lemire and gave a lecture on the health of the workers." Other speakers praised the virtues of the gardens set aside for workers and asked the people in attendance to adopt Drumont's motto, "France for the French."[28]

On December 22, with the agreement of Union Catholique, the incipient Comité Ouvrier Antijuif (Anti-Jewish Workers' Committee) called a meeting: "Citizen. You are requested to attend the private meeting that will take place Thursday, December 22, in Salle Gauschenot, at eight-thirty a.m. Agenda: constitution of a Comité Ouvrier Antijuif." At another meeting of the Union Catholique, attended by about fifteen workers, a former cobbler explained that, to oppose Jewish scheming, it was necessary to form, as in Algeria, an anti-Jewish workers' committee that would organize the unrest. "A collection made for the widow of Colonel Henry produced three francs."[29]

Under these conditions the right's electoral campaign was certain of broad success. *La Croix Meusienne* wrote on February 13: "Do you want to see these traitors to France disappear? Blacklist them and do not bring them the fruit of your labor any longer: do not pay a red cent to the descendants of Judas." In Marne the prefect reported the worries of the Jews of Reims, given that "for some time, signs have been displayed . . . on the walls bearing the words 'Never buy from a Jew. France must be for the French. Drive the Jew from the nation.' The signs were printed by the intransigent Catholic newspaper *L'Avenir*."[30] On February 22, 1898, in Pont-à-Mousson, most of the Jewish shopkeepers found, attached to their storefronts, a little sign from the Ligue Antijuive: "European and Arab Frenchmen, don't buy anything from the Jews."[31]

In the May elections, as people of Lorraine went to the polls, *La Croix de l'Est* gave a last piece of advice: "Whom not to vote for? Not for a Freemason. Not for an atheist. Not for a socialist. Not for a Jew. That is understood after the Dreyfus affair. The Jew, having no nation, insolently displays the pretension of squeezing ours dry." Among the candidates in Nancy the newspaper gave its support to Brice, a "moderate republican"; to Baraban, a "Catholic candidate, anti-Semitic republican"; and to Gervaize, an "anti-Semitic republican." In Lunéville it endorsed Corrard des Essarts, a "Catholic, anti-Semitic republican." In Toul it supported Piquart, a "Catholic," and not the unruly Abbé Hémonet, author of *Nancy juif,* who in his first declaration proclaimed, "Catholics and Frenchmen! Such is the cry of defense, the rallying cry, that *Nancy juif* raised five years ago and that echoed throughout France. Catholics and Frenchmen! Such is the grandiose and reassuring cry that France as a whole is voicing today and whose echo makes the old ramparts of Metz and Strasbourg shake. It is a program of deliverance because it means: Out with the foreign, lying, thieving Jew, a Judas and tormentor of Catholic France, just as he was for Christ. Lorrainians! Frenchmen! On your feet for the cross of Christ and the flag of France!" In lecture after lecture, Abbé Hémonet, who was running as a "French Catholic" candidate, had pronounced violent attacks against the Jews, using arguments drawn from his book, *Nancy juif.*[32]

In the third ward of Nancy, there was a difficult contest between Barrès and Gervaize, who enjoyed Catholic support; anti-Semitism turned out to be widely shared. *L'Est Républicain,* which opposed both of them, wrote, "The candidates Barrès and Gervaize replaced their platform statements with declarations that they were anti-Semitic. But it must be well understood that the republican contingent repudiates all solidarity with the cosmopolitan syndicate, which dared place in doubt the trust we had in the army, which we all associate with the holy idea of the great French nation. In Nancy we do not need to be taught to respect the army."[33] As a result it was possible to assert that "the Lorrainians are for the most part anti-Dreyfusards."[34] Thanks to his Catholic support, Gervaize defeated Barrès; Brice won too, and Baraban was defeated, though he received 31 percent of the vote in the first round. In Toul, Piquart was elected, while his rival, Abbé Hémonet, even more extreme in his anti-Semitism, drew 18 percent of the vote in the first round. In Lunéville, Corrard des Essarts received 38 percent of the vote but was narrowly defeated in the second round: he would nevertheless be elected a little later. He had declared on May 5, "I do not accept the idea that the Jews will continue to dominate our country, to sully France . . . Catholic, republican, and anti-Semitic, my platform can be summed up in these words: Peace, Work, Order, and Liberty. Long live France for the French!"[35]

The Union Catholique was not a passing fancy; it remained true to its values for a long time, very influential in Nancy, and very active. On April 10, 1899, before nearly three hundred people, the group denounced the overly ambiguous articles of *Républicain de l'Est*: "Certain people believe that *L'Est* is not more anticlerical than it is anti-Jewish. In reality, the priests are the main course at *L'Est*, and the Jews are only an hors-d'oeuvre or dessert. *L'Est* wants to make its little Semitic clientele forget what it published about the Dreyfus affair." On August 18, 1899, Gérard maintained that the Union Catholique had attracted four thousand people in Nancy. He celebrated Guérin's resistance to the Jews, defended "our valiant nuns," and played musical pieces on his phonograph—for example, Déroulède's *Le clairon* (The Bugle). On October 9, 1899, Gervaize and Brice conducted a meeting where the Jews were again accused of bankrupting France and of "contributing to the aberrations of the Protestants." On October 15 Abbé Jacquot, the new mayor of Saint-Sébastien, presided over a meeting of the Union Catholique that "reveled in the verdict at Rennes [where a court-martial of Dreyfus in September 1899 found Dreyfus guilty once again], which will not appease the families on the payroll of the Jews and cosmopolitans. There was applause." On October 18 eight hundred members of the Union Catholique participated in vespers at Saint-Epvre and Saint-Fiacre; "there were a large number in attendance." Afterward almost all the participants went to a large hall where the musical group of the Union Nancéienne performed "The Marseillaise." Gérard accused the government of obeying Joseph Reinach and hailed Paul Déroulède as a great patriot; he then returned at length to the Dreyfus affair and proclaimed himself the "friend" of Jules Guérin, "a sincere patriot, defender of all liberties in France," and he expressed the wish for "a hundred Fort Chabrols."* "People shouted 'Long live the truly French Republic!' and 'Down with the Jews!' "[36]

---

*Fort Chabrol: in April 1899 Jules Guérin and about fifteen of his fellow leaguists barricaded themselves in the offices of *L'Antijuif* on the rue Chabrol in Paris, leading to clashes with police and a six-week standoff. In the end Guérin surrendered to Prefect Louis Lépine. See Michel Winock, *Nationalism, Anti-Semitism, and Fascism in France*, trans. Jane Marie Todd (Stanford: Stanford University Press, 1998), pp. 231–33.—trans.

In the 1902 legislative elections, Gervaize, who had moderated his position, maintained that he now "respected the Protestant in his church and the Jew in his synagogue; the Catholic ought to have the right to go to mass if he so chooses." During an electoral meeting in Nancy on April 12, 1902, however, he presented himself as the anti-Jewish candidate. "The whole room was in favor of him," observed the police superintendent.[37] He was accompanied at that meeting by the mayor of Nancy, and everywhere shouts of "Long live Déroulède!" rang out. Gervaize was reelected in the first round with 10,054 of the 16,587 ballots cast. Brice, another anti-Semitic candidate, was also re-elected in the first round. In Lunéville, Corrard des Essarts won easily this time.[38] He had participated at a meeting in Blamont where the main speaker, after introducing him to the audience, "imitated with a rather nice comic talent the words and tone, as well as the accent, of an Israelite butcher or cattle merchant in the process of swindling a peasant."[39]

Nancy was the epicenter of fidelity to nationalist and anti-Semitic values. Not far away, in Bar-le-Duc, mobilization was also very strong and produced astonishing and powerful demonstrations against the Jews.[40] The Vosges department also experienced many anti-Semitic out-bursts. In Epinal on January 8, 1899, a poster announced: "Yesterday, at one o'clock, the 152nd Infantry was passing on the quai des Bons-Enfants. Just as the flag went past, the Jew Ulmann, a merchant on the rue Rualménil, exclaimed, 'Look at that rag going by.' That fellow who'd been baptized with pruning shears deserves the contempt of all good people. Down with the Jews! Death to the traitors! A group of patri-ots." Throughout that day the police had to intervene to prevent the crowd from attacking the Ulmann store. In the following days, small handwritten posters attached to the walls screamed, "Hang the Jew Ul-mann, who insults the flag! Death to the Jews! Long live the army!" And "Officers and soldiers of the 152nd, avenge the insult made to the flag: lynch the Jew Ulmann. Long live the army! Down with the Jews!"

On January 22 in Saint-Dié, a dozen young people ran through the streets of the city shouting, "Down with the Jews! Death to the Jews! Death to the Yids!" In early February shouts of "Down with the Jews!

Out with Zola!" could again be heard in Epinal. The police removed anti-Semitic posters from various streets. Other incidents occurred in the region. In Vincey, "in the evening, a troop of young people pursued a certain Isidor Marx, of the Jewish religion, a business representative in Charmes, who had come to sell the property of one of his debtors living in Vincey. To shouts of 'Out with Zola! Down with the Jews!' they struck Isidor Marx with canes and threw stones at him, as he headed toward the train station of Vincey."[41]

The police kept an eye on anti-Semitic activities and noted that one Raoul de Juglart had left Lunéville for Remiremont; there he took over the editorship of the clerical and anti-Semitic newspaper *La Volonté Nationale*, which in the 1902 legislative elections would support a reactionary and anti-Semitic candidate by the name of Flayelle. Flayelle held public meetings that attracted up to a thousand people in Remiremont alone: in the presence of the nationalist and anti-Semitic deputy of Bordeaux Charles Bernard, contradictory shouts of "Long live Flayelle! Down with the Jews!" and "Long live Méline!* Long live the Republic!" rose up. In the meantime, according to the police report, "Flayelle's speech was applauded by the nationalist faction of our city and the members of the Catholic club who had gathered near the podium." Altercations erupted; then Flayelle and Bernard were escorted out by three hundred young people who crossed the city, flags at the head of their procession, shouting, "Long live Flayelle! Down with the Jews!"[42] In Gérardmer as well, "the anti-Semitic unrest went on persistently but noiselessly." In January 1898 someone attached the following paper to the walls of the city:

AT THE LIDDLE BISSNISS OF

DREYFUS AND COMPANY

TRAFFICKING IN MOBILIZATION

DEPORTATION

KAHN, AARON, LÉVY, BLOCH, BLUM, AND COMPANY, PRINTERS,

ON DEVIL'S ISLAND.[43]

---

*Jules Méline: premier of France, 1896–98.—trans.

In the canton of Dompaire, within the context of the February 1898 cantonal elections, the attorney Léon Merklen conducted a violent campaign against "the Dreyfus syndicate" and "cosmopolitan Jewry." Although he was easily defeated, he received 23 percent of the vote.[44] The whole region was buzzing with anti-Semitic incidents, even the most modest towns. Thus in Mirecourt and Neufchâteau, the purchasing committee "refused to authorize the horse auction the Jews sought to conduct." As the police superintendent reported, "The Jew David Birgé became involved in the matter and concluded by saying that the Israelites were as good as other Frenchmen. Officers of the Ninth Light Infantry, finding David's [sic] intervention uncalled for, hastened to put him in his place . . . Everyone was indignant about the little Jew's audacity. That matter was not designed to calm people, who are already overexcited by the Zola trial." Another police officer remarked that "that incident produced a certain hilarity among the people present." In Avricourt in early April, someone posted accusing signs on the walls of houses inhabited by Jews: "Who has placed farming in jeopardy? The Jew . . . Down with the Jews! Long live France!" "Someone even climbed the outer wall of the synagogue to post the sign on that building," the police superintendent reported. On the Monday of Passover, a certain Lafrogne "threw a packet of these bills onto the carriage of Montoux, an Israelite butcher; the latter had had an altercation with Lafrogne in the street and pointed out to him, with good reason, that, in the canton, farming had been jeopardized by the bankruptcy of the banker Maizières, Lafrogne's uncle."[45]

As we move southwest from Nancy, to the vast zone stretching from Châlons-sur-Marne in the north to Besançon in the south and including Troyes, Dijon, and Vesoul, we find that this entire region experienced a great deal of unrest. In Châlons-sur-Marne, in Reims, and in Vitry-le-François, anti-Semitic posters were put up and meetings were held by Catholic clubs occupied with organizing the anti-Semitic campaign and creating L'Antijuif.[46] In Troyes, the chief city of the Aube departments as well as Bar-sur-Aube and Arcis-sur-Aube, the legislative contest was heated between the radical candidates and their opponents, supported by energetic Catholic groups. Almost all the radicals won, but as in other areas there were frequent aberrations.[47]

In Dijon the anti-Semitic fever lasted several months and reached an unusual intensity. In the early afternoon of January 23, 1898, a group of students and other young people marched, shouting until they were hoarse, "Death to the Jews! Down with Zola!" Several students were arrested, as was a certain Maurice Leclerc, who was wanted by the police for jewel theft; he had on his person a chisel and a large burin, with which he tried to strike the officers. All afternoon students, including many enrolled at the law school, repeated the invectives. A crowd of about four hundred shouted hostile slogans outside stores owned by Jewish tradespeople. They headed toward the synagogue but, upon seeing police protecting it, dispersed. Later, outside the café de la Concorde on the place Darcy, where the Jews of Dijon were accustomed to meet, merchants, vintners, and "industrialists" shouted, "Death to the Jews!" In the late afternoon and into the late evening, groups of several hundred people, "very overexcited," again made their way through the streets, tirelessly repeating the same slogans. On the twenty-fourth about a hundred medical and pharmacy students, coming out of their classes, headed toward the rue de la Liberté, led by an accordionist playing "The Marseillaise." One of the demonstrators, twenty-three-year-old Fernand Huguenin, a pharmacy student, was scolded by the police superintendent, whereupon he shouted, "I am a good Frenchman and the bitter enemy of the Jews. No one will prevent me from booing them. You will do your duty, Mr. Superintendent; as for me, I will shout what I like." People shouted outside Jewish-owned stores, threw stones, and destroyed windows. The police, prepared for violence, kept watch and limited the damage. All evening long other unlawful assemblies took place; the same cries were repeated, "followed by bursts of laughter or the stamping of feet or canes." Several arrests were made. Finally at about nine p.m., a group formed on the rue Chabot-Charny. It headed toward the synagogue and threw stones at the building, shouting, "On to the rabbi!" More arrests were made. The police superintendent's report indicated that "the special service provided during these last few days of demonstrations has exhausted the staff, which needs a deserved rest. It would be useful, if the unrest were to continue, if the gendarmerie could replace the police in maintaining order and the free-dom of the streets." On the twenty-fifth, students gathered in front of the Cirque d'Eté, then crossed the city before being dispersed. In re-sponse to "sensible advice" from the authorities, they withdrew. Later, workers—"ordinary troublemakers," according to the police, "who like to make use of the disorder in all the big cities"—also joined the fray: the windows of stores owned by Jews were shattered. On the twenty-sixth at about eight p.m., some four hundred workers and employees gathered on the avenue Victor-Hugo, then demonstrated until late into the evening on the rue de la Liberté, before being dispersed.

For several weeks things calmed down, and Dijon recovered its spirit. On March 13, however, Georges Thiébaud gave a lecture in the banquet room of town hall, attended by three hundred people including, the po-lice noticed, "several ecclesiastics." Forest, president of the anti-Semitic group in Dijon, "sharply attacked the Jewish race . . . He demanded measures in support of the workers and declared that people's minds had to be remolded to fit the national spirit. He acknowledged that the Jews were more intelligent than the Catholics, but they were also more crooked and thieving." Thiébaud, who followed him, launched into his usual diatribe, asserting that the Socialist Party was "subsidized by the Jews." Then the following motion was unanimously passed by the audi-ence: "The Dijonnais, several hundred of whom are gathered in Salle Flore, join with the ideas of the anti-Semitic speakers and demand from the government a more energetic repression of the foreigners. They send their hearty congratulations to Drumont, the originator of this great movement."[48] On April 12 in Dijon, the Union des Voyageurs Français Antisémites pour la Défense du Commerce et de l'Industrie (Union of Anti-Semitic French Travelers for the Defense of Commerce and Indus-try) was constituted. It sent the following letter to business representa-tives, tradespeople, and industrialists:

In the face of an economic situation that is worsening every day, in the face of the shameful commercial practices employed by cos-mopolitan Jewry to drain off national wealth to its own advantage, we felt that the moment has come for us, anti-Semitic French trav-elers, to unite . . . It is with that idea that a large number of busi-ness travelers, finding themselves in Dijon, held two meetings on

April 12 . . . We are thus appealing to all our anti-Semitic colleagues in France.

Shortly thereafter the organization had a poster plastered throughout France, from Dijon to Nantes, and from Charleville to Perpignan and Vienne. It was titled "The Monopolists. Where Are They?" and read as follows:

THE SYNDICATE OF WOE COMPOSED OF JEWS AND FREEMASONS,

SEEING THE TIDE OF INDIGNATION RISING AMONG ALL TRUE

FRENCHMEN, WOULD LIKE TO ATTEMPT A DIVERSION TO MAKE

US FORGET THAT, IN FRANCE, THE ACCURSED JEWS HAVE

MONOPOLIZED EVERYTHING. THEY REPEAT THAT THE TRUE

MONOPOLISTS ARE THE CLERGY . . . THE WEALTH OF THE CLERGY

COMES FROM THEIR FAMILY FORTUNES, THEIR PERSONAL

CONTRIBUTIONS OR GIFTS, AND THE ACTS OF GENEROSITY

FREELY PERFORMED TOWARD THEM. THE MONEY OF THE CLERGY

SERVES TO BUILD MANY HOUSES, WHICH GIVES WORK TO THE

WORKERS; IT SERVES TO GIVE REFUGE TO THE POOR, THE SICK,

THE ORPHANS, AND THE ELDERLY. THE MONEY OF THE JEW

COMES FROM PLAYING THE STOCK MARKET, FROM CONSTRICTING

THE MONEY SUPPLY, FROM THE MOST VILE AND SHADY SORT OF

DEALINGS. THE MONEY OF THE JEW GOES ABROAD. YES, THERE IS

AN ENORMOUS DANGER, BUT IT DOES NOT LIE IN THE WEALTH

OF THE CLERGY. IT LIES IN THE JEWS' MONOPOLIZATION

OF FRANCE.[49]

In the Haute-Saône department, where about six hundred Jews lived, the electoral campaign was particularly vigorous, given that a few of them held elective office. E. Schwob was mayor and general councilor of Héricourt; Blum was mayor of Jussey; and Lévy, the future general councilor and mayor, was municipal councilor in Gray. It also happened that, from 1887 to 1889, Eugène Sée was prefect of the department and Emile Waltz was Gray's subprefect. That relative political visibility intensified the traditional anti-Semitic rejection that reemerged at the start of the Dreyfus affair. As the 1898 elections approached, the tone was aggressive: on January 26 *Le Nouvelliste* denounced Zola, "the cynic, the filthy scoundrel who, after insulting the army by writing *La débâcle* (The Debacle), has just insulted it again by defending Dreyfus, who sold out to the enemy."

Like Nancy and Bar-le-Duc in Lorraine, Vesoul in Haute-Saône became a regional capital of anti-Semitism and remained so for several years. On March 13 a large anti-Semitic meeting, attended by a thousand to fifteen hundred people (including two hundred women, priests, and officers of the garrison), was conducted by Georges Thiébaud, who claimed mockingly that Dreyfus, by betraying France, was only doing "a liddle bissniss." He added, "We are anti-Semitic and nationalist. We say that the Jew is not French and that every Frenchman is aware of the Jewish peril, which is gaining a hold on the working class." He warned the population of Vesoul against the Jewish peril and committed himself to combat it in the Chamber. "We do not want the extermination of the Jews," he exclaimed in his speech. "We simply want France to be for the French, and for the Jews, who are not French, to be excluded." Eliciting laughter and cheers from the audience, that indefatigable nationalist leader demanded "the union of all the French of France against the Jewish and cosmopolitan influence, and . . . the emergency exclusion of the Jews from the army and public office." The motion was unanimously adopted.

Immediately after that meeting, the Comité Antisémite de Vesoul was created, and for several months in early 1899, it published the newspaper *Vesoul Antijuif.* The first issue declared, "The hour has finally come to stop the invading torrent of people of Israel and to extricate yourselves from the sort of slavery with which the descendants of Judas threaten you every day. You have finally felt the need to shake off the yoke and rid yourselves of that constraint." A little later this notice appeared: "For several years the big hooked noses and the big blue smocks of certain Jews from Feverney and Jussey have been making their hideous appearance in our peaceful countryside. Beware, all Jews of Feverney and Jussey, if you do not want to be scalded alive like the animals whose flesh you refuse to eat." The newspaper continued with its condemnation of a number of Jews, especially the pharmacist Blum, "that Yid, who is like certain night birds who come out only when darkness has spread over the earth." *Vesoul Antijuif*, upon learning that Blum had decided to leave the city, openly rejoiced: "Go then, you raggedy old man, leave quickly. Go adorn the sidewalks of some other city with your graceful person. You can go to Nancy, where people are already informed of your arrival, and you will be loved there on the basis of your merits. Never see you later, Miss'r Blum." In September 1899 the newspaper attacked one Dr. Jules Dreyfus, and when he too decided to seek refuge in Paris, it erupted in joy: "We will no longer have before our eyes that flushed red face, that monumental nose, that person with the dirty paws. So we will no longer see that Yid walking up and down every day on the sidewalks of our city. Oh, if he only knew the pleasure we feel in seeing him vacate a place he has occupied for too long! He would be very astonished, and perhaps, in his Hebrew brain, the idea would come to him to continue to pollute our good city." In the last issue of *Vesoul Antijuif*, after Déroulède was tried and convicted for plotting against the Republic, the newspaper published an outburst of anger:

> *There it is! It's the Republic of Jews!*
> *My hatred has grown by degrees.*
> *At the start of the affair, I was anti-Dreyfusard.*
> *For a while now, I have been anti-Parliament.*
> *Today, I am anti-Jew.*
> *Down with the Jews!*

Here too a large portion of the press slipped into an extreme anti-Semitism. On February 13, 1898, *La Croix Meusienne* wrote, "We would be curious to know whether the Jewish campaign, whose goal was to rehabilitate a traitor, has had repercussions in Meuse. The time is approaching for the major fairs, where the merchants used to bring their hooked noses, their big smocks, and their insolence. What kind of welcome will they receive? And in our cities where so many stores belong to them, will we continue to see that scandalous procession of Catholics buying their crucifixes, their first communion gowns . . . and all the rest from those who crucified Jesus Christ? French Catholics, let us save our money and our handshakes for our brothers of France."

An astonishing quantity of diverse and imaginative propaganda—remarkably preserved in the National Archives—flooded Vesoul. On various blotting pads and on many posters circulated by the anti-Semitic committee of the city came the warning: "The Jew is not French—he betrays his country." "Stand back dirty Jews, spies, thieves!" "Toss the Yids into the water! We don't need any more of them." "There may be scoundrels who are not Jewish, but there are no Jews who are not scoundrels." "Don't buy anything from the Jews, for the honor of France." As a police superintendent noted, on the walls of all the train stations in the vicinity of the Haute-Saône prefecture, banners appeared: "By whom have you been cheated in your purchases? By the Jews. Don't buy anything from the Jews." In his biweekly report of August 15, 1898, the superintendent observed that "the members of the Ligue Antisémitique are very excited in Vesoul; they are even becoming provocateurs and are attacking without reason the Israelites they encounter in the streets."[50]

The electoral contest in the city pitted the republican and anticlerical Genoux, the incumbent deputy who was also mayor of Luxeuil, against the industrialist Colle, a moderate republican, behind whom a conservative and clerical front rallied. The Dreyfus affair played a determining role in the outcome. Genoux was bold enough to write, "I have always believed in Dreyfus's guilt, and I have never doubted the military judgment, but there were irregularities." And he courageously added, "The ministry, through its equivocal, wavering attitude, is responsible for the campaign conducted by clericals and reactionaries, which exploits the most sacred feelings of patriotism. A deviant political current has established itself, against which I have the duty to warn the republicans; on the basis of an infamous act they want to build a religious war in favor of a caste." Depicted as the "champion of the Jews," accused by his opponents of taking money from the Jews, Genoux was easily defeated by Colle.[51] The same thing happened in the neighboring ward of Lure, which had long been held by the left. The incumbent deputy, Chaudey, faced a raging nationalist anti-Semitic campaign because Schwob, the mayor of Héricourt and a distant relative of Captain Dreyfus, whose name appeared among those who advocated giving a medal of honor to Zola, was on Chaudey's support committee. The rightist candidate, Salignac-Fénelon, easily won. His candidacy received the support of *La Franche-Comté*, which "hailed Salignac-Fénelon as an opponent of the Dreyfusard scheming, against which good Frenchmen have risen up." He was also supported by *Le Petit Saônois*, which, just before the elections, wrote, "Logic dictates that those who are Catholic vote for Catholics and buy from Catholics, and that those who are Jews, Protestants, and Freemasons vote for Jews, Protestants, and Freemasons and buy from them."

Anti-Semitism flourished in Vesoul. In his report of February 1900, following the senatorial elections, the prefect observed, "A nationalist current has established itself in Haute-Saône, and in Vesoul in particular, where, as a result of the presence of a small circle of Israelite families, anti-Semites are extremely numerous. The anti-Dreyfusard campaign conducted on the occasion of the elections has made strong inroads among the republicans."[52] In January 1900 a new champion of anti-Semitism, the prosperous industrialist Outhenin-Chalandre, headed a list that won two out of three senatorial seats. In March he also won the position of deputy for the arrondissement of Vesoul. "It is in troubled times, it is when the perils are the greatest, that it is most meritorious to fulfill one's civic duty," *Le Nouvelliste* wrote. "One of our major industrialists, Outhenin-Chalandre, is one of those. He saw the peril, and with a disinterestedness that does him honor, he sacrifices in defense of his country through his activities and his intelligence." In the 1900 legislative elections, the left lost a seat that it had held since 1876. The right received its highest share of the vote (44.3 percent) in support of Fachard, a *rallié* and a conservative who ran as an "anti-Dreyfusard republican." His opponent, the republican P. Morel, was called the "candidate of the Jews, of the friends of the traitor, of the opponents of the army, the candidate of the lodges, of the synagogue, of cosmopolitan radicalism." *Le Républicain de Gray* reported that Morel's candidacy "hatched after a slow incubation in the lodges and synagogues," while *Vesoul Antijuif* claimed that Morel benefited from the support of the Jews of the arrondissement. "Into the sewer with the Jewish and cosmopolitan filth," it admonished. "Into the sewer with the Masonic finery and those who wear it." Celebrating Fachard's victory, *La*

Franche-Comté reveled in "the crushing defeat of the Jewish, radical, Masonic coalition . . . in death sentence of the Jewish-Dreyfusard party."[53]

In reality, the entire east of France was stirred up. The regions of Franche-Comté and Lorraine vied with each other for the crown of anti-Semitism. In Poligny on the eve of the 1898 election, the following poster appeared: "Think of your children, your families. Think of France, the Republic . . . If you want nothing to do with a friend of those who support Zola and the Jews, vote against M. Drumont." In Saint-Claude even the moderate republican entreated "patriotic voters" to vote for him, while opposing the "anti-French campaign undertaken by the cosmopolitan Jews." In Lons-le-Saunier, according to *La Croix du Jura*, "the workers are sympathetic toward an anti-Semitic poster they have read, because they are true Frenchmen and have not sold their consciences to the Jews."[54]

Besançon, the capital of the Jura department, almost rivaled Vesoul in anti-Semitism. On January 19 the anti-Semitic wave hit that city: about five hundred people in the streets shouted, "Down with the Jews!" Then they gathered outside the synagogue and demonstrated outside the chief rabbi's home and various Jewish stores. "Everything took place in a very peaceful manner," observed *La Franche-Comté*. On January 21 another anti-Semitic demonstration erupted. About five hundred young people, including many students, headed for the synagogue via Grand-Rue and the quai de Strasbourg, shouting, "Out with Zola! Down with the Jews!" They continued in that way to the military club on the rue de la Préfecture, before reaching the home of Chief Rabbi Auscher, where they screamed, "Death to the Jews!" For more than ten days, groups of students crisscrossed the streets of Besançon, demonstrating loudly. "Nothing serious," the police superintendent noted in his report.[55]

Anti-Semitic posters covered the walls of the city. Horrible anti-Semitic brochures entitled *Gare aux Juifs!* (Woe to the Jews!) were decorated with a spider spinning its web and the caption "Yid lying in wait for its prey." These booklets made every effort to demonstrate that Jews dominated the French economy, state, and press, stating that "among the telephone customers in Paris, one third are Jews."[56] In the legislative elections, Adrien Bonnet ran under the "anti-Semitic conservative" label; although he lost, he conducted a very active campaign with posters and public meetings. Edouard Drumont awakened a particular sympathy in Besançon, since he had singled out the Jews of that city in *La France juive*. In *Mon vieux Paris* Drumont had portrayed traditional Paris subjected to the modernist yoke of the Jews; Abbé Hémonet gave a similar diagnosis in *Nancy juif*; and Jean Baffier had celebrated old Bourges. Similarly, Gaston Coindre, a painter and engraver, published *Mon vieux Besançon*, with a preface by Drumont himself.

North of Besançon, Belfort and its environs were not free from anti-Semitic schemes. In Delle, *La Croix de Belfort* wrote, on the occasion of the 1898 cantonal elections, "the entire tribe of Israel holds a certain number of votes . . . The three elected officials owe their majority to the Jews, of which they are the prisoners. It is therefore a band of fifteen circumcised men who are dictating the law to the citizens of Delle, and it is a circumcised man who is in control of municipal harmony."[57] The anti-Semitic wave, stirred up by local newspapers, took over the Franche-Comté region as a whole.

Chapter Four

Storm on the Coast:
Algerian Marseilles

On March 17, 1898, a particularly comical scene unfolded in the brasserie Castellane in Marseilles: Jean-Baptiste Reynaud presented to his audience his platform statement for the imminent legislative elections. "He was inspired by the principles of 1789," the police superintendent reported, "called the current government a thief, admitted to being a committed socialist, proclaimed himself anti-Jewish, and ended with the cry of 'Long live France for the French!' A member of the audience asked Reynaud to prove he was not Jewish. The candidate, after climbing onto a chair, displayed, before the eyes of everyone present, his genitals, thus committing the crime of public indecency."[1] A report composed by another police officer makes that colorful comedy a little less shocking; after pronouncing himself in favor of the emancipation of women, the revision of the Constitution, and the expulsion of the Jews, Reynaud, in response to the accusation against him, "asked that the women in the audience remove themselves and, once that was done, climbed onto a chair and displayed his nudity without letting a moment go to waste."[2]

A little later on the place Saint-Michel, a troupe of actors illustrated the dramatic aspects of the Dreyfus affair in three *tableaux vivants*, carefully described by a police report: "Dreyfus's treason: he is depicted giving a book of documents to a Prussian soldier with one hand and, with the other, receiving a sack of money from this same soldier. —Loss of military rank: a noncommissioned officer rips off his stripes and a soldier breaks his saber over his knee. —The punishment: The former captain is represented collapsed on his right side, half his jacket torn off, amid a group of soldiers from every branch of service. Behind him a woman symbolizing Alsace-Lorraine holds a sword horizontally above the head of the condemned man. The entire group of soldiers is pointing contemptuously at Dreyfus." The crowd roared with appreciation.[3]

Between January 16 and January 20, Marseilles and the surrounding cities were about to adopt the especially violent anti-Semitic ways of Algiers. *Le Petit Provençal*, which described itself as a "socialist republican newspaper," denounced "Jewish money," which supposedly led to "civil war"; in the same breath, it commented on the concert of the day given by the pianist Madame Roger-Nicolas, who "expresses herself in a luminously colored language, tenderly and poetically melodious by turns . . . You rediscover in it the glow and cheerfulness of the southern sky." The Marseillais particularly appreciated music. That same day at the students' ball at the Grand Théâtre, "people in picturesque, multicolored costumes danced to the sounds of the orchestra; groups spun till morning in a wild saraband." In these particularly lively days, concerts could be heard in Saint-Raphaël and in many cities of the Mediterranean region; magnificent balls and carnivals enlivened the streets of Hyères ("a delicious evening in every respect") and Toulon ("the evening of dancing was superb—people amused themselves with charming gusto"). Beyond music and balls, people enjoyed the most varied pleasures. In Aigunies a dramatic boar hunt unfolded ("a hunter, arming himself with great courage, aided by his dog, caught the boar by the ear and finished him off on the spot"). Residents of Vidauban, mute with admiration, attended "an electrical projection using Edison's cinematograph. It was marvelous. The public was amazed."[4]

Though Marseilles's cultural life was studded with various leisure activities, anti-Semitism was still rampant. On January 16, at the initiative of the Ligue Antisémitique, more than five hundred people in the Mathon hall brought the house down with virulent speeches. The comte d'Hugues, deputy of Sisteron and president of the Parti Agraire National (National Agrarian Party), explained that "the Jewish question exists, whatever may have been said. It is a question of race, and the only foundation on which that question must be discussed is the national foundation." After the lecture a motion was passed: "The assembly, numbering a thousand people, maintains . . . that it is indispensable to form a truce among all the divisions sown in the country by the Jews . . . to create chambers of agriculture to defend farmers vis-à-vis the government, against the Jewish monopolists." A demonstration of more than two thousand people, led by d'Hugues, shouted in anger as it passed stores whose owners were Jewish. They arrived at the Canebière, shouting, "Long live the army! Down with Zola! Long live Drumont! Out with the Jews!"[5] On the seventeenth at six o'clock, hundreds of students went to the rue Saint-Ferréol via the rue du Jeune-Arnacharsis and gathered on the place de la République, shouting, "Down with the Jews! Out with Zola!" A band of three to four hundred headed toward the synagogue, where they cried, "Long live Drumont!" Things almost took a turn for the worse: "A few hooligans attempted to rip off the door; others attempted in vain to climb the gates . . . Hissing, tooting of bicycle horns . . . Goodness, just imagine the most recent performances at the Grand Théâtre, and you will have an almost accurate idea of the din." A crowd of a thousand managed to reach the rue Saint-Ferréol; "as they passed by the stores owned by Israelites," the police superintendent explained, "there was jeering and whistles, but guards were outside these stores, and the demonstrators, after a few scuffles, headed toward the Canebière . . . Everything occurred peacefully until they got to the officers' club, where things did take a turn for the worse. Numerous bands of thugs had joined the students, and groups tried to force their way into Israelite stores. Brawls with the police occurred, and we had to endure violent blows while struggling energetically to protect the stores. Arrests were made, but they did not hold up, since the very large crowd managed to carry off the prisoners." The gangs reformed and broke the windows of Schul's notions store, attacked the jewelry store belonging to Pollak, and finally, on the rue Saintes, smashed in the window of the Blum store. A few troublemakers managed to grab jewels and precious objects. "Several officers were seriously mistreated, and a great number were punched and kicked. Brigadier Martel was knocked to the ground and trampled. In the face of such serious demonstrations and the considerable number of individuals who took part in them, the police were absolutely powerless to maintain order. If scenes similar to those of yesterday are repeated, we will need additional forces."[6] Several tradespeople whose stores had been stoned went to *Le Petit Provençal* to entreat the newspaper to let the population know they were not Jewish. One store owner published the following press release: "For our personal peace, and without concerning ourselves with the rest of it, we would like to declare to the entire population that we are not Israelites, much less Germans." Other tradespeople placed a sign on their store windows announcing to everyone: "Catholic business."[7] Many arrests were made, mostly of artisans but also of a few tradespeople, employees, and students.[8]

With violence threatening a local Jewish population of about thirty-five hundred,[9] the mayor of Marseilles, on January 18, asked the prefect to "be kind enough to make the necessary requisitions so that the line and cavalry troops confined to their respective quarters will be kept available to the chief superintendent, as well as the gendarmes on horseback assigned to the prefecture. Finally, see that a certain number of gendarmes on foot are distributed among the various police stations to join the peace officers." The city seemed to be in a state of siege. Violence was feared, particularly since the anarchists, who were very numerous there, were resolved to fight the nationalists. In the evening about a thousand demonstrators thronged outside the stores owned by Jews and outside the synagogue on the rue Breteuil and shouted anti-Semitic slogans. But, in one police superintendent's smarmy observation, "in spite of the crowd, no disturbance occurred. In fact, the closing of all the Israelite businesses removed any reason for the demonstrators to be there."[10] In reality, the demonstrations had begun at nine in the morning. Medical students, then law and business students, joined by students from the girls' high school and finally from the boys' high school—in spite of "a fatherly talking-to from the headmaster"—ran through the streets shouting anti-Semitic slogans before dispersing. Until seven p.m., parades, which grew in strength "when the workshops let out," booed Zola and tirelessly denounced the Jews. *Le Marseillais* wrote with satisfaction: "That was how the demonstration went, when the youth of our city demonstrated their indignation at the recent scandals

. . . Youth and the common people have spoken."[11] For its part, *Le Petit Provençal* wrote: "As much as we have been and remain the bitter adversaries of the infamous machinations of the Dreyfus band and his syndicate, we are equally opposed to the violent attacks on certain storekeepers and industrialists of our city. They are absolutely not associated with the antipatriotic machinations of the traitor's friends in France."[12]

On the twentieth the local committee of the Ligue Antisémitique had a poster put up: "Citizens of Marseilles! The Jews have monopolized wheat, petroleum, leather, copper, silver, and gold. We no longer have anything. Thanks to our excessive kindness, the Jews have introduced themselves into our finances, our administration, our justice system. Enough! Frenchmen of France, you have risen up en masse to defend the army! Take heart—the hour of the downfall of the 'stateless' has sounded. Citizens of Marseilles! Do you want to see these traitors to France disappear? Blacklist them, and do not bring them the fruit of your labor. Long live France for the French! Long live the army!"

The same day bands of students, "joined by a fairly large number of thugs and idlers," again went up the Canebière and arrived at the rue Saint-Ferréol. Some threw stones at the building housing Dreyfus and Company on the rue Breteuil; others attacked the windows of the offices of Mosès Borgel, a merchant on the cours Pierre-Puget. "A huge crowd shouted, 'Down with Zola! Down with the Jews!' The crowd was so tumultuous that the police had to charge. It was only thanks to the energetic measures taken by the police that a grave and regrettable incident was averted . . . A large number of arrests were made, almost all of students." Anarchists also attempted to take control of the street and protested to shouts of 'Down with religions! Down with property,' " confronting the anti-Dreyfusard demonstrators several times in the streets of Marseilles.[13]

Eventually the wave subsided, and the area seemed to become calmer. Nevertheless tempers remained on edge, especially since "it is not an exaggeration to say that the majority of the population of Bouches-du-Rhône has long been anti-Dreyfusard,"[14] as the biweekly reports of the police superintendents affirmed. As students from the colleges and graduate schools of Marseilles actively organized charity festivals for mid-Lent, which were to occur in mid-March, and received the cooperation of the garrison's military bands, 250 infantrymen, and a picket of gendarmes called in to maintain order during the traditional mid-Lent flower fight,[15] the animosity was far from gone. For example, *La Voix de la France* denounced the good-hearted festivities on March 6, claiming that "the working-class population has other things to do besides help these gentlemen live it up. It is not permitted to misuse charity by calling by that name the depravity of a public ball or the unwholesome exhibition of third-rate actors, snobs, and prostitutes. The tribe of Israel has given the word that it will greatly help in financing that filth." In the next column, the same newspaper attacked Jewish domination and rejoiced:

> They're scared. Ever since the demonstrations that booed Drey-fus's friends and Zola's comrades on the rue Saint-Ferréol, no one in the Jewish band has gotten any sleep. The stench of the ghetto is king. No one dares let his nostrils stray into it. If a few customers were to wander into their lair by accident, the Kikes, in the grip of a raging terror, would inevitably take them for demonstrators and have them expelled by the police, who keep watch all day long . . . The students are sacrificing their opinions for the joy of drinking a beer on the Canebière. From now on they will not open their windows and wave their handkerchiefs on the balcony except to salute a cavalry charge, the main costs of which will be assumed by Israel.[16]

Incidents erupted at every moment. In his October 16 report, the police superintendent expressed gratitude that "the wine harvest, the main resource of the region, is over. Although not extraordinary, the crop is good and the landowners appear satisfied." In the same report, he described a special patriotic ceremony: On the occasion of commemorating a hero of the 1870 war with a plaque, "a considerable crowd cheered the army to shouts of 'Long live the army! Down with the Jews!'" He added, "The arrondissement is very patriotic and very anti-Jewish and showed it all day long."[17]

During this time Marseilles was consolidating its ties to anti-Semitic Algiers, which was in the hands of Deputy Edouard Drumont, Mayor Max Régis, and their zealots. And the constant exchanges between the two port cities, the anti-Semitic uproar passed from one side of the Mediterranean to the other. When deputies in the anti-Jewish parliamentary group and their allies traveled from one to the other, their supporters passionately awaited them. On May 29, 1898, Drumont and the recently elected anti-Semitic deputies landed in Marseilles from Algeria, accompanied by a number of major figures of anti-Semitism: Marchal, Morinaud, Firmin Faure (all new anti-Semitic deputies), and most important, Jules Guérin and Jean Drault. More than five thousand admirers came to greet them warmly. "Anti-Semitic groups were positioned either on La Joliette or on the Canebière," said the chief superintendent, "and a fairly large number of individuals are recognizable by blue badges they wore on their lapels."

In the face of the disturbances, the police charged, and the anarchists harshly attacked the nationalists. *La Libre Parole* reported that "savage scenes have just occurred in Marseilles. A mob of paid assassins mingled with the enthusiastic crowd cheering the valiant anti-Jewish Algerian deputies. [The Algerian deputy] Marinaud was hit in the temple. A blow struck Drumont, and his wound was serious. The assassination attempt was typical. And it is with the complicity of the police, headed by the Jew Schrameck, that these abominations occurred!" A police officer noted that "the cane that attacked M. Morinaud was deposited at the police station." *La Voix de la France*, the newspaper of the Ligue Antisémitique, denounced the scheming of the anarchists, who, according to the newspaper, obeyed the Jews: "Those people prefer cold hard cash. And the Jews have lost no time providing them with it. Sunday morning, outside the stores of the Kike Montus on the rue Saint-Ferréol, we saw a Yid offer a hundred-sou coin and a whistle to a young worker, whom he wrongly took for an anarchist-of-all-trades." And the newspaper denounced "the monstrous coalition of anarchy from above, that of gold, and of anarchy from below, that of the knife."[18] For his part Drumont accused his old enemy Schrameck of having "let Rothschild's agents do as they liked."[19]

On July 16 Morinaud, the deputy from Algiers, was to give a lecture; in a number of articles, *La Voix de la France* made every effort to attract railroad workers and employees as well as port workers.[20] At the event shouts of "Long live Drumont!" were drowned out by the boos of the counterdemonstrators; "oranges and dung were thrown." Upon reaching their hotel, Le Petit Louvre, "the [Algerian] deputies continually appeared on the balcony to greet the crowd that was cheering them . . .

M. [Jules] Guérin appeared on the balcony and shouted, 'Down with the Jews!' The applause and boos increased; [Guérin] made threatening gestures at those who were booing, holding his hand to his ear and pretending to pull it." After Drumont gave a lecture in town to six hundred people, they passed the following motion: "The gathered assembly of six hundred congratulate the anti-Semitic deputies for their success in Algeria, challenge them to battle the Jewish race relentlessly, and promise all their devotion to the cause they are defending." The meeting let out noisily; as a report noted, "Drumont's and Guérin's car was followed to the hotel by everyone who had attended. They continued to shout, 'Long live Drumont! Down with the Jews! Death to the Jews!'"[21]

The same scenario would be endlessly repeated. On December 22 Max Régis, mayor of Algiers and editor of *L'Antijuif d'Alger*, arrived in Marseilles, provoking the usual scuffles. On the twenty-fifth Deputy Morinaud also returned. Shouts of "Down with the Jews!" were raised as he passed. "This was met with the words 'Long live liberty, down with the Jesuits,' shouted by nineteen-year-old Louis Radix, who was taken to the station and shortly thereafter set free." On February 4 Henri Rochefort arrived at the Marseilles train station from Monte Carlo, en route to Algiers in the company of Max Régis himself. Deputies Ernest Roche, Charles Bernard, and Marcel Habert and delegations from the Ligue des Patriotes and from anti-Semitic groups welcomed him, a touching demonstration of joint action. The crowd cheered the nationalist and Boulangist anti-Semitic leaders. Brawls erupted when anarchists attacked the delegations of the radical right. "People hit one another with canes" and projectiles were thrown onto the cars, but finally their occupants managed to embark on the *Général Chanzy*, which immediately weighed anchor for Algiers. On March 1 Drumont landed again from that city; two hundred people were waiting for him and shouted the usual "Long live Drumont! Down with the Jews!" A procession of more than fifteen hundred people accompanied him noisily back to his hotel.[22]

From mid-January to December 1898 and even later, Marseilles experienced similar large-scale anti-Semitic unrest, which met either with a police force firmly committed to maintaining order or with well-established anarchist groups. The last giant demonstration in 1898 occurred on December 8, on the occasion of a lecture given at the

Alhambra by Francis de Pressensé, the passionate president of the Ligue des Droits de l'Homme et du Citoyen, who had been won over to Dreyfusard ideas. That lecture was the occasion for a huge confrontation between socialists, now convinced of Dreyfus's innocence, and the particularly active anti-Semitic groups. For several days the Ligue Antisémitique and the Jeunesse Catholique had put up posters on the walls of the city denouncing the meeting. The Union Nationale also had a strong presence in the region and received the support of Abbé Garnier, who in late October, with a dozen priests in attendance, claimed at a meeting that "France is greatly threatened by the Jews and Freemasons, who obey [the former British prime minister Henry] Palmerston's plan to make France disappear from the map of Europe . . . The Dreyfus affair is nothing other than the sequel to Palmerston's plan; the Jews would gladly spend their millions to arrive at their goal . . . To oppose it, intransigent Catholics must join the Union Nationale."[23] Similarly, *La Voix de la France*, which presented itself as "the newspaper of the Catholics of Marseilles," had more than three thousand copies of this text posted:

CITIZENS OF MARSEILLES!

IT IS THE DUTY OF THE SIMPLE GOOD PEOPLE AND OF THOSE
WHO STILL HAVE SOME CONCERN FOR FREEDOM AND
THE NATION
TO DENOUNCE THE COWARDICE AND THE MONSTROUSNESS
OF THE MEETING AT THE ALHAMBRA.
LET US NOT DWELL ON THE KNIFINGS AND CLUBBINGS
OF A MOB OF PIMPS ON THE PAYROLL OF THE JEWS
AND THE PREDICANTS.
THOSE WHO MUST BE ESPECIALLY REPROBATED ARE THE
IGNOMINIOUS PEOPLE WHO HAVE
HIRED THESE SPECIALISTS IN PROSTITUTION AND MURDER!
LET US PILLORY
THE GLOVED JEWS WHO BENT DOWN TO LISTEN

TO THE REFLECTIONS

OF THE PATRIOTS, THEN SLYLY POINTED OUT THESE

WARM-HEARTED PEOPLE TO THEIR PALE HIRELINGS!

LEADERS OF THE FASHIONABLE CLASS,

WHO YESTERDAY FRATERNIZED WITH THE HOOLIGANOCRACY,

WILL COME TOMORROW WITH A SIMPER

TO OFFER, FOR AN EVENING, THE EPAULETTES

OF RESERVE AND TERRITORIAL OFFICERS,

IN EXCHANGE FOR THE RED ARMBANDS OF THE DREYFUSARDS.

JEW-SYMPATHIZING BOURGEOIS, WORTHY COLLEAGUES

OF PASTOR PRESSENSÉ,

TEAMED UP WITH THE REVOLUTIONARIES

BEFORE WHOM THEY TREMBLE,

AND WHO, TOMORROW, MAY NAIL THEM TO THE WALL.

SENSUALISTS OF THE UPPER CRUST, WHO TODAY ALLY THEMSELVES

WITH THE REVOLUTIONARIES AND WHO, TOMORROW,

ALONG WITH THE FRIENDS

OF *LE JOURNAL DE MARSEILLE*, WITH YVES GUYOT AND TRARIEUX,[*]

WILL STRANGLE THE LABOR UNIONS

AND WILL HAVE THE COMMON PEOPLE

MASSACRED, JUST LIKE THE JEW ISAAC IN FOURMIES.

TO EACH HIS SHARE OF SHAME AND RESPONSIBILITY.[24]

"Imposing police forces" were present to insure the maintenance of order. In the vast hall of the Alhambra, more than four thousand people—five thousand, according to some police reports—supporters and opponents of Captain Dreyfus combined, took their places. When the leader of the Ligue des Droits de l'Homme appeared at the podium, "people came to blows. Canes were waving in the air, and nationalists and anarchists struck one another."[25] *Le Provençal* described it this way:

---

[*]Yves Guyot and Ludovic Trarieux: Dreyfusard leaders.—trans.

"At various places people came to blows, empty spaces formed where human shadows tussled; the brawl was so intense that it did not seem possible that the meeting could take place. Citizen Nevierre ran to the podium to display 'what the priests understand by freedom.' Blood was streaming down his face; a gaping wound was open along his skull." Finally plebiscitarians and anti-Semites "who had placed themselves in the middle of the hall" were expelled. Many people were wounded, some in the head, and were taken to the pharmacy. Courageously, Francis de Pressensé took it upon himself to once again demonstrate the captain's innocence, the diabolical character of the machinations against him, the undeniable responsibility of the general staff, and the complete innocence of Picquart. He attacked the "imbecilic vanity" of the president of the Republic and criticized "the entire Chamber, the majority of which is more concerned with its own interests than with justice." He defended Picquart, "the apostle of truth," and paid tribute to Bernard Lazare, Zola, and Jaurès. "I hope," he declared, "that if the crime comes to pass, more than a thousand people will go to the court of the military school to prevent Lieutenant Colonel Picquart from being stripped of his rank, which would damage France as a whole." The lecture ended at about eleven p.m. As the attendees were leaving, anti-Semitic groups demonstrated. Police squads intervened to minimize the clashes; "nevertheless skirmishes occurred at several places: hats flew through the air, and people hit one another with canes."[26] A brawl erupted when anarchists attacked a municipal councilor from Algiers, accompanied by Réaux, vice president of the Ligue Antisémitique. The police, under the leadership of Schrameck, head of the prefecture and Drumont's sworn enemy, effectively intervened, but groups formed again, and the same cries erupted against Picquart and the Jews.

Populism and anti-Semitism were given free rein in Marseilles, especially since rival ideological camps made surprising alliances there. Boulangists, nationalists, and socialists—sometimes even strict ones— with the help of certain Catholic groups, joined forces to bring down the Republic of Opportunists and to combat the Jewish presence, before turning against one another near the end of 1898. *La Croix de Provence* continually spread a bitter anti-Semitism. "Ever since Judas and so many others," according to that newspaper, "it has been known that the Jewish race is on familiar terms with treason . . . From now on *Jews*,

Dreyfus, and *treason* are words that evoke the same idea in all French souls." Championing the boycott of Jewish shopkeepers, it wrote, "With the wicked laugh of a Yid who has cheated Christian dogs, he locks up in his safe heaps of loot that his overly credulous buyers have come to bring him. He is happy, that Jew." It denounced Dreyfus as a German Jew and a traitor to France, and exclaimed, "Long live the French people of France! Down with the German Jews!"[27]

Even though "the Catholic faction counted little in Bouches-du-Rhône,"[28] Marseilles and nearby Aix-en-Provence witnessed a renewal of Catholic religious fervor. During a national congress on Christian democracy, headed by leaders such as Lemire and Garnier and attended by the founder of *La Croix de Provence* and Edouard Drumont, young Catholics held a regional congress in Marseilles and created study groups linked to the Union Nationale. They warned the citizens of Marseilles on many posters:

YES, THERE IS A PERIL.

THE PERIL IS NOT CLERICALISM, BUT BRIBERY.

THE PERIL IS THE LIST OF BRIBED OFFICIALS,*

IT IS THE PANAMA SCANDAL REBORN

UNDER THE WEIGHT OF EVER-INCREASING TAXES.

THE PERIL IS THE JEWS, WHO CONSTITUTE

ONE THREE-HUNDREDTH OF THE POPULATION

OF FRANCE, YET WHO POSSESS NEARLY A THIRD

OF OUR TOTAL FORTUNE, THE JEWS, WHO GRAB EVERYTHING,

WHO ESTABLISH THEMSELVES EVERYWHERE,

WHO HAVE THEIR HANDS IN EVERYTHING.

THE JEWS, THOSE BIRDS OF PREY

THAT GROW FAT ON OUR DISASTERS.

THE PERIL IS FREEMASONRY, WHICH HOLDS FRANCE

UNDER ITS OCCULT POWER.

---

*Bribery, bribed officials (*chéquardisme, chéquards*): these terms refer specifically to the bribery in the Panama scandal.—trans.

During the countless meetings of the revisionist plebiscitary party, people denounced both the Jews and the Republic, praised Drumont, and attacked secularization, since it targeted the Catholic religion and threatened the priests' salaries. On April 15, 1898, four hundred people meeting in Salle Chrétien passed a motion in support of the candidate Giraudon, who was waving the banner of nationalism and was supported by the Ligue Antisémitique.[29] Giraudon's platform statement attacked "moral and material decadence" and protested "the support of the fortune thrown out as fodder to feed the gluttony of shady dealers and cosmopolitan Jewry." Giraudon also became the apostle of "national defense, compromised by the syndicate of the stateless," and claimed to be the protector of "the Catholic religion, which is that of the majority of French people." He concluded with the traditional "France for the French!"[30] *La Croix* stood beside him, as did part of the clergy and, according to the police, the brothers at the Christian schools on the rue d'Hozier and M. Lacroix, priest of Saint-Laurent, who provided them with aid. They were joined in that battle by the Ligue Antisémitique, which published the following appeal in support of Giraudon:

CITIZENS!

THE LIGUE ANTISÉMITIQUE,

CONDEMNING THE INFAMOUS ACCUSATIONS

OF THE SYNDICATE OF JEWS

AND JEW SYMPATHIZERS, WISHES TO DECLARE

THAT IT HAS NO RELIGIOUS CONNECTIONS. BUT, PROFOUNDLY

DEMOCRATIC, IT WANTS TO OVERTHROW

THE JEWISH FEUDAL SYSTEM.

TO THE VOTERS, IT RECOMMENDS GIRAUDON,

THE ONLY ONE WHO HAS LOYALLY

DECLARED THAT HE WOULD DEMAND THE CONVICTION

OF THE ARMY'S INSULTERS AND ZOLA'S ACCOMPLICES, AND WHO,

AS A SUPPORTER OF THE ABROGATION OF THE CRÉMIEUX DECREE,

HAS COMMITTED HIMSELF

TO DEFENDING OUR GLORIOUS FLAG AGAINST THE ATTACKS

OF THE COSMOPOLITANS OF HIGH BANKING

AND OF THE STATELESS PERSONS

OF INTERNATIONALISM.

LONG LIVE MARSEILLES! LONG LIVE FRANCE FOR THE FRENCH![31]

Giraudon himself ran as the Catholic candidate and participated in the Catholic study groups of Marseilles, but he was defeated in the May 1898 elections. Other nationalist candidates also braved universal suffrage at these elections, such as the lawyer François Tassy, who ran as a "nationalist socialist," and the obscure Edouard Pastorel, whose posters advertised his "anti-Semitic absinthe" and his "Drumont aperitif." Beginning in the 1890s, the Bouches-du-Rhône department saw socialist and Catholic currents come together in a shared rejection of the Jewish presence. On numerous occasions workers solicited the participation of anti-Semitic leaders to support strike actions.[32] That complicity was still apparent at the end of 1898 during the Pressensé meeting, which united Catholic notables from the populist and sometimes socialist-leaning movements, against the committed Dreyfusard militants of the Socialist Party and against anarchists resolved to fight the nationalists.[33]

Other major figures of anti-Semitism attempted to take root in the department, such as Joseph Dubosc, a Boulangist turned socialist who founded *Le Réveil Social*, the Marseilles equivalent of *La Libre Parole*. He failed in his electoral plans and finally rallied behind official collectivist socialism. The anti-Semitic press of Marseilles proved very active: *L'Antijuif Marseillais* and *La Parole Libre du Midi* actively conducted an economic boycott of the Jews, and *La Voix de la France*, whose editorial staff included representatives of the Catholic groups, mercilessly attacked the supposedly exorbitant influence of the Jews and endlessly pushed for anti-Semitic mobilization.

In the streets of the city, "La Marseillaise antijuive" could be heard:

Onward, children of the nation,
The day of vengeance has arrived.
Against us the obscene standard
Of Yiddischry has been raised;

Do you hear, in their lairs,
Those infamous swindlers howling loud,
Who, even on our flags,
Will spit their viper's slime!

Tremble, Yids, and all you traitors,
The opprobrium of every party:
Tremble! Your patricidal plans
Will finally get their reward.
Everyone's a soldier to combat you:
If our young heroes should fall,
The land will produce new ones
At the ready, rogues, to destroy you.

Sacred love of the nation,
Lead, support our vengeful limbs!
Freedom, O cherished freedom!
May victory, under our flags,
Rush in to hear your male cries!
And may all the expiring Yids
See your triumph and our glory.

We will join the service
When the Yids have all been hanged.[34]

In Aix-en-Provence, although the republican camp won despite intense nationalist activity, things were quite different. In 1896 the Catholic faction had supported the socialist Gabriel Baron against the incumbent mayor, Benjamin Abram, a radical and anticlerical Jew, who was defeated. *La Semaine Religeuse de l'Archidiocèse d'Aix* took keen delight in Esterhazy's acquittal, exulting that "Jews, Protestants, and pornographers such as Dreyfus, Scheurer-Kestner, and Zola are experiencing such a moral collapse that they are obliged to return to the shadows. May France recover its strength and take advantage of the coming elections to bar all the perpetrators of scandal and all those foreign agents from public affairs."[35] In 1898 the Catholic faction again succeeded in getting its candidate elected. *La Parole Libre du Midi* supported the socialists against radical Jews such as Abram and Bédarrides. For several years anti-Semitism was given free rein in Aix, where about three hundred Jews lived at the time.[36] When the socialist Baron became mayor of Aix, he immediately met with the archbishop of that city,[37] to the great satisfaction of *La Croix de Provence.* Here Guesdism,* to which Baron had rallied, lent itself to unnatural alliances, even though the Catholics would distance themselves from that movement in 1898.[38] Running against Baron, who became the official candidate of the Parti Ouvrier Français (French Workers' Party) that year, was Camille Perreau, chosen by the moderates and Catholics. This time it was Perreau who benefited from the support of *La Croix de Provence.* Addressing the Catholics, who seemed to want to abandon him, Baron's supporters distributed a tract that read, "We must at all cost continue the work of cleansing ourselves of the Jews. Yes, whatever may happen, everyone must vote for the anti-Semite Baron, who is following in the footsteps of the leader of anti-Semitism, the intrepid Drumont." The tone remained the same in another tract:

VOTERS!

WORKERS IN THE FACTORY AND IN THE FIELDS,

WOULD YOU LIKE TO CONTRIBUTE

TO THE VICTORY OF A COTERIE THAT HAS MADE NO EFFORT

TO IMPROVE YOUR FATE?

CITIZENS OF AIX,

THAT JEWIFIED COTERIE HAS PUT YOUR FATE

AND YOUR MOST SACRED INTERESTS INTO THE HANDS

OF THE JEWS, LETTING THEM

INVADE YOUR COURT OF TRADE, THE CIVIL COURT,

THE AGRICULTURAL UNION, AND OTHER THINGS.

TRADESPEOPLE, IT IS TO JEWRY THAT YOU ARE INDEBTED

---

*Guesdism: the Marxist views espoused by Jules Guesde.—trans.

FOR THE SIDEWALK SALES

AND THE PERPETUAL LIQUIDATIONS THAT RUIN YOUR BUSINESSES.

VOTERS!

IT IS NOT A POLITICAL VOTE THAT YOU HAVE TO GIVE

BUT A VOTE

OF REPROBATION AGAINST ALL THOSE JEWIFIED EXPLOITERS

AND THOSE SECOND-RATE OPPRESSORS.

BARON, IN TAKING ABRAM, NAQUET, AND COMPANY

OFF YOUR HANDS,

DESERVES TO SWELL THE RANKS OF THE DEPUTIES

WHO TRULY WANT

FRANCE FOR THE FRENCH.[39]

In a letter to *La Croix de Provence*, the archbishop of Aix wrote: "We want our representatives to worship and serve God. We are a Christian people . . . Spread the word everywhere that we accept without reservation the republican regime. But we, along with the pope, condemn its legislation, which is bad . . . May 8 is the feast of Joan of Arc: let us go to the polls repeating her holy warrior's cry. Let us do battle, God will give us the victory."[40] Baron was defeated; the Catholic world preferred his rival, who was elected to the great satisfaction of *La Voix de la France.* But Baron—a Guesdist, a collectivist, and an equally anti-Semitic candidate—was reelected general councilor in 1901. In 1902, with the support of the Comité Nationaliste d'Aix, which embraced the Republic but was under the patronage of Henri Rochefort, Godefroy Cavaignac, and Paul Déroulède, he even became a deputy. He was reelected without difficulty in 1906, thus benefiting from a strange coalition unified around a virulent anticapitalist-style anti-Semitism. Clearly, anti-Semitism was a view that was very broadly shared.

Though Provence was committed to the Republic and sometimes even to socialism, anti-Semitism came in torrents. Salon-de-Provence, a city dominated by the leftist radicals under the leadership of Camille Pelletan, got a rude shock when Alfred Anastay, mayor of the city, became a candidate of the Comité Républicain Radical, in defense of the region's interests, in the 1898 legislative elections. He was supported by *Le Progrès de Salon* and by the municipal council as a whole. Anastay conducted a violent anti-Dreyfusard campaign. Although Pelletan was easily reelected in the first round, he was very soundly defeated in the city of Salon: Anastay enjoyed enormous success there, attracting 63.3 percent of the votes.[41]

On other parts of the coast the agitation was ever greater because, as in Marseilles, the republican forces that had rallied behind the Dreyfusard camp were willing to confront the nationalist mobilization. To varying degrees, from Toulon to Perpignan, that mobilization was in full swing toward the end of 1898. In Sète, however, as a police superintendent noted, "religious passions are not very keen. There are very few Jews here . . . Even though the young people in the schools are currently calm, I am keeping myself posted on the acts of a few ringleaders, whom the events unfolding in Algeria might again stir up and push toward further demonstrations against the tradespeople living on the rue Gambetta."[42] In Montpellier and Perpignan, the situation was more alarming. In January 1898 Montpellier saw numerous demonstrations uniting hundreds of people who insulted Zola and the Jews while denouncing the mayor. The anti-Semitic mobilization, fanned for many years by *La Croix Méridionale*—which tirelessly denounced the Jewish presence in Montpellier—and by *L'Eclair*, came about quickly. On January 18, according to *Le Petit Méridional*, "four hundred young people departing from the entrance to the Esplanade ran through [the streets], chanting 'Out with Zola! Down with the Jews!' and striking storefronts . . . The demonstration took place under the paternal eye of the police and the central police superintendent, M. Hitte, who had taken the sensible view of letting things go on so long as the demonstration did not become more aggressive." On the nineteenth, also according to *Le Petit Méridional*, young people ran through the streets, again shouting, "Down with the Jews! Down with Zola! Long live the army!" The outcry increased as they passed by the stores owned by Jewish shopkeepers. On the twentieth a large strip of white fabric was found attached to the monument commemorating 1870. It bore these words: "Down with the Jews! Down with Zola! France for the French!" On the twenty-first, as *Le*

Petit Méridional reported, four hundred students gathered at the Grand Gambinus, "waved tricolor flags, and speared copies of *La Libre Parole*, *Le Libertaire*, and *L'Antijuif* with the tips of their canes." A student proposed adopting the following motion: "The students of Montpellier, gathered at the Grand Gambinus, regretting that they came into the world three hundred years too late, demand the reestablishment of the Holy Inquisition." In the face of such demonstrations, some of their republican comrades condemned anti-Semitism, protesting on January 22 and shouting, "Down with the Jesuits!" Statements from the most polarized groups appeared in succession in *Le Petit Méridional*. Other groups, "independent and sincere republicans," distanced themselves from the republican students but broke ranks with the openly anti-Semitic students, publishing the following press release addressed to the latter: "We object to Jewish conduct as much as you do, but we do not recognize the right to cast anathema on an entire race, which our fathers welcomed in 1792 . . . You have demonstrated to us that anti-Semitism was nothing but a pretext for you to resuscitate disruptive and outmoded religious quarrels for the benefit of the clerical outlook . . . Repudiating Jewish conduct, but above all republican and anticlerical conduct, you have prevented us from following you."

Montpellier was covered with various anti-Semitic posters, signed by "a group of anti-Dreyfusard Frenchmen," whose true author, according to the police reports, was Abbé Fourié, chaplain of the local Carmelite convent. On one of these posters, the figure of "a committed anti-Jew" addressed "M. Populo," aka "Jacques Bonhomme," a workman by trade:

THE KEPT MEN AND WOMEN OF THE JEWISH PIMPOCRACY

CONTINUE TO SWEAR

UP AND DOWN THAT THERE IS NO JEWISH PERIL . . .

THERE IS A JEWISH PERIL: THAT IS WHAT HAS COME

OUT OF THE DREYFUS AFFAIR,

WHICH THE ANTI-SEMITES DID NOT ORGANIZE.

SO A JEW WHO HAD STRAYED

INTO THE RANKS OF THE FRENCH ARMY

TOOK A DUMP ON HIS CAPTAIN'S STRIPES

BY TRAFFICKING IN SECRET DOCUMENTS

OF NATIONAL DEFENSE. THAT JEW WAS CAUGHT RED-HANDED.

IMMEDIATELY THERE ROSE UP, FROM THE FOUR CORNERS

OF THE GLOBE,

A REGULAR PACK OF BARKING HOUNDS,

A BAND OF YELLOW JOURNALISTS,

BIG MASTIFFS AND LITTLE CURS WHO BEGAN TO YELP

THIS LITTLE REFRAIN:

DREYFUS IS A MARTYR

DREYFUS IS A HERO

AND HIS DOO-DOO IS ROSE WATER.

AND GIVE ME A BONE . . .

CAN THERE BE ANY MORE PALPABLE DEMONSTRATION

THAT THERE IS A JEWISH PERIL,

THAT A COSMOPOLITAN FINANCIAL POWER EXISTS,

AND THAT IT IS URGENT

TO CURB IT THROUGH A "GUT LIDDLE GONFISCATION"?

THAT WOULD BE

A TREAT FOR JACQUES BONHOMME.[43]

At meetings with various local elected officials, participants denounced the "Jewish mind" and protested the arrest of Régis, who was supposed to give a lecture in that city. Drumont, still as active as ever in the region, gave a lecture at the racetrack.[44] Another meeting, attended by about four hundred people, took place at the Eden concert hall; it was devoted to the "unfair competition with Montpellier business in which the Jews engage" and began with a defense of the marquis de Morès; honorary chairmanship of that meeting was unanimously bestowed on Drumont. According to the police superintendent, the main speaker "begged the Montpellier tradespeople to unite against the invasion of opera glass and carpet merchants (alluding to the Jews) who arrive in the city without money and kill business . . . He declared he was sickened by a circular that a Jewish store sent to all the presbyteries, recommending itself for religious supplies."[45]

As in Marseilles, the entire year in Montpellier was punctuated by demonstrations. On July 3 the socialists held a major lecture in the Théâtre Municipal; before more than eight hundred people, Jean Jaurès denounced "the bourgeoisie in decomposition, lying and hypocritical, which has not even been able to apply the law to one of its own," and he invited the proletariat to do something healthy by getting rid of the exploiting capitalists." As cries of "Down with the Jews!" resonated, the speaker responded that he made no distinctions between capitalists, and he shouted, "Down with the Christian Jews when they are exploiters like the others!"[46] On October 25 a lecture held by anarchists at the Grand Gambinus was "interrupted by a rowdy and threatening crowd."[47] On October 31 it was the royalist youth of Montpellier who called for a demonstration; nearly a thousand people assembled in the hall on the rue Plantade and cheered its leaders and their incendiary speeches against the Jews. Here, as L'Eclair recounted, "the young Adonises were solid boys from our rural areas of Hérault, farmers and laborers."[48] Real miracles were said to have occurred: "a group of mutes who were in the hall began to gesticulate upon hearing the peroration by Chauvet, one of the royalist speakers," a police officer observed. Someone wanted to appeal to the duc d'Orléans to save France from the cosmopolitan syndicate; cries of "Long live the king! Long live the army! Down with the Jews!" echoed as the crowd set off for the place de la Comédie.[49]

The year ended with a very animated lecture given in support of Captain Dreyfus by Pressensé, head of the Ligue des Droits de l'Homme, on December 6. Many posters on the city walls summoned "all true Frenchmen, all patriots, all those who are not Dreyfusards" to come out and protest. The lecture took place in front of a tumultuous audience of almost five thousand. Nearly two hundred students interrupted the speaker with shouts of "Long live the army! Down with the Jews! Long live Rochefort!" Demonstrations occurred every day, and "the decision was made to answer [the students] by recruiting workers from the outlying districts and neighboring regions." "Very serious brawls are to be expected," the police noted. Things were calm in the end, however: the public prosecutor wrote that "last week's demonstrations will not be repeated . . . Professor Charamont of the law school has asked the students to refrain from demonstrating in the streets. The many citations for disturbing the peace given to certain students has had a salutary effect on those who were harboring the desire to continue the demonstrations."[50]

To the southwest in Aude, a department committed to the republicans and home to a particularly strong socialist impulse, the Dreyfus affair also elicited anti-Semitic demonstrations, fanned by the Catholic camp, in the city of Carcassonne. *Le Courrier de l'Aude*—whose motto was "Long live Christ, who loves the Franks"—excoriated Jews on a daily basis and in January 1898 published an article by Drumont against the "Jewified Zola." Month after month it denounced "Jewish wealth," a "force of corruption" that differed in every way from "Christian wealth . . . a source of benefits and agent of productivity." At the end of the year, when a review of the Dreyfus case seemed in the offing, the newspaper exclaimed, "The Prussians have just seized France. A band of Jews and a few politicians they have bought off have handed us over to them . . . In France, thanks to the gold of the Jews and of Prussia, Dreyfus now has a powerful faction, which is imposing its will on an entire people." In January 1898 *La Semaine Religieuse de Carcassonne* also pointed an accusing finger at the Jews' gold, and on February 25 it published the following text: "For several days we have been witnessing an astonishing spectacle. Men tried to drag our French officers through the mud and worked to rehabilitate a scoundrel who was a traitor to the nation. Cosmopolitan Jews had formed a syndicate and were providing gold, which they thought could buy France. An Italian of immeasurable arrogance is lending—or selling—his pen to that syndicate. But Zola's pen is a shovel that moves only rubbish."

In the view of *La Semaine Religieuse de Carcassonne*, the Jews, because they betrayed Christ, "have been cursed . . . for nineteen centuries. They wander, despised, hated everywhere, bearing something like a sign of malediction on their foreheads. With no nation, no altar, no offerings, they mingle with every people and exploit them with their insatiable greed. Enemies of the people among whom they live, they have their hand in every shady affair . . . The hand of God is thus clearly upon them." The right, in order to win in the legislative elections, adopted a clear anti-Semitic tone. Thus M. de Belfortès (who would nevertheless be defeated) held many meetings denouncing "invading Jewry . . . In the Dreyfus affair, the government became the accomplice of the Jews. We must save France, wrest the nation away from Jewish finance." The audience cried out, "Down with the Jews! Long live the army!" His platform statement read, "Today it cannot be denied that the French are no longer the masters in France and that they are subject to the orders, the snubs, and the exploitation of the Jews . . . For a century, and particularly for the last twenty-five years, we have endured the exploitation of the Jews without saying a word . . . Do you want to tolerate those insults and allow those dangers to persist?" The moderate republican candidates were more cautious and confined themselves to defending the army. On the left the same anti-Semitic tone could be found as in other cities. On January 30 *Le Radical du Midi,* the republican newspaper of radical and socialist unity—published in Carcassonne—examined "the Jewish question" and ended with a resounding "Long live the army! Down with the Jews!" Though it attacked clericalism for its agitation against the Republic, in several articles it equally rejected "the cosmopolitan syndicate, the Judeo-financial machinations." In Castelnaudary as well, the radical Saba, who called himself "the friend of the poor," wrote in his platform statement: "It is time for the Jew Shylock, ancestor of Dreyfus, to no longer exact his pound of human flesh from the people he is starving and squeezing."[51]

Let us complete our slow descent toward Spain by visiting Perpignan. Here on January 19 an anti-Semitic demonstration of about four hundred people erupted. It targeted the Jewish tradespeople and their businesses, but the gendarmerie rapidly intervened to calm things down. Troubles resumed the next day, when the demonstrators gathered outside the prefecture and offered a bouquet of flowers to the major general to honor the army. A large white flag adorned the column on the promenade des Platanes, bearing the inscriptions "Long live the army!" and "Down with the Jews!"[52] Once again the campaign for the legislative elections produced many anti-Semitic declarations, such as that of the marquis de Dax from Axat, who declared in his platform statement, "The Republic is abandoning the lost provinces and is groveling at the feet of the foreigner; it is prostituting itself to the Jew, who supports it with his gold; it obeys Freemasonry, of which it is the deserving and contemptible daughter. Long live God! Long live France!" On May 6, before six hundred people gathered in Salle Arago, the candidate Bourrat boasted that he had voted against "the Dreyfus syndicate."[53]

An anonymous poster went up on the walls of the city:

CANDIDATE, GIVE US AN ANSWER!

IN YOUR PLATFORM STATEMENT, YOU MAKE US

BEAUTIFUL PROMISES.

YOU PROMISE US YOU WILL TAKE DOWN THE MOON

WITH YOUR BARE TEETH.

BUT APART FROM THE FACT THAT THAT EXERCISE IS PERILOUS

AND THAT YOU MIGHT

DISLOCATE YOUR JAW, IT IS NOT THE MOON

WE WANT.

IT IS RATHER THE GOOD OF OUR NATION.

DO YOU BELIEVE THAT PRIVILEGES SHOULD BE REESTABLISHED

SOLELY IN FAVOR OF THE FREEMASONS, THE FOREIGN JEWS,

THE PANAMAISTS, AND THE SECTARIANS?

CANDIDATE, GIVE US AN ANSWER!

ARE YOU THE FRIEND OF THE JEWS?

THE FRIEND OF THE JEWS IS NOT OUR FRIEND.

THE FRIEND OF THE JEWS IS LISTED ON THE STOCK MARKET,

HE IS BOUGHT AND SOLD . . .

WE DON'T WANT ANY PART OF THAT COMMODITY.

IN YOUR FRIENDSHIP WITH THE JEWS, YOU LOSE YOUR FREEDOM,

YOU TURN TO BRIBES.

WHAT DO YOU THINK OF ZOLA?

WHAT DO YOU THINK OF THE TRAITOR DREYFUS

AND THE SYNDICATE?

VOTERS MUST KNOW, BECAUSE IT IS SAID

THAT THE WEAKLINGS IN THE GOVERNMENT

HAVE PROMISED TO CAPITULATE,

RIGHT AFTER THE ELECTIONS,

TO THE JEWISH, PROTESTANT, AND FOREIGN INFLUENCES

AND TO REVIEW THE DREYFUS CASE.

IF YOU WERE A DEPUTY, WOULD YOU BE PART OF THE

SYNDICATE'S FLOCK OF SHEEP?

WOULD YOU BE WITH THOSE

WHO WOULD LIKE TO GIVE UP ON THE ARMY?

WOULD YOU BE AMONG THE SILENT DOGS?[54]

In September 1899, when the Rennes court once more found Captain Dreyfus guilty, "the Jewish stalls and stores in the city remained open as usual," but some people amused themselves by exploding four bombs on the place Vauban, across from the mayor's house, "to thumb their noses at the municipality." The local incidents pitted Dreyfusards against anti-Dreyfusards. One brawl pitted Henri Farrès, an editor at *La Croix des Pyrénées-Orientales*, against the anarchist Seignolles, who "appeared to want to force him over the balcony railing." Farrès managed to break free after "getting hit in the eye and losing a button from his cuff." The pardon granted Dreyfus ten days after his final conviction was nevertheless welcomed with "satisfaction. The public, which reasons coolly and which, for its business and industry, asks only that people calm down, sees that clemency as an act of good policy capable of satisfying all parties."[55]

Our journey from Marseilles to Perpignan is at an end; let us now return to Provence, a region that had been open to the Jewish presence for centuries. More specifically, let us move away from the Provençal coast, and the constant exchanges with anti-Semitic Algiers, and return to the cradle of Provençal Judaism, Aix-en-Provence, Avignon, and Carpentras.

Carpentras embodied the spirit of Judaism characteristic of Comtat Venaissin; it was the Jerusalem of the Midi Jews, a city attached to the religious traditions and practices observed by important families, such as the Naquets, the Lunels, and above all the Valabrègues, Alfred Dreyfus's in-laws. In Carpentras, which the captain had visited often since his adolescence, the affair immediately acquired a particular resonance. The city became a special target of anti-Semitic attacks, especially since, according to *Le Mont Ventoux*, "the Jews brought anti-Semitism upon themselves by making common cause with the traitor instead of handing him over for his heinous crime." That republican newspaper remained hostile to Dreyfus until June 1898: "I don't like the Jews any more than I admire Zola," a journalist wrote. "But it seems to me that, at a time when a storm of religious persecutions has been let loose, it would hardly be fitting to demonstrate against those who are persecuted in this country, which has proclaimed the rights of man."[56] A few months later he nevertheless added, "The Jewish question is not a religious question. What we all see is that, in France, Jewish citizens have a preponderant position, which they owe to their cohesiveness. Government service, big business, industry, and especially finance are in the hands of Israel. I know a few Israelites who would like their co-religionists to blend in with the French nation, but they are the exception. The Jews continue to marry Jews, to live among themselves, to back one another up against the rest of the nation. They should not be surprised that they are a race apart . . . that they constitute a state within the state. The day will come when these antipatriotic residents will disappear."[57]

The reaction, for its part, was able to draw upon a clergy solidly rooted in the most reactionary arrondissement of the department of Vaucluse, where the conservative right flew its flags. The Catholics were an essential element in the anti-Jewish struggle. For example, there had always been anti-Semitic jeers on Good Friday, chanted by children at the sight of the yellow hats worn by Jews. These insults reappeared during the months of anti-Semitic mobilization and were shouted under Jewish windows and outside Jewish stores, whose panes were shattered. *La Libre Parole* and *La Croix d'Avignon et du Comtat*, for their part, had their wary eyes fixed on Carpentras. *La Croix* thought that that city had "a real bed of ghetto flowers . . . a Carpentras yiddischry." *La Tribune Libre* made fun of the "tribe of Isaac" that had established itself there.[58]

On January 20, 1898, anti-Semitic signs were posted on the walls of Carpentras: "Citizens, in view of the national demonstration taking place throughout France, the city of Carpentras cannot lag behind. All patriots who are sickened by the underhanded schemes of the Jewish vermin will gather today at the place du Théâtre to form a procession to the town hall, shouting 'Down with the traitors! Down with the Jews! Down with Dreyfus! Long live the army! Long live the republic!' " The police superintendent's report stated that "on the houses inhabited by influential Jews such as the Lunels and the Valabrègues—one of whom, a certain Joseph, is Dreyfus's father-in-law—a sign appears bearing the inscription 'Down with the Jews. Down with Dreyfus. Down with the syndicate of treason.' " The police made every effort to cover up these posters, but in any case, "the reception given to that proclamation was so cool that this appeal to the residents remains without effect."[59] The Carpentras newspaper, Le Mont Ventoux, wrote, "Hoaxes. A few practical jokers displayed a handwritten sign appealing to the residents of Carpentras to go to town hall shouting the things ordinarily shouted at these sorts of demonstrations. Our population, as usual very sensible, did not respond to that appeal, and the smart alecks who wanted to play the joke were not even seen at the place they had themselves set for the rendezvous."[60] The Vaucluse prefecture was nevertheless concerned, and the prefect alerted the subprefect of Carpentras, "If there are fears of attacks on the Jewish stores, see that they are warned to close on time in the evening." The most disturbing rumors circulated, and the mayor of Carpentras told the subprefect of the "fears inspired in him by the views expressed in cafés concerning the Israelites." He asked him to take "measures necessary to protect individuals."

But these fears turned out to be unfounded: the unrest seemed to exist only on the surface, and no violence occurred. Anti-Semitism was nevertheless palpable. During the campaign for the May 1898 legislative elections, Edouard Drumont himself considered running as a candidate here. Georges Thiébaud, that violently anti-Semitic Boulangist, replaced him at the last minute, supported by certain republican circles in the city and by La Tribune Libre, La Croix d'Avignon et du Comtat, and Le Journal du Comtat. In April a Comité de la Jeunesse Antisémitique et Nationaliste (Committee of Anti-Semitic and Nationalist Youth) was created, and its meeting room was at the café du Siècle. In town and throughout the region, Thiébaud gave many lectures on the Jewish threat. He ran as a republican and, in his platform statement, committed himself to sit on the extreme left of the Chamber. On April 26 in Sault, he attacked the Jews and denounced their economic power in the arrondissement of Alfred Dreyfus's father-in-law, Joseph Valabrègue. Valabrègue lodged a complaint in the criminal court of Carpentras. Thiébaud then stormed against "that Jewish trick to prevent me from being elected . . . That syndicate is bringing an action against me, I who am slandered from morning till night in the Jew-sympathizing hotbeds of Carpentras."[61] On May 5 Thiébaud was convicted of disorderly conduct, then released; when he came out of the Palais de Justice, a crowd cheered him. The same day in Salle Brémond-Genin at the porte d'Orange, the atmosphere was electric, and brawls erupted. When court let out, Thiébaud, accompanied by a crowd, returned to the place du Palais, as shouts of "Down with the Jews!" reverberated. The nationalist leader continued his harsh electoral campaign, which was disturbed, strangely, by revolver shots fired in the middle of the night into the casement window of the room at the Hôtel de l'Univers where he was working late.[62] The ambience was highly charged.

Although Carpentras remained "sensible" and refrained from any visible excesses, the candidacy of Thiébaud, the true leader of the nationalist anti-Semitic movement, attracted a great number of Carpentras residents; but they usually preferred to stay behind their blinds rather than demonstrate openly. In the second round of the legislative elections, Delestrac, the radical republican candidate, defeated Alfred Naquet—deputy of Carpentras since 1893—who was accused of "selling out to the Jews." Delestrac, who had clear anti-Semitic opinions, attracted a large part of the Catholic electorate. In Carpentras itself Thiébaud was very successful. Carpentras, the symbolic site of French Judaism, was a long way from Marseilles, the Algiers of France, but it was not completely immune to anti-Semitism. This part of Provence did adopt the ideas of Drumont and company.

Local unrest continued into 1899. In September, after the verdict against Dreyfus in Rennes, Alfred Dreyfus himself came to Carpentras, where the threats were so serious that the police took strict protection measures and placed a guard around his residence. Everywhere the agents of Sûreté were vigilant.[63] Malicious graffiti appeared, and in late

September Dreyfus received particularly disturbing anonymous letters, one of which read, "Scoundrel: It is too bad that you did not long ago receive twelve bullets in your flesh, like all the loathsome fellows like you . . . You will perish by the dagger of a true Frenchman of France, who will not regret spilling your blood for his dear nation. There are only twelve of us, but believe it, we will not retreat, even though you are protected by the scoundrels. See you soon. Long live France! Death to the Jews! [Signed:] The twelve." Another letter read, "Dreyfus, you are the traitor . . . Dreyfus, the time has come . . . Buy a revolver and six cartridges, and use them. If you do not obey, 153 Frenchmen have voted for your death. Death to the traitor Dreyfus, Alfred, Jew . . . A Frenchman is writing you and will do you in if you do not obey. I give you four days to consider. Death. Death. Death. Death. [Signed:] The one who must kill you if you refuse." And finally, "It may surprise you, Dreyfus, to receive a Frenchman's letter. Because, you know, it's not a Jew who is writing you . . . I am French, but I am not rich like you and the Jews. The little I have, I earned honestly—not like you, by selling out France to those cursed Prussian Jews. But patience, the hour of your judgment, of your death, of your traitor's, your bandit's, your scoundrel's end will soon come . . . I, a man, a Frenchman, I ought not to take the law into my own hands, but I will not pardon you. Long live France. Down with the Jews."[64]

The Catholic youth association held a conference in Avignon on January 22, 1898, during which Pierre Tournel, an editor at *La Croix*, accused the mayor of being close to the Freemasons and the Jews and then attacked the Jewish race. To spice up the meeting of three hundred, a satiric comedy in two acts by Jean Drault, an adherent to Drumont's philosophy, was performed to the great joy of the audience, which, according to a police report, "applauded the allusions to the Jewish race."[65] The anti-Semitic demonstrations reached Avignon, the city of popes, later than elsewhere. On February 23, 1898, more than six hundred people ran through the streets, sang "The Marseillaise," and shouted, "Long live the army! Long live the Republic!" The cafés displayed the tricolor flag. The police superintendent reported that "at the division building, the aide-de-camp, addressing the crowd cheering him, exclaimed, 'I do not have a flag at hand, but I am wholeheartedly with you in shouting. Long live the army! Long live France!' " As the meeting seemed to become threatening, the superintendent took preventive measures. "At my invitation," he reported, "all the Jewish merchants closed their stores; only M. Roos (Le Petit Paris) felt he ought to leave his store open. Everything took place without serious incident. M. Dubourguier, a law clerk, and M. Dioanons, who repeatedly struck the storefront of M. Ben Carcassonne, on the rue Sainte-Garde, with his cane, were taken to the station . . . Tomorrow evening another demonstration, larger no doubt, will take place, because of the candlelit procession that will occur for the republican holiday of February 24."[66] During the night young people from the Groupe Catholique d'Etudes Sociales d'Avignon (Catholic Social Studies Group of Avignon) put up posters calling for a demonstration.[67] To avert the worst outcome, Rabbi Bauer also asked the Jewish shopkeepers to close their shops and to stay calm; for its part, the prefecture compiled an exhaustive list of names of Jewish residents and shopkeepers, accompanied by their home addresses. It added, in conclusion, "thirty available officers and two gendarme brigades"—an indication that violence could have erupted.

On February 27 *Le Courrier du Midi* gave the following account of these two demonstrations:

> The news of Zola's conviction produced among people of every station, without distinction of class or condition—one can even say in every political party—a unanimous movement of inexpressible satisfaction. This feeling manifested itself with a demonstration that emerged spontaneously from the crowd. A thousand times the cries were repeated: "Long live France! Long live the army! Down with the Jews! Out with Zola!" That unplanned demonstration received great applause as it passed through the streets. The entire population of Avignon seemed to join in. It appeared particularly agreeable to the military element, which publicly expressed its gratitude. The gendarmerie and the police did nothing to impede it but let it go on with conspicuous benevolence. The next day, on the occasion of the candlelight procession held by the municipality to celebrate the anniversary of the revolution of February 24, 1848, the demonstration took on an even

more expansive character. Several thousand people, belonging to every class and point of view, without distinction, as on the previous day, followed the procession and expressed their feelings with shouts, dominated by "Down with the Jews!" Someone carried a flag inscribed in bold letters with Drumont's motto, "France for the French!"

That account is not totally slanted, since *Le Radical du Vaucluse* also wrote on February 27, "Like almost everywhere else in France, the Avignon population welcomed the jury's decision in the Zola affair with enthusiasm." *La Libre Parole* rejoiced; its correspondent sent a telegram describing the scene to Paris headquarters: "Magnificent anti-Jewish demonstration. Five thousand demonstrators preceded by brass bands and flags passed through city. Shouts: Long live France! Long live the army! Long live Drumont! Death to the Jews! Down with the Jews! On the place Horloge, ten thousand spectators cheered the demonstrators, reproducing yesterday's demonstration."[68]

That was not the end of it. During the legislative election campaign, the rumor spread that Zola was hiding in the Vaucluse department, and anti-Semitism again surfaced. During an electoral meeting held by the radical-socialist republican mayor Pourquerey de Boisserin, a listener shouted, "You are the ally of the Jews." The mayor took the floor and, according to a police report, "defended himself against the accusation of having supported the Jews. He declared that Dreyfus ought to have been shot. He nevertheless repudiated religious hatred and affirmed his republican convictions."[69] Once again a certain ambiguity reigned in republican ranks, and as in other localities, a republican political label did not always prevent the expression of prejudices. Something similar occurred in the anti-Semitic camp. When Drumont, in the company of the deputies from Algeria and of Jules Guérin, entered the Avignon train station on their way to Paris on May 30, 1898, members of the Catholic clubs, flanked by about twenty priests, waited for him and actually gave him an ovation. The police superintendent recounted with unintentional humor that "M. Drumont replied with the cry, 'Down with the Jews! Long live the Republic!' This last sentence was not cheered, because the atmosphere was clearly essentially reactionary and clerical." A commanding officer of the gendarmerie noted, amusingly, that "order was not disturbed."[70] This time it was the conservative and Catholic anti-Semites who refrained from repeating the slogans of their hero, who too openly embraced the values of the Republic.

In Nîmes as well, anti-Semitic signs were displayed: "My children, citizens of Nîmes, take arms for France. Wage war on the Jews, both for our bread and for that of our children. Take arms, take arms, war, war, war." And again: "Down with the Jewish syndicate and long live the army!" Scenes of unrest occurred on January 22 and 23. Young people wore masks "belonging to the royalist youth," and "children who were members of the parochial schools" brandished an effigy of Zola and paraded, shouting, "Down with the Jews! Out with Zola!" On February 22, handwritten posters were plastered on the market wall: "Tuesday evening, six-thirty. Rendezvous the place des Carmes. Anti-Jewish demonstration. All patriots will be there to shout down the Jews, that filthy race and scourge of France." Other posters proclaimed, "Down with the traitors!" Several hundred people gathered and were dispersed by the police. *Le Petit Provençal* denounced these "sectarian and religious struggles" but rejected the claims of the "Semites," while *L'Eclair* protested this "new slap in the face to all patriots" and congratulated the residents of Nîmes for standing up to fight the Dreyfusards. The newspaper condemned the police measures decided upon by the mayor to protect "his good Jewish friends" and described a comical scene: on the place des Carmes, as the bell on the clock of the Saint-Baudile church was chiming, the police officers present were on the watch. A nearby demonstrator, "doubtless overcome by cold feet on that rain-drenched square, sneezed a few feet away from one of the principal police officers. 'Without a doubt, that's the signal,' the good officer said to himself, and immediately collared the demonstrator. What an excess of zeal, Messeigneurs!"[71]

Among the candidates for the legislative elections, the presence of Fernand Crémieux, the former deputy of Uzès, and a distant relative of Adolphe Crémieux,* fanned the flames of bitter strife. His nationalist opponent, Léonce Pascal, signed his electoral posters "Léonce Pascal,

---

*Adolphe Crémieux: crafter of the Crémieux decree.—trans.

candidate of the Ligue Antijuive de France," and ran as a "Catholic republican." One of Pascal's election proclamations, posted between the two rounds of the election, read:

> At such a critical moment, it was necessary to rally around the flag of "the Republic of all and for all." And now onward to complete and affirm the victory. This is a decisive moment . . . In the face of the patriotic movement that is moving the country so deeply, it is up to you to say if you want to march behind the national flag, so nobly held by Drumont, Déroulède, and many other courageous patriots, or if, forgetting your proud traditions of independence, you want instead to mingle with the Jews and the stateless, and, obeying the watchword of the synagogues, make this arrondissement, still resonating with patriotism, the last refuge of the syndicate, condemned and executed by France as a whole. Take heart, patriots, and go to the ballot box with shouts of Long live France! Long live the Republic! Long live the army![72]

According to the subprefect, "Crémieux, the incumbent deputy, has . . . little chance of success, as much because of his opinions—which are not those of the vast majority of voters—as because of the discredit that has befallen everything relating to the Israelite question." *Le Petit Méridional* reprinted excerpts from *La Libre Parole*, which called for "getting rid of the Jew Crémieux." Léonce Pascal, supported by the Catholic electorate, won easily in the second round.[73] In the first days of 1899, posters covered the walls of Nîmes, distributed by the local branch of the Ligue Antisémitique: they claimed that it was necessary to "protect the nation against cosmopolitan Jewry." The many lectures given in the Gard department by Célestin Bouglé and especially by Francis de Pressensé in February and March launched further unrest, but it now bore witness to the domination of the Dreyfusard camp. Violent acts occurred, and *Le Journal du Midi* railed against "the Huguenots and the Yids."[74] In Vauvert and in Alès, Saint-Jean-de-Garde, Lédignan, and Anduze, the head of the Ligue des Droits de l'Homme drew large audiences of several thousand people but provoked a violent reaction from royalist groups, who mercilessly attacked that "Huguenot," that "apostate" friend of the Jews, bringing to the surface the religious antagonisms of the past. Bourthoumieu, a royalist journalist, wrote, for example, "To follow M. de Pressensé and his men, one must belong to a religion other than the Catholic religion or be the avowed enemy of that religion . . . It is not possible for a Catholic conscience to associate itself unequivocally with the acts of hatred recommended by M. de Pressensé against the Catholic religion, without falling into absurdity."[75] After the verdict against Dreyfus at Rennes, a poster again addressed the population: "Patriots of Nîmes. The mob of troublemakers has its back to the wall. Once again the gold coins that the Jewish syndicate threw by the handful at the fanatic followers of the Dreyfus case could not prevail over our officers . . . Patriots of Nîmes: let us be calm. To the insulters of France, to the last-minute revolutionaries, to those who sold out to the Jewish syndicate, let us reply only with contempt . . . Like Déroulède and Guérin, let us know how to unite and how to wait and, if necessary, how to sacrifice our freedom to save our France from the peril in which a Jew-sympathizing and Masonic government has cast it. Long live France, long live the Republic, long live the army."[76]

In Alès as well, about sixty young people from Jeunesse Royaliste, accompanied by about three hundred others, marched in February 1898, brandishing an effigy with a caricature of Zola. In March 1899 a poster signed by "a group of patriots" and printed on site was put up on the walls of Alès to protest a lecture by Pressensé: "Will you allow a few STATELESS persons on the payroll of foreign nations to trample all your most cherished sentiments?" In the May elections M. de Ramel, an anti-Dreyfusard royalist and mayor of the city, was reelected. On September 9 and 12, 1899, violent brawls erupted, pitting royalist groups against socialists; and on September 12, 1899, the disturbances between the Dreyfusards and the anti-Dreyfusards were so serious that the gendarmerie intervened to harshly repress actual riots.[77]

Far to the east, in Digne, conscripts ran through the streets on January 25, shouting, "Down with Reinach! Down with the Jews! Down with Zola!" In Valence as well, in the northern part of the Drôme department, conscripts demonstrated under the windows of *La Revue de la Drôme*, shouting, "Down with the Jews! The magazine has sold out to the Jews." The police superintendent on the scene said this incident was "without importance."[78] The affair left long-lasting traces in the southeast region of France. On October 4, 1908, for example, at the initiative of Action Française, a meeting was held in Nîmes with Léon Daudet and Louis Vaugeois: "Once it was the freedom of the bullfights that the fanatics from the lodges and the synagogues attempted to suppress; today it is freedom of conscience, the rights of fathers and mothers, which they want to take away . . . Everyone in Nîmes, then, shout, 'Down with the traitor Dreyfus! Long live the nation! Long live our freedoms as Catholics and as French citizens!' "[79]

Chapter Five

Radical Toulouse,

Nationalist Bordeaux

Toulouse, capital of the Midi-Pyrénées region, seemed to maintain its composure and did not give in to the boisterous anti-Semitic temptation. The police reports from January 1898 tirelessly repeat the same message: "The population appears indifferent . . . That is the attitude it seems obliged to take every time the question of the Dreyfus trial is raised in its presence."[1] Here the Republic was truly at home, and in the Adour valley and in the nearby Ariège department, the openly nationalist reactionary forces kept a low profile. To be sure, in parts of the Southwest, the streets were not so quiet. In Dax, a city in Aquitaine, Théodore Denis, a deputy who conducted a virulent anti-Semitic campaign in the Chamber, was easily reelected as a "radical republican" in the May 1898 legislative elections. Armany Jacquey was also elected as a "republican" from the Landes department, and Joseph Massbuau, a new deputy from the Aveyron department, was elected in Espalion as an "independent republican." The Bonapartist Paul de Cassagnac, who opposed the Republic, won in Mirande, receiving 9,128 votes after a campaign during which he did not miss a chance to denounce the power of the Jews.[2] Jean Delpech-Cantaloup represented the Gers department after winning Lectoure under the plebiscitarian label, and Marie Lasies won Condom, also as a plebiscitarian. All of them hastened to join the anti-Semitic group in the Chamber. What a paradox, then: on the whole, the enormous republican Southwest turned its back on anti-Semitic nationalist candidates—yet it alone sent a third of the eighteen deputies to the Chamber who joined the new anti-Semitic group. Whether Bonapartist or royalist, they all used anti-Semitic rhetoric and won the elections in the name of a Gascony liberated from a Republic supposedly dominated by Jews. Beside them two radicals, Paul Decker-David and André Delieux, who also played a prominent role in the Gers department, did not miss a chance to denounce "cosmopolitan financial Jewry," warning their rural voters in their platform statements that the Jews were more dangerous than phylloxera. That anti-Semitic atmosphere was fostered by *La Croix du Gers*, which published a large number of anti-Semitic caricatures, such as a little comedy on January 30, 1898, that depicted a military lottery. A robust and straightforward peasant addresses the subprefect, who is presiding over the lottery, "I have number 22, Mr. Subprefect." The latter replies, "Gut vor tree years of serfice; long lif Vrance!" Stunned, the peasant exclaims, "Why, he talks like a Yid, our subprefect does."[3]

The Pyrenean region around Toulouse nevertheless remained largely safe from the nationalist unrest affecting nearby areas—which almost wholly overtook Bordeaux, the capital of Gironde. In Bordeaux two out of the three deputies, Charles Bernard (the "republican") and Albert Chiché (the "socialist Boulangist"), joined the Chamber's anti-Semitic group, headed by Drumont. But Toulouse took pleasure in its own sense of time and clung to its particular rhythms, which accentuated its highly atypical character. Although anti-Semitism was just as—and perhaps more—oppressive there than elsewhere, it asserted itself less in the streets than in the press and the parties. Above all, its anti-Semitism revealed itself in radicalism.

In the heat of events, the streets of Toulouse seem to have remained peaceful, and the overt anti-Semitic mobilization, the resolute collective actions of angry crowds, could only be restrained: against the all-powerful Republic, it was the royalists who monopolized street anti-Semitism as a form of protest. *L'Express du Midi*, the royalist newspaper of Toulouse, was its ringleader. From December 1897 to January 1899,

that paper urged people to demonstrate; managed a local Ligue Antisémitique (that however was fairly weak and lacking in autonomy); and
stirred passions against "the Jewish Republic." These aristocrats of the
Southwest controlled the minuscule Ligue Antisémitique branch that
was created in Toulouse in December 1897 by M. de Boëry, a member
of one of the most ancient noble families of Agen, who was later
succeeded by M. de Baud.[4] In *L'Express du Midi*, Paul de Cassagnac
announced a major anti-Semitic demonstration in Toulouse for December 15, 1897, and appealed to everyone who "does not bow down before the Golden Calf of modern Jewry" to participate. Also on the
fifteenth, according to the police reports, eight hundred people gathered
on the place du Capitole outside the officers' club and shouted, "Long
live the army! Down with Zola! Down with Dreyfus!" They "struck the
facades of several stores belonging to Israelites with their canes, causing
some damage to the store Paradis des Dames."[5] On January 7, the Feast
of Epiphany, Toulouse was once again out of step with the demonstrations unfolding at the national level: two hundred people toasted the
health of the duc d'Orléans. The comte d'Adhémar and the marquis de
Panat castigated the republican regime. People shouted, "Long live the
king! Down with the Republic!" At about eleven p.m., with a white flag
in the lead, a group of young people ran through the streets of the city
shouting, "Long live the king! Long live the army! Down with the
Jews!" On the rue Alsace-Lorraine they clashed with young socialists.
On the nineteenth the Ligue Antisémitique held a meeting at the Pré-
Catelan, where about three hundred people heard Boëry, president of
the league local, then Renaud d'Elissagaray, a local nationalist candidate,
deliver "long diatribes against" the Jews, the cosmopolitan financiers,
the Rothschilds, and Joseph Reynac [sic] . . . All the speeches were repeatedly interrupted by shouts and outbursts." They denounced the
politicians who "have groveled before the Jews." In a report not without
irony, the police superintendent wrote: "The speeches were just a series
of clichés, fabricated out of phrases cut out from Drumont's articles,
with an insipid mixture of socialism . . . Although the hall applauded
wildly, it is certain that the majority of listeners did not hear a thing."
When the meeting let out, the demonstrators headed toward the place
du Capitole, shouting, "The Jews are pigs! Death to the Jews! On to the
synagogue!" People marched in procession, preceded by a small sign,

about "80 by 40 centimeters," depicting "a little man with a Jewish profile considering a pile of some sort placed at his feet." The sign read, "It
is not shit." Hostile shouts rose up outside houses inhabited by Jews;
stones were thrown at Jewish-owned stores. People cheered the newspapers *La Dépêche* and *L'Express* and milled around the place du Capitole,
where they burned *L'Aurore* and a bale of straw. Then via the boulevards
Harbourg and Lazare-Carnot, they went to the headquarters of the nationalist organizations, where they shouted, "Long live the army! Down
with the Jews!" Then left again via the rue Alsace-Lorraine. Stones were
thrown at the store Au Gaspillage, "which is supposedly Jewish." Fog
covered the city, dampening the enthusiasm. "Noise, unanimity in their
animosity toward the Jews," the police report concluded, "but nothing
serious to note." In the eyes of the police, that "ridiculous ceremony"
organized by "idle" students verged on a mere "racket to amuse themselves . . . The population did not take part in the demonstration, which
did not appear to meet with much approval." Two Jewish shopkeepers,
Ernest Léon, owner of La Mascotte, and Lévy, owner of Au Gaspillage,
and a money-changer, Molina, lodged complaints.[6]

In the months that followed, anti-Semitic notices covered Toulouse.
Calls for boycotts were broadly distributed in tracts near Jewish stores.
One of them, signed by the committee of the Ligue Antisémitique et
Nationaliste de Toulouse, denounced "Jewish tricks" like fake clearance
sales designed to swindle the customers: "The Ligue Antisémitique et
Nationaliste de Toulouse intends to found a newspaper to defend the
interests of honest and loyal local businesses against Jewish enterprises.
It denounces the extremely dangerous Jewish tricks, the cheap goods for
which the Jews are paid dearly thanks to the magic word 'clearance.'
When the good Yid has completely lost his reputation on the square, he
clears out. Immediately some Moses or Isaac of one kind or another arrives and takes over the business . . . Buy French, you are forewarned. Do
not serve as suckers for those cosmopolitan exploiters." *La Croix du Midi,
La Semaine Catholique, Le Clairon Antisémite*, and even *La Dépêche* supported
that campaign, as did *Le Messager de Toulouse*, which devoted space to the
following incident that took place in faraway Remiremont: "A Jewish
butcher in the city gave his shop the name 'Joan of Arc's Butcher Shop' "
and thereby easily fooled the Catholics. "A good Frenchman opposite

his shop found a witty way to put an end to the charade," the newspaper reported. "He had a huge billboard made with gigantic letters: 'Apraham's Putcher Shop.' The Jew turned red with anger. His pals came to his aid and moved heaven and earth. But the witty patriot stood fast and had the last laugh. The Jew, seeing he was unmasked, painted over his sign; the Catholic saw no disadvantage to imitating him. You have to defend yourself."[7]

On March 9 about eight hundred people attended an anti-Semitic meeting in the Pré-Catelan. Thiébaud, Drumont's faithful servant, made the trip from Paris, and as a "child of Toulouse who had his first dance at the Grand-Rond," he attacked "Jewish clericalism," exclaiming, "Isn't there a danger in that for the nation? Do you want to end up the way Poland has?" He denounced the influence of Jews and Protestants over the government and even over the Sûreté Générale: "If you peel away the surface, you find the whole clan of Jews making up that staff." "In the legislative elections," he declared, to the general applause of the audience, "every candidate must make a commitment in his platform statement to demand the purging of the Jews." Another speaker, André Jacquemont, exclaimed, "The patriots must keep watch; the Jews must be driven off . . . Since the Catholic religion is the French religion, we must prefer a national religion to a foreign religion. This must end. We want France for the French." A police superintendent in attendance maintained that "the vast majority of those present were clerical reactionaries." Another speaker, Bouissou, showed a handkerchief belonging to the marquis de Morès and recalled his words: " 'As for the Jews, we will kill them.' Remember France, so beautiful and powerful during ten centuries of monarchy, the France of Philip Augustus, of Saint Louis, of Henri IV, of Richelieu . . . Cosmopolitanism is the enemy! Long live France for the French! Long live France for France!"[8] On May 4 at the café Espagnol in Saint-Simon, sixty people listened to an anti-Semitic speech by Elissagaray. On May 7 at Salle Tivoli in Saint-Cyprien, seven hundred people attended another of Elissagaray's meetings, where his opponents provoked scuffles. The anti-Semitic declarations were "frequently applauded" by the audience. The same day Elissagaray held another meeting in the Pré-Catelan, attracting between twelve and fifteen hundred enthusiastic people.[9]

At the end of the year, in December 1898, and then in January 1899, the last gasps of unrest echoed in the streets of Toulouse. On December 22 in the Pré-Catelan, Pressensé held a meeting in support of Captain Picquart. Threatening posters in the colors of the French flag were put up on the city walls, and disturbing rumors were circulated. The prefect received an anonymous letter: "Friends of mine have asked me to go with them on the evening of Pressensé's lecture to break windows in the Israelite stores. Since I find that a very bad thing, especially since I am an employee of Israelites and have no complaints about them, I believe I am doing the right thing in warning you of what is about to happen." Even before the meeting began, a thousand shouting people left the Théâtre des Variétés, preceded by a flag, and gathered outside the officers' club on the place du Capitole. Mounted gendarmerie charged and cleared the plaza. People then headed toward the Pré-Catelan. Inside Octave Mirbeau took the floor and denounced anti-Semitism, which "was gnawing away at the country." At that moment an altercation broke out in the hall; a brawl erupted; people fought with canes and chairs; and a band of three hundred people, preceded by a flag, charged at the sound of the bugle and invaded the hall. Shouts of "Long live the army! Down with Pressensé! Down with the Jews!" erupted, interspersed with shouts of "Long live Picquart! Down with the Jesuits! Down with the priests!" As a police report indicated,

> there was a free-for-all. Tables, chairs, sticks, and stones were thrown from every point in the hall; several individuals were wounded; others were trampled. Everything got broken: bleachers, chairs, doors, curtains. The partitions in the loges were demolished; bottles and glasses were thrown in the hall. During the tumult the bugle was still sounding the charge. An anti-Semite attached a white scarf to the end of a pole and paraded it around like a flag. A group of revisionists rushed to tear it away. The brawling increased in intensity. The superintendent gave the order to evacuate the hall; the gendarmes and the police officers grabbed MM. de Pressensé and Mirbeau and dragged them off. Friends intervened, and MM. de Pressensé and Mirbeau were shoved and knocked to the ground. The nationalists surrounded them in great numbers.

Finally the police had the combatants evacuated. About four hundred people went on to demonstrate in the streets. The police intervened: gendarmerie brigades, municipal guards on horseback, and squads of officers went into action. Several were wounded in the melee. The police believed that "the population remains indifferent, and that is the attitude it seems obliged to take every time the question of the Dreyfus trial is raised in its presence," but four thousand nationalists actually demonstrated, according to *Le Télégramme*. *L'Express du Midi* described "eight thousand parading militarily between two thick rows of sympathetic spectators."[10] Feeling outnumbered by the crowd, which they estimated at only twelve to fifteen hundred, the police in charge asked the army to intervene. In concert with the general who commanded the seventeenth corps, they planned to have the troops intervene, and all the available forces of the gendarmerie were placed out in the field. The crowd attacked several stores owned by Jewish tradespeople. Counter-demonstrations clashed with them in a free-for-all.[11] Smaller nationalist meetings were held in Toulouse in late December: on several occasions, Dürbach, a professor at the law school, was attacked, and Frédéric Rauch, a Jewish professor at the school of letters, was also shouted down.

Before they were definitively stifled, anti-Semitic passions found noisy expression one last time, in January 1899, in demonstrations that attracted a few hundred people each. On the eighth about a hundred demonstrators from the Ligue Royaliste went down the rue Alsace-Lorraine shouting, "Out with the Jews! Long live the army!" A brawl occurred when they ran into supporters of Picquart; one demonstrator, Pierre Bourdieu, was wounded in the head. Demonstrators hired fighters and even tried to procure weapons. The anti-Semitic nationalists gathered on January 9, then on the twelfth and thirteenth, to carry out their battle plan. A police inspector in attendance warned that the city was heading toward "serious disorder," especially since another anonymous letter, composed by the same informant as the previous one, had reached the prefect: "Someone has proposed that I take part in a procession that is to pass through the Israelite stores. They recommended that I come armed, preferably with a revolver, and led me to understand that if I don't have one, I will be provided with one. The last time I had the honor of warning you, there was only physical damage. This time it is more serious." A third anonymous letter followed shortly: "Ten residents of Toulouse are sacrificing their lives and are resolved to go kill Dreyfus upon his arrival in France." On the fourteenth, therefore, a final demonstration occurred. Nearly five hundred people confronted Dreyfusard counterdemonstrators before nine thousand onlookers who were considered by the police to be mere "curiosity seekers" but who nevertheless closely followed the nationalist troops. *Le Télégramme* estimated that there were five thousand nationalists among them, whereas *La Dépêche* estimated them at only two thousand. The gendarmerie on horseback evacuated the place du Capitole, where they had assembled. Other brawls erupted outside the Théâtre des Variétés, and a group of four hundred counterdemonstrators organized at the café de France, then headed for the place Saint-Germain, singing "The Marseillaise" and "La Carmagnole," before clashing with nationalists. Arrests were made, particularly since several people were found to be in possession of revolvers.[12]

Toulouse did not in any way stand as a haven of civil peace within a heated France, as a number of police reports mentioned above claimed. The city of radicalism par excellence, a key site for the triumphant Republic for more than a generation, nonetheless remained atypical. In January and February 1898, at the peak of the anti-Semitic mobilization, it barely experienced a few ripples. The four hundred or so Jews who lived there (out of a total population of about 150,000) enjoyed relative calm: their possessions were not systematically destroyed; they escaped physical assault; and their synagogue and rabbi were not targeted by demonstrators. The Republic was at home in Toulouse, as was the socialist movement. And here more than elsewhere, after Jean Jaurès became the herald of Dreyfusism in late 1898, socialist militants would learn how to confront the nationalist groups and get the upper hand. As a result, the central confrontation more clearly pitted the republican camp against solid royalist troops, openly benefiting from clerical support.

Nevertheless, Toulouse did see a long period of anti-Semitism shared by Catholics and radicals alike. However hostile they were to each other, the opponents of the moment shared almost identical prejudices. If the Catholic press demonstrated a bitter anti-Semitism, so did the radical press. Anti-Semitism brought together opponents who had nothing more in common than a rejection of the Other, of anyone who persisted in displaying an identity that did not result from a simple cleavage between republic and monarchy, or between clericalism and anti-clericalism. More strikingly than other cities, then, Toulouse bore witness to unexpected points of contact between opposing ideologies.

The Catholic press, spurred perhaps by its alliance with the royalist camp toward a radical opposition to the Republic, delivered anti-Semitic insults by the cartload.[13] *L'Express du Midi*, the finest feather in its cap, openly called itself the "daily organ of social and royalist defense" and acted in concert with the region's royalist leaders. It systematically defended every anti-Semitic initiative, particularly since most of its militants shared royalist ideas. With a daily circulation of seven thousand, sold almost exclusively in Toulouse, it was the third-largest newspaper, after *La Dépêche* and *Le Télégramme*. Although *Le Messager de Toulouse* was more moderate, representing Catholics who rallied to the Republic, it too remained within the royalist sphere of influence, regularly publishing articles from *La Libre Parole* and reproducing all the local and national speeches of the various spokesmen for anti-Semitism. Weeklies, such as *La Croix du Midi* and *La Semaine Catholique*, whose print run of six thousand made it the largest-circulating weekly in the region, constantly spread aggressive anti-Semitism.[14] That anti-Semitic press, very visible, was backed up by several more short-lived newspapers, such as *L'Avenir de Toulouse et du Midi*, *Le Commerce*, and *Le Clairon Antisémite*, which made anti-Semitism their sole issue. That gives an idea of the strength of that press, which was allied to the royalist camp in a shared rejection of the "Jewish Republic," which, according to it, held exclusive power in Toulouse.

We need only look at issues of *L'Express du Midi* from late 1897 and early 1898 to understand the scope of its anti-Semitism. On December 8, 1897, the newspaper wrote: "The Jews, having become the gods of gold, are in the process of expropriating the French little by little. They have already taken their châteaux, heroic relics of feudal times; they have taken their baronies; and they want to take over the army . . . The soldier is the priest of patriotism, just as the priest is the soldier of God . . . Keep your hands off, Jews, and false Christians who broadcast the Jews' voices: we forbid it."[15] At the height of the events, *L'Express du Midi* rejected the idea of massacring the Jews (which was supported by

Drumont's precepts) but on numerous occasions it quoted and adopted Drumont's "sociological" analyses. It wished to treat the Jews as foreigners, as was done during the monarchy. It was not possible to overthrow "Jewry except by overthrowing the Republic," since the Jews had to be put back in the place belonging to them in a Christian society.[16] *Le Messager de Toulouse* was less cantankerous than *L'Express*; but its editor in chief left no room for ambiguity when he wrote calmly, "We know that Jewry is not exactly in the good graces of *Le Messager de Toulouse*." In 1898 in particular, that newspaper attacked the "big Jews"; it wrote ironically of "Judaic reasoning" and protested "Jewish vengeance." "The entire race of Israel has risen up to seek revenge for one of its sons, to slur France's name in the eyes of foreign nations. The race of Dreyfus has truly avenged itself well." *Le Messager* believed that "the Jew is of the Semitic race, the European of the Aryan race. There is the same difference between the Semite and the Aryan as between the Negro or the Chinese and us." Making every effort to unmask the plots devised by the new "wandering Jew" represented by Dreyfus, the newspaper also wrote, "By virtue of his origin and his education, Dreyfus can only be an internationalist, stateless or belonging to every country, whichever you want to call it. His attitude during his military career and his act of treason peremptorily demonstrate it. He does not share the sacred love of hearth and home that lies in every good Frenchman's heart, and he possesses the arrogance of his race to the highest degree. What is in the blood does not change." The misdeeds of the "Jewish sabbath" were infinite in number.[17]

Issue after issue *La Croix du Midi* pointed a vengeful finger at the "Jew sympathizers" who were enslaving "Catholic France." Anti-Semitism was said to be legitimate since it consisted of "a first effort on the part of the native Frenchman to once more take control of native soil." It led to the repression of "the Jewish leprosy," of that "horde" with "hooked noses," those "nasty faces with bent noses." Celebrating "the resurrection of the French soul," *La Croix* added, in the spirit of Joseph de Maistre, "the Jew is unmasked. The French people have seen through his games; they will henceforth be on their guard, they will look at both hands before shaking the yellow hands of the syndicate's gold. And once more Providence, which always watches over France, will have allowed good to come out of an excess of evil." The result was this feat of logic:

"If France remains Christian, the Church, without becoming the police-man of extortion and pillage, will reduce the shock of the reprisals. If not, triumphant socialism and Freemasonry will no more spare the Jews than the Reign of Terror will spare the terrorists." In the view of *La Croix du Midi*, the Jews were safer as foreigners in a Christian France than as citizens in a republican France, since the latter would inevitably lead to a victorious reaction by humiliated Catholicism. They thus had to break their alliance with the Republic and return to their former status as protected persons.[18] Similar views appeared in *La Semaine Catholique*: "Let us repeat again and again that Alfred Dreyfus is not French. He is a Jew and a Freemason. These two marks of shame on his forehead suf-fice to explain his treachery . . . The Jew has a hand in all our disasters." And it added, "It can be said that we are being exploited by the sons of Israel. Drumont is very right to demand that France belong to the French."[19]

The viewpoint expressed by the journalistic stronghold of the radical left, *La Dépêche du Midi*, was almost the same. Under the editorship of Arthur Huc, this radical daily of the Southwest, the embodiment of all-powerful Toulousian radicalism, held a more or less dominant position over its rivals and was so strongly implanted at the local level that it was crucial to political candidates' efforts to capture votes. Yet surprisingly, this very newspaper spread anti-Semitism, which linked it to its monar-chist and Catholic rivals of a nationalist bent.[20] We have already en-countered that curious alloy of anti-Semitism and the left in various regions of France: in the Southwest, which was stalwartly republican, it acquired a particular shape, given that it was spread on a large scale by *La Dépêche*. For many years *La Dépêche*, with its hegemonic position, did not alter its vision one iota. On November 4, 1894, it wrote regarding Dreyfus's arrest: "His very accentuated Jewish typology, which gave him the air of a foreigner disguised as a French officer, undoubtedly played some role in that irrational dislike." A few days later, on November 9, Arthur Huc, who was private secretary to Allain-Targé—minister of fi-nance in the Gambetta ministry and an integral member of the republi-can political staff most open to Protestant and Jewish allies—wrote:

The moral is that the traitor is an Israelite, and in the pure and simple observation of that fact lies a sign of the times in which we are living . . . The Jewish caste is becoming a considerable danger in a country that still insists on defending its old mores, its traditions, its history, and that, without the ideal that made it glorious, would inevitably be condemned to disappear . . . I know that I am risking a great deal in going against many received ideas that seek the cause of all the iniquities of Israel in the matter of race . . . I am hardly persuaded that a Russian Jew freshly escaped from the ghetto or some Negro recently emancipated could so quickly claim to be the equal of a man whose ancestors were on familiar terms with Diderot, Condorcet, or Voltaire and who prepared the way for the Revolution.

Although Huc considered himself faithful to the Enlightenment, his prose was identical in this case to that of Drumont in *Mon vieux Paris* and to that of Jean Baffier, the champion of Berry. Both men were counterrevolutionary supporters of a revolution that had finally become French once more. In the end, it was difficult to distinguish his prose even from that of Abbé Hémonet, who lamented the disappearance of his old Nancy.

Strikingly, the editor in chief of *La Dépêche* was anxious to distance himself from Drumont from the outset. He protested that he was not anti-Semitic "in the manner of M. Edouard Drumont," and he justified his hostility to Jews with considerations more economic than religious or racial. Still, *La Dépêche* also propagated the most well-worn religious and racial anti-Semitic imagery. The paper's anti-Semitism, founded on a socialist tradition that encompassed the entire nineteenth century in France, was not above resorting to figures and metaphors identical to those of its opponents. *La Dépêche* even received the support of Jean Jaurès, who wrote: "We have come across a phenomenal deployment of Jewish power to save one of its own, that is all." Even though Jaurès took the precaution of rejecting "the religious war" and "the race war" in January 1898, in his newspaper *La Petite République* he maintained that Drumont was "a profound sociologist" who had seen that "the Jews manipulate our Civil Code with diabolical skill." In *La Petite République* on December 13, 1898, even though he had now definitively joined the Dreyfusard camp, Jaurès compared Drumont to Marx, of all people: the former was simply less "clear-sighted" than the latter in not clearly attacking, behind the Jews, capitalism itself.

Throughout these years *La Dépêche* was not above reprinting word for word numerous articles from *La Libre Parole* and *L'Intransigeant* and citing its sources. In late 1897 Arthur Huc and Camille Pellatan again mercilessly attacked "Jewish tenacity," the "Jewish syndicate," and "cosmopolitan financial Jewry." On January 19, 1898, Huc warned the people of France against "all the tribes of Israel." On February 17 he evoked the "race that claims to dominate us . . . from the top of its piles of money." Anti-Semitism in this particular case did not correspond to a relentless defense of Catholic religious identity, and *La Dépêche* did battle clericalism and its royalist allies as well. In the first months of 1898, Huc rejected "Jewish methods," protested the domination of France by "the usurers of Israel," and also protested "Jewry," which dominated the state. In an incredible article on February 19 entitled "The Jewish Question"—which anti-Semitic demonstrators posted on the city walls with explicit mention of its origin—he thundered against "that inferior race" and denounced

> the ardor that pushes the Jews toward the acquisition of gold, which constitutes the inferiority of their race . . . It has renounced generosity, the passion for the Ideal, which have made for the greatness of our Aryan race. The worship of the Golden Calf has canceled out all other religion among the Israelites . . . The Yahweh of Moses is a miserly, cruel, jealous God brimming over with a strange mercy for his chosen people, inexorable toward the infidels and preaching the extermination of foreign races . . . The Israelite, who is born a merchant, visibly differs from the Arab, who is born a soldier. The race is the same. The tribes are different. There is no question of anti-Semitism, therefore, but there is a question anti-Jewry.

The opposition between the warrior Arab and the merchant Jew, which haunts all French anti-Semitic literature of the time, was formulated most explicitly by Drumont himself.[21] Huc drove the point home, formulating a comparative theory of the assimilation process: "We have opened our civilization and our ranks to them. If they decline to join it, is it our fault? . . . A hundred years was sufficient for our common people, our workers, our plowmen, to transform themselves and no longer resemble in the slightest the common people before 1789."[22] The Jews persisted in their culture. Like the author of *La France juive*, Huc wrote in *La Dépêche*, at the heat of the anti-Semitic outburst, "For my part, I doubt that M. Reinach's physical appearance, however picturesque it might be, bears witness in any way at all to the supremacy of Israel; nor do I find any greater proof of that supremacy in the fact that the curve of Jewish noses has braved persecutions and the centuries . . . Modern-day anti-Semitism came into being at the spectacle of Jewry asserting itself as class consciousness and in the power of its money." This passage gives an idea of how faithful the author remained, during these years, to his racist convictions. Indeed, in his astonishing article of November 1894, already quoted, like Drumont he elaborated on the opposition between the Aryan, concerned with "glory" and "nobility," and the Semite, who displayed his "subtle intelligence" in the service of money, "the weak spot of the Israelite race."[23]

The anti-Semitism of *La Dépêche* would disappear after the trial in Rennes, as did the increasingly precise threats that the nationalist camp wielded against the very survival of the Republic. But *La Dépêche* did not join the Dreyfusard camp until very late, nearly a year after Zola's "J'accuse" and shortly after Dreyfusard demonstrators took to the streets. It did so as well in reaction to the threat represented in its eyes by clericalism and the "black-robed hordes." A coalition committee that henceforth united the Dreyfusard forces proclaimed on December 28, 1898:

> Since representatives of monarchy expect to ban free speech among the French people; since they allow anti-Semitic gangs to import the savage practices of Algerian gangs into our city; since aspergilla are being exchanged for truncheons; and since the thugs in the barracks and the sacristy call for revolutionary methods—it would truly be strange if the party of the Revolution were to remain behind . . . We intend to be the masters of the street, and we will be it at any price . . . Has history, then, not taught these imbecilic bandits that progress cannot be checked and that it would

be both futile and dangerous to oppose it? Take heart, citizens! And onward against clericalism and militarism![24]

Clearly, the republican shift to the Dreyfusard camp, brought about both by the political organizations and by La Dépêche, hardly took the fate of the Jews into account.[25] The specifically Jewish dimension of that Franco-French war was cautiously relegated to the background. As if miraculously, anti-Semitism evaporated from the pages of La Dépêche without any theoretical clarification having taken place. Writers condemned the anti-Semitism propagated by Catholics and by Drumont but glossed over the anti-Semitism that had so often surfaced in the radical camp. People now proclaimed that anti-Semitism represented a "maneuver" on the part of Catholicism, which was "plotting" against the Republic. Now La Dépêche defended the Dreyfusards, to whom the fate of the Republic was linked, but these radicals or socialists kept quiet regarding their own erstwhile anti-Semitism. As the battle between monarchists and nationalists came to the fore, the defense of the Republic prevailed over every other consideration. The struggle against "Jewry," the efforts to beat off that "inferior race," were suspended, as it were, just as the desire to attack capitalism was put off indefinitely. The cleavage between monarchy/clericalism and Republic/anticlericalism took precedence. Anti-Semitism, having become the official ideology of the nationalists and clericals who were now placing the Republic in danger, lost its power to mobilize in the radical and socialist camp.

Open anti-Semitic demonstrations, moderate in scope in Toulouse, barely affected the other cities of Haute-Garonne, with the exception of a tiny incident that occurred in the streets of Revel, to which the mayor quickly put an end.[26] Not far away in Agen, on January 23, 1898, about a hundred people demonstrated on the boulevards and outside the house inhabited by a Jew.[27] In the Tarn region anti-Semitism increased, fed by La Croix du Tarn and La Semaine Religieuse, which published many hostile articles and thundered against the Jews' supposed Protestant allies, to such a point that La Voix de la Montagne openly worried: "Fanaticism against the Protestants, not to mention the Jews, has once more returned to France." During the May legislative election campaign, as in many other places, Catholic circles were often behind these forms of intolerance. *L'Union Républicaine* observed that "the influence of the clericals has incontestably grown. Not since the Restoration have we observed such an active propaganda campaign on the part of the monastic community. Anti-Semitism itself, which is merely a form of clericalism, is developing." Unrest in Tarn reached crisis proportions on October 15, 1899, when more than five thousand nationalists, including more than four thousand from outside the area (fourteen hundred from Carmaux and one thousand each from Toulouse, Castres, and Paris), and leaders of the Ligue de la Patrie Française flocked to the city of Albi. *La Semaine Religieuse* commented favorably on the events, concluding: "May God see fit to support this generous enthusiasm!"[28]

That vast republican Midi-Pyrénées region did not, however, support open anti-Semitic demonstrations. The Ariège department did not experience any at all;[29] nor did the Hautes-Pyrénées and Pyrénées-Atlantiques departments. In the cities of Tarbes, Lourdes, Vic, and Bagnères-de-Bigorre, no anti-Semitic unrest was perceptible. The streets remained calm, with no signs of mobilization. Tarbes went about its business: people worried about their stallions; discussed the presence of wild boars nearby; and celebrated the butcher boys' ball. As everywhere in France during that season, the music scene was relatively lively. On January 16 the Schola Cantorum gave a concert of sixteenth-century music at the Sainte-Thérèse church, playing pieces by Tomás Luis de Victoria and Orlando di Lasso. A few days later the Fifty-third Infantry performed *Coriolanus* and *Peer Gynt*. Theaters put on comedies by Georges Courteline and Ernest-Aimé Feydeau.[30] Lourdes experienced no unrest and was particularly preoccupied with organizing the processions. With all eyes turned toward the grotto, the heart of the city beat to the rhythm of the miraculous cures, endless lists of which were given day after day in the Catholic newspaper *L'Echo de Lourdes*. There were digs at the Freemasons, of course, but no trace of anti-Semitism was visible. Nothing, not a word about the Jews.[31] *L'Ere Nouvelle*, one of the major dailies of Tarbes, seems to have given up the provocative anti-Semitic phrases it was so fond of in 1895 and 1896. Nevertheless, a practiced eye might stumble over this advertising jingle from a perfumer, sung throughout France and adapted to particular regions and tastes:

An ironmonger told the prefect of police:
"Dreyfus! Only Congo could make him white."
"Very possible!" replied Mr. Blanc. "In any case,
It's the only soap that will make one's skin smooth."[32]

Blanc was the name of a moderate conservative candidate from Bagnères, whom the newspaper supported as the elections approached. With these lines anti-Semitism, previously hidden, made its appearance in the public debate in the heart of that quiet region. In his platform statement, Blanc, supported by the Catholics, attacked "the coalition of cosmopolitans" who supported Dreyfus—but he was not too insistent. He ran against the republican Frédéric Ozun, who declared in *Le Courrier Républicain*, "Blanc has behind him all the clerico-creeps of Bagnères, who, along with *La Croix*, have made a supreme effort, thanks to the support of M. Raynal* and Jewry and thanks to the complacency of the administration."

La Croix des Pyrénées also frequently and harshly attacked the Jews. One day in 1898, the front page read, "Down with the Jews!" On the eve of the legislative elections, the newspaper "increased its prayers and Ave Marias." It added, "This will be the day of victory."[33] Wishing to drive Blanc "from our mountains and valleys," Ozun forcefully attacked the "syndicate of Dreyfus" and hoped that Dreyfus "will be as shot he deserves." In his platform statement, the republican candidate wrote:

He who has little must pay little, and he who has much must pay much. Everyone acknowledges this is fair, but there is a league of Jews of all types and of cosmopolitan financiers who resort to the most hypocritical and roundabout methods to keep that necessary and humane reform from being carried out . . . Come on! On your feet, valiant voters of valiant Gascony! Awaken your sleeping consciences! Do not bow your heads any longer before the contemptuous insolence of money. Vote for a child of the land.

Addressing the voters in the canton of La Barthe, where he was general councilor, Ozun attacked the mayor, Montagnan: "You know this capi-

*David Raynal: deputy of Gironde and important member of the Republican elite.—trans.

talist too well—he could teach the most hardened Jew a thing or two—to take his ridiculous flights of fancy into account."[34] Another candidate in Bagnères, Robert, also made his feelings known, posting on election notices: "We are being squeezed and plundered by the stateless Jews who are strangling us. Theft and cowardice constitute the entire system of the Jews and of the Jews' associates. No Opportunists, no *ralliés*, to use the pompous term, no democrats, not even any radicals. In voting for them, you are voting for the supporters of the Jews, of the Panamaists, for the supporters of the Dreyfus syndicate." Blanc won with 10,218 votes, but Ozun received 7,612. The left, which was not above vigorous anti-Semitic arguments, again found itself eliminated, as it had been in 1894, when the teacher Dupin ran against Blanc, all the while attacking Gaston Polonais, editor in chief of *La Petite Gazette*, who supported the conservative Blanc. In *Le Courrier Républicain*, Dupin wrote, "Learn, O *Croix*, that Gaston Polonais, editor in chief of *La Petite Gazette* in Bagnères, is Jewish, as Jewish as can be. Yet he has been seen to thunder with all his might against those he calls the Freemasons of Bagnères and has appealed to the Catholics. Well, these good Catholics of Bagnères are bowing down at that appeal; they say they will vote for Blanc, thus giving the sad example of Catholic leaders marching hand in hand with the Jews, the worst enemies of our beliefs."[35] The republican left, which also did not recoil from prejudice-laden language, would finally take control of Bagnères with the 1902 election, when Ozun drew 11,929 votes and his new conservative opponent, Becq de Fouquières, only 5,250; each vied with the other to win over the Catholic electorate. Ozun vigorously affirmed, "I love the army. I love religion. In my family, everyone is Catholic." And Becq de Fouquières declared, "Look around the room: do you not see all those good and brave peasants, all of them Catholic, who love their religion?" He concluded with a ringing: "Stand aside for the French of France against the foreigner!"[36]

In Tarbes an electoral committee attached to the Union Nationale, whose secretary was Abbé Fontan, eagerly solicited the Catholic electorate. Along with Abbé Lafforgue and Abbé Tayan, he attempted to mobilize the Catholic electorate but had no great success, according to the police report.[37] In Tarbes as well, there were anti-Semitic rumblings during the May legislative elections. In the first ward, Léon Frulin ran as the "candidate of the workers" and loudly proclaimed a platform encapsulated as "equality and fraternity." On his election poster, he proposed a "revision of the Constitution of 1875 by a Constitutional Assembly stipulating that no one would have the right to hold public office if he did not prove that he had been French for at least four generations. The Jews ought to be excluded by law . . . We French are being squeezed and plundered by those stateless Jews who are strangling us." He then drifted toward locally essential proposals such as "In the interest of the livestock breeder, I will ask the stud farm administration that half the first-class licenses be saved for third-class mares. To reach that result, I will insist that the number of capable stallions be increased in the stud farm in Tarbes. I will also ask that the purchase of stallions take place in Tarbes, the center of production, instead of obliging the stock breeders to go to Toulouse, which is costly and dangerous . . . Long live the Republic of the workers!"

Leaving Tarbes and its environs and moving closer to the Atlantic Ocean, we reach Pau, a city that appeared to be dozing. The bulletin board, in the first months of 1898, reveals a very rich music scene: *Mignon*, *Carmen*, and the overture to *Die Meistersinger* were being offered, as were Aleksandr Borodin's *On the Steppes of Central Asia*, the overture to Hector Berlioz's *Les Francs-juges*, Richard Strauss's *Death and Transfiguration*, and Paul Vincent d'Indy's *Trilogie de Wallenstein*. In rehearsals were *The Barber of Seville*, *Faust*, and even Jacques Halévy's *The Jewess*. Other forms of musical expression were not neglected either, such as the Béarnaise melodies offered by the group Estudiantina Paloise. As far as theatrical plays were concerned, the spectator had far too many to choose from. Socially the coming weeks were expected to be thrilling: "Evening gowns, ball gowns, glittering or diaphanous, the season will be sparkling, and soirees and balls, concerts, fetes of all sorts, must follow one after another . . . A word on the neckline to be worn this winter: tight, very straight across the chest. The ball gowns are accompanied by heavy coats, also very luxurious."[38] The streets of Pau maintained their calm, and it was not until the night of the premiere of *Faust*, at the Grand Théâtre on March 28, that the first stir of anti-Semitism was audible. As he did everywhere in the region, Renaud d'Elissagaray, the anti-Semitic candidate in the legislative elections in Toulouse, gave a lecture: approximately a thousand people, according to *Le Mémorial des Pyrénées* (half that, according to the police), in Salle Chilo "cheered" his speech against "the cosmopolitan gangs." Though the arteries of Pau thereafter returned to their tranquil state, anti-Semitic prejudices spread. In mid-January *Le Mémorial des Pyrénées*, for example, the most influential newspaper in the region, launched a lively campaign against Dreyfus. On the fifteenth it claimed that Zola defended "Dreyfus, the holy of holies, the anointed of the chief rabbi, the big chief rabbi," and added, "Zola's frenzy shows the ravages of the Jews' actions in our French circles." On the twenty-first it inveighed, "There are truly two Frances today: the Christian France, the national France, and the other one . . . The politicking Jews, the flashy-looking Jews, the Jews without patriotism—for the good reason that they have no nation—hold the country under their boot heels." On February 3 *Le Mémorial* diagnosed the situation: "The Jews have remained in the state of a foreign tribe in our country . . . The Jews are, so to speak, stuck to the Republic. We Frenchmen do not want to be governed by a foreign tribe." Throughout the year the newspaper remained faithful to these convictions and conducted an anti-Semitic campaign in the Olorun ward, where future premier Louis Barthou was nonetheless victorious.[39] It had the support of its readers, one of whom sent the following message: "I am not a socialist, but if I had to choose between Yiddischry and socialism, I would choose socialism. As for the Jews, I execrate and despise them."[40] But here again, mixed feelings showed through: in the May legislative elections, the winner was de Gontaut-Biron, a royalist who had rallied to the Republic and was the friend of the "politicking abbots," according to *L'Avenir de Pau*, a republican newspaper that supported his opponent, Doleris, but he was also "the friend of the Jewified."[41]

In Bayonne anti-Semitic demonstrations in the streets were rare.[42] Like the Southwest as a whole, Bayonne was out of sync with the rest of the nation. Nothing noteworthy seems to have occurred inside the city walls unless perhaps one counts an impressive fire at the Saint-Louis-de-Gonzague Catholic high school on May 4, 1898, during which Father Dubourdieu distinguished himself by saving a large number of students. The fire caused a stir, and the local press gave it an enormous amount of coverage.[43] In February an incident had erupted during the election of Dr. Delvaille (who was also president of the consistory of a Jewish religious organization) to the council of the order of physicians. For the first time, a great number of members refused to vote for the man,

whom *La Semaine de Bayonne* criticized for his "utterly Hebrew modesty."
L'Avenir worried, "Is anti-Semitic unrest, which has been spared our city,
now going to manifest itself here?" Similarly, the Basque newspaper
L'Eskualduna, widely read in Bayonne, continually attacked Dreyfus and
the Jews of France, repeating, "Kick the Jews out"; it took care to translate the name *Dreyfus*—"three-footed," according to it—into the Basque
language, as *Hiru-Zango*. *La Semaine de Bayonne*, no laggard, had long spread
an intense anti-Semitism.[44] Not until June 14, 1899, did anti-Semitism
suddenly surface. During a reprise of military retreats set to music, a
crowd followed the soldiers. Shouts of "Long live the army!" reverberated. "For the rue Victor-Hugo, which contains Jews, the crowd reserved
the Hugolatrous cry 'Down with the Jews!' " That unexpected anti-
Semitic demonstration elicited a complaint to the mayor from the
Israelite consistory. To the fifteen hundred Jews in Bayonne, the demonstration came as only a partial surprise.

Bordeaux, capital of the Southwest and epicenter of triumphant radicalism, had been a symbol of the left since 1888. But Bordeaux joined
the anti-Semitic mobilization early on and in the legislative election gave
two wards to the nationalists, including one to the local leader of the
Ligue Antisémitique. The local press fanned anti-Semitism, particularly
the influential and royalist *Le Nouvelliste, Bordeaux-Journal* (the newspaper
of Catholics rallied to the Republic), and *La France de Bordeaux et du Sud-
Ouest* (a radical newspaper). The last-named wrote on November 6,
1894: "Spain got rid of the Jews in 1492, then the Jews of Portugal arrived in Bordeaux. They are as faithful to their beliefs as the day they arrived." Only *La Gironde* refrained from any excesses.[45] On January 14,
1898, *Le Nouvelliste* made fun of the "fit of delirium tremens of the
Jewified Zola." In a wrathful article entitled "Down with the Jews!" it
wrote, "Opportunism is the triumph of Jewry. The regime was created
by the Jews and for the Jews . . . Despite the warnings that were given
them, it pleased them to wage a fight to the death; defeated in the first
encounter, they now have the effrontery to continue it. We accept:
moreover, it is time to be done with it. Down with the Jews and long
live France." Every day on its front page, *Le Nouvelliste* pursued an anti-
Semitic campaign that quickly found a favorable response.[46]

Bordeaux thus entered the storm just as the weather itself was abruptly changing. For the first two weeks of 1898, the sun was still shining and everyone celebrated these beautiful, unexpected days. On January 15, however, "the darkness of the day barely allowed a glimpse of the sun through the thick fog." A heavy atmosphere settled on the city. That same day, the central superintendent alerted the prefect, "An anti-Semitic demonstration is to take place this evening, sponsored by the students. I am taking all measures useful for maintaining order . . . I discreetly warned Israelite store owners that it will be a good idea for them to close their establishments this evening."[47] No demonstration occurred, however—life went on. That night, after *Lakme* and *Lohengrin*, rehearsals for *Othello* began at the Grand Théâtre; the Bouffes Bordelaises celebrated the brilliant debut of Pi-Ouit, from the Folies Bergères in Paris; the Nouveau Théâtre put on a dramatization of Eugène Sue's *Les mystères de Paris*; and the Alcazar staged *Les pêcheurs de Venise*. In the public park could be heard Massenet's *Les Huguenots*, Carl Maria von Weber's *Oberon*, Signard's *Le vieux ménétrier*, and a polka for oboe. The next day, as the press reported in great detail the anti-Semitic demonstrations that were then igniting Paris, everything remained calm in the Bordeaux region: "On Sunday our fellow citizens took advantage of the exceptional weather to indulge in the pleasures of the traditional Sunday stroll."[48] The Arachon Lawn Club held its ball at the Grand Hôtel on Médoc road in Le Bouscat. In soccer Bordeaux faced the Toulouse team. At numerous balls "the salon chandeliers shone with the magical brilliance of electricity on the veils, spangled and embroidered with gold and beads . . . Fashion was all aglitter; the pretty spangled fan, which has become the elegant accessory of every ball gown, joined the party. Like so many twinkling stars in the hands of the pretty women, they cast a lovely reflection on their faces . . . One novelty on the evening gowns was the crosspiece of satin ribbons veiling the bodice and sewn onto the skirt at a certain height."

Things took a turn for the worse on the seventeenth, however. In the evening the variety shows were in full swing: *Les mystères de Paris* attracted a full house; Feydeau triumphed at the Théâtre des Arts in *Champignol malgré lui*; and "the fortune teller" Carlos Tchingo "performed remarkable feats of sleight-of-hand" at the Alcazar. In addition, "the Duffauts made everyone laugh with their Chinese duet 'Stam-Stam.'" The first concert of the Cercle Philharmonique took place in Salle Franklin, with Tartini's *The Devil's Trill* along with a mazurka by Chopin, then Berlioz's *La prise de Troie*, Fauré's *En prière*, and Saint-Saëns's *La cloche*. Twenty-one prostitutes, "debauched girls," languished at Saint-Jean hospital, and twelve others, accompanied by three children, spent a long night in jail. Meanwhile more than four hundred students left the place Magenta and headed toward the rue Sainte-Catherine, shouting, "Out with Zola! Out with the Jews!" Jostled by police on the place Saint-Project, some of them regrouped on the place de la Comédie and made their way through the cour de l'Intendance. They repeated their slogans on the place Magenta, the rue Cursol, and the rue des Trois-Conils. Outside the home of Charles Bernard, municipal councilor and future national-ist deputy, they shouted, "Long live Bernard! Down with the Jews!" Then, outside the offices of Raynal, near the allées de Tourny, they shouted, "Down with Raynal! Down with the Jews!"

In the barracks yard, the gendarmes on foot and the horsemen, their horses bridled and saddled, awaited orders. The police intervened. There were many wounded, and Officer Prévôt was seriously injured by a cane. Among those arrested were Jean Agard, twenty-five, a postal employee; Jean-Marie Mourra, twenty, a mechanic; Arthur Nicouleau, nineteen, a business employee; Hippolyte Fébrenon, twenty, a tapestry maker; and Ernest Milleroux, eighteen, a baker.

The next day, the eighteenth, "was beautiful but, toward evening, a thick fog descended on Bordeaux." People rejoiced that "the bullfighting rings in Bordeaux are going to be considerably enlarged. It is anticipated that next season will cause a sensation since the best swordsmen of Spain will parade in our new arena." In Salle Franklin people prepared to hear Joseph, Francis, and Jacques Thibaud, "sons and students of our distinguished professor Georges Thibaud." Students met in Salle de l'Athénée, while a thousand people, particularly employees and workers, gathered on the place de la Comédie. Via the place Puy-Paulin, the rue Castillon, and the rue de Cheverus, the demonstrators headed toward the synagogue, taking the rue des Trois-Conils, the rue du Loup, the rue Sainte-Catherine, the cours Victor-Hugo, the rue Sainte-Eulalie, and the rue Labirat, then left again via the rue Sainte-Catherine and were dis-persed by the police. "A clash occurred: fortunately the wall of horses did not give way, but for more than ten minutes, it was a terrible struggle, an effort, an enormous push on the part of the students and of the people who swelled their ranks." Once dispersed, the rioters regrouped on the place Saint-Projet; at the time they numbered more than a thousand. You could still hear "Out with the Jews!" "Outside the stores whose owners were believed to belong to the Israelite faith, people shouted ear-splitting screams." Several times the gendarmes on horseback passed back and forth through the cours de l'Intendance to disperse the demonstrators. The latter still shouted anti-Semitic slogans; some of them thought they recognized a Jew in a carriage and rushed at him. Fortunately, he was not a Jew, and "the traveler got off with only a fright." Among the people arrested were Jean Andrieux, twenty-two, a business employee; Pierre Lansarde, forty-five, a baby-wear manufac-turer; Louis Raynaud, seventeen, a barber; Paul Caudesaygues, seven-teen, a waiter; Lagrolet, eighteen, a waiter; and Pierre Fagardie, nineteen, a cabinetmaker.

On the nineteenth at the Grand Théâtre, *Les Huguenots* made a fa-vorable impression, "in spite of an accidental fall by the very brilliant Mlle Magliani and a rather careless production." At the Bouffes Borde-laises, audiences found amusement listening to "Elles en veulent." The Olympia and the Alcazar also provided entertainment. Meanwhile, a new upsurge of violence caused serious damage. At about eight-thirty a.m. on the place de la Comédie and the cours de l'Intendance, a group of "kitchen boys and pastry chefs, which swelled and swelled and swelled" in number, suddenly emerged. The group set off with the shout "To the synagogue!" Pursued by four gendarmes on horseback and about a hun-dred police officers, the group destroyed the windows of Nouvelles Galeries, whose owner was believed to be Jewish. (Two days later the owner's furious press release would be published in *Le Nouvelliste*: "I, sir, am simply French. I am also Catholic.") On the place de la Comédie, to curtail the ominous demonstration, eight more horsemen and two hun-dred officers were called in as reinforcements; they attacked the demon-strators, who scattered on the place des Quinconces, to get away from the horses. But the cavalry charges produced a general stampede. As people fled, a very dense fog descended on the city as a whole, hardly propitious for continuing demonstrations.[49]

On the twentieth at about six p.m., fifty pharmacy students joined two hundred students from other schools and, escorted by close to three thousand people, went to the rue Sainte-Catherine, where they clashed with officers. Regrouping on the rue Porte-Dijeaux, they shouted, "Down with the Jews!" Once more clashing with police, they reassembled on the rue Bouffard, still shouting the same slogans, and finally dispersed during a final police charge. It was not over, however: at about nine o'clock, an enormous crowd was loitering on the place de la Comédie and on the allées de Tourny. A demonstration formed, with shouts of "Out with Zola! Down with the Jews!" Until eleven-thirty, amid several thousand sympathizers and onlookers, the demonstrators repeatedly crisscrossed the streets, shouting, "Down with the Jews!" When they were dispersed, small groups gathered outside the synagogue, where the police pushed them back. They then returned toward the allées de Tourny, where the game continued. At that moment Delmas, the police superintendent, was struck several times with a cane, and his assailant, an unemployed waiter, was arrested. The superintendent in charge of peacekeeping operations observed that "the entire police staff was on its feet for four days, and at present the men could not be more exhausted." There were forty-seven arrests, including twenty-three students; three cabinet-makers, eighteen or nineteen years old; a nineteen-year-old painter; a twenty-year-old locksmith; a heating engineer, age twenty-nine; two law clerks, ages nineteen and thirty-two; a laboratory assistant, age twenty-nine; an accountant, age thirty; and two unemployed men, both twenty years old.

Worried, the chief rabbi, Lévy, wrote to the prefect: "Posters inciting hatred of the Israelites have just been put up in all the neighborhoods of the city. In the state of mind in which the population finds itself, such incitements could become dangerous and bring on serious trouble. We are taking the liberty of asking you to please give orders that these posters be removed . . . With confidence in your vigilance." In another letter to the police, a certain Cahen maintained that the incitements were "actual calls for civil war" and requested that the posters be removed, as had been done in Toulouse. The prefect responded: "Mr. Chief Rabbi, no legal purview authorizes me to have the posters you indicate removed. The police reports that have come to me note, in fact, that the incitements contained on the notice have up to now left the Bordeaux public indifferent." In that respect the prefect agreed with the chief of the gendarmerie who, in his report to Paris concerning the anti-Semitic demonstrations, maintained that "everything was limited to shouting, making a racket, and scuffles between the police and the demonstrators."[50]

The mayor, however, did not share their view and had an appeal plastered on the walls of the city and circulated in the press:

> My dear fellow citizens, for a few days now, the public peace has been disturbed by tumultuous demonstrations. Were they to continue, serious disorder could be the consequence. Slipping in among sincere demonstrators are usually shady gangs, whose only goal, unrelated to any political or patriotic feeling, is to take advantage of the incidents to engage in malicious or criminal acts. The duty of the municipality is to ensure peace for all, the safety of persons and of their homes . . . I entreat you, my dear fellow citizens, to return to the state of calm and dignity befitting free men. I count on you, on your public-spiritedness, on your dedication to honor and duty, on that old local good sense that our city has demonstrated so many times.

On the twenty-ninth, as thirteen hundred spectators attended the Grand Théâtre, fourteen hundred attended the Théâtre des Arts, nine hundred and fifty the Olympia, nine hundred the Bouffes Bordelaises, three hundred and fifty the Alcazar, and two hundred the Nouveau Théâtre, nearly three thousand people, including a large number of students, came to the hall of the Athénée to hear the star performers of anti-Semitism, Lucien Millevoye, the Parisian anti-Semitic leader, and Charles Bernard, general councilor and secretary of the Ligue Antisémitique de Bordeaux. Numerous and precise police reports describe how the evening unfolded. Bernard began by congratulating "the Bordeaux population, which has noisily demonstrated in the street its contempt for the cosmopolitans . . . At a time when France is in the grip of a handful of Jews . . . the people of Bordeaux" ought to listen to Millevoye, since "we do not want our country to remain in the hands of a band of people, who have come to France from Judea or elsewhere to make a fortune selling pornographic etchings and transparencies. It will not be said that the flag of the French Republic lies in the hands of cosmopolitans." As the frenzied assembly shouted, "Down with the Jews!"

Millevoye made every effort to demonstrate the international origin of the Dreyfus affair. Germany was trying to end the rapprochement between France and Russia and to divide the nation and weaken it. Speaking of Reinach, Zola, and the Dreyfusards, he exclaimed, "There are ropes and street lamps ready . . . Our names may be too modest, but they are more French than those of Reinach and Company . . . We wrote Reinach that we wish to know the color of his blood, but we see only that of his money." That peroration produced "three bursts of applause from the audience." As blows were exchanged with a few socialist and anarchist hecklers, applause thundered and cheers reverberated. When the meeting let out, a group of young people chanted the traditional slogans: "Out with Zola! Down with the Jews!" and attempted to form a procession. They were rapidly dispersed by the police.[51]

At last the anti-Semitic mobilization subsided. The city caught its breath; a police report observed that "the markets are well stocked. Active selling." In the flood of daily news, random events regained their importance: the theft of rabbits and pigeons on the rue Catros; of cigars on the cours d'Alsace-Lorraine; of two volumes of *Don Quixote de la Mancha* on the allée de Tourny; of three lambs from the slaughterhouse; of forty-six bottles of wine and liquor on the rue Judaïque; of chickens and a rooster on the quai Deschamps; of nightingales on the cours Saint-Jean; of white pigeons on the rue de Rome; of shirts on display belonging to Mlle Lévy, a haberdasher on the rue Michel-Montaigne; as well as nighttime assaults and battery; begging offenses; arrests of "debauched girls"; and other minor acts of delinquency. Prejudices continued to be expressed nevertheless, and the legislative election campaign launched new agitation. *Le Nouvelliste* supported all the candidates who did battle with "the Opportuno-Masonic and Jewish coterie of Bordeaux," in particular Albert Chiché, the incumbent deputy in the first ward. In the second ward, it backed Charles Bernard, the dynamic chairman of the local Ligue Antisémitique who had once been editor in chief of *La Victoire de la Démocratie*, a Blanquist newspaper; Bernard "called himself a socialist but rejected collectivism with allegiances to international Jewry." Finally in the third ward, it supported the fiery Colonel de Vitré. *Le Nouvelliste* was delighted with the "Bordeaux pact," which united royalists, radicals, and certain socialists through a common rejection of Opportunist power, and it denounced the unnatural alliance between the Opportunist leaders and certain collectivists: "They are held together by Jewry and Freemasonry." *La Petite Gironde* maintained, on the contrary, that "the red rose and the white rose* are united fraternally, like the two sister stalks of the clerical rosebush." *La Gironde* condemned that "monstrous coalition bringing together, under the banner of the Sacred Heart, all the royalists, a few misguided radicals, the mass of clericals, and former Bonapartists who have not lost their rough edges and who, as Boulangists in 1889 and as socialists or nationalists in 1898, are quite simply former narrow-minded militarists who have cut off the tails of their legendary redingotes to turn them into revolutionary *carmagnole* jackets." *La Démocratie* also denounced those strange "Siamese twins," maintaining that "unlike what is happening in other cities of France, Bordeaux has the sad privilege of seeing disparate alliances forming," which explained the strong nationalist impulse.[52] *La France* reveled in that pact, as did *Bordeaux-Journal*, which launched a resounding "Appeal to the Catholics": "We believe we should point out to the Catholic voters the shameless maneuvering of Opportuno-Jewish society against [nationalist candidate] Albert Chiché." It was also through that newspaper that Cardinal Lacot, archbishop of Bordeaux, sent a letter to the clergy: "We are interested, out of the purest feeling of patriotic love, in requesting from Heaven good elections for France as a whole."[53] In reality, that altogether exceptional coalition ran an electoral campaign that provoked anti-Semitic incidents.

Let us set aside capricious candidates such as J.-G. Rouleau, who, on enormous colored election posters, denounced "the entire Jewish gang at Nouvelles Galeries, that whole gang of Kikes that has held court at the café de Bordeaux . . . They must be driven out, since that vermin, which was once penned up, tends only to propagate itself and to lead to our decay. Long live the nationalist Republic." To understand the role of anti-Semitic incidents, we need only follow the electoral campaign of three stars of nationalism: Bernard, Chiché, and Vitré, the first two being elected without difficulty. Bernard's dizzying campaign hit the ground running. On two occasions he "declared himself anti-Jewish but not anti-Israelite, wanting to make war not on a religion but on a race": first on January 19, at the Touge tobacco shop, in front of cemetery em-

*The red rose and the white rose: the socialists and the royalists.—trans.

ployees and laborers; and again on January 27, in Salle Solo on the quai de la Douane, before about a hundred people who, according to a police report, "are allied with the working class." Deriding his opponent, Gruet, as "not Jewish but Jewified," Bernard maintained that "the question of the workers' internationalism does not frighten him; that of the cosmopolitan Jews is more troubling." On February 3 on the rue Mouneyra, he was asked to better distinguish the Jew from the "Kike," and he responded that it was "only the money-grubbing Jews" whom he called "Kikes." He would nevertheless make "war on the Jews, who do not have callused hands and belong to a foreign race and are associated with the Dreyfus syndicate." Several times "he thundered against the Jews and spoke out against their pretension to become the masters of France": on February 13, in Talence, in the Plume-la-Poule neighborhood; on the twenty-first, in front of three hundred people, in the establishments of La Cape; on March 5, in the hall of the Athénée; on the tenth, on the chemin Dupuch; and finally on April 3, before six hundred people on the rue Villeneuve, again in Talence. On both April 21 in Le Bouscat and on April 23 at the school on the rue Dupaty, before nearly three thousand people at the port of Bordeaux, he attacked the Jew Pereire, whose port of Pouillac monopolized the unloading of merchandise at the expense of Bordeaux. On several occasions he accused *La Gironde* of being the ally of the Jews and the Germans: on April 29, to four hundred people assembled in the school on the rue Pelegrin; on the thirtieth, at Arlac school, to eight hundred people, including many workers; on May 3, on the rue Solférino, to eight hundred people; and finally, on May 6, at the Saint-Augustin school. On May 7, during a large meeting at the Athénée that attracted two thousand people, he "declared [himself] the opponent of the department stores, the big bazaars that belong only to Jews," and concluded, "Citizens, let us all shout: Down with the Jews! Long live the social Republic of clean hands! Long live the Bordeaux pact!" On May 8, at the Athénée, he again referred to himself as an anti-Semite, and the crowd accompanied him back to his home to cries of "Bernard's the one we need." He spoke on the fifteenth in Talence and on the seventeenth at the school on the rue d'Arlac, before eleven hundred people. On the nineteenth he held a meeting in front of four hundred people at the Saint-Augustin school. Meanwhile *Le Nouvelliste* maintained that "all the Jews in the second ward are conducting a bitter campaign against Bernard, as if it were a matter of saving Dreyfus and Zola." He finished off his campaign on the twenty-first, on the eve of the second round, in the hall of the Athénée, in front of five hundred people who were stirred by emotion and who frequently applauded as he repeatedly attacked his opponent Gruet, "the infamous Jew."[54]

Chiché's campaign was just as dizzying and resolute. Several times "he took to task the Jews, who have only one goal—to become the masters of France—and demanded social laws to protect the workers": on April 15, in the school on the rue du Jardin-Public, in front of eight hundred people; on the twenty-third, before nine hundred people in the school on the rue Pelegrin; on the twenty-eighth, in front of a thousand people in the hall on the rue Tresareru; and on the thirtieth, in the school on the rue Croix-de-Leguey, before three hundred people. People shouted the classic "Down with the Jews!" and the spectators triumphantly accompanied him home, shouting, "Down with the Jews! Chiché's the one we need." Chiché declared in his peroration that "all races have the same value; men are equal; the Jews must be equal and not our masters; Jewish domination must be rejected." Several times he thanked the voters of Bacalan who, by supporting his candidacy, had pronounced themselves against "the exploiters, the Jews, the Dreyfus gang, and *La Gironde*."[55] The campaign of Colonel de Vitré, who capitalized on the quarrels between the other two candidates, also attracted a large audience, galvanized by *Le Nouvelliste*, which on May 6 published an appeal signed by a number of joiners, hatters, engravers, grocers, lithographers, coopers, butchers, employees, landowners, and merchants. On the seventh it ran another appeal: "Stand back, you stateless people! Make room for the true friends of the workers!" It was signed by a new list of joiners, soldiers, cooks, stonecutters, cobblers, fitters, soap makers, carters, smiths, ironmasters, carpenters, typographers, waiters, sawyers, bakers, accountants, packers, farmers, gardeners, and so on. The newspaper urged conservatives and Catholics not to vote for the collectivists, who "are held together by Jewry and Freemasonry." In his platform statement, Vitré wrote, "A vote for me means: Stand back, cosmopolitanism, stand back, Jews and Jew sympathizers! Long live France for the French!" He too held many public meetings. On April 1, to a thousand people at the Théâtre des Menuts, he declared himself both anti-Jewish and anticlerical, both a constitutional royalist and a republican. On March 26 at the Petit Matelot on the avenue Thiers, he declaimed, "It is you the people, you alone, who foiled the appalling plot of the cosmopolitans, the Freemasons, and the Jews! May honor be paid you!"

Vitré was nevertheless defeated. Jourde, the publicly disgraced socialist, won decisively. Following the second round, on May 23, before twelve hundred people gathered at the Nouveau Théâtre, Vitré repeated his anti-Semitic and nationalist diatribes. After achieving an unprecedented success in the first round, Bernard was two votes shy of the majority needed to avoid a run-off. When the president of the election bureau announced the run-off election, anger and indignation erupted: shouts of "Down with the thieves! Down with the Jews!" "Silence, gentlemen!" shouted the president as the crowd repeated, "Down with the Jews! Down with the thieves! Down with the Opportunists!"[56] Bernard was elected in the second round. A police report observed that, at the school on the rue d'Arlac, which was very favorable to Bernard, "the workers came in great number this morning; there were also many priests and monks; the Franciscans from the rue de Pessac voted in twos every few minutes."[57] Bernard was cheered by thousands of people, who waited for him outside the town hall while, as *Le Nouvelliste* reported, a large crowd welcomed him with open arms, escorting his car along the rue Montbazon, the cours d'Albret, and the cours Cicé, and shouting, "Long live Bernard! Down with the thieves! Down with the Opportunists! Down with the Jews!" Thanking his voters from the balcony of his home, near the section of Arlac where he had received few votes, he presented himself as the defender of the humble, asking the crowd to repeat after him: "Long live the honest and liberal Republic! Down with the Jews! Down with the thieves!"

Chiché also won, with 7,805 votes to his opponent Chaumet's 6,886, and thousands of their supporters ran up and down the city, but a heavy rain limited the size of the demonstration, which the police kept under close surveillance. *Le Nouvelliste* noted that "the Opportunists, being cautious people, and especially the Jews, have avoided making themselves conspicuous."[58] In the days that followed, receptions to honor Chiché and Bernard were offered in countless halls, where both men declared that they intended to take their seats among the new group of anti-

Semitic nationalists. The celebrants joyfully raised their glasses, gave their heroes long ovations, and cheered, accompanied by the usual slogans. On the walls of the city appeared this "Great Lamentation: The Electoral Crime of Place Mériadeck":

> GOOD PEOPLE OF LA ROUSSELLE,
> OF TALENCE AND OTHER SITES,
> COME HEAR OF THE ODIOUS CRIME
> THAT, IN ITS CRUEL AUDACITY,
> WAS COMMITTED BY A SCOUNDREL
> MORE CRIMINAL THAN MARAT!
>
> IN BORDEAUX, THE METROPOLIS,
> THERE LIVED A GOODLY MAN,
> FRIEND OF THE JEWS, A GOOD CHRISTIAN,
> WHO SOLD OIL RETAIL,
> ODORLESS OIL, APPARENTLY
> RECOMMENDED BY ROTHSCHILD.
>
> GRUET WAS THE NAME HE BORE,
> DRESSED LIKE AN ENGLISH LORD
> MORE SMASHING THAN FÉLIX FAUR'!
> HIS BEARD WAS DELIGHTFUL,
> AND HE KNEW—HERE'S THE PITFALL—
> HOW TO WEAR A MONOCLE IN HIS EYE!
>
> THE OTHER DAY, IT WAS A SUNDAY,
> THE TWENTY-SECOND IN THE MONTH OF MAY,
> BREATHING THE FRAGRANT AIR,
> SNIFFING THE WIND, HAND ON HIS HIP,
> FOR HYGIENE'S SAKE, HE WALKED ABOUT,
> THE EXCELLENT MR. GRUET.

AS CHANCE WOULD HAVE IT, HIS STROLL

LED HIM IN THE PARCHED WEATHER

TO THE CORNER OF MÉRIADECK!

OH LORD, WHAT A SICK MAN HE IS,

FOR THE MURDERER IMMEDIATELY

APPEARED INCOGNITO.

HE WAS A VERY SHORT MAN,

ROBUST AND VERY BROAD-BACKED,

VALIANT AND VERY WELL BUILT;

BERNARD IS HOW HE WAS NAMED.

COMING UP TO THE WALKER,

HE TOLD HIM: DON'T BE AFRAID!

I AM NOT A CUTTHROAT,

I AM A PHARMACIST FROM THE CORNER

TO SERVE YOU IF NEED BE.

I WANT ONLY YOUR SASH,

OH, AND YOUR MEDAL AS WELL.

HAND THEM OVER WITHOUT A WORRY!

THE COMMON PEOPLE MUST

FINALLY BE REPRESENTED,

I MUST BE A DEPUTY.

TO DISSIMULATE HIS CRIME,

THAT BERNARD, INFERNAL CREATURE,

PUT THE BODY IN A JAR

LIKE A MINUSCULE FETUS,

HERMETICALLY SEALED IT

WITH NO FEAR OF PUNISHMENT!

DESPITE HIS CRAFTINESS,

THE GUILTY MAN WAS ARRESTED.

BUT IN THE MAJORITY,

TO THE STRAINS OF THE RUSSIAN HYMN,

THE GREAT JUDGE POPULO

RENDERED THE ODDEST VERDICT.

BY EIGHT THOUSAND AND FIFTY VOTES,

HE CONDEMNED WITHOUT DELAY,

THE ACCUSED MAN CHARLES BERNARD,

WHO HAD SUCH A SHOCKING ATTITUDE,

TO FIVE YEARS OF DETENTION

IN THE CHAMBER OF THE PALAIS-BOURBON.

MORAL

LITTLE SCHOOLCHILDREN,

YOU PARENTS, AND FOLKS FROM AROUND HERE,

LEARN FROM THIS TALE

THAT OIL MERCHANTS MUST,

ACCORDING TO THE ANCIENTS,

BEWARE OF PHARMACISTS.[59]

Thenceforth the streets of Gironde's capital remained calm, with the exception of a final outburst of public anti-Semitism on July 23, at the funeral of the rector Couat. A crowd of about fifteen thousand people surrounded the rectorate building on the cours d'Albret, the rue Dauphine, the avenue d'Arès, and the place Saint-Bruno. With General Varaigne, commander in chief of the Eighteenth Army Corps, in attendance, Paul Stapfer, the dean of the school of letters, praised the deceased for his Dreyfusard sentiments. This produced outrage. Many professors from the school of letters and sciences protested. On the twenty-eighth the minister of public education suspended the audacious Stapfer (to whom the noted sociologist Emile Durkheim, to the great anger of *Le Nouvelliste*, offered public support), for which he was rewarded by becoming in turn the target of an anti-Semitic disturbance. Again, on January 11, 1899, as Stapfer was about to give a private lecture, shouts immediately erupted: "Long live the army! Down with the Jews!" Protected by the police, the former dean returned home, where a few student supporters surrounded him. A larger group spilled out one last time onto the cours Victor-Hugo and the rue Sainte-Catherine, shouting, "Long live the army! Down with the Jews!" before being dispersed, one last time, on the place Saint-Projet.[60]

To be sure, as in Caudéran, Bègles, Blaye, and Arcachon, anti-Semitic posters still covered the walls from time to time, but not enough to launch new demonstrations. Nevertheless, *La Citadelle Blayaise* supported Bernard and Chiché: "We want to participate, as much as our strength allows, in ridding the Republic of the Jewish leeches and Opportunist bugs that, for too long, have sucked the purest of its blood. Long live the Republic! The committee of workers of Blayais."[61] In Blaye as well, a handwritten poster proclaimed, "A so-called clerical peril must not make us forget another, very real one. It is true that the convents possess the colossal fortune of 500 million francs, but that sum is distributed among 150,000 individuals, which comes to about 3,400 francs apiece. But Rothschild on his own possesses 10 billion, almost as much as 3 million monks and nuns. Add to that the billions of Camondo and Hirsch,* and those of the Jew-sympathizing Christians, and you will say: where is the most pressing peril? Long live France for the French!"[62] Similarly, *Le Médocain* wrote, "When the brass, the leather, the coffee, the sugar, and the wheat are monopolized by the big Kikes, the Frenchman pays a slightly higher price for his shoes, his coffee, his sugar, and his bread." After a meeting in Caudessan with Duperier, a candidate in the legislative elections, the newspaper commented: "M. Duperier, because he did not reply to any of the questions asked him, is convicted by his own silence. M. Duperier refused to support Paul Déroulède's letter regarding the review of the traitor Dreyfus's case. M. Duperier is thus a Jew sympathizer who has made common cause with the enemies of the

*Camondo and Hirsch: Jewish financiers, like the Rothschilds.—trans.

army and of France. Further, he is the friend and protégé of the Jew Raynal. Down with Duperier."[63] In Bazas as well, because Halphen managed to attract a large number of votes in the 1898 municipal elections, Le Nouvelliste wrote, "Isaac placed his money at 90 percent interest." Later, in 1901, during the cantonal election of Captieux, there was a local revolt against "that rich Parisian Israelite who sees the voters only as a commodity." The election unleashed considerable anti-Semitic violence, even if it did not translate into demonstrations.[64] As we leave Bordeaux, the violence—but not the prejudices—gradually vanishes. The storm abates as we head north toward calm Charente-Maritime. Libourne, for example, hardly allowed itself to be drawn into the chaos of Bordeaux, somewhat the way La Rochelle, compared to Nantes, remained an oasis of peace.[65]

Chapter Six

Take Arms, Citizens of Vendée!

In rural, Catholic, and conservative Vendée, so long opposed to the Republic and still marked by the opposition of white Anjou, land of the irascible Monsignor Freppel, anti-Semitism rumbled (almost effacing this ancient cleavage) and nearly ignited the city of Angers, which had once looked "blue."* From Anjou to the heart of Vendée, an entire region of Pays de la Loire, now almost unified, rose up in a nationalist frenzy. A police superintendent from Nantes warned Paris, "The anti-Semites are not going to focus their efforts solely in the department of Loire-Inférieure; they have a broader ambition. Above all they want to address the population of Vendée and, under the cover of anti-Semitism and patriotism, awaken their profoundly Catholic feelings in order to use them against the Republic."[1] On January 19 a procession of students formed on the rue Chaussée-Saint-Pierre in Angers, shouting, "Out with Zola! Long live the army! Down with the Jews!" At the theater they attacked the director, who was Jewish, as well as Cahen, owner of La Grande Maison. Then, via the rue Saint-Martin, they gathered at

*Blue: color of the republicans.—trans.

the newspaper *Le Patriote*, whose director, Raphaël Hennecart, "was allegedly an Israelite," and proceeded to the boulevard de Saumur to cheer the army outside the military club. Approximately six hundred people passed through the rue d'Alsace, the place du Ralliement, the rue Lenepveu, the rue des Poëliers, the rue Bodinier, and the rue de la Roë, headed toward the rue Saint-Laud and the rue de l'Aiguillerie, and finally came to the carrefour Rameau, shouting with increasing frequency, "Death to the Jews!" The procession continued through the rue Plantagenêt and the rue de la Parcheminerie, the place de la République, the rue Saint-Evroult, the place Marguerite-d'Anjou, the rue Denis-Papin, the rue des Lices, and the rue Voltaire, ending its long journey on the place du Ralliement while constantly shouting the same slogans in that usually peaceful city. The next day, January 20, a new procession formed, led by "three individuals wearing ecclesiastical costumes," and rapidly grew to four thousand people. As on the other evenings, it took the main arteries; the crowd again shouted, "Out with Zola! Down with the Jews! Death to the Jews! Long live the army!" "Hooligans" led the demonstration; stones were thrown at stores (often pieces of schist from the nearby slate quarries) owned by Jewish tradespeople. Line troops—a company from the 135th requested by the central superintendent—intervened to put an end to these "excesses," even though "the people did not understand how they could be shoved around by the army." At about ten p.m., a group invaded the gare Saint-Laud, and to shouts of "Out with Zola! Down with the Jews!" its members "set fire to copies of *Le Figaro* in the courtyard." Again at midnight, when the theater let out, shouts of "Down with Zola! Down with the Jews!" erupted.

On the twenty-first between four and five thousand people assembled on the place du Ralliement and in the adjacent streets, while the three priests observed earlier again proved to be very active. In the courtyard of the Ecole des Arts, students repeated the same shouts in a chorus. Several young men were arrested and others received citations for "disturbing the peace." On the twenty-second nearly two thousand demonstrators again crisscrossed the streets of Angers. On the afternoon of the twenty-third, Cahen and Crémieux, downtown merchants, received the following message: "My dear little Cahen, for your own sake, I recommend that you close at noon tomorrow, Sunday, because I believe that your windows will no longer be standing at three o'clock. We drew lots to see who would do it. I'm the one, and I swear to you that I will do it without fail. Prison does not frighten me, since I feel I will have done my duty as a Frenchman. And my three hundred friends who are behind me would do it if I did not. I can warn you that you must expect tomorrow, at about two o'clock, a large anti-Jewish demonstration. Take advantage of it; you see, we will not take you by surprise. A word to the wise. [Signed:] The executor of the committee of anti-Jewish employees." That evening several hundred demonstrators went to the place du Ralliement, with particularly high participation by the members of the Catholic club. "A number of hooligans" and workers from the Trélazé quarries were noticed there as well. A few hours later more than fifteen hundred people were protesting.[2] Other anti-Semitic mobilizations erupted in Cholet and Saumur, where conscripts and other demonstrators shouted, "Down with Zola! Down with the Jews! Long live the army!" The unrest affected even the smallest villages: in La Romagne, near Cholet, about a hundred people paraded "for the army and against the Jewish syndicate," finally burning an effigy representing Zola, as was done in so many other localities.[3] On January 23 in Ancenis, day students from the secondary school shouted the same slogans. The newspaper La Vendée congratulated them: "Ancenis was again spared the invasion of the Kikes; along its journey, the young band did not run into any Jewish stores. A word of congratulations to the young students."[4]

Angers, a city with a population of 77,164 that was led for two years by a republican municipal council, thus experienced anti-Semitic and nationalist demonstrations that for several days attracted between two thousand and five thousand people. They invaded the narrow arteries of the city and tirelessly passed through them in all directions, in the silence of the night. It is hard to understand how Le Patriote could congratulate itself on the absence of unrest in Anjou and write that the residents "are moderate people with a friendly spirit."[5] In the Maine-et-Loire department, which counted no more than some hundred Jews, the press as a whole—with a few hesitations by the republican Le Patriote de l'Ouest, which was caught between the defense of its ideas and the need to keep its readership—slipped into anti-Dreyfusism and anti-

Semitism. There was a difference, *Le Patriote* maintained, between "murdering the Jew passing in the street like the first dog you come across and letting the Jews infiltrate our general staff and get hold of the banks."[6] In reality, even after the September 1899 Rennes trial, "there was no newspaper" that displayed the belief that Captain Dreyfus was innocent.[7] *L'Indépendance*, the newspaper of the radical-socialists, was very isolated, explicitly condemning, on January 23, 1898, "the bashing endured by the Jews." The republican newspaper *Le Petit Courrier*, which struggled against the region's omnipotent right wing, nevertheless celebrated, on May 12, 1898, the failure in the legislative election of the "Dreyfusard Yid Reinach." *Le Petit Courrier d'Angers*, also a self-proclaimed republican paper, nonetheless demonstrated a keen attachment to Catholicism, writing on January 29: "The Jew, the cosmopolitan, second-rate Jew, engages in usurious lending practices against the Arab. He lives like a rat in the garrets and sewers, gnawing, devouring everything he can get his teeth into." The newspaper remained true to this vision of the world on February 23, when it maintained that "France is invaded by the cosmopolitan vermin, which is trying to gnaw away at it"; and on August 20, when it denounced the petitions supporting a review of the case, distributed "in a hypocritical form to tempt the peasants." It opposed Zola's letter to the president of the Republic "in support of the Jew on Devil's Island" and declared, "All good Frenchmen now have only to cry in chorus the energetic response, and that response is: Shit." On November 5 it exclaimed, "With what tenacity all-powerful Jewry seeks to exonerate the modern Judas!" In its view, then, the slogans "for the Republic" and "against the parasitical Jews" were not contradictory.[8]

If the role of the Catholics in these demonstrations has been clearly established, the role played by a number of republicans, in newspapers open to anti-Semitic prejudices, is no less clear. "For the first time since the Revolution," observed one historian, "the citizens of Angers, republicans and monarchists, seemed to consider their membership in the French nation more important than their political differences; that reconciliation could take place only because the two camps had discovered a common enemy: the Jews."[9] In August a strange hunt was staged: people were hunting Zola as if he might be in Maine-et-Loire. This poster appeared on the walls of Angers: "In search of Zola . . . who might have taken refuge in the department: 59 years old, about 1 meter 70, slightly stooped, graying hair, thinning on the neck, large, somewhat elongated head, bony face."[10]

The following notice appeared in the streets:

LONG LIVE THE CHURCH

LONG LIVE THE SLAUGHTERERS OF THE JEWS

LONG LIVE LOYOLA

LONG LIVE THE INQUISITION[11]

In April 1898 other signs, with the title "The Nation in danger! The Jewish peril," alerted the residents: "We have had the monopolization of wheat and of brass, and we have had Panama. It is done. Poor France! The Jews have monopolized everything. Universal Yiddishry! Down with the syndicates, the Jews, the traitors!"[12] A royalist poster emphasized that "monarchy is divine in essence: it is for that reason that the Jews, through the organ of Freemasonry, deny the history of France prior to the Revolution . . . With the king, God was the base of power; with the Republic, it is everyone and no one. How powerful the people are, then, who let themselves be cheated, looted, murdered by 28,000 masons, the instruments and slaves of 60,000 Jews! . . . There is darkness, a cataclysm; the Republic itself is howling at death. A sword appears out of that chaos, and like Joan of Arc standing on her mount, the one holding it shouts: 'Onward! Onward! They are ours.' It is the king of France . . . Let us follow him, for God and for France."[13]

Intransigent Catholicism favored a social plan that would integrate the workers into French society but exclude the Jews; Abbé Bosseboeuf based his candidacy for the legislative elections on this plan. In 1894 the Notre-Dame-des-Champs Society, a group of Catholic adult and youth clubs from which followers of Christian socialism were recruited, exerted an unquestionable influence on working-class families by providing care for their children. Many public meetings were held, during which people supported Abbé Lemire and priests denounced "the law of money, which has overtaken religious law. It is the fight between the fat people and the skinny people . . . We cannot resemble the Jews, who are seizing our wealth . . . They are strong thanks to their capital, their union, and their hatred of the Christians, but they lack local capabilities."[14] Every year these clubs organized a pilgrimage from Anjou to Lourdes. In 1896 and 1897, the Catholic group that distributed *L'Usine et l'Atelier*, a bulletin whose motto was "For God, for France, and for the workers," was active in Angers, attracting crowds of fifteen thousand to ceremonies held in front of churches. Abbé Segrétain addressed a forceful message particularly to the workers and called for laws against the money-grubbers, against the "Jews, who are to be feared." "France will become stronger provided that Christian principles are not stamped out."[15] Near Angers in August 1898, the pilgrimage to the Field of Martyrs, a memorial for Catholics killed during the French Revolution, organized by Abbé Segrétain, took place. The ceremony was presided over by Monsignor de Kernaëret, and five hundred people chanted the canticle "Hope of France: Workers, Let Us Be Christians." Abbé Segrétain declared on that occasion that "if the religious struggles resurface, as everything suggests they will," he hoped that all good Catholics would do as their fathers had done and passionately defend their flag and their faith. "France is divided into two camps," he said, "and the frightening thing is that the larger camp is the one opposed to our ideas; so, my dear friends, we must make an effort to bring as many as possible who have gone astray back to our Holy Mother the Church, the eldest daughter of France."[16] In the same vein, *Le Journal du Maine-et-Loire* said people faced a choice between "a Republic where the Freemasons, the Jews, and the freethinkers occupy all the offices, and an honest government where children would be brought up as Christians."[17] That large local newspaper warned that "even though we live under majority rule and the Jews constitute only a tiny minority in the nation, they have been placed everywhere. Out of hatred for the Catholics, they have been called to the highest and most varied offices. They populate our higher administrations."[18] Similarly, students in the philosophy class of the private Mongazon secondary school in Angers published a declaration in *La Libre Parole* protesting "against the Jews, slanderers of the army" and committing themselves to defend a Christian society.[19]

In Angers as in Lorraine, in Bordelais as in Bouches-du-Rhône, the campaign for the legislative elections aggravated prejudices. Abbé Bosseboeuf ran in the first ward of Angers by rallying a large reactionary following behind him. Although he was one of the rare conservative candidates defeated in the second round in the department, he nevertheless attracted 8,816 votes with his violently anti-Semitic and nationalist platform; Jean Joxé, the republican candidate, won with 11,429 votes. In early May, during countless public meetings, Abbé Bosseboeuf presented himself as "a child of the land [and] made himself the defender of the farmers but also of the working class." He declared himself a "patriot," condemned Dreyfus, and denounced "the perfidious Jews." *La Croix Angevine* celebrated the impact of Bosseboeuf's words, which, in Saint-Lezin, for example, held "the very respectful and very kind attention of four to five hundred quarry workers."[20] On May 1 *La Croix Angevine* held a meeting at the circus theater in Angers that attracted two thousand people. On May 2 eighteen hundred again crowded into the circus theater to listen to him; hecklers, and especially anarchists, made their presence known with loud interruptions that left the abbot impassive. A police superintendent noted that "he crossed his arms over his chest and lifted his eyes to heaven. 'The Holy Spirit is about to descend!' a voter screamed. 'There is certainly a need for it,' Bosseboeuf retorted." The same day he conducted a meeting at Sept Sonnettes, on the route de Paris and, in front of that smaller audience, declared "that the Church [recommends] praying for the perfidious Jews, that the Jew [sells] everything for money. The Jew is a traitor out of atavism. As a priest, I could have only words of forgiveness toward them, but as a deputy, I would call for laws putting the country out of reach of these traitors, foreigners to the nation and to our race."[21] In an interminable platform statement entitled "My Program," he wrote, "Every day the foundations of our social edifice are furiously attacked by a band of sectarians who seem to wish to tear it down at any cost and to bury us under its ruins. Jews, Freemasons, the stateless, and the revolutionaries pursue us with both their implacable hatred and their perfidious attacks." He asked for the freedom to choose between parochial and secular teachers for the schools; condemned divorce; defended the army and "working-class interests"; and attacked "Jewish and antipatriotic corruption."[22] On May 14 he received the support of Abbé Lemire, who sent this letter to him, published by *La Croix Angevine*: "You are valiantly struggling to show that the priests are in the service of their country. The voters of Angers have confidence in you. I intensely hope we can work together in Parliament and, through our devotion, bring the Church and French society closer together." The same day *La Vérité* declared, "The duty of Catholics is wholly spelled out by the circumstances. In all conscience they cannot excuse themselves from doing everything to attain the success of the candidacy of Abbé Bosseboeuf."

Among the other conservative candidates was Baron Le Guay, who engaged in a sharp polemic with the Freemasons. Let us get a real taste for that polemic. Le Guay wrote in his platform statement, "Now a band of Jews and Freemasons is seeking to drag the French army, as admirable in its devotion as in its discipline, through the mud." The response from the Freemasons merits quotation:

> Mr. Baron, we have attentively read and reread your circular. You deign to write, Mr. Baron, that a band of Jews and Freemasons is seeking to drag our army through the black mud. In that, you are, knowingly or unconsciously, doing a bad deed. We give you the Jews—money-grubbers and shirkers whom we care nothing about; but as for the Freemasons, we dispute the validity of your slander. The Freemasons, Mr. Baron, are patriots, and they claim to be so as much as you . . . You are wrong, Mr. Baron, to place under suspicion people you don't know. They might reply that there are many barons among the Jews and very few among the Freemasons. They might further tell you that dukes, marquises, counts, and barons are not above restoring their family fortunes by marrying Jewesses. For them, does money save one's origins? [Signed:] The Freemasons of the lodge Labor and Perfection of Angers."[23]

In the face of that reply, the baron did not hesitate to proclaim once again, "A band of Jews and Freemasons is attacking the army and our safety. Is that not true? Are not all the members of the Dreyfus syndicate Jews and Freemasons? . . . If their entire program were to be carried out, we would see the sanctuaries where so many aged workers and orphans find refuge disappear from Angers." In the first round, Le Guay earned 4,231 votes, Bosseboeuf 5,147, and Mitonneau 1,653. Mitonneau ran under the socialist label, but as a police report noted, he did not shirk from "making nice with the reactionaries and the clericals while also knowing how to flatter the workers." According to another report, he had "a real influence in working-class circles. Like Bosseboeuf, [Mitonneau] engages in 'Christian socialism.' [He] will be able to bring together a very respectable minority, at least in terms of numbers, including reactionaries alongside the purely working-class vote." He announced his candidacy in 1897 at a socialist banquet where he professed internationalism and adherence to the socialist platform of the town of Saint-Mandé, before abruptly breaking that ambiguous commitment. During a large socialist meeting in Angers, the Parisian socialist deputy Paul Chauvière attacked the three enemies threatening modern society, namely "Caesar, Shylock, and Loyola." Shylock was the embodiment of "the Jew, that is, Rothschild, the golden calf before which they all prostrate themselves, because he holds the power of money." "Our soldiers," added Chauvière, "are not slaves parading under the eye of a Dreyfus who will betray them tomorrow." The second round might have gone well for Bosseboeuf, who seemed capable of surviving it, but, as the police superintendent emphasized, "Baron Le Guay displayed a certain bitterness regarding Bosseboeuf. Many of the baron's friends are aristocrats, who do not consider Bosseboeuf part of their 'world.' " Like the bishop of Angers, they rejected "that ecclesiastic unknown to the diocese, always in the way, an apostle of Christian socialism." From then on it was all over for Bosseboeuf. Part of Baron Le Guay's electorate went over to the republican Joxé in the second round. Joxé was easily elected by that heterogeneous coalition, especially since, in his platform statement, the mayor of Angers had written, "I will defend with all my energy the French nation and our faithful army against the odious maneuvering that makes trouble in the region, that disrupts business, and that my Lorrainian heart reprobates and highly condemns."[24]

Accommodations with republican ideas were necessary in this case, given that the Pays de la Loire region remained profoundly conservative. In the arrondissements of Cholet and Segré, as the prefect's office noted, "the voters have such an allegiance to the lords of the manor that, as yet, no serious republican candidate dares wage battle. The mass of rural voters is under the complete domination of the large property owners." Hence in the first ward of Cholet in the Anjou region, Jules Baron, the openly reactionary incumbent deputy, won with 10,600 of the 18,169 votes cast. In his platform statement, he declared, "Does it not seem to diminish the moral greatness of France to continue to refuse religion its legitimate share of influence in society? . . . The current of public opinion—which in France is increasing every day—against the interference of the foreigner has not escaped any of you. The country, which has lost so much of its savings as a result of the bankruptcies of businesses launched by the coalition of Jewish and cosmopolitan financiers, sensed the danger that the influence of such a power posed to its independence . . . We owe it to our nationals to give them preferential treatment." In that ward, a police report observed, "one finds essentially a reactionary and especially a clerical population . . . The clergy is all-powerful, and the candidate who has its support is certain of his success." Similarly, in the second ward of Cholet, the vicomte de La Bourdonnaye, who espoused reactionary ideas, was reelected. In his platform statement, that deputy wrote, "In whatever name the enemies of society cloak themselves, whether Freemason, Jew, or socialist, I want, with the help of God, to fight for the defense of the ideas that will make France great and strong . . . The enemies of law and order are made more audacious through the weakness of an unstable power: they want to destroy everything. The army itself is not spared. A syndicate of Jews has dared commit the most insulting slander against it . . . Your deputies can better serve your interests by ensuring the worker, through more moral and more Christian legislation, the dignity of the home." In the arrondissement of Segré, Laurent Bougère, the incumbent deputy who, according to the police, "distributes handshakes, wine, and gold with the same largesse," easily defeated his republican opponent, Pertué.[25]

The example of Grandmaison, an incumbent deputy who easily won in the arrondissement of Saumur with more than 14,000 votes, illustrates that ambiguities were indispensable for electoral success there. He claimed to be a republican, but as the police maintained, "his fortune and his special propaganda methods do the rest." In Saumur the newspaper *L'Avant-Garde* proved to be resolutely republican but also antiSemitic. Similarly, *Le Courrier de Saumur* embraced republican ideas but opposed incumbent deputy de Grandmaison in these terms:

Why this peculiar alliance between M. de Grandmaison, the submissive and docile creature of the Jesuits, and the Jewish or Jew-sympathizing financier deputies? In spite of all the glasses of champagne and white wine consumed in private, all the fishing expeditions, all the wedding dinners, M. de Grandmaison belongs to that reactionary coalition that is the enemy above all of universal suffrage . . . He is above all the protégé of the Jesuits . . . There is a cordial understanding to crush democracy between the Church and Israelite, Protestant, or Catholic finance . . . Sometimes the Jesuits shout very loudly against Jewry, but immediately these partners calm down and recognize they have the same interests—they agree to divide up the power and the benefits . . . That is how the votes of M. de Grandmaison can be explained.[26]

To top it all off, on August 14, 1899, in Montreuil-Bellay, the township where Grandmaison was mayor, a monument was dedicated to honor Alphonse Toussenel, an anti-Semitic figure who, in the nineteenth century, had exerted a strong influence on the left and on Edouard Drumont himself. The ceremony was presided over by Grandmaison. Sitting on the speakers' platform were various deputies and senators—Marlet, Jules Baron, Ferdinand Bougères—as well as Abbé Bosseboeuf. Drumont was expected but canceled and was replaced by his faithful Gaston Méry. Before a large crowd, Méry expressed admiration for Toussenel, "the so very original and so very French storyteller who, well before Drumont, pointed out the Jewish peril, that is, the invasion of the old races by the Semitic element." He emphasized that while Toussenel "denounced Jewry, Drumont has given the Jew a thrashing at a time when the Jews are staking everything to save a traitor."[27] On October 16, Grandmaison held a banquet at the town hall of Saumur, attended by five hundred people, in honor of Jules Quesnay de Beaurepaire, the former presiding judge in the civil chamber at the Cour de Cassation who had overseen the course of the Dreyfus affair in that chamber. Quesnay de Beaurepaire was born in Saumur; an anti-Dreyfusard magistrate, he had resigned when the chamber relinquished the case in favor of a court with all chambers combined, which was to open the way for a review of the case. The press was represented by La Libre Parole, Le Gaulois, and Le Petit Journal, which always displayed a particular anti-Dreyfusard zeal and made no mystery of its anti-Semitism. The presence of Henri Vaugeois, of Action Française, was also noted.[28] During that splendid ceremony in honor of a child of the region who had kept France from "being handed over to the predators and the mobs," the luncheon was sumptuous:

> *Butter, sausage, radishes, sardines*
> *Fish from the Loire with caper sauce*
> *Filet of beef with mushrooms*
> *Salt-meadow leg of lamb à la bretonne*
> *Peas à la française*
> *Young valley turkey roasted on a spit*
> *Seasonal salad*
> *Cake*
> *Fruit*
> *Coffee and liqueurs*
> *White wine in carafes. Sparkling wines graciously offered*
> *by Maisons Ackerman-Laurance,*
> *Bouvet-Ladubay, and de Neuville*

L'Avant-Garde reported that during this feast Grandmaison gave a long speech celebrating the courage of Quesnay de Beaurepaire, who had been able to resist "the public criminals bribed by foreign nations and cosmopolitan finance." In his peroration he declared, "I lift my glass to Quesnay de Beaurepaire, to M. de Mahy, our president of the Ligue de la Patrie Française, to the *Petit Journal*, and to Judet, whom we are sorry not to see here; I drink to the Frenchmen of France, to the army, to Anjou, our little homeland." Mahy followed him and denounced cosmopolitan foreigners as many in the audience shouted, "Down with the Jews!" Quesnay de Beaurepaire himself then took the floor: "I have stood up to this new invasion. It was no longer Goliath I had to battle, but Judas. I laid down my robe, I left everything behind, I made myself the champion of our dear army . . . The barbarians are at our gates, they have seized hold of the Republic . . . Let us clink our glasses, therefore, as in the good old days. Drink with me to my native city and to my old friends from the land of Saumur." Grandmaison, the "moderate" republican, would remain true to his prejudices: first elected deputy of Saumur in 1893, he was regularly reelected until 1933 with impressive shares of the vote, ranging from a low of 47 percent in 1893 to a high of 72 percent in 1902. A prefect's report maintained that his altogether extraordinary political longevity could be explained by his double-dealing: according to the superintendent, the deputy, "who feigned rather liberal opinions in Paris, in Saumur came off as the representative of the reactionaries."[29] The "mild climate of Anjou" was thus the result of compromise.

Before we arrive at the heart of Vendée, let us briefly note that in Le Mans, to the northeast, in December 1898 four hundred people hailed General Auguste Mercier, shouting, "Down with the traitors! Down with the Jews!"[30] And let us briefly look eastward to Tours, whose calm made it closer to the center of France than to vehement Anjou. The demonstrations there were almost harmless: on January 24 and 25, 1898, students, some in medicine and pharmacy, paraded on the streets outside the synagogue, striking with canes the fronts of stores owned by Jewish tradespeople and shouting the usual anti-Semitic slogans. That was all—little to speak of—and that would be the end of it, at least in the city itself. Posters ("The cursed race of the Jews must be exterminated") and press articles nevertheless kept stirring up anti-Semitic unrest, especially several newspapers that did not hide their intense hostility. *Le Journal d'Indre-et-Loire* claimed that "it is easier to stop the sun than to stop Jews from committing an infamous act"; *L'Echo d'Indre-et-Loire*, though republican, celebrated the anti-Semitic demonstrations in faraway Marseilles. *L'Eclaireur*, the socialist newspaper for western France, denounced "the Jews' gold," made fun of nobles who married Jewish girls, and finally launched the following threat: "The day Jacques Prolo comes out into the streets, it will be to make the good Jewish and the good Christian capitalist despoilers pay restitution."[31]

Let us now resume our slow journey southwest toward the Atlantic, which will take us to Vendée and then La Roche-sur-Yon and finally to La Rochelle. On the way to Vendée we stop in Nantes, an industrial and republican city of more than 120,000 that differed fundamentally from Angers. In early January 1898, however, its anti-Semitic mobilization was just as overwhelming, perhaps more so. On the fourteenth "a large band of factory and shop workers got a response from the crowd by chanting rhythmically, 'Down with the Jews! Down with the Jews! Down! Down! Down with the Jews! Down with the Jews! Down! Down!' " In his report the superintendent observed, "The response that these cries and threats got from the crowd was enough to elicit fear for public order in the streets."[32] On the sixteenth *L'Espérance du Peuple* announced a new demonstration, in which the crowd was to burn a straw effigy of Dreyfus. The mayor, worried, posted a resolution to prohibit "the parading of the emblem considered to be the representation of the Jewish people." On the seventeenth more than fifteen thousand people gathered in the streets near the rue Crébillon. Between two and five thousand gathered outside the post office, then on the rue d'Orléans and at the place de la Cathédrale and outside the prefecture building. They finally dispersed on the place Royale. With canes they struck the storefronts of businesses owned by Jewish tradespeople. They proved to be particularly aggressive, and a young man named M. de Charette displayed extreme violence. The demonstrators gathered on the rue Kléber outside the home of the rabbi, whom they insulted and threatened. On the rue Copernic, they attempted to break down the gate leading to the synagogue, broke the windowpanes of Lévy's store, and looted the sheds of the nougat merchants, who were considered likely to be Jewish. The police superintendent noted that "a considerable number of well-dressed men and young people, tradespeople, and business employees, very sincerely demonstrated their hostility toward the Jews."[33]

The next day, January 18, the demonstration turned even more acrimonious. To face the situation, the Nantes municipality provided three brigades of gendarmes on horseback and two on foot to reinforce the city's police officers. Nearly three thousand people again made their way through the main streets of the city, shouting, "Down with the Jews! Out with Zola!" "Noisy bands composed of workers and children gathered outside a few isolated shops of Israelites. Stones were thrown; a storefront was broken down, the store was invaded, and the owner, M. Szezupack, was brutalized as the shelves were looted. The troops had to intervene right away to protect him."[34] A man identified as Jewish was jostled and struck and got away thanks only to the rapid intervention of the police. Patrols of gendarmes on horseback tirelessly crisscrossed the arteries of the city and were carefully avoided by the demonstrators. Many stores were posted "Catholic owner"; shopkeepers had notices published in the press saying they were Catholic, that their sons had served in the military, that they were truly French. As a result, "in Nantes, which had become a little Algiers, the 'tricolor terror' reigned."[35] *La Fronde* observed that "the scenes of savagery occurring against the Jews in Nantes are indescribable. Everything you read will give you only a weak idea of the state of mind here, which harks back to the Middle Ages."[36] On the nineteenth the city was in a state of siege; the dragoons went through the streets, barred the large arteries, or stood on the alert. A few groups of more than five hundred people apiece attempted to assemble and demonstrate, but the police intervened immediately and dispersed them. Many arrests took place; workers as well as lawyers and shopkeepers were promptly taken to the station. On the twentieth dragoons prevented the demonstrators from beginning their usual course: the students had wanted to gather outside the home of Bachelot, vice president of the civil tribunal, to protest the severity of the sentences imposed on the previous demonstrators. New arrests were made, as patrols of gendarmes and police officers circulated until two o'clock in the morning. Organized by the seven superintendents, the police forces were omnipresent, fanning out to all the potential targets. As a detailed account made in preparation for the evening of the twenty-third meticulously indicated, a guard plus a brigadier stood outside "the rabbi's" and "at the synagogue." A police report observed: "The extreme fatigue of the police, the gendarmerie, and the local troops" made urgent the intervention of two squadrons of gendarmerie from Pontivy. Cavalry detachments guarded the entrances of the city, since groups of students from Angers and Rennes were expected to arrive.[37]

L'Espérance du Peuple could not conceal its joy at the size of these demonstrations. Inflating the numbers somewhat, it estimated the number of participants "shouting against the Jews" at twenty and even fifty thousand. In its enthusiasm the newspaper meticulously described

that compact wave of demonstrators shouting at the top of their lungs, "Death to the Jews! Into the water with the Jews! Out with Zola! Down with the Yids! Long live the army!" It was a veritable and formidable army on the march, in close order and impetuous, an impetuous wave at flood stage flowing through the streets lined with another crowd, combining its shouts for death with the shouts of those passing . . . And in that army of demonstrators, all viewpoints and social ranks fraternally rubbed shoulders: workers, shopkeepers, students, nobles, laborers, bourgeois, persons of private means, and so on. There was a real delirium in that crowd, down to the old people who followed close behind and shouted at the top of their lungs, "Death to the Jews."[38]

In a more moderate tone, *Le Soleil* expressed regret at the "Death to the Jews" shouts and rejoiced that "fortunately that threat against an entire race remained platonic since, apart from a few broken windowpanes and a damaged store, the demonstrators did not go too far in their commotion." And the editor added: "To be sure, I do not claim that the Jews should be manhandled in any way . . . France can require that they not infringe on the rights of others, that they not confiscate private fortunes after usurping the public fortune in its entirety, that they cease to try to dominate in a country where they number 100,000 out of 36 million . . . They can be seen everywhere, in the prefectures, in the courts of justice, in civil, military, and maritime engineering, in the army, everywhere, everywhere!"[39]

The anti-Semitic clamor thereafter lost intensity, but it remained present in a residual form. Until 1900 the incidents in the streets of Nantes barely paused. On January 29, 1898, on the place de Bretagne, young people shouted, "Death to the Jews!" and attempted to stir up the crowd against the stall merchants, who were quickly protected by soldiers. On February 16, when the attorney Bricard was acquitted by the Rennes court of appeal after he had insulted a police officer during the January unrest, a demonstration of sympathy spontaneously erupted, lead by M. Padioleau, head of the order of Nantes attorneys. Toasts were made; "violent words were pronounced against the Jews and against Zola"; and 150 students, friends of Bricard, expressed their sympathy to Drumont, Rochefort, and Judet.* They resolved to hold a large anti-Semitic meeting on Saturday, February 26, to which they invited Drumont himself.[40] On March 5 on the place Kléber, several people sang at the top of their lungs, "Long live Déroulède! Death to

---

*Ernest Judet: anti-Dreyfusard editor of France's largest newspaper, *Le Petit Journal.*—trans.

the Jews!" Some of them, like the law student Raymond Levrault, who "was considered a fanatic," were in fact members of the Ligue des Patriotes; they were taken to the station and fined for "disturbing the peace." On March 6 Rabbi Korb lodged a complaint at the police bureau because, the previous night, several people had shouted under his windows, "Down with the Jews! Down with the rabbis!" then struck the door to his house with canes. On June 29 about five hundred people gathered outside Le Grand Bazar and shouted, "Down with the Jews! Long live the army!" brandishing a French flag. One of them when arrested had a loaded six-shooter and a blackjack on him. On October 26, as the Fourth Battalion of the Sixty-fifth Artillery Regiment left for Brest, a crowd assembled at the train station, alongside two generals and many other officers, and screamed, "Long live the army!" and "Down with the Jews!"

Let us return to the first months of 1898, shortly before the campaign for the May legislative elections. The local press as a whole displayed a virulent anti-Semitism: *Le Populaire*, *L'Espérance du Peuple*, *Le Nouvelliste*, *Le Progrès*, and *La Croix Nantaise* all inveighed against the Jews. Moreover, "in Nantes and Saint-Nazaire, the Dreyfusian crisis led to a manifestation of the religious spirit and determined, more or less consciously, the positions taken."[41] *L'Espérance du Peuple* enjoyed itself to the fullest, writing on January 13 that "today it is once more the living God who has won, the God who issued the terrible curse against the Jews." On April 29, on the eve of the first round of the elections, *L'Espérance du Peuple* exclaimed, "May the elections be national above all else! That is the supreme exhortation. Deliver us from the Jews!" In the 1896 municipal elections, the conservatives had seized ten out of seventeen seats. This time the contest in the second ward pitted the republican Roch and the socialist Brunellière against the nationalist Gireaudeau. Roch finally won, but almost everywhere else the reactionaries won, in both Saint-Nazaire and in the little town of Paimboeuf.

In one ward in Nantes, the anti-Semitic nationalists made every effort to obtain the support of the socialists, on condition that the latter do the same for them in the other ward. Brunellière, the socialist leader, probably could have gotten himself elected in that manner, but he refused any rapprochement without hesitation. Nevertheless, during certain socialist electoral meetings he conducted, in a supercharged ambience where any metaphor could reinforce a prejudice, people did not hesitate to denounce the gold of the Rothschilds; and although some objected to any new Saint Bartholomew's Day massacre between the Jews and Catholics, they did so while maintaining that "both are equal; the only difference is that salt has been put on the tongue of one, and the other has been snipped somewhere." On April 6, 7, and 13, before assemblies of eight to twelve hundred people each, the socialist speakers showed they were convinced that "Dreyfus is guilty and he betrayed his country." Again on September 22, during a meeting held by the socialist revolutionary committee in Salle Gendron, Séraphine Pajaud declared that God did not exist and that Catholicism was "the most absurd religion of all." She maintained that Dreyfus was innocent and that "anti-Semitism is an indirect means to arrive at the enslavement of the worker; the Jews and the reactionaries are equally hypocritical and thieving. The revolutionaries have been accused of being part of the Jewish syndicate. There are two syndicates: that of wealth and that of poverty; the revolutionaries are part of the latter." On the twenty-fifth Pajaud repeated the same speech in Chantenay-sur-Loire, addressing it to approximately two hundred workers and even a few ladies who got in free.[42]

The great Atlantic port of Nantes was thus the context for hard political struggles, echoing oppositions from the past as well as new class antagonisms. They unfolded even at the end of 1898 and beyond, against a background of old prejudices that expressed themselves with more or less restraint. In 1900 General Auguste Mercier entered the Senate race. At the end of the bitter campaign, he managed to be elected despite his crucial role throughout the Dreyfus affair as one of Dreyfus's most determined opponents. *L'Espérance du Peuple* ardently defended his candidacy, maintaining that "the Catholics will make it a strict duty of conscience to vote for Mercier." The newspaper published the following poem:

> *To General Mercier, who made our hearts feel light,*
> *When trembling France went forward to beseech him,*
> *You will give your votes, Bretons who are stopped by nothing,*
> *Subdued by nothing, and to nothing bowed down!*
> *You will cast many of them in the avenging ballot box*

That weapon of combat placed in your hands,
And the sons of Judas, that traitorous race,
Will pale upon seeing the senator of tomorrow.[43]

In late January 1900 Mercier became a senator, attracting 703 votes; his republican opponent received only 287. The day before the balloting, to clarify his views, he boasted of wanting "to overthrow the financial tyranny of the Jews and the political tyranny of the Freemasons. To achieve these results, what does it matter if one is a republican, a Bonapartist, or a monarchist! We must rally together and unite our efforts."[44] Without question he was heard.

Of all the cities of France, Nantes, burdened with so many prejudices, was indisputably one where the anti-Semitic movement set up the strongest institutional structure and most deeply penetrated community life. An association of shopkeepers was rapidly constituted that openly called for a boycott on stores owned by Jews. In September 1897 the words "Death to the Jews" were posted night after night on Jewish shopkeepers' signs. According to a police superintendent, in January 1898 "important merchants in the city, not being able to bear the Jewish competition . . . want to take advantage of the events that have just occurred and the current of public opinion presently unfavorable to the Israelites to found an association in Nantes whose goal would be to defend their interests against the Jews." On February 1 someone distributed handbills in the main streets of the city: "Caution! Monday and days following, *DO NOT BUY* from any but *CATHOLIC STORES.* That is the best demonstration." As the police noted, the shopkeepers and students who undertook that campaign belonged "to families in the city well known for their clerical opinions."[45] In April a league of defense against Jewish businesses, called the Ligue Patriotique Antisémite, was officially created by 257 people who published their names and addresses on the back of their manifesto. "Dear citizen," it proclaimed,

as a Frenchman and a patriot, your heart must have pounded with indignation in seeing an occult syndicate place in doubt the act of justice carried out by the war council [Dreyfus's condemnation], with the entire Semitic race following close on its heels . . . A

group of Nantes citizens believe the moment opportune to organize a patriotic league of Nantes . . . Already several cities in
France—Paris, Lyon, Bordeaux, Poitiers, and others—have preceded us on that path, and we, the citizens of Nantes, must stand
firm and not lag behind in that healthy French work . . . to return
France to the French; to require an anti-Semitic platform from
candidates in the next elections; and to struggle by every legal
means against the invasion of public affairs and public office by
the Jewish race.

L'Espérance du Peuple lauded that initiative and wrote on April 27: "In our
department anti-Semitism is making rapid progress. Not only has a
league been established on solid foundations in Nantes, but word has
come back to us from all sides that, in the rural areas, people are exasperated with the Jews." Very quickly the first members received the support of eight hundred more. The police superintendent emphasized that
"the league is recruiting from all social circles, without distinction of
party . . . People sound out the public figures who are up for office . . .
Four prominent socialists have supposedly agreed to be part of the
[league's] bureau. That would be evidence, already given through the
publication of the names of 257 of its members, that the league is
practicing the greatest eclecticism in political matters; all viewpoints are
combined in a single hatred of the Jew." In another report the superintendent maintained that it was all a "business question . . . The shopkeepers want to take advantage of this more or less sincere and
spontaneous movement of public opinion against the Jews to divert customers from stores operated by Israelites into their own shops . . . The
moral and material advantages that each of the members expects to enjoy will silence many a scruple." Again in late December 1898 the
president of the league, the shopkeeper Ganuchaud, declared during a
meeting, "That business question is one of the most effective means for
succeeding in the struggle we have undertaken against Jewish society."
Another speaker added, "The struggle is between the French shop and
the Jewish shop. We certainly have the right to defend our own."[46]

    In addition to the boycott, other actions were undertaken against the
Jewish shopkeepers. A system of photographic surveillance was set in
place in front of certain Jewish stores to discourage potential customers:

if they entered one of the stores, their pictures would be put up on a bulletin board. A police report observed that "several individuals equipped with cameras were posted in front of the stores on the rue du Calvaire run by the Deutsch brothers (of the Israelite religion), under the sign Sans Pareil, and pretended to photograph people entering these stores." A tract was widely distributed: "Coming soon. Silhouette and biography of the customers, men and women, of Dreyfus the Traitor. Snapshot! Snapshot!" The optimistic superintendent maintained that that approach "may perhaps bother many anti-Semites who are so in name only." Hostility toward Jewish shopkeepers left its mark in many other ways as well. In late April, a police officer noted, "after several Israelite businesses sent contributions to the organization committee for the Joan of Arc festivities, said committee unanimously refused to accept these funds and any other contribution from the same source." The son of a Jewish shopkeeper named Sexer, who had long been part of a musical group called La Symphonie, which was headed by a businessman, was expelled from the group without ado. The police superintendent emphasized that "the true reason for the expulsion may be his status as an Israelite."

In Nantes, then, the nationalist and anti-Semitic protest in politics and the professions took on such intensity that some saw the city as the "center for a new Chouan revolt."[47] The police reports accumulated on the prefect's desk as surveillance of the activities of the Ligue Antisémite heavily mobilized officers throughout these two years. On April 18, 1898, many public meetings were held under the chairmanship of Deputy de Pontbriand, who had just submitted a bill to the Chamber aimed at granting French citizenship only after an immigrant family had been in the country for three generations. In his view "the Nantes league is against the Jews. It would be equally against the English, the Americans, or other foreigners if they were threatening the French nation." A motion was passed unanimously: "The members of the Ligue Patriotique Nantaise send their most sincere respects to Edouard Drumont, valiant director of La Libre Parole, for the distinguished service he is rendering to the French nation by working to deliver it from the degrading yoke of the Jews." According to the superintendent, the members of the league launched "a relentless campaign against the influence of the Jewish colony, so powerful in Nantes," and benefited from the considerable support of several newspapers, which published vengeful press releases. They were combated explicitly only by *Le Phare de la Loire*, whose editor, Maurice Schwob, became the favorite target of the local anti-Semitic movement.

In early August Grimaux, a chemist, vice president of Le Ligue des Droits de l'Homme, and one of the most famous signers of the Dreyfusard motions in defense of Dreyfus, arrived in Nantes to preside over the congress of the Association for the Advancement of Science at the Théâtre Graslin. But his presence at the congress unleashed something close to nationalist hysteria, orchestrated by the Catholic clubs, the Jeunesse Royaliste, *La Libre Parole*, and one of the latter's main journalists, Raphaël Viau, a native of Nantes. The police feared events identical to those that had occurred in Algiers.[48] Twenty-five thousand of the Ligue Antisémite tracts were distributed. In response, the following poem was widely circulated:

> *Unsavory captains, pious lambs,*
> *And the noncoms and priests with dirty feet*
> *Close their doors to Grimaux.*
> *And all in an outburst bellow like calves.*
> *Because the provinces, with astonishing morals,*
> *Value Judet, Boisdeffre, and Pellieux.*
> *The miracles of Lourdes and the angel Esterhazy*
> *Gladden the imbecilic heart of Nantes.*
> *That is why the tuna merchants, the country squires,*
> *Strike back like wild bulls,*
> *Abominating the Jew on the Loire and the Erdre.*
> *To them, holy water is a "liquid spell":*
> *Whatever wit they might have had trickles away in Drumont.*
> *In response to his causes, it is fitting to say, with Ubu,*
> *For rhyme and reason: Long live the armanure.*[*49]

In the hall the interruptions were so violent that Grimaux could not take the floor, and the session was abruptly adjourned. Grimaux left by

---

*Armanure (*armèrdre*): a portmanteau word consisting of *armée* (army) and *merdre*, the famous first word of Alfred Jarry's play *Ubu roi*, which adds a second "r" to *merde*.—trans.

a concealed door, but nearly fifteen hundred people surrounded him, booing. There were shouts of "Out with Grimaux! Down with the Jews! Down with Zola!" *Le Nouvelliste de l'Ouest* described the scene this way: "Some of the editors of the Jewish newspaper *Le Phare* and a certain Portais, municipal councilor in the sixth canton, were brutally manifesting their Dreyfusard sentiments. They were flanked by two or three Jews with hooked noses and shifty eyes, who took part in the Semitic concert by conscientiously shouting: 'Long-a lif Grimaux! Long-a lif Grimaux!' " A police report noted that "most of the people out walking, attracted to that place by a musical concert given on the square, joined the demonstration." Three thousand people (five thousand according to *La Libre Parole*) denounced Grimaux and the Jews, sang "The Marseillaise," and wound their way through the arteries of the city, intending "to take a little tour through the Jewish stores." All the gendarmerie brigades in the department were concentrated in Nantes, which was crisscrossed by dragoons. Brawls erupted between demonstrators and counterdemonstrators. According to a police superintendent, "among those who vociferated the most were people of the best society, bourgeois, persons of private means, shopkeepers, reactionaries such as de Charette the younger . . . Finally, among those who were shouting the most against the Jews, I made out a certain Douillard, a socialist . . . I would not be surprised if he paid off workers with money from the reactionaries to get them to demonstrate against Grimaux . . . The viscount of La Janselière and a few other royalists bought a funeral wreath and pruning shears on the place Lafayette, which they intended to offer to M. Grimaux." *Le Nouvelliste*, satisfied with that memorable day, concluded: "Decidedly, apart from the Jews living in Nantes, a dozen intellectuals, and the Jew Maurice Schwob, editor of *Phare de la Loire*, the syndicate of treason counts no friends in our dear city of Nantes." In the August 5, 1898, issue of the latter newspaper, its editor pointed out that during these demonstrations: "The police did not believe it should intervene or even attract too much attention by its presence." The same day *Le Nouvelliste* paid "tribute to the great majority of officers, who had a delicate task to perform" and condemned those who had struck certain demonstrators opposed to Grimaux.[50]

In autumn the militants of the Ligue Patriotique Nantaise widely distributed posters from the federated branches of the Jeunesse Antisémitique et Nationaliste, proclaiming, "Like our fathers, the heroes of Bouvines, Rocroi, Valmy, and Fleurus, we will drive the foreign hordes from France." On October 14, in Salle du Lion d'Or, one speaker attacked "the kike gangrene." The main speaker boasted that he had named his dog "Kike" and that he himself "was not circumcised." On November 9 nearly "three hundred gentlemen" attended a banquet in honor of Ganuchaud, the president of the league. They accused the new prefect, M. Helitas, of being Jewish and maintained that it was out of the question to "tolerate, in Nantes, a prefect of the Israelite religion." The guests called for the abrogation of the Crémieux decree and impatiently awaited "the day when France would be rid of the cosmopolitan Jews who are exploiting it." The attorney Chéguillaume took the floor next and argued that "the league was founded to fight the cosmopolitans. The goal we are pursuing is essentially French and must be inspired by the bloody riots of Drumont in Algeria. To achieve such a noble task, Bretons have to be in the front lines, since good blood does not lie . . . The leaguists must go to the people and show them what this Jew is who has caused so much misfortune in our country." To that end, the leaguists decided to hold lectures "in the countryside, in order to warn the peasants against the machinations of the Israelite businesses," and committed themselves to fight "Jewish gold," which was allegedly being used to save the traitor Dreyfus. Before the meeting dispersed, a speaker "praised a deceased anti-Semite who left behind a large family, whose situation is worthy of interest. He proposed that the leaguists come to the aid of the widow and her children." As the guests left, they shouted, "Long live France for the French!"

On December 8 the Ligue Patriotique Nantaise held another meeting. It modified the leadership committee and allowed two socialist workers to join it. "The goal of those appointments," remarked the police superintendent, "is to prove that the league has no allegiance to any political party." He continued, describing the meeting: "A report was made of an action taken by a delegation of the league, begging the bishop of Nantes to use his influence over the Catholics, through the mediation of the priests, to commit them to blacklist Jewish businesses. The bishop responded with a categorical refusal." Close contacts nevertheless existed between the league and certain Catholic circles, contacts that had been established, in particular, during preparations for the Joan of Arc festivities. Many police reports emphasized that connection, as did *La Semaine Religieuse de Nantes*, *Le Nouvelliste*, and *L'Espérance du Peuple*. In fact, present on the committee charged with preparing for those festivities were the Catholic club, the religious boarding school Fidèles de Jésus, the Louis XVI club, and in full force the league president's family, the Ganuchauds. A certain number of priests also worked on that committee, including Abbé Lefeuvre, an "intimate friend" of Abbé Garnier, the national leader of the anti-Semitic leagues. They joined to undertake of a number of pilgrimages together with more than eight thousand faithful; feasts of Saint Louis and impressive meetings to fight pornography—which even some officeholders were accused of supporting—all followed in quick succession.[51]

These connections appeared clearly on December 11, when the league held a huge meeting in Salle Leduit and addressed the population, distributing fifteen thousand tracts denouncing "those on the payroll of cosmopolitan Jewry." The league was aided, a superintendent noted, "by the clerical camp, which, thanks to the events relating to the Dreyfus affair, conducted an active propaganda campaign on that issue and put its best agents on the case. Libraros, a Catholic bookseller and spokesman for the clergy, told me this morning that he was again going to chide the members of the league for the inadequacy of their zeal." To this end Libraros distributed the newspaper *L'Antijuif Nantais* (The Anti-Jew of Nantes), which was a local cousin of *L'Antijuif de Lyon et du Forez* (The Anti-Jew of Lyon and Forez). The tone was extremely virulent: on October 1, 1898, *L'Antijuif Nantais* denounced on its front page "the grasp of the Jew, who holds France upside down and whose bony hand grips its neck and bruises its flesh . . . We will begin to rummage through the pile of crooks, panderers, procurers, and swindlers who compose the Jewish dungheap. And even if we face asphyxiation by the putrid miasma that will be released from the rot we are going to shovel away, others will come to relieve us and allow us to breathe a little pure air before we go back down into the cesspool."[52] Several nationalist anti-Semitic deputies, such as Lasies (deputy of Gers), Lucien Millevoye (deputy of Paris), Magne (deputy of Dordogne), Raphaël Viau (editor of *La Libre Parole*), and Jules Guérin (editor of *L'Antijuif*), led the great anti-Semitic celebration in Salle Leduit, beside numerous nobles who are members of the organizational committee: deputies Pontbriand,

Montaigu, L'Estourbillon from Morbihan, and Armand Baudry d'Asson from Vendée.

On the day of the meeting in Salle Leduit, the stores and the private homes of Jewish shopkeepers were protected by the gendarmerie, which was omnipresent in the city. A crowd of more than eighteen hundred assembled outside the hall; violent brawls erupted both inside and outside. Socialist militants managed to get in, singing "Ça ira!" "Le chant du départ," and "La Carmagnole," and attacked the anti-Semitic militants. At the podium Guérin called for denying "Jews the status of Frenchmen and maintained that once they had been driven from France, there would soon be understanding between the social classes." Socialists shouted, "Long live the socialist Republic! Long live Picquart! Down with the priests! Down with Drumont!" Shouts of "Down with the Jews! Out with Picquart! Out with Zola!" came in reply. Dreyfus supporter Aristide Briand took the floor, to an enormous uproar. Blows were exchanged. According to the police report, the anti-Semitic militants committed "acts of revolting brutality." People struck out with canes. The municipal police and the mounted gendarmerie intervened. A group of about five hundred anti-Semites left the hall and demonstrated in the streets. Outside the building of the army corps, they shouted, "Long live the army! Down with the Jews! Down with the traitors! Down with the accepters of bribes!" Following that memorable evening, the police superintendent argued in his biweekly report that "according to impartial onlookers, the Dreyfusards were unable to drag the sound portion of the population of Nantes into their antipatriotic campaign. But the fishers in troubled water, the extreme anti-Semitic and revolutionary portions, revel in that unrest, which paralyzes business and holds France hypnotized in a fatal status quo . . . The population lives in a state of breathlessness and worry."

The meeting at Salle Leduit probably marked the swan song of the nationalist and anti-Semitic movement in Nantes. In late 1898 it encountered sharp resistance from the socialist movement, which contended with it for possession of the streets. The movement pursued its activities, but in a minor key. On December 17 the Ligue Antisémite held a meeting and expressed concern that some of its friends, such as the newspaper *Le Populaire*, was turning its back on it. Two lines now faced off: according to the police superintendent, "although a certain number of members, especially distinguished tradespeople, would like to pursue their work in silence and without noisy demonstrations outside, the militants of the league, especially the clericals and members of the Jeunesse Royaliste, would on the contrary like to give free rein to their aggressive mood by continuing the unrest. To do so, they wish to bring the Algerian agitators Régis and Drumont to Nantes . . . Conversely, M. Ganuchaud, the president, considered that their coming to Nantes would compromise the best of causes." Not knowing which way to turn, the members of the league decided to at least contribute to the Henry monument [the fund for Hubert Henry's widow]. On December 18 *Le Nouvelliste* emphasized that "rich and poor send their widow's mite to the noble wife insulted like a coward by the Jew Reinach. We note a certain number of Nantes citizens who insisted on publicly protesting the machinations of the cosmopolitan gang. Sincere congratulations to our fellow citizens." On the list of contributors, next to "the poorest," appeared a considerable portion of the department's nobility: La Ferronnays, La Bourdonnaye, Le Cour-Grandmaison, Villebois-Mareuil, and so on. The movement to bar Jewish shopkeepers continued, and as *L'Espérance du Peuple* revealed on December 28, even the "patriotic cyclists" added their two cents' worth. On December 26 the league held lectures in all the villages of the region, and a letter, signed, "a civil servant who is sorry he cannot sign his name," was read aloud. In the letter, according to the police report, "even while violently expressing anti-Semitic feelings, the author indicates that most of the civil servants approve of the league's attitude." On January 21, 1899, of the seven hundred people who were still members of the league, 120 gathered to name their new staff, which again included Pucel, who had boasted of naming his dog "Kike." Here the editors in chief of *La Croix Nantaise* and *Le Nouvelliste de l'Ouest* as well as Du Bouays de Couësbouc, attorney at the Nantes bar, again discussed the Jewish question.

The league pursued its activities throughout 1899 and held anti-Semitic meetings on March 18, March 22, April 11, and June 10. During that last meeting, someone anticipated "going at the Jew." A speaker "shouted death for the Israelites" and praised Drumont, "the man of thought and action, the head that studies and the arm that strikes, the

adviser and the good giant." Month after month the league held nationalist banquets. It arranged for the publication of an *Annuaire Commercial
Antisémitique* (Anti-Semitic Business Registry), under the particular responsibility of Frémont and Du Bouays de Couësdouc. The names and
addresses of the city's Jewish shopkeepers appeared in it, and it was generously distributed throughout the entire department. An action group
was set up, composed exclusively of "young people known for their
anti-Semitic or Catholic opinions," whose goal was to heckle their socialist opponents.

In Nantes and in Paris, on December 9, 10, and 11, 1898, socialist
meetings brought together more than eight thousand people and proclaimed Dreyfus's innocence loud and clear. Between those meetings and
the major demonstrations of June 22 and 29, 1899, Sébastien Faure
noted with satisfaction, "in Nantes and in Paris, we are the masters of
the street in spite of the nationalists." The Socialist Party, which had attracted fewer than two hundred militants in early 1898, transformed
itself into a force to be reckoned with. It gave a new impetus to the social struggles, leading, for example, in November 1899 a long strike of
working men and women from the Manufacture Nationale des Tabacs
(National Association of Tobacco Manufacturers). (The strike came in
response to a comment by its director, who supposedly declared to the
female workers, "When the bulls leave, the cows follow." The central superintendent denied the words had been uttered: "It is very doubtful
that the director expressed himself in that way, and everything leads us
to suppose that a few spiteful women are seeking to aggravate the situation.") In any case, in Paris and in Nantes, the Socialist Party now threw
its forces behind Dreyfus and the Republic, though without neglecting
the social struggles. In the streets of Nantes, socialists distributed a
tract addressed to the "workers of Nantes":

> When the anti-Semites tell you that the Jews have monopolized
> everything, they are lying . . . The owners of the mines, the major
> glass-makers, the billionaires in the metallurgical factories, the
> aristocrats who own the land and oppress the peasants—all these
> parasites are not Jewish but good and fervent Catholics . . . If the
> anti-Semites incite you against the Jews, it is to take you back to

the horrors of the religious wars during the Middle Ages; after the Jews it will be the turn of the Protestants, then the free thinkers—all those, in a word, who refuse to bow down before the aspergillum.

It now seemed that the socialists were being heard. To face these increasingly enterprising opponents, Ligue Patriotique Nantaise almost openly sought the support of certain Catholic sectors that were propagating ideas identical to its own. On March 19, 1899, the Fédération des Travailleurs Chrétiens du Centre (Federation of Christian Workers from the Center of France) held a conference in Nantes, where speakers accused the forces in power of being only "puppets with the Jews pulling the strings . . . If we are not careful, the Jews will make French blood flow . . . We must drive them from old French soil, just as Joan of Arc once drove out the English." Together the anti-Semites and clericals controlled the organization of both the Joan of Arc festival and Carnaval, as *Le Populaire* accused on March 19. They undertook a number of actions and participated in military parades; their rapprochement was openly desired by Abbé Peigné, who even in late December 1898 expressed keen admiration for Judet.

As a police report observed, nevertheless, "the league has settled down a great deal, either from lassitude or from good sense." *Le Nouvelliste de l'Ouest,* the league's usual mouthpiece, eased its nationalist vigilance to such an extent that on March 31, 1899, the Deutsch brothers, Jewish shopkeepers, and the owners of Sans Pareil, the store so often targeted by the anti-Semitic movements, managed to "play a good joke" on that newspaper. It had a large advertising notice published: "The weather, which was a little menacing this morning, has subsequently proved milder, and a large crowd thronged to the display windows on Maundy Thursday. Needless to say, one of those that attracted the most attention was Sans Pareil . . . Especially noteworthy was the display of stylish hats, the ready-to-wear clothing for ladies and girls, and the new high fashion fabrics. A marvel! The conclusion that must be drawn is that any woman wishing to be elegantly dressed must go to Sans Pareil." The "joke" was so successful that, according to the police, "the owners of Sans Pareil distributed *Le Nouvelliste* free to the many from the general public who filed past their windows yesterday."[53] That is a good indication to what extent the "citizens of Vendée" had finally decided to lay down their weapons and abandon the noisy surveillance of the street.

Once we leave Nantes, the epicenter of the Pays de la Loire region, and arrive in La Roche-sur-Yon, we find ourselves at the legendary heart of the rebellious Vendée, which had nevertheless resigned itself to accepting the Republic. Along the way, while still in Loire-Atlantique, we passed Boussay, not far from Clisson, where on February 26, as *La Vendée* pointed out, "the residents have strikingly contradicted those who claim there is no Jewish question in the countryside."[54] More than fifty people demonstrated that day on the place Jeanne-d'Arc, burned an effigy of Zola, and shouted, "Down with the Jews! Long live the army!" Curiously, the streets of La Roche-sur-Yon remained calmer. Little more than a demonstration was noted on January 24, made up of conscripts singing "The Marseillaise" and shouting, "Death to the Jews!" Three days later they took it up again, making fun of one of their comrades and repeating their previous slogan.[55] The Republic now seemed well accepted in Vendée; republicans like Marchegay, a deputy and the mayor of La Roche-sur-Yon, seemed unruffled, as did Georges Batiot, deputy of Sables-d'Olonne, and Prosper Deshayes, deputy of Fontenay-le-Comte, republicans all. The situation remained so much in hand that the prefect was not at all concerned. In his biweekly reports for April 1898, including the last, dated the thirtieth, he confidently predicted that these deputies would be reelected in May without any great problem, and he anticipated as well the reelection of Paul Bourgeois, the well-established royalist deputy of La Roche.[56] Nevertheless, in late 1897 many police reports pointed to a special effort by the royalists, supported by the Catholic election bureau of Vendée, to win back the electorate, especially since Monsignor Catteau, the bishop of Luçon, was manifesting "an unusual bitterness toward republican ideas." The Catholic Comité Justice-Egalité proved to be particularly aggressive. The prefect reflected that "in Vendée religious questions and the political question are of a piece; the royalists and the Bonapartists make up the bulk of the clerical camp and, while fighting for the Church, they also intend to fight against the Republic. That explains why republican

Catholic views are almost unknown in Vendée; the two terms are con-tradictory here."[57] Numerous newspapers spread Catholics' anti-Semitic ideas. Hence in January 1898 *L'Etoile de la Vendée* observed that times were "bad for the Synagogue . . . The solution to the Jewish question will be bloody." In February L. de La Grandière, municipal councilor of La Roche-Servière, published a letter to Zola in that newspaper, ending with "You dirty Kike, you are a rogue, a scoundrel, a villain."[58] Similarly, in January *La Vendée* went to war against the "Kike's gold," with one reader attacking the mayor of Fontenay-le-Comte, who "shows signs of sympathy toward the Yids. He has thus just provided a policeman with clothing from the store of a Jew recently established in the city."[59] Simi-larly, in its first issue, *L'Electeur Vendéen* announced its convictions: "The Jews constitute a people. They will never be French."[60]

On the other side, the republicans benefited from the support of *Le Patriote de la Vendée*, *Le Libéral de la Vendée*, *Echo de la Vendée*, and *La Vendée Répub-licaine*. But all their support did not gain electoral victory for republi-cans. Marchegay, deputy and mayor of La Roche-sur-Yon, had been sure of his reelection, but to the surprise of all, he was soundly defeated by the marquis Zénobe de Lespinay (9,347 votes to 8,688). The latter thanked his voters by proclaiming on a large orange sign, "France for the French." That major property owner was well established: he was the director of the Société d'Encouragement pour l'Amélioration de la Race du Cheval Français (Society for the Encouragement of Improving the Breed of French Horses), the Union Colombophile de La Roche (Asso-ciation of Pigeon Fanciers of La Roche), and the Société de Tir Mixte de La Roche (Society of Mixed Marksmanship of La Roche), and he ran Catholic charitable clubs with his wife. He was able to attract the workers of Chantonnay, winning the canton back from the left. Close to Abbé Lemire and a *rallié*, he proved a formidable opponent and would be reelected deputy in 1902 and 1906.[61] In the second electoral ward, Paul Bourgeois, a reactionary, was the only candidate to run: he was elected with 13,614 votes. In the first ward of Sables-d'Olonne, Georges Batiot, the incumbent republican deputy, was defeated by the city's mayor, Fernand Gautret. Batiot had ended his platform statement with a resounding "Long live Vendée for the Vendéens! Long live the Republic!" But it was not enough: he was defeated, 7,725 votes to 7,042. Throughout the campaign *L'Etoile de la Vendée* maintained that Ba-

tiot was "the friend of the Jews and traitors." A huge yellow poster asserted that, by contrast, "Gautret is the enemy of the Jews, whom Batiot
supports. Long live France for the French!" Gautret straightforwardly
proclaimed himself "the enemy of the Jews," and a little later, in 1900,
his slate won the municipal elections.[62] In the second ward of Les
Sables, Armand de Baudry d'Asson, who shouted a sharp "Long live
Catholic France! Long live France for the French!" was elected with
89,495 votes, versus 7,127 for his republican opponent, Lucien Dodin.
In Fontenay-le-Comte, the republican Gaston Guilleminet barely managed to be reelected in the first ward, receiving 9,849 votes; his opponent, Raymond de Fontaines, received 9,318 votes after a violently
anti-Semitic campaign. In his platform statement, Fontaines wrote, "I
share the indignation of honest people at the campaign undertaken by
cosmopolitan Jewry for the rehabilitation of a traitor." He constantly
attacked Guilleminet, "the friend of the Jews," and made fun of
"Guilleminet's soft spot for the Kikes."[63] Finally, in the second ward of
Fontenay-le-Comte, the contest pitted Prosper Deshayes, the incumbent
republican deputy, against the Bonapartist attorney Anatole Biré. The
latter was finally defeated but also received a more-than-respectable
share (7,896 votes to his opponent's 10,548). Biré's campaign was
marked by virulent anti-Semitism: on April 17, in the small locality of
Nalliers, for example, in front of three hundred people applauding and
shouting, "Down with the Jews!" he attacked "the band of cosmopolitan Jews who want to sell us out to Germany." In his platform statement, he wrote, "Order must be assured. The government must no
longer tremble before the Jews. Silence must be imposed on Dreyfus
and his accomplices both inside and outside the country." The editor of
L'Electeur Vendéen mercilessly attacked his opponent: "It is not at all clear
to me that Deshayes wants nothing to do with the Jew. Yet the main
concern of patriotic voters is to get rid of the tyranny and treason of
the Jews." Biré agreed, confirming in the same newspaper that "the Jewish people are unassimilable; precautions must be taken against an invading race." Thus a tidal wave swept Vendée, and the four elected
officials of La Roche-sur-Yon and of Sables-d'Olonne made no mystery
of their anti-Semitic feelings. Although Fontenay-le-Comte resisted
with difficulty, the openly displayed hatred attracted several thousand
votes in each ward. In Vendée the anti-Semitic tide of 1898, moving

against a recent evolution, almost completely effaced the republican message.

Farther to the south, the region of Poitou-Charentes looked tranquil by contrast. To be sure, in Niort on January 21, 1898, a dozen isolated young people could be seen crisscrossing the streets of the city, stopping outside stores owned by Jewish tradespeople, uttering threats, insulting them, and breaking windows.[64] But in La Rochelle everything remained calm. Here, as the superintendent's biweekly report observed, in these first months of 1898, so agitated elsewhere, "absolute silence reigns everywhere . . . Dead calm." The same could be said for Rochefort and Marennes. In February and March 1898 in Marans, as the superintendent noted repeatedly, the main concern was that "the public is demanding a glass roof to shelter travelers when crossing the tracks in the train station of Saint-Jean-d'Angély," where only a few street hawkers lingered.[65] The campaign for the legislative elections seemed to be about nothing but grain rights, the regulation of the central marketplace, port entry fees, "the scourge of vagrancy," and the education question. Not a word was whispered about the Dreyfus affair in La Rochelle. Moreover on May 4, 1898, five hundred people gathered to hear the candidate Delmas; when one of them asked an unexpected question concerning the Jews, Delmas "responded, to unanimous approval, that the Declaration of the Rights of Man had made all citizens equal, that the Jews were French in the same capacity as all other citizens, and that as such no measure could be taken against them."[66] Certainly in Saintes and La Rochelle, day after day the press reported in detail the events of the unfolding Dreyfus affair, reported the demonstrations elsewhere, and joined in the unanimous condemnation of Zola. The republican newspaper *L'Indépendant de la Charente-Maritime* wrote that Zola had "dirtied everything in our country, soiled it, ridiculed it . . . That is because the man is not French." And it concluded, "M. Barrès has given us the atavistic secret of that contemptuous ignorance of our race and country . . . Leave the Venetian Zola to his muck heap, his pile of dung." *La Charente-Inférieure*, the republican newspaper of La Rochelle, also condemned the "criminal piece of work . . . the anti-French declaration" of Zola, who was "Italian by birth."[67] But for the rest there was nothing noteworthy. Unlike Angers and Nantes, the region seemed to stand apart from the anti-Semitic mobilization. There was one alarming headline in *La Charente-Inférieure* on January 26, 1898: "Anti-Semitism in La Rochelle." A minuscule incident had just occurred. *La Charente-Inférieure* commented, "It's all been blown completely out of proportion. A sales representative left the theater and shouted, 'Down with Dreyfus!' He was followed by a few spectators, very young people, for a length of about twenty meters, then suddenly disappeared. That was all for that evening. The day of the military lottery, conscripts treated themselves to a lavish supper in a hotel, . . . indiscriminately struck all the storefronts on the rue des Merciers, and banged on the windows. M. B. lodged a complaint. The guilty party, along with his comrades, asserted that he was not professing anti-Semitism . . . Once again, there was nothing to make a fuss about, and our population has once more demonstrated its calm, its level-headedness, and its wisdom." That was all. It was very unlike Vendée.

Chapter Seven

The Battle of Brest

On January 1, 1899, Brest became a disaster area. A cyclone hit the city, overturning trees and breaking storefronts. Tiles pulled off roofs were transformed into dangerous weapons. As people were preparing for the theatrical performance that evening of Fromental Halévy's grand opera *La Juive*, an incident erupted at about four p.m. on the battlefield of Brest. According to the report of the central superintendent, dated January 2, "a few young people had stolen nougat from a foreign merchant, and the latter's clerk tried to foil the theft. The young people then threw objects from the display case at the merchant's head . . . A brawl followed. The crowd stood up for the little thieves and got them free, to the shout of 'Down with the Jews!' These events attracted a crowd of two hundred people. The demonstration expressed itself as a defense of the thieves out of hatred for the Jews. Six individuals were arrested."[1] In the superintendent's view, the crowd protected the "little" thieves "out of hatred for the Jews." We learn little else, except that the nougat merchant was a "foreigner." Was he a Jewish or non-Jewish foreigner, a French Jew, a stranger to the region and perceived as different, a stranger to the country? The report does not say. The court records contain no trace of that confrontation or the arrests that followed.[2]

The press also had no knowledge of the incident. It is as if the authorities, too touchy about this type of trouble now that it had been ravaging France for a year, had dreamed it up. But with a little perseverance, I was finally able to confirm its veracity. On January 3 in *L'Express de Brest*, the following short item appeared: "The misadventures of a nougat merchant. A certain Badi, saying he was the victim of a theft on the part of a few children, came out of his stall to pursue them. But Badi had not reckoned on the crowd, which turned against him. A considerable crowd formed, and the officers had to intervene. One of them was kicked in the legs, and his assailant, a port worker, was taken to the station." This republican newspaper (which was created to combat the strong clerical influence but would vanish that same month, January 1899) tells us little more than the name of the nougat merchant and the presence of port workers in the angry crowd. Did the reporter not hear the shouts of "Down with the Jews!" that the authorities noted? Did he deliberately choose to be silent about them? What happened to the particularly aggressive worker who joined the crowd acting "out of hatred for the Jews"?

The day after that sudden outburst of violence, Brest recovered its good nature: the orchestra of the Second Infantry Regiment installed itself peacefully on the site and played Esprit Auber's *Le Lac des Fées*, then Edmond Audran's *Le Grand Mogol*, Léo Delibes's *La Source*, and *Richard Wallace*, a military allegro.[3] The city returned to peace and quiet, devoid of any public form of anti-Semitism. The biweekly police report (June 1 to June 15) nevertheless noted that inscriptions of "Down with the Jews! Death to the traitor!" were written by hand on posters announcing the judgment of the Cour de Cassation annulling Dreyfus's conviction. In this same report, a sword duel between Lévy, a high school teacher, and Amingue, sublieutenant of artillery, was also noted: "The adversaries failed to hit each other. That duel is connected to the Dreyfus affair." The subprefect wrote directly to the minister of the interior: "The unmarried high school teachers take their meals in a room of the Hôtel de l'Univers, a closed room available especially for them. In a nearby room the lieutenants and sublieutenants of the navy artillery gather." As the teachers were exchanging views about the affair, an officer named

Amingue, challenged by the "jingoistic" attitude of one of his colleagues, "knocked on the door leading to the dining room, entered, and made it known that, from the next room, he had heard remarks that were offensive to the army and that he had come to ask for an explanation." The officer then quarrelled with Lévy, a mathematics teacher. The situation calmed down until the next day when "Amingue took an aggressive stance in front of Lévy in a café. More words were exchanged, and a duel was arranged. It took place on Wednesday; Amingue received a slight wound in the arm. The two adversaries reconciled and sealed that reconciliation by sharing a friendly glass of punch that evening."[4]

Although Brest did not experience the major mobilizations that struck many cities and towns throughout France, the Dreyfus affair nonetheless elicited a long string of minor incidents nearby. In Lorient, for example, on January 21, 1898, a blacksmith from the dockyard reeled from one café to another shouting, "Down with the Jews!" The next day, again in Lorient, on the cours de la Bôve, bulletins that read "Down with the Jews! Out with Zola!" were distributed.[5] The same day in Quimper, during the military lottery, after singing and dancing, "a certain number of young people tried to stage a small anti-Semitic demonstration . . . The attempted demonstration had disturbing consequences for only one demonstrator who, in fleeing the police, fell and broke an arm."[6] On the north coast, in Saint-Brieuc on January 27, about fifty high school students and conscripts gathered on the boulevard Thiers, outside the home of Lucien Foubert, an instructor of history and geography and, along with his colleagues Celestin Bouglé and Robert Muffang, the signer of the petition in support of Dreyfus in L'Aurore. They shouted with all their strength, "Down with the Jews! Resign! Resign!"[7]

In Saint-Malo, the situation got rather serious. On January 21 handwritten signs were posted on the ramparts, on the place du Pilori, and on the warehouses of the South Western Company: the signs invited everyone to participate in an anti-Semitic demonstration that evening on the square Duguay-Trouin. Two hundred young people, preceded by about a hundred children, gathered outside the navy office and went down the rue Porcon-de-la-Barbinais, chanting, "Down with the Jews!

Long live the army!" They assembled outside a store, the Cristal Palace, whose owner was suspected of being Jewish. They yelled, struck the shutters of the store, and left again for the Au Petit Paris store on the rue de Dinan, where the same scene was repeated. On Sunday the twenty-second, signs again urged people to demonstrate: more than five hundred people—close to a thousand, according to the gendarmerie report—went down the rue Pocron-de-la-Barbinais. They stood outside the Grand Bazaar and shouted again. But the police superintendent pointed out to them that its owner, Giraudeau, "was French and that his silent partner, the comte de Kermovan, belonged to one of the oldest families in Brittany." The demonstrators "understood" him and, as a result, headed toward the Cristal Palace, where they pulled off its shutters. The procession tirelessly crisscrossed the streets, repeating the same slogans. Overwhelmed, the police superintendent asked for troops to intervene: about fifty soldiers with bayoneted rifles took their positions and stopped the demonstrators, who nevertheless managed to throw stones at the Cristal Palace, twice hitting the police superintendent and an assistant to the mayor. In the midst of the cheering on the place du Pilori, the crowd burned an effigy, "a symbol of Jewry and the Dreyfus syndicate," before finally dispersing. *L'Union Malouine et Dinannaise* reported that "at the request of their owner, Mme Guillemard, the foreign shopkeepers who ran the Cristal Palace store left the city of Saint-Malo."[8] In its account of these very tumultuous days in Saint-Malo, *La Libre Parole* concluded its report with the following query: "When will we decide to arrest the Jews en masse, the primary cause of the uproar?"[9] Over the next few days, more small demonstrations occurred and threatened to get worse. To deal with them, the police set up an artillery battery on the place Bouvet and a brigade of mounted gendarmerie crisscrossed the city. Police officers equipped with clubs dispersed the demonstrators "by twirling [the clubs] around."[10] On September 27, across the Gulf of Saint-Malo in Granville, Louis Baudoin was seated at the terrace of the Grand Café. The police report noted that "three Arabs came by selling carpets. M. Baudoin called them 'Jews' and shouted, 'Down with the Jews! France for the French!' A few customers stood up for the merchants. A fairly large uproar began, during which shouts of 'Long live the army! Down with the Jews!' could be heard. Baudoin went back into the café, paid for a few soldiers' drinks, and shouted, along with a few onlookers, 'Long live the army! Long live the police! Down with the Jews!' "[11]

In Dinan on the same day, *La Rose de France*, a two-act play by Drumont's friend Jean Drault, was performed. *L'Union Malouise et Dinannaise* described the performance:

> God of Israel, Abraham, and the rest, how heartily we laughed! . . . It is the eternal story of the Jew and his gut liddle bissniss, two things so absolutely inseparable that one cannot be understood without the other. A young artist, M. Mercier, admirably plays the part of the Jew, who, through wily and perfidious scheming, and with the sly tone of voice that characterizes the Jew so well, is about to drag a good but . . . somewhat weak man, the gut misser Tupois, as he is called, into a very bad liddle bissniss. Yidman (that's the name of the Jew) is going to have him sign a partnership agreement, when, on the accusation of one of his own coreligionists, he is arrested in the home of M. Dubois himself, and accused of spying. That play was an out-and-out success, both because of the performance, which was perfect in every detail, and because of the topical overtones it acquired in the unfortunate circumstances we are going through.

Beginning in the morning, the residents could read posters proclaiming:

CITIZENS OF DINAN!

WILL WE REMAIN INACTIVE AND INSENSITIVE TO THE

INDIGNATION THAT HAS TAKEN HOLD OF ALL THE FRENCH

PEOPLE, AFTER THE MACHINATIONS OF THE JEWS, THE WORST

ENEMIES OF OUR DEAR HOMELAND?

YOU ARE FRENCHMEN AND PATRIOTS!

SO, FRIDAY EVENING, EIGHT-THIRTY, THE PLACE DE LA GARE.

LONG LIVE THE ARMY! DOWN WITH THE YIDS!

That evening a group formed on the rue de la Gare and assembled outside the gendarmerie and then outside the barracks. After a few minutes, as *L'Union Malouine et Dinannaise* reported, "the lieutenant of the gendarmerie told the demonstrators: 'Gentlemen, it is late; where do you want to go? You are from good families, you are going to disperse and not make it necessary for us to book you for disturbing the peace. Let us take our leave and see you tomorrow . . . It is ten-thirty; the cafés are about to close. Citizens of Dinan, sleep, under the protection of the police and the gendarmerie, which watch over your persons and your property."[12] The next day a new sign covered the walls of the city:

PATRIOTS OF DINAN,

WE CANNOT, IN THE SPACE OF A FEW HOURS, DEMONSTRATE ALL

THE CONTEMPT AND HATRED WE FEEL FOR THE JEWISH RACE

AND THE ARMY'S DETRACTORS.

WE ARE EXPECTING A NEW SHOW OF PATRIOTISM FROM YOU.

SEE YOU THIS EVENING ON THE PLACE DU CHAMP

AT EIGHT-THIRTY PRECISELY.

Despite penetrating cold and intense fog, more than five hundred people gathered on the place du Champ and headed toward the barracks, shouting, "Down with the Jews! Long live the army! Down with Zola!" "Peaceful strollers followed the procession as they would have followed a torchlit parade," noted the police report. The demonstrators resumed their march toward the Grands-Fossés and shouted, "Long live Algiers!" They passed through the rue de l'Ecole and briskly climbed the rue de l'Abbaye, returning to town by way of the viaduct, where the superintendent, who was following the procession, slipped and fell. The troops were confined: the Thirteenth Hussars and the Twenty-fourth Dragoons were in their barracks to avoid provoking the demonstrators. "A certain number of horses were saddled with soldier's packs, and the horsemen stood ready to rush into the street in case of serious unrest." The mayor sent out a notice inviting his fellow citizens to cease their activities, since "the expressions of sympathy for the army that are being given in this way are missing their target, by imposing on the garrison the great annoyance of being confined." The next day a new sign appeared:

ANTI-JEWISH DEMONSTRATION

CITIZENS! A NOTICE FROM OUR HONORED MAYOR IS TRYING TO
LIMIT OUR FREEDOM. THEY WANT TO STOP OUR PATRIOTIC AND
ANTI-JEWISH DEMONSTRATIONS. LET US SHOW WITH THE
STUBBORNNESS OF BRETONS THAT WE KNOW HOW TO RECONCILE
OUR RIGHT TO FREEDOM AND OUR RESPECT FOR AUTHORITY.
COME, THEREFORE, ALL OF YOU, DEMONSTRATE THIS EVENING
UNTIL TEN O'CLOCK. UNTIL THAT HOUR WE ARE WITHIN OUR
RIGHTS. WE INVITE THE GENTLEMEN OF THE GENDARMERIE TO
CURB THEIR ZEAL . . . THE ANTI-DREYFUSIAN, ANTI-JEWISH,
ANTI-GENDARME ASSOCIATION. THIS EVENING,
EIGHT O'CLOCK, PLACE DUGUESCLIN.[13]

That evening the police and the mounted gendarmerie circulated in the streets, but there were no new disturbances. It was over; Dinan had recovered its calm.

Brittany as a whole was buzzing with anti-Semitic incidents. Not far away, in Châteauneuf, a demonstration took place against Béquet, a candidate to the arrondissement council. An effigy representing him was paraded in the streets by 150 people, with a placard reading "Down with the Jews and Zola!" The demonstrators sang patriotic songs, then burned the effigy, before the gendarmes intervened to disperse them.[14]

In Rennes demonstrations took place that have hardly received the attention they deserve. They were triggered when Jules Andrade, a professor of mathematics at the school of sciences sent an open letter to General Mercier, a former schoolmate of his at the Ecole Polytechnique, for publication in *L'Aurore* on January 15th: "If Dreyfus is innocent, which, I am not afraid to say, appears more and more probable to me, I would pity you with all my heart." On the seventeenth people could come to hear, in Salle Victor-Poirel, Mozart's Symphony in

E Flat, Charles Leconte de Lisle's *Nell*, and Fauré's *Shylock*; meanwhile about three hundred students, according to *Le Journal de Rennes*, "wanted to make the professor expiate his soft spot for Israel." They massed outside his home and caused a great racket, shouting, "Out with Andrade! Down with the Jews!" Soon more than twelve hundred were parading, including a thousand students. A circle formed around a wicker effigy stuffed with straw depicting Dreyfus; demonstrators struck it with canes, stoked a fire, and jumped boldly over the blaze while singing. Then the group, down to somewhat more than six hundred students, ran through the streets. The next day, the eighteenth, about three hundred students invaded the school of sciences. Seeing Andrade was not there, they ran to his home, where they shouted in indignation, "Out with Andrade! Down with the Jews! Long live the army!" They circled the place du Palais-des-Sciences and attacked Victor Basch—"Professor Bâche" or even "Bach," according to police reports—whom they ran into by chance. They came back to the school of sciences, where a farandole was organized. *Le Journal de Rennes* harshly denounced Professors Aubry, Andrade, Victor Basch, and Henri Sée, who had joined *L'Aurore* in condemning Esterhazy by signing the manifesto of intellectuals: "Did the signers count on impunity because at least two are Israelites, that is, Frenchmen of recent date? And might we, the sons of France, descendants of those who made the nation at the cost of their suffering and sometimes of their blood, be obliged, for a long time yet, to hang our heads in the face of Israel's insolence and the insulting behavior of all those creatures baptized by pruning shears? Let them beware!" The next morning, the nineteenth, posters announcing another demonstration covered the walls of the city.

That evening at the Carlis, before an assembled crowd, a letter was read, addressed to the director of the university. "You were no doubt grieved to see the letters and signatures of MM. Andrade, Basch, Sée, Aubry, and so on . . . We judge them unworthy to teach sincere French people who love their country. Those antipatriots should leave the university! The comrades of Dreyfus should resign! The youth in the schools are counting on the government to sanction their generous ideas and finally make the true French people of France free and dignified." Giraud, the son of the attorney general, took the floor and backed the measures undertaken by the prefect in that regard; then a demonstration of more than a thousand people headed toward the home of Victor Basch. At its head students carried transparencies reading "Out with Andrade! Out with the Jews!" Brandishing paper lanterns on the tips of their canes, they marched through the streets and demonstrated outside Andrade's home. On the place de la Mairie, an enormous circle formed around a bonfire burning issues of *L'Aurore*. Someone threw on an effigy representing Andrade, along with the banners and the paper lanterns, giving cries of joy as the sparks rose toward the sky.[15]

On January 21 Offenbach's *Orphée aux Enfers* was playing to a full house, with "absolutely awful choruses . . . The operetta might have been passable if there had been no singing in it," wrote one reviewer. The Association Artistique et Littéraire de Bretagne was preparing for the evening of the twenty-sixth, when its members would perform arias from Saint-Saëns's *Samson et Dalila*, Bériot's *Scènes de Ballet*, Vidal's *La Bonne Journée*, and the comte de Bellevue's *La Cruche Cassée*.[16] Meanwhile, the prefect, worried, sent a letter to the interior minister:

It is certain that the peculiar letter from Professor Andrade to General Mercier, whom he does not know and has never seen, was the cause of all the demonstrations that have just occurred in Rennes. The working-class population asks for nothing more than to participate, and the clerical camp, very powerful in Rennes, is fully prepared to take advantage of that movement among the youth of the schools to organize anti-Semitic unrest there. That is a situation that could become serious. I have begged the minister of public education to order M. Andrade's transfer . . . His transfer, I believe, will calm these very agitated souls; nevertheless, I feel that the situation of Israelite professors such as MM. Basch and Sée, who joined the protest by the newspaper *L'Aurore*, will always be wrong in an environment as Catholic as Brittany, and that their presence at the University of Rennes can only gravely damage its development. Undoubtedly, it is the Catholic university of Angers that will benefit from that administrative mistake.

The same day the prefect sent another letter to the minister of public education to complain that Andrade had "elicited legitimate feelings and whose effect has been to call attention to his colleagues of the Jewish race."[17] On several occasions the prefect wrote the rector to point out to him that he intended to take measures to prevent Andrade from resuming his classes. In early February Andrade slapped one Régnier, a law student and son of the vice president of the prefecture council, who had been demonstrating against him. The instructor appeared in criminal court, and the prefect urged the minister of public education to transfer him without delay: "His attitude is extremely regrettable, especially in an environment like that of Rennes, which he ought to know and where the Dreyfus affair has taken on great importance and upset people . . . The solution would satisfy the university students but would also give satisfaction to the population, which is outraged by the professor's behavior." On February 5, in a courtroom packed with students, Andrade paid a fine of fifty francs, plus one franc in damage and interest, to Régnier. The students brought down the house with their applause. The public prosecutor condemned "very severely" Andrade's letter to General Mercier and his attitude toward the students.[18]

We now possess good evidence of the climate reigning in Rennes at this time thanks to the very recent publication of the correspondence of Henri Sée, who wrote many letters to André-Ferdinand Hérold, a poet and the son of the notorious Hérold, prefect of Seine. On January 25 Sée emphasized that the son of the attorney general and the sons of the appeals court judges had been the ringleaders in the student demonstrations:

> The students decided to go to Basch's house. There were at least fifteen hundred of them, some of whom were not students. You could make out the most staid people in the city: attorneys, bourgeois of every sort, even priests. At the head was the cream of Christian and royalist youth. All the factions of the reaction were present. They began by booing and insulting Basch, shouting, "Down with the Jews!" But soon stones were thrown at windows where light could be made out. All of a sudden, seditious cries of "Long live the Republic! Down with the clericals!" were heard. This counterdemonstration was composed of about thirty people, including, in the forefront, our own students marching.

The last demonstration, as Sée described it, began at the Carlis and was attended by six hundred students; more than a thousand gathered outside. "Attached to the front of the rostrum was a sort of banner decorated with a nondescript Jewish figure with the names of several professors . . . Adam, the son of a magistrate at the court of appeals, presided . . . Fifteen hundred people left for the place de la Mairie . . . They burned the Dreyfusian banner on a fire improvised from paper lanterns." Sée continued:

> We have the impression that we are suffering the effects of a real reign of terror. The vast majority of the bourgeois and civil servants throw stones at us. We have unfriendly relations with a host of people, are looked down upon, called pariahs. You hear publicly that the Jews must be slaughtered, and it is the officers who are the most bitter, or at least some whose views we have heard. Life is going to become intolerable, and I am seriously thinking of clearing out. But the whole province is just as intolerable. Hatred of the Jews can be easily explained: along with the Protestants, they are the only bourgeois who escape the grip of the Church. Hence the Dreyfus trial. I have come to realize that they are monitoring my correspondence, that my letters have been opened. We are already suspect: when will we be banished?[19]

These letters give an idea of the climate of intolerance and threat that reigned in Rennes: the few professors, Jewish and non-Jewish, who took Dreyfus's side lived in terror. The anti-Semitic atmosphere even penetrated the barracks. Hence in July two cooks from the Tenth Artillery Regiment shouted in protest, "Dirty Jew! Down with the Jews!" after a Jewish sergeant found fault with them. *Le Patriote Breton* published the following commentary: "Although the soldiers, who are all good Frenchmen, know how to submit to the harshest rules of discipline, it pains them to receive orders from those who, *pace* the Crémieux decree, do not have the right to the status of French citizen. If the government had not sold out to Jewry, it might have excluded Israelites of all stripes from the army long ago; in that way we would not have the dreary Dreyfus affair on our hands at this moment."[20] These threats would be repeated during the Rennes trial in August and September 1899. On June 6 various anti-Semitic demonstrations erupted: during a torchlit march of the Forty-first Regiment, a large group of students from

Champ de Mars shouted, "Long live France! Long live the army!" A Jewish shopkeeper, Saxer, was brutalized. A police report noted that "as these demonstrators passed in front of the seminary, the students who were perched on the surrounding wall cheered. Moreover, among the demonstrators were several ecclesiastics who, though they did not shout, manifested their joy by waving their hats." In another dispatch the police officer explained that "the great majority of young people belong to or come out of the Saint-Vincent seminary, which is run by priests. It is to that institution that the officers of the garrison send their sons."[21] Many anti-Semitic meetings were held in June and July, attended by deputies such as Le Gonidec, an elected official of Vitré, and they frequently ended with swift parades into town. In mid-July things again turned serious, although *L'Avenir Hebdomadaire* tried to minimize it: "Nothing serious, but improper and childish pranks, which ought to be cut short. This morning, at about eleven o'clock, approximately sixty young people led by supervisors met in front of the Hôtel des Trois Marches and shouted, 'Out with the Jews!' They threw stones at the windows of Victor Basch's apartment. One stone broke a windowpane and dropped into his work office. M. Basch, without losing his composure, came out of his house, and the band of naughty children did not dare attack him. They dispersed." Basch described the incident to his wife: "As is my habit, I placed myself at the window. Someone spewed all the insults you can imagine in my face . . . A moment of silence, then someone shouts, 'Speech, speech.' I did not deign speak to those brutes . . . With the racket, rocks flew and broke one of my windowpanes." Many young men were arrested, but for the most part were fined only one franc on August 14.[22]

The police maintained strict surveillance over the anti-Semitic groups, which remained very active in late July. For example, at Les Lices the groups held a nationalist banquet presided over by the Boulangist René Le Hérissé and attended by the mayor of Rennes and a number of municipal councilors. It ended with a torchlit procession, during which they chanted, "All the Kikes to the lamppost, all the Kikes, we'll hang them!" The police report is all the more reliable because "the cross bearer for the Notre-Dame church, who was implicated in the July 14 demonstration, is reportedly prepared to denounce all those who were with him, including a certain number of students from the Sainte-Anne workshop run by M. Lebreton." Also "the young Leroy, who took part in the Basch demonstration, is reportedly prepared to denounce his comrades in addition to saying how he was led to demonstrate." The police maintained that "the true focus of the unrest that the clericals sought to create is allegedly the Catholic club headed by Huchet, one of whose nephews was arrested on July 14. It was to the hardware shop run by Huchet's son-in-law, Gourdon, that the young anti-Semite Robin, a scholarship student at the Rennes secondary school, came to get the password." Each day further confirmed the role of the priests in fomenting the unrest. The priest of Moussaint was said to be one of the most militant. He was very rich and devoted part of his fortune to clerical and anti-Semitic propaganda, housing *Le Patriote Breton* in one of his buildings. On July 24, on the place Sainte-Anne, a meeting of the Ligue Antisémitique in Rennes was held, with about a hundred people present. They took a wreath to the monument to those who had died in the 1870–71 war. As people were giving speeches in front of the monument, the group of anti-Semites sang "The Anti-Jewish Marseillaise," before being dispersed by the police. On the twenty-ninth another meeting was held, again on the place Sainte-Anne, but this time it was disrupted by—in the expression of the police—"Semitic socialists," who started a brawl. On August 1 the anti-Semites again assembled and expressed concern about the outburst of the "Semitic socialists" at the previous meeting. In exasperation President of the league L.-H. Petit, an important Boulangist leader, declared that they "must no longer argue with the Dreyfusards but hit hard; that is the only way to prove we are right." The wounded anti-Semites received, as a gift, a portrait of Paul Déroulède mounted on cardboard. A merger between the local nationalists and anti-Semites was expected as soon as possible, but for the moment they confined themselves to selling portraits of Déroulède for 0.20 francs apiece and to arranging for the distribution of *Le Péril Juif* in Rennes and the rural areas. On August 8 another meeting of the Ligue Antisémitique was held, attended by about eighty people. There they made plans to shout, "Long live France! Long live the Republic! Down with the Jews!" when the generals passed on their way to the second court-martial of Dreyfus. On September 1, on the faubourg d'Antrain, the police arrested Pierre Philouze, municipal councilor of the commune of Saint-Grégoire. Philouze, in an advanced state of inebriation, had followed Jaurès and Basch out of a restaurant and taken "advantage of the moment when these gentlemen were on their doorstep" to shout noisily, "Long live France! Down with the Jews!" On September 9, at the moment of the verdict, customers at the café de la Paix sang "The Marseillaise." They shouted, "Long live the army! Down with the Jews!" and "Oh, it will happen! it will happen! All the Yids, we will hang them."[23] In October many police reports mentioned the increasing strength of the Ligue Antisémitique, with which Edouard Dubuc was involved: the students of Rennes were joining. "One of the most active members is a young man of eighteen," a report indicated, "the close friend of an independent priest who is preparing the [previously] unsuccessful candidates for the *baccalauréat* exam."[24]

From Brest to Rennes, from Quimper to Saint-Malo, from Lorient to Saint-Brieuc and Dinan, and particularly in Rennes, Brittany experienced a string of anti-Semitic demonstrations in the streets of these usually calm cities. Paris was unaware of almost all of them, but they did mobilize crowds. Catholic domination and the clash between royalists and republicans truly paved the way for a structured anti-Semitic populist movement. In a general way, Brittany remained a place where the Drumont movement could find recruits for their cause, and the presence of anti-Semitism was easily palpable, even though the mobilization could not threaten synagogues since there were none. In this region, where the Jewish presence was almost nil, it was always "foreigners," Catholics from somewhere else, or even "Arabs" who bore the brunt of the anti-Semitic unrest. Hatred of the Jews was nevertheless constant and striking in its intensity. Although Brittany's republican movement repudiated anti-Semitism, particularly since Blanquism and a certain type of radicalism remained very weak there, the rejection of the Jews remained a leitmotif in the speeches and positions of reactionary and clerical politicians and officials.

This can be demonstrated if we linger briefly with the legislative elections. In Brest Abbé Gayraud, a social Catholic and friend of Abbé Lemire opposed by the royalists, had long given openly anti-Semitic speeches. He was elected in 1897 in the third ward of the department of Finistère, but the election was voided. The same year, despite the campaign of the comte de Blois, who accused "the Jews of rigging the stock market" and ended his platform statement with "Brittany for the Bretons!" he was reelected. Gayraud, who maintained that "the Jews own the press and high banking" and that the Jewish question was "insoluble for anyone who does not believe in Christ," would be reelected in 1898 and in every legislative election until World War I.[25]

In Rennes, Le Hérissé won after conducting a campaign devoid of all ambiguity. On April 3, 1898, in Cavaignac, at a banquet in the main dining room of the town hall—with Guiyesse and Pontallis, the deputies of Lorient and Fougères, respectively, in attendance—Le Hérissé distinguished Dreyfus's ideas from "the opinion of every good Frenchman . . . The remedy to that Jewish policy is simple. We have universal suffrage." On May 5, before fifteen hundred people in Salle Laimu, he declared to repeated applause, "There is a serious question, and that is the high cost of bread; the market has been monopolized by the Jews. We have seen them, these Jews, trying to save their most traitorous one, Captain Dreyfus . . . We must act against those who unite with the Jews. I do not want to compromise anyone's conscience. I am a liberal." On the tenth, on the rue Thiers, Le Hérissé repeated the same speech. Another candidate, René Grivart, proclaimed on enormous blue and pink signs, "Natives of Rennes, the old Gallic blood has awakened. A few people—and I am among them—had long pointed to the existence of the Jewish question. May this peril, now clearly glimpsed, serve to rally all the sons of France to the shout of 'France for the French!' "[26] In Vitré, Le Gonidec de Troissan, a royalist who participated in meetings opposing the Jews (for example, in Rennes), won without difficulty, receiving 11,900 votes. Similarly, in Redon, Lieutenant Colonel du Halgouël was easily reelected. On May 5 in one of the warehouses of the Garnier factory on the quai Jean-Bart—in the presence of Garnier and Lagrée, arrondissement councilors, attorneys, bankers, notaries, dealers, and "almost all the workers in the Garnier factory and the Mebon and Richer construction yards"—he emphasized that he "was particularly devoted to the farmers and workers, whose fate is the constant object of his concern." He was "the sworn enemy of the stateless, of the Jews and Freemasons, whom he will always bitterly fight," and he directed "our religious faith against the attacks led by the cosmopolitan syndicate."[27]

In Fougères anti-Semitism was shared by almost everyone. Throughout the year, *Le Journal de Fougères* denounced "the money-grubbing, corrupting, thieving, traitorous Jews, the un-French Jews." On February 5, 1898, it proclaimed the need to "de-Jewify France" and admonished, "Does the blood of the Gauls and the Franks no longer flow in our veins? . . . Come, old Gallic cock, flap your wings and give your war chant." Here Jenouvrier ran as a liberal against Mayor Bazillon, a progressive republican, and called for setting in place "an anti-Jewish policy so that France will be for the French." He was an attorney at the court of appeals in Rennes and intended to fight against "cosmopolitan Jewry." "Have you noticed?" wrote *Le Journal de Fougères*. "M. Bazillon never dares say a word against those cosmopolitan Jews who are ruining us and who want to starve France by monopolizing the wheat. That is because M. Bazillon is the prisoner of the Jews, who support him, and who oppose M. Jenouvrier, because he has publicly denounced their power and their misdeeds." To escape that accusation, Bazillon declared in *La Chronique de Fougères* on April 30, "It is not only against the Jews that one must go to war but against the Jewish spirit . . . It is unfortunately not the monopoly of the circumcised. France must truly be for the French." He won with 10,400 votes, versus 9,316 for Jenouvrier.

In Cornouaille the election campaigns regularly revealed the force of anti-Semitic prejudice—for example, in Douarnenez.[28] Not far from there, a poster signed by "a group of sailors from Concarneau" denounced a candidate "supported by the Jew Reinach"; in Quimper E. de Chabre, municipal councilor, asserted on enormous blue, white, and red posters that "we need a Republic delivered from the connections to international Jewry and Freemasonry."[29] In Morlaix the comte de Guerdavid proclaimed on huge posters, "Catholics, I am honored to share your faith. A band of cosmopolitans, supported by Jewish finance, is aspiring to stain the honor of the flag and to ruin the military hierarchy . . . Long live France for the French! Long live Finistère!" His candidacy was vigorously supported by *La Résistance (Croix de Morlaix)*, which maintained that "all Israel is in the fray at the current time." On the front page of that newspaper, he published his platform in the Breton language and repeated his accusations. Although he was defeated by Jaoeun, a radical-leaning republican, he received 6,838 votes in the first round.[30]

Brittany did not experience the violent anti-Semitic mobilization that shook several other regions, but the events retraced here were not inconsequential. We see this clearly in the following police report: "The [Dreyfus] affair has had repercussions on the use of vacation time. A number of Parisians who have not yet decided on where they will take their vacations are preoccupied with whether, at this time, they will be able to enjoy the healthy air in peace, without the affair ricocheting around them."[31]

Chapter Eight

In the Region of Normandy

On the night of January 18 to 19, 1898, fog literally enveloped the city of Rouen. The populace waited for daybreak in their rooms. The evening before, the privileged had headed toward the Grand Théâtre, to attend a performance of Mozart's *Don Giovanni*; the same day *Le Patriote de Normandie* had published a long summary of the libretto. In the dark of night, the city was covered with anti-Semitic proclamations: anonymous people displayed overactive imaginations and expressed the violence of their rejection in every way possible—and suddenly plunged the residents, when they emerged, into profound anxiety. On the store windows, walls, and city properties, an incalculable number of banners proclaimed, "Death to the Jews," "Let's drive off the Yids," "Down with the Yids," "Long live the army! Get the Jews," "Down with the Jews," "Get the usurper! Death to the Jews," "Down with Hendlé!!! Death to the Jews," "Into the trash heap with the Jews," "Into the sewer with the Jews," "Death to the Jews," "Send Scheurer to Charenton, send the syndicate to the sewer," and so on. There were countless variations on this theme. Prefect Ernest Hendlé, a

Jew and forceful high official, was particularly singled out for attack.[1]

Jewish shopkeepers received anonymous letters. A disconcerted Lévy, who ran a store at 99 rue du Gros-Horloge, forwarded this threatening text to the central police bureau:

Mr. Lévi, you old hypocrite,

I warn you in advance that tomorrow, at fifteen minutes before seven, you will hear from me. You will do well, old Jew, to lock yourself in, because you could get debris from your windows and the storefront may get a stomachache and you as well.

We are all going to equip ourselves with clubs and we will start with you and the others. Then, Blum, Bloch, *Le Petit Paris*, and all the Jewish businesses like you.

We will do more damage to you than to Ravel, who is not Jewish like you, see, you dirty old lout. Your daughters will be married to Jews like you, see, you dirty pimp. If we catch one of them, we will rape her, especially the oldest one. Now, work it out, and, old pal, tomorrow evening, Saturday, seven o'clock.

Down with the Jews. We will hang them all, those future Dreyfuses. Devil's Island awaits you all, Jews, and the guillotine afterward, see, you pile of good-for-nothings. And now, see you tomorrow without fail. You can warn the cops.

[Signed:] A committee of demonstrators.[2]

The lawbreakers kept their rendezvous. At approximately ten-thirty on the night of the nineteenth, about a hundred people gathered on the place de la Haute-Vieille-Tour after leaving the Ecole des Beaux-Arts, then ran through the streets shouting, "Down with Zola! Out with the Jews!" They went to the rue de l'Epicerie and assembled outside the store of a certain Rosenberg, breaking the windows. They then headed to a store owned by Blum, a shoe merchant, on the rue des Augustins, where they hit the door with canes, then on to the place du Vieux-Marché, where they were dispersed by the police. The police superintendent considered the demonstration a "regrettable childish prank," but it was remarkably organized. Witness this letter addressed to the president of the students' association of Rouen:

A great cry of protest is rising up from one end of France to the other, against the infamous schemes of traitors hired by foreigners ... I come to beg you to tell your comrades that tomorrow all students are requested to gather at the place de la Basse-Vieille-Tour, where the students of the Ecole des Beaux-Arts, who began to demonstrate yesterday, will depart from their school. A large anti-Semitic demonstration in support of the army will take place. You are requested to leave in an orderly manner and in rows of four, which should reform quickly if they happen to be broken up.[3]

At the designated moment, three hundred demonstrators broke into two groups, one headed toward the place de la Basse-Vieille-Tour to take the quays, the other toward the cathedral. On the rue de la République, the demonstrators gained momentum and chanted anti-Semitic refrains at the top of their lungs, as the police made arrests. Among the arrested were Lucien Vieulle, seventeen, an employee; Abel Franqueville, eighteen, a high school student; Maurice Touzet, eighteen, a student at a private boarding school; Jules Marest, seventeen, a business employee; Albert Triquet, an accountant; and Joseph Massa, a painter. *Le Patriote de Normandie* exulted at the scope of the demonstration: "We must celebrate the fact that the fine fervor for noble causes, known in earlier times, still quickens the heart of French youth." The next day, after the arrests and the police intervention, the newspaper raised its pitch: "Is it true that, in one of our schools, someone threatened to take away the students' ID cards if they were associated with an anti-Jewish demonstration? Is it true that, in another school, someone subjected the students to a sort of inquisition, that they were made to submit to an interrogation?"[4] On January 9 that large regional daily denounced "the Judaic concerns of Dreyfus's attorneys." The day after the publication of Zola's "J'accuse," it mercilessly attacked the "folly of that auxiliary to Israel." The same was true for *La Semaine Religieuse du Diocèse de Rouen*, which day after day denounced the "Jewish sectarians," the "cosmopolitan Israelites," the "Jews who abuse their preponderance."[5]

On the evening of the twenty-first another demonstration seemed about to take place. As another performance of *Don Giovanni* was under way and the Union Catholique held an evening of music and literature, the prefecture displayed its concern: "the evening shows signs of becoming very eventful. It is payday for the workers. It is anticipated that workers from the outskirts of Rouen will come to join the demonstrators." Already the day had been marked by various incidents. Officer Fauvel noted that, on the rue Saint-Lô, an individual had pointed at a passerby and declared, "There's another one, he's a Kike." On the walls of several houses, a little sign was put up: "The current ministers are puppets whose strings are in the hands of Jewish financiers." Tension was high, and the police were omnipresent. At about six-thirty a procession assembled at the corner of the rue Saint-Fardeau and the rue Grand-Pont; accompanied by many curiosity-seekers, the demonstrators headed toward the place de la Cathédrale, then dispersed and regrouped outside *Le Patriote.* A considerable crowd was now present and more or less participated in the demonstration. Until close to midnight, it shouted the traditional "Down with the Jews! Out with Zola!" with ringing shouts of "Long live Joan of Arc!" They moved from the place de la République to the place de la Cathédrale and the place des Carmes and loitered for a long time outside the department of public records. More than two thousand people joined that protest. Mounted gendarmes combed the streets and constantly intervened to move the curiosity-seekers along. As the arias of *Tannhäuser* rose up before an attentive audience, the din increased. A cavalry squadron charged several times and made several arrests of the same sort it had two days before. Officers Lécuyer and Poisson were suddenly "surrounded by individuals who struck them violently with their canes and managed to release the prisoners." The prefect's office gave notice to the police "not to have too heavy a hand and to avoid accidents," particularly since women and children were present in the crowd. Maintaining order became all the more delicate a task given that, "with the help of very mild, clear weather, a good part of the population of Rouen had gone out to look at the demonstrations. The gawkers followed the groups en masse as they went by." On January 27 the people arrested were fined one, two, or three francs. "Apprehended were people whose only crime was to have expressed this theme aloud: France must remain for the French. That seems unbelievable to us," lamented *Le Patriote de Normandie.* "Their true crime is to have shouted, 'Out with the Jews!' They wanted to have them pay the penalty."[6] Daniel de Folleville, deputy of the department of

Seine-Maritime and honorary dean of the law school, praised the convicted students: "Bravo, my dear friends. You have demonstrated that
you are good Frenchmen. I recognize you, once again, as the worthy suc-
cessors of those valiant generations of students."[7]

In his report to the minister of the interior, the prefect emphasized
that he was going to "punish" an arrested prefecture employee, and he
accused "people belonging to the reactionary, clerical faction" of being
behind the demonstrations.[8] A few days later, on January 24, he believed he had new signs of the clerical influence. Several young people
had fastened small signs onto gaslights with the following text: "The
enemy is the Jew!!! The enemy is the traitor!!! Long live France! Long
live France for the French!" After a pursuit on foot through the streets,
officers managed to arrest Massenet de Marancourt, age sixteen, son of
the general of the gendarmerie and a student at the Rivage private
school. In late March "lists of Jews of Rouen" containing, in alphabet-
ical order, their names and addresses were distributed at the doors of
churches. The police collared Georges Ledanois, twenty-eight years old,
for distributing the lists. In the eyes of the central superintendent, they
were "the work of the clerical camp, since Georges Ledanois is the son
of the servant woman who works for the priest of Boisguillaume."[9] On
April 2 *Le Petit Rouennais* firmly condemned "anti-Semitism in Rouen" as
"a call for religious war" and related that the previous day now-released
Ledanois had visited the paper, claimed responsibility for his actions
outside the churches, and proclaimed himself a member of the Ligue
Antisémitique.[10] *L'Antijuif* published protest letters from Rouen Jews like
Alphonse Picard, who "formally opposed his name being published in
that registry and declared that, should it come to pass, he was ready to
sue for damages and interest." A certain Bloch also protested the publication of his name and added, "Certain people must be very poor
and destitute—and devoid of the slightest scruples—to seek to make
a mint through the beastly procedure of serving up a minor category
of good citizens for the consumption of a few thousand bloodthirsty
idiots!" In response, *L'Antijuif* made fun of "Misser Ploque . . . that
funny Jew."[11]

The May legislative elections launched new unrest. In April the
Rouen branch of the Ligue Antisémitique de France held several public
meetings. Gigantic signs plastered on all the walls of the city pro-

claimed that "the French must unite against the cosmopolitan Jews." *Le Patriote de Normandie* reproduced part of the text in between an article on the damage produced by a mad horse and another devoted to swallows, "those gracious messengers of spring."[12] *La Semaine Religieuse* expressed its preference for the nationalist candidates: "One must be a patriot above all else, nationalist, French to the marrow . . . To counter cosmopolitanism, let us go to the polls as men of faith, for God and country."[13] The electoral posters of Knieder, a republican candidate, who would receive only 3,609 votes, were defaced with the vehement slogan "No Jew in the Chamber." The comte de Pomerau, a candidate in the second ward who pronounced himself against "cosmopolitan speculations" and the "attacks directed against the nation," was elected with 8,659 votes.[14]

Throughout the rest of the year, endemic anti-Semitic unrest persisted. In May and in October, anti-Semitic posters were put up on the walls of the city, and in July Henri Corroyer, an agitator sent by the Comité Antisémite de Paris, held a conference at the Baubet château, with the duc de la Ferté as honorary chairman. The police, alerted, heard from "the landlord's maid, who certified that she had seen a book entitled *Death to the Jewesses* in the count's room." At the end of the year, however, the tide turned: in September, each of several conferences held by the Dreyfusard camp attracted three to four hundred people. Drawing inspiration from Francis de Pressensé's formulations, speakers asserted the innocence of Dreyfus and Picquart, praised Zola and Jaurès, and denounced "the alliance of the saber and the aspergillum." "The sons of '89" rose up to defend Dreyfus, who "was arrested only because he was Jewish."[15] Still, the anti-Semitic moment was not over: virulent "anti-Jewish leaflets" against "the traitor Dreyfus" were spread throughout town, proclaiming, "Let's drive off the Yids! Always the Yids."[16] The conflicted relationship between church and state sparked hatred, and at the turn of the century new Catholic demonstrations vehemently attacked Protestants and their Jewish allies. According to Ernest Renauld, author of the pamphlet *Le péril protestant,* "Today Protestantism, hiding behind the Jews and the Freemasons, wants to seize power and substitute sectarian education for the Catholic religion. That is where we stand, as Catholicism lies on its deathbed, as the people are starving, as the government is composed of renegades, Dreyfusards, and protectors of the thieves of Panama."[17] Nearly ten years after the outbreak of the Dreyfus affair, speeches linking the captain to the allegedly harmful role of the Jews in French society could still be heard.

If we leave Rouen and head north to the coast, we find that Dieppe indisputably experienced very intense anti-Semitic unrest in the region. It reached that city rather late, in February. On the twenty-fourth of that month about twenty students from the school of hydrography made their way through Grand-Rue chanting, "Out with Zola! Long live the army! Down with the Jews!" According to the police superintendent, "more than a thousand people, including many young people not yet twenty years old, soon joined them. In front of the clothing store run by a certain Lévy, an Israelite, the demonstrators kicked the storefront and tore off the iron rail." As officers intervened, "the crowd gathered outside the store belonging to Blum, also an Israelite, and a great number of demonstrators came back from the beach with stones, which they threw at the storefront." The officers apprehended Georges Aubert, an eighteen-year-old law clerk, and Charles Baust, a sixteen-year-old student, for throwing stones. They were released shortly thereafter. According to a police report, "the population seemed absolutely indifferent." Nevertheless, measures were taken "to prevent the return of that minor unrest." On the next day, the twenty-fifth, a crowd, estimated by the police at two thousand, circulated on Grande-Rue until eleven p.m. shouting, "Down with the Jews!" Meanwhile, as Le Patriote de Normandie reported, "applause emanated from a good number of windows." Twenty-one arrests were made. The twenty-sixth was market day on the place Duquesne, which was frequented by a few Jewish merchants from Rouen; tension was high from morning on. Scuffles occurred, leading to arrests. The mayor appealed for calm, but starting at about nine p.m. more than five hundred people again crisscrossed Grande-Rue and continued until late in the evening. The subprefect, the attorney general, the captain of the gendarmerie and his troops, and the local police restored calm without difficulty. Nineteen people were arrested, then later freed after being given a citation. The law forces were very vigilant, because they feared that "a few rogues would break into a store to rob it." On March 1 the court fined thirty-six individuals one franc and two individuals fifteen francs. It also fined two people for throwing stones (one and two francs) and one person for drunk and disorderly conduct (two francs). *La Libre Parole* reproached the police for being too brutal with the demonstrators, but the subprefect of Dieppe wrote to the prefect of Seine-Maritime to assure him that, on the contrary, the police had proceeded with "tact and extreme moderation."[18]

In a long article, *L'Impartial de Dieppe* expressed regret at these demonstrations, even though they had maintained a certain decorum.

A demonstration, more noisy than serious, occurred on Grande-Rue. Normans need time for reflection—and then it is never too late to behave badly. That little scuffle, which was absolutely inappropriate, was brought on by lively and unreflective young people . . . Soon all the evening strollers, regulars on the sidewalks of Grande-Rue, young clerks, employees, students, and so on, increased the strength of the procession. There were five hundred people after a quarter hour. Nothing to be concerned about. The demonstrators, inciting one another, had the troublesome idea of moving from words to acts. They kicked M. Lévy's storefront and threw stones at M. Blum's . . . That brawl is regrettable because of the material consequences for which the city is ultimately responsible, and because of the troublesome state of mind it revealed. The chief authors of these disturbances ought to know that their fellow citizens, in front of whom they shouted "Down with Zola! Down with the Jews!" are peaceful people and honorable merchants of Dieppe. Sectarians want to establish a rift between men belonging to different religions. That is a narrow, antidemocratic, antiphilosophical idea . . . Yesterday the incidents of the previous day were repeated with less gravity and fewer curiosity seekers. All Dieppe went out into the street so as not to miss an eventful and sensational spectacle . . . We are addressing all the young people. The army and the public conscience have been avenged by the jury's decision. It is wise to return to silence and calm, to go back to work, which the agitation of these recent days has interrupted.

The newspaper *La Dieppoise* also disapproved of the demonstrations against Lévy, "a resident of Dieppe for about twenty years," and against Blum, "a native of Dieppe." "The young citizens of Dieppe tried to imitate the students of Paris. They did it too late and with very little relevance. In town, there is unanimous disapproval."[19]

In Dieppe as elsewhere, the May legislative elections allowed prejudices to be expressed publicly. The local press published the platform statements of the candidates. Albert Jubault, "a child of the land," who signed as a "republican candidate," wrote, "Steel your hearts against financial cosmopolitanism, which, having attempted in vain to dishonor the nation, was not afraid to challenge its very existence in a recent and painful affair. Long live France for the French! Long live the Republic!" In the second ward, the independent republican Folleville, an incumbent deputy, wrote, "Teach the Jews that they are not your masters . . . If you want the prosperity of agriculture, of industry, and of commerce, if you want the greatness of the army, choose an energetic representative to put down any new attempt by the cosmopolitan and Jewish syndicate against the military forces and the fortune of France. Long live the Republic!" Folleville was barely defeated by Roulard.[20] In late 1899, after Dreyfus was pardoned, the anti-Semitic turmoil was so great that the police again went on the alert. Thanks to their preventive measures, the planned anti-Semitic demonstrations were canceled.

In the other parts of Normandy, in Neufchâtel-en-Bray, Yvetot, and Sanvic, other forms of prejudice could be heard. Yvetot, south of Dieppe, did not experience any anti-Semitic demonstrations in early 1898. During the legislative campaign, however, Montfort, the incumbent deputy who ran as an independent republican, came out against the tax on apples, against the increase on duties for brandy, and against margarine, which was competing with butter. He also boasted that he had "submitted an important legislative bill aimed at allowing public office only to Frenchmen born of Frenchmen. That bill, supported by a large number of deputies of all parties, would have the effect of putting an end to the dangerous invasion of foreigners of all races in the affairs of our country." He was easily reelected.[21] In December a branch of the Ligue Antijuive de Le Havre was created in Yvetot, at the instigation of the director of *L'Abeille Cauchoise*. They met at the café Lefèvre and distributed brochures entitled *Manuel de l'antisémite* (Manual of the Anti-Semite) and *La question juive* (The Jewish Question). The police transmitted to the prefect the names of people who participated in these so-called secret meetings. The branch was headed by Adam, an attorney and law official; the subprefect of the city immediately called for his dismissal.[22] The same month small signs were put up on the walls: "For the salvation of France," one read, "do not buy anything from the Jews." *L'Abeille Cauchoise* was intensely anti-Semitic: on April 2, 1898, when Zola emerged from his trial, its headline was "Jews Victorious." The Yvetot branch of the Ligue Antijuive proved to be fairly active: police reports described the different local demonstrations for which it was responsible. On October 8, 1899, almost twenty young people ran through the streets of Yvetot shouting, "Down with the Jews!" The police officer responsible for the report depicted one of the leaders of that little organization as being of "a violent temperament."[23]

In Le Tréport as well, handbills entitled "Frenchmen, do not buy anything from the Jews" proliferated. In Sanvic the municipal council sent the minister of war a resounding declaration of support for the army. On February 20, 1898, *L'Echo de Neufchâtel*, a progressive republican newspaper, denounced "the Jewish prefect we are suffering under" and wrote, "Yes, the name Dreyfus is an insult, like that of Judas, his ancestor in the Gospel, and it is easily imaginable that public opinion in our cities and rural areas understands the accursed race with a feeling of contempt equal to that which the two traitors inspire. The race that embraces them is now ravaging the country that did not drive them off, after having first stolen from it." During the electoral campaign, Santupéry, mayor of Mesnières-en-Bray, ran as a candidate "to defend the Catholic camp" and denounced his opponent, Bouctot, as "a Jew who must either be combated or embraced."[24] Later, in Bolbec, Francis de Pressensé was energetically interrupted during a lecture in support of Dreyfus.

Le Havre did not experience the excesses of Dieppe or Yvetot. On January 19, 1898, however, handbills reading "Drive off the Yids" and "Residents of Le Havre, shake off your torpor, throw off the yoke that oppresses you. The enemy is the Jew" were plastered on many shops, including that of Lang, a clothing merchant on the rue de Paris. On the store of Quatre Nations, someone wrote in chalk, "Down with the Jews! Death to the Jews!" The shutters of the store belonging to Crémieux, a tailor and dealer on the rue Thiers, were also defaced with "Down with the Jews!" Other posters signed by "a group of Le Havre patriots" proclaimed, "Citizens! We have seen men drag through the mud the French officers who are the glory of our country. They have dishonored the nation. To these men we forever refuse the status of Frenchman. We have a feeling of sadness and shame in thinking that they have found, even in our proud and loyal city, vile creatures for their base acts . . . The people perceive that the Jew wants to make France morally bankrupt. They finally understand that the enemy is the Jew! The enemy is the traitor! Long live the army! Long live France for the French! Long live the Republic!" "The young people, fairly well dressed, appeared . . . between twenty and twenty-five years old, but having seen them only from a distance and from behind, the officers were unable to identify them."[25]

Le Havre remained implicated in such incidents, which, though sporadic and limited in scope, were nevertheless repeated from one year to the next. On March 12, 1900, in an anonymous letter to the police prefect of Paris, signed "XYZ 9009," an informant, in exchange for a payment of four thousand francs, offered to provide information on the anti-Semitic groups in Le Havre. Not without humor, the denouncer added, "The sum I ask from you may appear high, but let me remind you that officers are much better paid and give much less information than I could transmit to you." He invited the prefect to respond by general delivery in Le Havre.[26] In 1900 the city experienced many anti-Semitic demonstrations, such as the one held on April 8 by the nationalist club with, in attendance, Edouard Dubuc, one of Drumont's close friends. The speaker, eliciting unanimous applause from the audience of about fifty, attacked the Jews, who "bought French civil servants such as [Pierre] Waldeck-Rousseau, Galliffet, and Millerand, vile servants of the Jews," and accused them of being responsible for the retreat of Fashoda and the cruel fate of Captain Marchand.*[27]

Farther to the west, on the western bank of the Seine, the department of Calvados also joined in the turmoil. As in Rouen, fog hung

---

*Fashoda: in 1898 Captain Jean-Baptiste Marchand commanded an African expedition that occupied Fashoda, a town in the Sudan, unleashing a crisis in Anglo-French relations.—trans.

over the good city of Caen. In January 1898 the inclement weather was such that many collisions between boats occurred and some sailors drowned. During the last days of the month, a snowstorm in Calvados stopped traffic. Mist, fog, and snow, however, did not prevent anti-Semitic demonstrations. The first one erupted on the seventeenth: students crisscrossed the rue Saint-Pierre and the rue Saint-Jean, shouting hostile slogans. "We warmly applaud the expansive enthusiasm," wrote *La Croix du Calvados*, "which proves to us that the youth of this country understand where the true enemies of France are." The newspaper was delighted that "a violent blast of anti-Semitism is passing among us." On the same subject but in a different tone, *Le Moniteur du Calvados* reported that "the demonstrators, impelled by the officers, vanished into the thick fog, hardly propitious for parades."[28] On the twenty-fifth a lecture given by Lerolle, an attorney and councilor of Paris, sparked a crisis. To more than three hundred people, including, as the superintendent emphasized, several priests, the speaker denounced the government's anticlerical policy and added that, conversely, the rabbis "are privileged persons whom the government does not dare touch, for example, Chief Rabbi Zadoc-Kahn, whose attitude in the Dreyfus affair seemed to [Lerolle] to be punishable but who nevertheless was left in peace." When the lecture let out, the students, joined by business employees, took to the streets of the city, stopped outside stores run by Jewish shopkeepers, and shouted, "Death to the Jews!" A crowd of more than four hundred formed and let its hatred erupt outside the stores of Crémieux, Haguenauer, Bine, and David. *La Croix du Calvados* opined that "the demonstrators were able to prove to the Jews that France has had enough of them and of their commerce. Will they take the hint? If not, France must sooner or later shake off those vermin, which are gnawing away at it." That large anti-Semitic demonstration almost ran into a small procession of about twenty young people who shouted, "Long live Zola! Down with Drumont! Long live the Jews!" Everything finally turned out well: people preferred to take no notice, and the balance of power was reestablished on its own.[29] The next day, the twenty-sixth, the students again gathered, but given the numerous police forces present, they chose to not protest.

A lecture given by Drumont's fanatical supporters Thiébaud and Dubuc relaunched Caen's unrest on the thirtieth. Drumont was unable to make the meeting; so before six hundred residents of Caen, a letter of apology from him was read, to their sustained applause. Thiébaud proclaimed himself Catholic and attacked "the Jews," the band of cosmopolitans who allegedly dominated the French nation. One audience member exclaimed, "Yes, we want the Jews to be banned from public office; we have a secretary general who is Jewish!" The following motion was passed: "The population and the students of Caen believe that the Republic is the property of the nation. They say that France is for the French and not for the foreigners, and demand the formation of a nationalist republican party." The crowd now exceeded eight hundred. It left the hall and divided into two processions that crossed through the city. One followed Dubuc via the rue Saint-Jean, while the other accompanied Thiébaud back to the train station. *La Croix du Calvados* reported that "the enthusiasm is indescribable. People chanted, 'Thiébaud's the one we need.' More than eight hundred people then went up the rue d'Auge, the rue de Vaucelles, the rue Saint-Jean, and the rue Saint-Pierre, shouting, 'Death to the Jews!' " Outside stores run by Jews, they "made threatening gestures with their canes."[30]

If we read the local press and follow attentively the biweekly reports composed by the police superintendent, however, we have the impression that the early months of 1898 unfolded in accordance with a normal rhythm. Daily life appeared immune to the unrest. *Le Bonhomme Normand* lamented, "Mardi Gras is sad this year in Caen, as a result of the rain and cold. Nevertheless, there was a large crowd in the streets and a passionate confetti fight." Life continued its normal course: several people died as a result of the cold weather; the train from Trouville to Dozulé was stuck on the tracks after the locomotive collided with an ox standing in its path; crooked firefighters were arrested; there was a call for "the reestablishment of street urinals next to the covered market. The street and the sidewalk are contaminated"; carpets disappeared as if by magic on the rue Saint-Pierre, and the police investigation made no headway for a long time; the clairvoyants of Tilly were up to their old tricks; and the entire region was ravaged by an indefinite number of thefts. In Folletière cider disappeared; in Croissanville, sheep; oxen at the Saint-Martin market of Caen; rabbits in Fontaine-Etoupefour, Mondrainville, and Sannerville; ducks in Epinay-sur-Odon; chickens in Lavigny. Elsewhere it was mares and colts that disappeared, stacks of wood that were attacked by stones, flour that was adulterated. Throughout the region fines were levied every day for drunkenness, assault and battery, breaking and entering, fraud, and vagrancy. There were countless sex scandals: incest, adultery, even prostitution. Although the papers endlessly reported such incidents, they remained silent about the social climate. The biweekly reports composed by the police in March and April observed that the absence of strikes and unemployment, the level of salaries, and "the good harmony that reigns between the worker and the employer" explained the serenity of that climate. As a result, since "the spirit of the population of Caen is republican, everything suggests that nothing will be changed regarding representation in the Chamber" in the May elections. "Everyone is very calm; moreover, the Norman is not effusive, it seems that that is his character . . . The Socialist Party is a nonentity in Caen. M. Hervieu, president of the Jeunesse Caennaise, will probably be supported by *La Croix du Calvados* and *Le Moniteur du Calvados*, reactionary newspapers."[31]

Georges Lebret, a republican, had a firm hold on the mayor's office and was supported by *Le Journal de Caen* in the legislative elections; in opposition to him, the reactionary papers were, in fact, preparing to use the events to secure a victory for their candidates. A police search of the home of Abbé Masselin, owner of *La Croix du Calvados*, revealed his close ties to the Ligue Antisémitique; tracts and anti-Semitic literature were found there.[32] His newspaper, founded by Abbé Garnier himself, wanted to be more resolutely on the offensive than the Catholic clubs, which had a relatively significant local presence.[33] Day after day it spread vicious anti-Semitism. Let us take two examples. On the front page of February 6, 1898, the paper devoted a great deal of space to the following "joke":

> The son of a well-known Jew of Mandeville appeared a month ago at the home of a merchant on the quai Saint-Jean. "I have brought you a good many clients during the year," he said, "so you ought to give me a liddle bonus." The merchant pointed out that such was not his business practice, but the Jew was so insistent that the merchant, to get rid of him, handed him a free season ticket for the velodrome [a racetrack for cycling] on the cours Montalivet. Our Yid pocketed it, quite delighted, and that very

evening went to the velodrome. Alas, he had been tricked; the velodrome was open only to the wind that year.

On February 13, again on the front page, the following text appeared:
"Can the Jew be a good patriot? No, and here is why. Like the Rhône,
which crosses through Lake Geneva without mixing its waters with it, so
the Jewish people have wandered for two thousand years. The Jew is in-
capable of founding anything lasting. For him, religion is a secondary
matter, and only the memory that he belongs to the once-powerful Jewish nation, now vanished, is alive in him. The Jew has created nothing,
invented nothing, discovered nothing. He is a parasite who sucks the last
drop out of his victims."[34]

Hervieu, whom the newspaper supported in the first ward against
Mayor Lebret, attracted crowds. On May 5 more than a thousand enthusiastic people came to a large electoral meeting to applaud him. Vigorously supported by *La Croix du Calvados*, which accused Lebret of "not
having broken the thread that attaches him to the people of Israel," and
by *Le Moniteur du Calvados*, which condemned "the alliance between Lebret and the Jew Reinach," Hervieu declared in his platform statement:
"Having lived in Caen for thirty years, having been born in Pont-
l'Evêque, where I have agricultural holdings, I know the needs of this
region . . . France, rid of its rastacouères and finally returned to the
French, will now form a single family out of love for the Republic." He
received only 1,855 votes, however, and had to withdraw in favor of
Delarbre, now supported by *La Croix du Calvados*. Delarbre was an anti-
Dreyfusard Catholic who declared he wanted "to reestablish the credit
of France, which is at the mercy of the Jewish bankers," and who spoke
out "against the monopoly on alcohol, for the continuation of full privileges for home distillers, for the prosperity of the port of Caen, and
for respect for the *res judicata*. Long live the Republic, long live France!"
Lebret would finally be reelected, earning 6,726 votes to his opponent's
5,693. Nevertheless, as the final consequence of these disparagements,
Lebret, an apparently undefeatable mayor, lost his legislative mandate in
1902.

Though Calvados was very open to republican ideas, it barely
avoided a political upheaval. Republican personalities as deeply implanted as Georges Lebret and Conrad de Witt, the deputy of Pont-

l'Evêque, found themselves harshly attacked as accomplices of the Jews. De Witt, a Protestant, was also the target of public obloquy for his religious convictions, which, it was said, necessarily made him an ally of Dreyfus. Anti-Protestantism, which had been awakened throughout France, designated him as an ideal victim. Although he was reelected along with Lebert in 1898, he would be eliminated from the political game in the 1902 legislative elections.

La Croix du Calvados left no stone unturned. In the first ward of Caen, it went after Saint-Quentin (who was still reelected); it vigorously attacked Henri Chéron, a candidate in the second ward of Lisieux, by asking, "Do you want to have the Jews obtain the good graces of the government? Vote Chéron." It supported Baron Gérard, the incumbent deputy of Bayeux and a declared anti-Dreyfusard, and it also supported Charles Paumier, the incumbent deputy of Falaise.[35] Although some of these candidates went down in defeat, they obtained more-than-respectable shares of the vote. In the cantonal elections of August 1898, several of the councilors supported by La Croix du Calvados were elected. This means that the newspaper's positions had found a following within the context of these local elections.

As the results of the legislative and cantonal elections demonstrate, the anti-Semitic ideas supported by La Croix du Calvados spread widely. Under the highly symbolic patronage of Abbé Garnier, the newspaper proved highly effective: "Let us boycott these drainers of national wealth," it beseeched its readers; "let us desert their stores, let their merchandise collect mildew on their shelves, let us buy only from true Frenchmen, and in a little while, all these cosmopolitans will be reduced to seeking their prey elsewhere. Christians, that is the true war: do not buy anything from the Jews. In ten years we will be rid of that vermin." "Small businessmen," it also enjoined, "make a threatening gesture in the darkness against the silhouette of the Semitic vampire passing by!"[36] As in Rouen and many other cities, a guide to the Jews of Calvados was put up for sale in the bookstores and tobacco shops of Caen. L'Antijuif supported La Croix's demands: for example, writing to a merchant named Bine living at 38 rue Saint Pierre, it pointed out, "Bine, aka Myrthil, aka Bibine, clothing merchant. A Saint-Pierre [Saint Peter's]. So tell me, Jew Bibine, couldn't you change the name of your shop to A Dreyfus, for example? . . . In the meantime, we are putting a barrier up outside the door of your shop so that true Frenchmen will no longer go in. Think about that, you old Kike!"[37] A tract entitled "Reflections of a Small Businessman of Caen" was distributed in the streets toward the end of the year:

> All of you, workers, employees, shopkeepers, retirees, citizens of Caen of every condition, do you know where evil comes from? Yes, you know! Evil is the money-grubber! Evil is the Jew! . . . French-women, you who are most often responsible for the shopping: the weapon to fight the money-grubber, the Jew, is in your hands! You are making the Jew rich, wives and daughters of shopkeepers, housewives, bourgeois women, patronesses, nuns, the Jew is driving your fathers and husbands to ruin, and thanks to his people's soli-darity, he is invading everything—positions, offices, jobs—and throwing your sons out on the sidewalk. The Jew you are support-ing, daughters of France, with the money he has stolen from you, has believed it right to form a syndicate to exempt from deserved punishment the traitor Dreyfus, who sold the blood of your brothers! You will oppose the Judaic invasion. For your purchases, go exclusively to shopkeepers of Caen, to Frenchmen![38]

Suddenly throughout western Normandy, from Caen to Cherbourg, shopkeepers took anti-Jewish measures, and business travelers had Jew-ish tradespeople expelled from the hotels where they were staying. *La Croix du Calvados* reported smugly that "a mutual society of business employees has just been founded in Caen. At the first general meeting, on the proposal of the founders, the seventy members present decided to prohibit Jews from joining the society. That decision is greatly to the credit of the young people who were its promoters, since it proves that they have well understood the damaging role of cosmopolitan Jewry. The Jew, who knows nothing but loot, does not seek to get into all the associations out of charity or camaraderie. Masked by these sentiments, too lofty for the Kikes to ever think of, are little self-interested benefits to be drawn from their presence."[39] Anti-Semitic incidents multiplied, revealing a broadly shared state of mind. In Cherbourg the municipal council argued over a subsidy that was to be given to Hertz, one of the former editors of *Le Bonhomme Normand*, to pay for his quiet retirement in Cherbourg. *Le Bonhomme* reported that "a little white paper was circulated whose content was revealed aloud: 'Is it true that M. Hertz's true name is Hertzemberg? Is he not a Jew of German origin?' And M. Loben, one of the municipal councilors, exclaimed, 'For my part, I do not want to give city financing to a Jew! Let's find out.' *Le Bonhomme Normand* has found out: M. Hertz is really and truly French; he even served in the military!"[40] The story does not say whether Hertz finally obtained that modest subsidy. Always passionate in his efforts, Abbé Garnier, year after year, tried to become a driving force in Calvados. Hence on April 9, 1900, he gave his umpteenth lecture in Caen at the Ecole Saint-Pierre, which was owned by religious interests. Before 350 men (women were not admitted), he attacked, always with the same outrage, Dreyfus and his co-religionists, whom he accused of betraying France in collusion with the English. "Organize little committees among yourselves that will extend first into the canton, then into the arrondissement, and then into the department," he urged. "That is the only means by which you will effectively fight all these persecutors of France . . . The Saint-Pierre parish is resolved to form action groups; the parish of Vaucelles is ready to join it; and soon the whole city will follow the same movement." After the priest of Saint-Pierre thanked the speaker, applause greeted Abbé Garnier, and the audience, still fervent, promised to act without further delay.[41]

Chapter Nine

Good Superintendent Leproust:

Peacekeeping and Prejudice

Among the Police

In Paris and the provinces in 1898, the police were constantly on the move. As the tempest swept through French society, the police remained the last rampart against a nationalist mobilization that never seemed to subside. The mobilization seemed to be whipped up by sudden changes of fortune typical of a bad serial novel or of one of those burlesque dramas that were enjoying success in the variety shows. The forces of law and order (the police and the gendarmeries, which I deliberately combine into a single group despite their different status), omnipresent in the field, exhausted by so many days of intense surveillance, assumed the heavy burden of defending, almost on their own, the rights of man and of the citizen. Before the republicans in the government and the socialists pulled themselves together and came to the aid of the meager anarchist troops who had dared fight the nationalists every inch of the way, and while the anti-Semitic moment was still white-hot, it was the police who transmitted their political interpretation of the events to the authorities. It was the police who were able to identify the adversary, to fight him, and to protect the victim, often against the latter's will. Nevertheless, they too were prone to prejudice, capable of participating in the abuse of power even while defending those assaulted by the nationalists.

On October 29 the Paris prefecture received the following report from one of its informants: "Guérin's release has given him confidence . . . Last night at the brasserie Maxeville, Guérin and his friends proposed, in the event that a review of the case is decided on, to go serenade the magistrates and to thrash all the Jids [sic] they might encounter and the Dreyfusard police officers."[1] Guérin and his troops had no illusions about the determination of their toughest opponent, "the Dreyfusard police officers." But were the police Dreyfusard in the full sense of the term? Did they really share the humanist values of the former captain's supporters? It hardly matters. They must simply be considered Dreyfusards because they came forward as defenders of equal rights for all citizens.

The central superintendent of Caen had no doubt about his role: he arrested street hawkers for selling songs and shouting, "Buy our songs, they will not poison you, they will poison only the Jews." He claimed they "were disturbing the public peace by fomenting the contempt or hatred of one group of citizens against another . . . It would be suitable to take measures to stop that campaign directed against one category of citizens."[2] In Dax, after someone put up an anti-Semitic poster, the superintendent took pen in hand and wrote to his minister, "Even though the jurisdiction in which I find myself is calm, I believe that this sign is of a nature to open controversies painful for the region and perhaps damaging to the harmony of all good Frenchmen."[3] Similarly in Narbonne (on the Mediterranean coast), the superintendent sent the director of the Sûreté Générale the following observations: "The irritation appears to me, at least in my region, to be neither superficial nor fleeting. The incitements of the press can have no other result than to transform the animosity against the Israelites into blind hatred, and should the occasion arise, it could lead to regrettable deeds."[4]

Opposed to an ideology that upset the harmony among "all good Frenchmen" and that pitted "one category of citizens against another," a number of police superintendents clearly designated the troublemakers. The superintendent of Nancy felt that "basically, this affair has been deeply unfortunate and may be considered a work of discord, in which only the enemies of France and of the republican institutions can take delight. It is obvious that in the future, and especially during the upcoming electoral campaign, anti-Semitism is going to serve as a mask for clericalism and that, in the state of overexcitement into which that affair has thrown the country, it will constitute a convenient platform for opponents pleased to find in it an unhoped-for element of success."[5] His analysis is lucid: anti-Semitism destroys the indispensable unity of citizens and favors the clerical assault on the Republic. The superintendent of Delle (in Franche-Comté) said the same thing: "The practicing Catholics and a good number of conservatives who call themselves republicans are rejoicing because they believe it is the beginning of a strong reaction against the Protestants and the Israelites. That frame of mind is astonishing and demonstrates that the great principles of broad religious tolerance have not yet penetrated where one ought by rights to find them, and that explains the bitterness of the political struggles."[6] That insight, which appears to have escaped so many politicians—government republicans, radicals, and socialists; that analysis of political and religious realities, which seems to have been inconceivable to a number of observers both past and present, acquires the ring of undeniable truth in these police reports. The analysts at the prefecture gave the most refined interpretation of the historical circumstances and even used sociological vocabulary. As far as political circumstances were concerned, the analysts at the prefecture of Paris emphasized the parallel between Boulangism and anti-Semitic nationalism. According to one observer at the prefecture, the same movement, favoring a heterogeneous alliance of ultraconservatives, clericals, and certain socialists—for example, Blanquists—anxious for social revolution had arisen ten years earlier during the Boulangist movement, even more strongly than during the Dreyfus affair: "The people, who are simplistic above all else, easily took up the chorus. It was nevertheless easy to sort out that the true objective was a search for the supremacy of Christian capitalism over Jewish capitalism and that, to attain that goal, it was necessary to appeal to race hatred and denominational wars." The author, a faithful republican and experienced politician, added, "If we seek with impartiality the circles from which the majority of the men most firmly attached to the current regime have been recruited for the past quarter century, if we examine who has constituted its strongest support, we find a considerable proportion of them among the free thinkers, the Protestants, and a few Israelites . . . Must we alienate those faithful to the Republic? Must we, out of kindness to opponents of the current regime, or out of fear of them, perhaps lose considerable strength?" Such lucidity is astonishing, though the "sociological" explanation regarding popular participation in that reactionary undertaking was less discerning. As far as sociology was concerned, in fact, this observer from the prefecture, who composed his report near the end of 1898—the very year Emile Durkheim, founder of French sociology, and his team published *L'Année sociologique*—used a vocabulary that had been in vogue (though only moderately so) in the schools of letters since the publication of Durkheim's masterworks, *De la division du travail social* (On the Division of Social Labor) and *Le suicide* (Suicide). For that police observer—half political strategist, half novice sociologist—"the sly form in which anti-Semitism was presented explains why it was able to recruit a certain number of supporters among the many—too many—who, in the current social order, know nothing of the past, are dissatisfied with the present overwhelming them, and head blindly toward the future, unconscious of everything that surrounds them, whether men or things. They can be forgiven for having believed that Drumont was a socialist. For a time the leaders of anti-Semitism hoped to enlist the proletariat under their banner, counting on the fact that the latter were too wasted away by alcoholism and anomie to resist them."[7] The ingenious author delicately took apart the mechanisms that had made surprising political alliances possible. With panache he clearly articulated truths that are hard to accept. Therefore let us not quibble over his invocation of "anomie," which is so inconsistent with the conventions of the sociological discipline; let us rather point out the noble generosity of that inveterate republican, who pities more than he castigates those who "head blindly toward the future" and who, as "unconscious" creatures, participate in the clerical and reactionary forces that threaten to sweep away the Republic. Let us instead keep in mind his courage in unconditionally defending free thinkers, Protestants, and Jews.

That republican consciousness is all the more striking in that it was shared by other members of the police. One officer displayed an astonishingly complex line of reasoning that proves convincing. In his view "the clerical Caesarians seek to unleash reactionary forces on the pretext of defending the army, which only a few fanatics dream of attacking;

they stubbornly persist in the infuriated affirmation of Dreyfus's guilt and the absolute rejection of a review of the case, solely to disparage the state ministers of the Republic itself."[8]

Some police officers, daring in their reasoning and eager to drive out into the open the strategy of all the Republic's opponents, defended its legitimacy in the street. In Paris and Nancy, Bordeaux and Marseilles, Lyon and Dinan, Perpignan, Rouen, and so many other cities, the law forces were constantly on the alert, patrolling without respite, dispersing rioters, charging threatening crowds, guarding stores whose owners were Jewish, defending Zola or Captain Dreyfus, keeping a close watch on the intentions and movements of the leaguists, and maintaining an army of informants. Their operations made it possible to contain or prevent riots, to head off the anti-Semitic wave, and to curtail the new Boulangist uprising. They invented new forms of field operations. The police prefects and the superintendents, for their part, were not idle: they were constantly present at the hot spots, thinking up ways to respond to the discipline and mobility of the anti-Semitic gangs. In that sense the anti-Semitic moment stands as a high point in police strategy.

Some, in fact, among the peacekeeping forces were wounded. In Lyon on January 18, 1898, a municipal guard on horseback charged a crowd of demonstrators and fell onto the wet asphalt, breaking a leg under his horse.[9] The same day in Paris, two other horsemen fell under their mounts. Officers were wounded, several of them seriously, in Nantes, Rouen, Marseilles, Saint-Malo, and Lunéville. The following year, when the socialists finally confronted the nationalists, more officers took direct hits to the head with paving stones.[10]

Without a doubt, good Superintendent Leproust of the Paris prefecture deserves special mention as a courageous police officer who endured direct nationalist violence. His signature on a large number of prefecture documents attests that he played a crucial role in setting the city's surveillance system in place, but he achieved notoriety only with the events of October 25, 1898. That day the leaders of the Ligue des Patriotes and the Ligue Antisémitique, taking the new session of the Chamber as a pretext, threatened to launch an assault with their troops against the Palais-Bourbon, the symbol of parliamentarianism.

In the name of the Ligue des Patriotes, Paul Déroulède summoned his militants to the place de la Madeleine with the declared intention of going to the place de la Concorde to protest the prolongation of the Dreyfus affair, "to manifest loyalty toward the Republic, confidence in the army, and an aversion for the traitors." In *L'Intransigeant* of October 24, Henri Rochefort also invited patriots to come to the place de la Concorde "in close order" to denounce "the Dreyfusard mob . . . that sold its country out to the foreigner." Appearing in the same issue was an unambiguous appeal of the Jeunesse Blanquiste: "Neither God nor master. A ministry that has sold out to cosmopolitan Jewry, traitorous deputies regurgitating on our republican traditions, are returning to the house of money changers. Let them climb the steps of the Palais-Bourbon to jeers and shouts and boos. Long live the social Republic!"[11] The socialists, for their part, were resolved to thwart the plans of the leaguists and their allies. According to a police report, they were preparing themselves, in close alliance with the anarchists, for that "big day" and would go to the place de la Concorde in response to any type of "provocation."

Jules Guérin had carefully coached his troops, meticulously elaborating a battle plan with a secret rendezvous and military discipline. He ordered them to "avoid any conflict with the police, since the people composing it are not opponents but Frenchmen; war on the Jews and cosmopolitans only." "If we fall, we will fall for the nation and the honor of France." He asked the "anti-Jewish bosses to close their shops that day and send their employees to the demonstration."[12] The prefecture received reports portending the worst: they spoke of several thousand men, on the side of the nationalists and anti-Semites, who would be armed.

The socialists and anarchists had no less will to fight, since by common accord they refused to "let Drumont's and Déroulède's men control the street . . . The day will be extremely eventful," a letter warned the police, "and if you allow the two factions to occupy the place de la Concorde, you will witness a true pitched battle, whose outcome cannot be predicted." Another informant judged that the socialists and anarchists could count on "the idle, a few strikers, a few shops that have been out of work since this morning or afternoon, and bands of vagrants, fixtures at the trade union center. On the other side are the anti-Semitic patriots and the Catholic and Bonapartist groups that have embraced the anti-Semitic appeals of Déroulède, Drumont, and Guérin.

We cannot predict what may happen. Nor can I assure you that one side or the other will not be armed." A last informant warned that, if the nationalists were to assault *L'Aurore,* "it is nearly certain that blood will be spilled."[13]

The situation promised to be heated that day. An attempt at a coup d'état might even result. The precautions taken by the police authorities were reminiscent of January and February 1898 and even the heyday of the Boulangist movement. All the troops were ready for action; Charles Blanc, the police prefect, was constantly on the scene. Countless brigades made their way through various neighborhoods of Paris toward the quai d'Orsay. For their part, the mounted Republican Guards from the Mouffetard barracks took their positions on the rue Soufflot, across from the Sorbonne. At the Tuileries, Mouquin, the superintendent responsible for operations, had at his disposal three hundred police officers, a regiment of Republican Guards, and a squadron of cuirassiers. Numerous police officers guarded the place Beauvau and the Elysée. More than a hundred of them stood outside the Palais de l'Industrie. The rue de Bourgogne, on the Left Bank, looked like a regular encampment. The Ministry of War was heavily protected, the bridges closely guarded. A crowd massed outside the Madeleine, on the rue de Rivoli, along the quays, on the boulevard Saint-Germain, and on the Champs-Elysées. Several thousand people were thus assembled along a perimeter very close to the Chamber of Deputies, but how many were there exactly? The estimates were so different that we will never know: the lowest was four to five thousand, but some journalists spoke of thirty, fifty, or even—certainly a gross exaggeration—sixty thousand demonstrators. Some sported red carnations (Ligue des Patriotes), some blue cockades (Abbé Garnier's militants), and some the emblem chosen by Guérin. As Déroulède, Paulin-Méry, Millevoye, and Drumont arrived at the place de la Concorde one by one, a huge ovation greeted each of them. As usual, people shouted anti-Semitic slogans until they were out of breath, even though the slogans were prohibited because the prefectures considered them seditious. Platoons of guards on horseback crossed the place de la Concorde in every direction. Here and there, as *Le Temps* noted for example, people mercilessly attacked isolated individuals who had been designated by a peremptory sentence: "He's a Jew."

It was at that moment that the Leproust incident occurred. Leproust, a police superintendent and head of the first search detail brigade, approached a demonstrator who was shouting, "Down with the Jews!" and tried to apprehend him. Pointing at him, demonstrators exclaimed, "He's a dirty Jew!" A dozen people rushed toward him, beat him black and blue with their canes, knocked him down, and badly trampled him. He was bleeding profusely from a skull fracture, and his clothes were stained with blood. Police Prefect Blanc came to his aid. As a platoon of cuirassiers cleared the square, Superintendent Leproust, in spite of his wounds, had Guérin and several demonstrators arrested. Three more officers were subsequently wounded. The assault against the superintendent would cause a stir in Paris, especially since it would lead to the imprisonment of Jules Guérin, head of the menacing Ligue Antisémitique, who would be formally charged with being one of the police officer's assailants.[14]

The nationalists, pushed back, surged toward the Madeleine, shouting, "Death to the Jews! Down with Jaurès!" The windows of one Jewish shop were shattered, and someone burned the newspaper *Les Droits de l'Homme*, screaming, "Death to the Jews!" A certain humor persisted, however. *L'Intransigeant* reported the following incident. As Superintendent Mouquin furiously shouted, "Mass arrests!" [*Arrêtez en bloc*], some joker interpreted it as "Arrest Bloch!" "So, death to the Jews!" he added before being apprehended. Pursued by cuirassiers, the demonstrators left via the boulevard des Capucines. On the place de l'Opéra and the boulevard des Italiens, there was a regular ocean of leaguists; *Le Gaulois* described it as "an unforgettable spectacle, all the faces were radiant, inebriated with a patriotic joy, and the demonstrators felt that victory was theirs." The heavily falling rain facilitated the task of the police force.

In the late afternoon, more anti-Semitic demonstrations erupted when the Chamber let out. *L'Aurore* reported that "Drumont was noticed sending smiles and friendly gestures to a dozen priests, armed with leaded canes, who were standing on the sidewalk. They shouted: 'Long live Drumont! Down with the Jews!' It was apparently these priests who gave the signal for unrest on the place de la Concorde." In the evening more than three thousand people were standing on the boulevards and outside the *La Libre Parole* building, which was lit up for the occasion. An extraordinary state of agitation reigned, reminding many of the

Boulangist period. Half a squadron of mounted gendarmes dispersed the particularly fanatical demonstrators. Patrols of twenty-five men crisscrossed the streets. Reserve officers constantly charged, dispersing thousands of people. "The shout 'Death to the Jews!' rang in our ears," one journalist remarked.

During that extraordinary day, more than 250 people were arrested. It was October 1898, when a major alliance of leaguists of every stripe was being formed. In *La Libre Parole*, Drumont, reflecting on the events, was eager to be done with Henri Brisson, the premier of France at the time, and his government, which was abandoning power "to the claw-like hands of fanatical Jews"; he wrote an article that linked actors who were very far apart but had great esteem for one another: "Admit that the Habsburgs are having no luck with the Jews and that Lueger and his friends may not be entirely wrong to want to send truly harmful people back to Palestine, those people who, in one year, have found the means to give the Dreyfusard plague to France and the bubonic plague to Austria." So it went with Drumont, Lueger, and later Hitler himself—an incongruous comparison, since the eras were so different, but nevertheless of some significance.

Let us return to the courageous Leproust. For arresting Jules Guérin at the place de la Concycle, the superintendent was violently attacked by *L'Antijuif*: "It is the non-Jewified press as a whole that is being attacked by Leproust's abuse of power." Drumont, Millevoye, and other leading figures of anti-Semitism went to the Palais de Justice to secure Guérin's freedom. On October 27 Guérin appeared before the Eighth Criminal Court: after a short deliberation, the tribunal granted him provisional freedom, eliciting ringing shouts of "Long live Guérin! Long live Drumont! Down with the Jews!" inside the Palais itself. *L'Aurore* predicted that "presiding Judge Bernard will probably be named an honorary member of the legion of anti-Semitic slaughterers." A procession formed under the paternal eye of the guards, a few of whom added their voices to those of the screamers and headed for the cour de la Sainte-Chapelle, still shouting, "Long live the army! Down with the Jews!" The same shouts were voiced by the small troop on the quai de l'Horloge; then the din subsided near the pont Neuf. By contrast, Guérin's release elicited consternation and disapproval among the anarchists. *Le Père Peinard* wrote, "Imagine that, in place of Leproust, it was a poor prole whom the anti-Yid clique had attacked: the poor soul would have been collared by Leproust—on Guérin's orders—gotten a first-class beating, been hit with a blackjack by Guérin, and beaten by sergeants. His goose would have been cooked." *Le Libertaire* protested in similar terms, and *Les Temps Nouveaux* wrote, "The anti-Semites are fortunate: they can allow themselves many things that would come at a high cost to vulgar anarchists."

A few days later good Superintendent Leproust was awarded a gold medal first class by Police Prefect Blanc, to mark the latter's objection to the court decision that had freed Guérin. Guérin's trial was heard on November 10; Leproust testified, acknowledging that on October 25 he had not been wearing his superintendent's sash in a visible manner, but he declared that he had tried to prohibit demonstrators from shouting, "Death to the Jews," and that they had then rushed him. "I swear that Guérin shoved me and punched me in the chest. My memory's recollection is particularly accurate because I staggered backward. The scene did not last long, and I may have received thirty to forty blows with sticks. Everything spun around, something like in a kaleidoscope." During the court session, Leproust heard someone whisper, "Death to the Jews, he's a dirty pig, we'll get him too," as one of his witnesses went by. Leproust showed his anger publicly, but after a moment of excitement, the proceedings resumed. The witness, by the name of Calfon, asserted that he had seen the anti-Semitic leader strike Leproust. The major figures shifted; now Drumont and Deputies Lasies, Charles Bernard, and Firmin proclaimed Guérin's innocence. Deputy Public Prosecutor Lénard came next and exclaimed:

"Death to the Jews!" Is that a political argument, an economic argument? No, it is a death cry, a call for murder, for civil war. For the accused, that cry is a rallying sign, and what a serious one! What a dangerous one! M. Leproust, who has studied mob psychology, who has read books about it, who even knows its pathology, was not unaware of that. M. Leproust was acting as a good citizen . . . Are the defendants old scholars, driven solely by the desire for knowledge, having spent their lives studying the carapaces of insects? Did they go to the place de la Concorde as altruists? No, gentlemen, Guérin, Ottavaiani, Girard, and Chanteloube [the

other defendants] are not scholars or philosophers. They are politicians undergoing special training and are unlikely to indulge
in philosophy. M. Guérin is at the head of a veritable little army
that, at a single word from him, at a single sign, come together
equipped with canes; indeed, of the four defendants, only one did
not have a cane. On October 25 they went to the place de la Concorde armed with those playthings.

The magistrate ended by pointing out Superintendent Leproust's status
as an indisputable witness. But his efforts were in vain: nearly forty witnesses acting in collusion testified that at the time Guérin was not at
that location on the place de la Concorde. M. Ménard, the attorney for
the accused, was applauded when he claimed, with great imagination,
that "it is not accurate that 'Death to the Jews!' is a death cry. 'Death to
the Jews!' means 'Death to the power of the Jews, death to the shameful
syndicate that has taken shape, death to that power, which asserts itself
through gold, through the newspapers, by every means.' It also means:
'Death to the social power of the Jews, death to the state formed within
the state.' " The attorney then certified that Guérin had not struck Leproust, contrary to so many witnesses, and that although the defendants
had "brought canes, that fact does not establish that they used them to
strike." Guérin was found guilty of carrying a prohibited weapon; the
charge of assault and battery was dismissed; the penalty was a hundred
francs. The audience applauded repeatedly. Captain Dreyfus's attorney,
Ferdinand Labori, who was in the courtroom, was disappointed. The judicial system had little confidence in its own loyal police force.

   That little-known affair, so richly documented, deserves to become
part of history: it is the only precise evidence we have of legal action
taken in 1898 against a rioter who was determined to put hatred of
Jews into practice. Its unfortunate lesson is clear: the "Dreyfusard police
officers" who defended the republican order were not rewarded. Just as a
portion of the republican political staff did not hide the prejudices it
shared with its nationalist opponents, certain public servants sympa-
thized with anti-Semitic acts of violence.[15]

To say that the police did not always seem particularly zealous in apprehending those responsible for the violence is an understatement. Apart from a few "peaks," a few heated days when order seemed threatened, arrests of rioters were very rare in Paris, as they were in Bordeaux, Nantes, and Marseilles. Even when events of enormous gravity occurred, such as the looting of the Bernheim factory, the destruction of stores, the ransacking of synagogues, and the assaults on rabbis, shopkeepers, or mere passersby whose only mistake was that they were Jewish, hardly anyone was arrested. As in theatrical plays, the police always arrived too late. The slow reaction of the forces of law and order, who always appeared after the party responsible for a crime had departed, is astonishing. It is equally astounding to note the incredible leniency of the police superintendents who, in report after report, maintained that a particular anti-Semitic act—for example, the throwing of stones at stores run by Jewish shopkeepers in Paris in January 1898—was an "incident" and was in the end "nothing serious worth noting." We find that evaluation in Paris, during the violence on the rue du Cardinal-Lemoine, and in Besançon, Toulouse, and Nantes where, in spite of unbelievable violence, the superintendent indicated, "Order was not seriously disturbed . . . just a row."[16] In Rouen, when store windows belonging to Jews were destroyed, the superintendent considered it "just a childish prank."[17] After violence shook Dijon, the superintendent wrote calmly, "These demonstrations did not assume a disturbingly grave character. They did not give rise to acts of serious rebellion against the officers or to violence or assaults of any importance against private property. It was all limited to a few stones thrown through the windows of stores run by Israelites and through the stained-glass windows of the synagogue, several of which were broken."[18] Savor that "it was all limited to . . ."

In Avignon in mid-February, when several thousand demonstrators went through the city shouting, "Long live the army!" and "Down with the Jews," the superintendent wrote, "That demonstration did not give rise to any disorder and ended without incident." In Paris on January 6, the superintendent annotated in beautiful handwriting the report of one of his subordinates on the events of the previous day: "It was very harmless." In Narbonne the police superintendent wrote, "A very keen antipathy against the Jews is publicly manifesting itself. That situation, which until now has not been dangerous for public order, threatens to worsen and to degenerate into race and religious hatred."[19]

The arrests that were made almost never targeted individuals accused of attacking property or persons, of striking the Jews or looting their stores. The most frequent charges, both in Paris and in the provinces, were inevitably "refusal to move along," "assault and battery against police officers," and so on. The police apprehended demonstrators who were threatening public order, not those who were deliberately attacking Jews. In the Parisian and provincial archives, no list of arrests and convictions explicitly indicates arrests for acts motivated by anti-Semitism, and among the convictions participation in anti-Semitic violence is only rarely specifically sanctioned. All the mechanisms of the police, deployed impressively throughout the cities of France, all the patrolling brigades, all the charging cuirassiers, acted in the name of defending the state, the Republic, or more simply of ensuring the safety of residents. In addition, the vast majority of those arrested were immediately released after a mere "admonishment"; the few unlucky ones who went to trial were fined only one, two, or—rarely—five francs. Seen from the viewpoint of the police apparatus and the judicial institutions, the "anti-Semitic moment" had little reality. Only punishment for public disorder in general was meted out—and only with extreme leniency.

Such inertia in the face of anti-Semitic attacks proper was perplexing, so much so that Dufour, a good old shopkeeper who ran an embroidery business on the rue du Sentier in Paris, sent—not without courage—the following letter to the police prefect:

I am not Jewish; it is just that my business relationships are conducted in part with Jews.

The passivity or the encouragement that your officers show toward the anti-Semitic gentlemen when they shout "Down with the Jews" and toward the boycott these individuals are mounting against Jewish stores, without being disturbed by the public prosecutor's office, are prejudicial to my business.

Thus, Mr. Prefect, let me respectfully ask you: when will you put an end to the exploits of these screaming gangs who want to do in Paris what succeeded so well in Algiers?

Our walls bear the motto "Liberty, Equality, Fraternity"; therefore, we have the right to require that no one living in France can be slated to have his store looted in the near future on the pretext of his religious feelings.[20]

In Paris that police passivity was observed in several reports. On January 15, 1898, as hundreds of students shouted anti-Semitic slogans on the rue Soufflot and the rue Saint-Jacques, "an agent ran to alert the officers in a neighboring police station. The reply was 'We'll see.' And even though there were about twenty officers in the station, none came out to disperse the protesters."[21] On December 6, as the anti-Semites behaved like "beasts" in Paris, "officers were notable for their absence. What is clear is that, had they managed to take preventive measures, as they know how to do for strikers, the government would not have found itself accused of weakness and complicity with the troublemakers."[22] In Rouen in March, during anti-Semitic incidents, "the local police did not even write up a report."[23] After the events of great brutality in Nantes in late January, *La Fronde* published the following commentary: "The scenes of savagery that are occurring against the Jews in Nantes are indescribable . . . And how many Jews are there in Nantes? Perhaps a hundred. And the police are powerless to protect a hundred people! Can you understand that? All their stores have been looted; the women are not spared, not even one who had rushed in to save her husband, who had been knocked almost senseless by canes."[24] Similarly, when the demonstrations that shook Bar-le-Duc led to brutality against Rabbi Taubmann,[25] the destruction of many stores whose owners were Jewish, and constant violence over several days, *L'Univers Israélite* could not understand why the responsible parties, whose identities were known, had not been apprehended. In the same vein, *Le Rappel* wrote, "Just one thing to keep in mind: the inertia, in that deplorable affair in Bar-le-Duc, of the representatives of the central powers. In spite of urgent requests, the prefect did not intervene to reestablish order. He let things go on."[26] Beyond inertia the police seemed at times even to collude with the rioters. In Paris that is what *La Croix* itself observed: "the police are doing their duty . . . but they recognize that the demonstrators are in the right."[27] Joseph Reinach noted that "the police, composed in great part of former soldiers, smiled at the screaming mobs."[28] On May 9, 1898, "even as, the previous day, demonstrators were shouting outside the offices of *La Libre Parole*, 'Death to the Jews, down with Rothschild!' very respectable people criticized these provocations and the inertia of the police at the scene, who were fraternizing with the population."[29]

Even when they did not go so far as to fraternize publicly with anti-Semites, many officers made no mystery of their prejudices. The reports of the superintendents are irrefutable evidence and contain many extremely dubious expressions. In Rennes, when Dreyfusard students attempted to reply in kind to anti-Semitic assaults, the central superintendent designated them in several reports to the prefect as "Semitic students" or even "Semitic socialists."[30] Commenting on the close relationship that Major Esterhazy continued to maintain with a certain Lévy, a superintendent expressed astonishment: "It is hard to explain why the major places his trust in that individual, whose race and Semitic connections he must be aware of."[31] In Toulouse the superintendent commented on the machinations of the anti-Semites against "Jews installed in Toulouse for a certain length of time." In Nantes the superintendent sent the director of the Sûreté Générale an account of the activities of the Ligue Antisémitique against "the Jewish colony established in our city," an expression we find again in the report of the police superintendent of Lunéville: "People are very worked up against the Israelites, especially since the Jewish colony is very large and very rich in Lunéville."[32] One ironic superintendent commented on an informant's report of a demonstration held in Paris by students from Condorcet high school, adding in the margin: "There are many Israelites among the Condorcet students!"[33] Police informants also made use of a dubious vocabulary. In January 1898 one wrote the director of the Sûreté to warn him that Sébastien Faure, to obtain protection at a political meeting, had made an appeal to "friends of Jews on Dreyfus's payroll." Another imagined the most far-fetched plans: "The Jews have people who, at the opportune moment, will incite the crowd to loot, so that Drumont and his friends will be blamed."[34] On several occasions superintendents held Jews responsible for anti-Semitic violence. In Bar-le-Duc, for example, it was "the arrogance of Rabbi Taubmann" that provoked anti-Semitic violence. Similarly, in Dijon, if the anarchist Lucien Weil had not given his lecture, "it is more than probable that no demonstration would have taken place."[35] In Toulouse, a lecture by Francis de Pressensé "took on the character of provocation."[36]

Even worse, in a few cases police officers may actually have orchestrated attacks on Jews with unconcealed pleasure. During the Zola trial in February 1898, according to *Gil Blas*, near the Palais de Justice the journalist Armand Strauss shouted, "Long live Zola!" in response to the nationalist demonstrators. These demonstrators rushed over and chanted loudly at him, "Down with Zola!" Brigade officers made ready to intervene. " 'He's a Jew! Don't you see he's a Yid!' people shouted on all sides. And the good officers, who were preparing to execute a line charge, furiously turned back on the one who had just been pointed out to them. 'Oh, he's a Jew!' they shouted, and without finishing their sentence, they pounced on M. Strauss, who was immediately beaten up."[37] The police were also frequently accused of holding back when the nationalists—for example, during the heated days of January 1898—attacked the rare Dreyfusard newspapers. In Lyon an out-of-control crowd attempted for several hours to loot the offices of *Le Peuple*, which were defended by its journalists, some of whom were wounded. The police made a timid appearance more than an hour after the siege had begun: two police officers, then an agent on horseback, took their time showing up. Thereafter the forces of law and order finally decided to intervene in earnest against the assailants, who were throwing paving stones weighing more than three kilos![38] In Paris in February, when riots rumbled and countless processions tirelessly passed through the neighborhoods shouting, "Down with Zola! Death to the Jews!" the police seemed to be quite absent, leaving the area clear for the anti-Dreyfusards. *Gil Blas* commented that "since the beginning of this unfortunate affair, M. Blanc, the police prefect, has proved to be very unfit for his task. We trusted him for a certain period of time because he was new at the job, but it seems he is beginning to abuse our trust. M. Blanc would do well to take serious measures."[39] Does Police Prefect Blanc represent the opposite of good Superintendent Leproust, his subordinate, as a high-level police officer with few Dreyfusard feelings? We are tempted to believe so, since he came to the aid of his wounded subordinate only with reluctance, as many journalists noted.

On October 2, 1898, in Paris, militants from the Ligue des Patriotes and the anti-Semitic leagues attacked the Dreyfusards assembled in Salle Wagram with their leader Pressensé; the police response sheds light on the dealings of certain officers. The violence, let us recall, was extreme.

The prefect in person was on site to observe. But as *Le Radical* reported, "The police force wanted to be in the service of M. Déroulède . . . Screaming, 'Long live Déroulède! Long live Rochefort! Death to the Jews!' people received the approving smiles of the policemen. A single 'Long live Picquart!' or 'Long live Jaurès' provoked a terrible beating . . . M. Blanc thus appreciated and authorized the acts of his subordinates and could not or would not change their attitude." Such was also the interpretation of *Le Rappel*: the police knocked the republicans around; escorted Déroulède's troops; gave "a ride downtown" to the police station to the citizens who exercised their right to shout, "Long live the Republic!"; and let gangs go on shouting, "Death to the Jews!" and "Long live the king!" without intervening. *La Lanterne* also maintained that the hostility of Déroulède's troops "toward the Republic was to them a safeguard against M. Blanc's agents. It is high time to remind the officers of the police prefecture that they are in the service of the Republic and not that of patriots by trade and of the coup d'état." *L'Aurore* was outraged at the "police brutality" deliberately committed against the Dreyfusards and at the "scenes of savagery" that occurred in the street, where "number 165, a mean, violent man, his eyes ablaze with alcoholism, attracted attention with this relentlessness. He waved his saber in a frenzy. In front of us, one poor soul was struck in the neck and blood gushed out." These acts of brutality were repeated in the police stations: one officer struck the Dreyfusards over the head with the knob of a heavy cane, and they screamed in pain.

A comparison of the accounts of *L'Aurore* and *La Libre Parole*, in spite of their necessarily diverging evaluations, offers an idea of the specifically anti-Semitic dimension of the police violence. For example, *L'Aurore* reported that agent 194 collared a demonstrator who had shouted, "Long live Picquart!" and "while beating him up, said to him, 'Take that, you damned dirty Jew.' Another demonstrator was protesting those who were shouting, 'Long live Esterhazy!' He was arrested. 'Here, dirty Jew! This is for you,' said an officer, giving him a sharp kick in the kidneys. As we were protesting that odious conduct, an officer declared to us that it was all according to orders and that the Jews had to be eliminated!" A little farther on, *L'Aurore* reported that agent 253, referring to a charge that was taking place near the top of the avenue de

Wagram, said, " 'What do you know? They're having a good time up there. So it won't be our turn for a while!' With these words he took a top out of his pocket and placed it in the palm of his hand; then, showing one of the officers the sharp and polished head of the top that poked through between his closed fingers, he said, 'Those dirty Kikes. I've already missed them once; but the first one who falls into my hands, I'll knock him out with this.' "

The picture drawn by *La Libre Parole* is not very different, except for the commentary: "Just a quick glance: the superintendent's 'lockup' on the rue Fourcroy is packed with demonstrators, who are brought in minute by minute. Almost all have bloody faces; you recognize a good number of little Yids . . . 'Sir,' says one of them, 'der's a misunderstandink, I vas out valking beacefully.' " The police violence was such that protests against it erupted that very evening. Serious charges were filed against the prefecture, and sanctions were imposed. After much equivocation, Agent Loiseau had to take the fall: he was dismissed. *La Libre Parole* felt for him, and a reporter went to Agent Loiseau's home. His wife, in tears, confided, "Hitting a man that other officers were taking away—him, sir? . . . It's crazy: that giant wouldn't hurt a fly."

The day after that brawl, on October 3, Ulmann, a retired warrant officer in the navy infantry employed at the prefecture, in the company of Bloch, a personnel manager at a publishing house, headed toward the brasserie Maxéville on the boulevard Montmartre to have an aperitif. In this hotbed of anti-Semitism, both were insulted and threatened: "Dirty Jew, betrayers, traitors!" they heard. When Bloch shouted, "Long live the review of the case!" militants from the Ligue Antisémitique fell upon him and pummeled him, despite Ulmann's intervention. *L'Aurore* recounted the scene this way: "Officers, seeing the brawl, rushed over. They pushed aside the gang of anti-Semites and fell on M. Bloch, whom they brutally took down to the station on the rue Drout, along with his friend, calling them dirty Jews, dirty Yids, and so on." The two friends spent the night at the station, and the next day the superintendent told them, "When one is Jewish, one does not get mixed up in such demonstrations." "But when one is Jewish, can one not go have an aperitif on the boulevard?" "Shut up or I'll send you to jail." And turning toward Ulmann, he added, "You are an employee of the Seine prefecture. Nothing would be easier than to write up a report on you, which, if transmitted to your superiors, would undoubtedly lead to your dismissal."[40]

Though they were not necessarily defenders of Jews, the forces of law and order were able to withstand the onslaught, to overcome the nationalist and anti-Semitic wave, and to limit the damage. Here and there they rushed to the aid of people being threatened, and their presence kept demonstrators from sacking stores and setting fire to synagogues. Without their vigilant presence, Paris, but also Nancy, Bordeaux, Nantes, Lyon, Dijon, Angers, Dinan, and Avignon would have been transformed into so many Algierses or Orans, this time with murderously violent marches. The "Saint Bartholomew's Day massacre of the Jews," so frequently dreamed of by the nationalists, would have acquired a certain degree of reality. But it did not, and so much the better. Nevertheless, we cannot cast a knowing and ironic gaze on this anti-Semitic moment on the pretext that death did not have its day. All of a sudden, Kishinev* or Algiers moved curiously closer to sweet republican France. Though the Dreyfus affair took a different turn, there is no reason to deny, as people still do, almost with disdain and suspicion, the stupefying scope of the violence, to which so many citizens as well as police officers yielded. Good Superintendent Leproust was quite alone after all.

---

*Kishinev: a city in present-day Moldova where a massacre of Jews occurred in April 1903 at the instigation of Russian officials.—trans.

Chapter Ten

The "Arrogance" of Rabbi Taubmann:

Passivity and Resistance

Among the Jews

On February 24, 1898, the police superintendent of Bar-le-Duc sent the following report to the mayor of that little city in northeastern France, located not far from Nancy and populated with slightly fewer than eighteen thousand residents.

I have the honor of informing you that last night, Wednesday, beginning at seven-thirty, a demonstration occurred against M. Tauppmann [*sic*] in particular and the Israelites in general. A group of approximately eight hundred people, including a habitual criminal carrying an effigy representing the local officiating rabbi, ran through the various streets of the locality chanting, "The rabbi! The rabbi! Long live the army! Down with Dreyfus! Down with the Jews!" . . . At about eight-thirty, informed that masked people among the demonstrators wanted to pillage the building occupied by the officiating minister, I immediately had my agents occupy the place to prevent any disturbance . . . At about ten o'clock, after certain individuals had detached themselves from the group to strike the storefronts of the Israelites

Anchel, Lévy, and Salmon, officers who were following the demonstrators immediately arrived and kept them from doing any damage. At ten-fifteen, when the demonstrators attempted to get onto the place Reggio to burn the effigy representing him under the windows, I stood in their way. Then everyone shouted, "Long live the army!" with more than a thousand people present . . . M. Mayeur, a wholesale wine merchant, militant reactionary, and member of the Catholic club, was, it is said, the organizer of these demonstrations.[1]

The same day, in his report to the interior minister, the special commissioner for the railroads, who was in constant contact with Paris, gave an even more alarming account: "A column of twelve hundred demonstrators ran through the streets of Bar-le-Duc, stopping outside the stores and homes of the Israelites, singing the song 'Down with the Traitors' and shouting, 'Down with the Jews, death to the traitors! Long live the army!' They smashed up the storefront of Bloch, a hatmaker, Lévy, a joiner, Lévy, a butcher, Cahen, a tailor, Strauss, a café owner, etc."[2] "The group marching at the head of the procession carried an effigy representing former captain Dreyfus. The demonstrators burned the effigy amid great enthusiasm . . . The population here welcomed Zola's conviction enthusiastically."[3] Did the demonstrators brandish and burn two effigies, that of Rabbi Taubmann and that of Captain Dreyfus? Or was there only one effigy, and the police officers confuse Taubmann and Dreyfus, two individuals who did not have very much in common, simply because they saw only the caricature of the eternal image of the Jew and were indifferent to the true physiognomy of the rabbi and the captain? To anti-Semites, the silhouette of the rabbi in that eastern city was indistinguishable from that of the dashing captain, a Parisian and a graduate of the Ecole Polytechnique. The effigy's identity was probably not clear either to the demonstrators or to the police officers.

In February 1898 that peaceful little city, controlled by the republicans, experienced a moment of intense collective anti-Semitic mobilization. Between one thousand and twelve hundred people voiced the cry of hatred heard so many times—"Death to the Jews!"—and openly displayed their anti-Semitic zeal. A crowd, enormous in proportion to Bar-le-Duc's modest population, demonstrated day after day against Rabbi Taubmann (who, in the police reports, becomes indiscriminately "Tauppmann" or even "Tautmann"). What exactly did Taubmann do? That same day, at about two a.m., near the market, two street hawkers were selling the song "Down with the Traitors, or, We'll Kill Dreyfus," when Rabbi Taubmann approached them and asked them to stop. The radical-socialist newspaper *Le Républicain de l'Est* described the scene this way: "A man passed by whose friendly face embodied and exaggerated all the distinctive characteristics of Semitic ugliness. It was M. Taubmann, assistant rabbi in charge of slitting the throats of calves and cutting the little children of Israel." The small crowd grew indignant and threatened the rabbi. A police officer came to his aid and took all the protagonists to the police station. The rabbi expressed his regret for having intervened. But it was no use—the crowd ran through the streets of Bar-le-Duc singing:

Of Jewry
There are millions
Who in our nation
Support the spies.
Beloved France,
Will you wake up at last?
Drive from the army
Everything with a Yid's nose.

The Jews are the masters
Thanks to all their loot,
There are some of those traitors
Even on the quai Bourbon.
All of them eat among us
While we starve to death.
It cannot be, things must change.
Otherwise it's all over.

There's no mistake, Dreyfus is the only guilty one.
He shouted, wept,
Begged, but in vain,

He'll never come back from Devil's Island,
He'll stay there till he's dead from cholera.[4]

Emotions ran high. The city had reached the boiling point. The Jewish population remained in their homes while "masked people" beat forcefully with their fists and canes, resonating on the walls and windows. The Jew hunt was on. Several evenings in a row, many stores run by Jewish shopkeepers were attacked, windows were broken, merchandise was stolen, and considerable damage was incurred. A group of several hundred demonstrators, "their heads hidden in the hoods of their capes," rushed at the Jewish storefronts. The police constantly intervened to protect the victims; two brigades of mounted gendarmes dispersed the demonstrators and reestablished order. Several people were arrested, including "many reactionary militants, members of the Catholic club," and were prosecuted. Some of them, such as Marcel Mayeur, were denounced in the courtroom by "MM. Alphens Senior and Junior for having thrown stones through their storefront." The crowd of close to four thousand observers who had come to the hearing to support the rioters applauded the justice of the peace when he expressed "his agreement with public opinion,"[5] brushed aside the testimony, and imposed modest fines. These fines did not diminish the ardor of the rioters in the slightest, who left singing. The police superintendent noted that "the Israelites, contrary to their habit, have refrained from frequenting public establishments." In another report he emphasized that "people are very stirred up against the Israelites and especially against M. Taubmann, of whom several of his co-religionists disapprove and with whom they find fault. Further demonstrations are probably going to take place. It is really surprising and unprecedented in the city of Bar-le-Duc, usually so calm and peaceful."

Day after day in the remote provinces, far from the capital and its constant disturbances, anti-Semitic crowds rose up and took action. In Bar-le-Duc the person responsible for these unusual events was right at hand. In a report to the director of the Sûreté Générale, the police superintendent singled him out: "Such are the deeds that I bring to your attention and that occurred because of the arrogant attitude of the rabbi, M. Tauppmann, toward the public." The police commissioner, without the slightest trace of humor, referred to "M. Taubmann" as "the author of the demonstrations." Here, then, was a deed stemming from pure "arrogance": a Jew who had dared to protest publicly, to intervene so that the provocations would end! The crowds may have taken their revenge, but the Jews were really asking for it! And they were sorry to have "caused" it, according to *Le Républicain de l'Est*, which was told "that they [the local Jews] are literally furious at the recklessness on the part of their rabbi, who compromised the cause in that way, who blew their cover and provoked demonstrations for which no one, in a city as calm as Bar-le-Duc, would have taken the initiative."

It is an understatement to say that Rabbi Taubmann's conduct was astonishing. Some even claimed that he had been bold enough to raise his hand against the street hawkers, that, "aided by a respectable butcher at the market, M. Lévy [naturally], he rushed at the vendor and took him by the neck," an accusation Taubmann denied. Another police report gave a completely different version: "After M. Tautmann insulted the street hawker and threatened to strike him with his cane, the street hawker grabbed it away from him and struck him a few times on the back." Just like a scene from the commedia dell'arte. Shortly thereafter "a group of four superb Pierrots whose costumes were very fresh" passed by. They wore on their chests a sign printed in bold characters saying, "Death to the traitors," and on the back another sign reading, "Long live the army." Rabbi Taubmann's act of resistance dumbfounded the anti-Semites and, quite logically, elicited their anger and the discreet disapproval of the Jews themselves, who, noted a police officer, "prudently stayed home."[6] They stayed quiet, barricaded themselves, and waited for the storm to pass. Everything had suddenly conspired against the rash rabbi: republicans, Catholics, and socialists stood almost shoulder to shoulder to shout their hatred. Fearing a backlash, the Jews of Bar-le-Duc even arranged for the person at fault to leave town. Taubmann, who had been so "lacking in tact" (*L'Eclaireur Meusien*), deserted by all, abandoned ship. Similarly, a Jewish woman from Bar-le-Duc sent her friends the following letter:

We are all devastated; this evening, we are all escaping to X . . . For three days, there have been demonstrations here outside the homes of all the Israelites. We had our store window shattered. Others also had the windows broken and considerable damage. The same

314 The Anti-Semitic Moment

thing is happening here, in Bar-le-Duc, as in Algeria; we have no
one, you understand, no one, to protect us. The mayor and the
prefect, whom someone goes to see every day, promise to provide
reinforcements, but they do nothing. Oh, how unhappy we are!
Those who called themselves our friends shout in unison, "Death
to the Jews!" and incite the crowd. For three days we haven't had
any sleep, we haven't eaten. No one does anything for us here, and
everything is driven by the Catholic clubs. We are at the end of
our rope . . . Excuse my handwriting, I'm shaking. My eldest
daughter had three fainting fits last night: five hundred demonstrators from Ligny are said to be arriving this evening. My husband is
at the end of his rope. All my love to you. Oh, what a tragedy!
What a tragedy![7]

In the May legislative elections, the Bar-le-Duc candidates vied with
one another in their anti-Semitism. Henry Ferrette, a nationalist but
also a republican, supported by Drumont's La Libre Parole, started things
off. During a public meeting of fifteen hundred people, he declared,
"An evil is raging through France, whose ravages extend to all portions
of national activity. This evil is international, cosmopolitan speculation." And the audience responded, "Jewry."[8] The candidate declared his
desire to fight "the cosmopolitan financiers" who financed the "syndicate of treason." "So that our civil servants may be sincerely devoted to
the interests of the party," he wrote in his platform statement, "it is necessary henceforth to set aside elective office only for those who are
French and the grandchildren of French people . . . Long live France for
the French! Long live the army! Long live the Republic for the workers."
In his official platform statement, Major Angelini, another parliamentary candidate, to whom the liberals rallied, protested "the criminal monopolies of cosmopolitan Jewry." All of the candidates denounced the
republican Jules Develle, the incumbent deputy and himself a fierce defender of the army, as "the candidate of the Jews and Freemasons, the
councilor of the Dreyfus family." Develle, however, took care to keep his
distance from any Dreyfusard connection. Neither Angelini nor Develle
found favor in the eyes of La Croix Meusienne, which called for "the
Christian citizens" to battle "Yiddischry . . . Chief Rabbi Zadoc-Kahn,
the lower rabbis, and the other little rabbis of the Taubmann kind." In

that overheated atmosphere where anti-Semitism was broadly shared, Henry Ferrette easily won in the first round.[9]

The "arrogance" of Rabbi Taubmann was truly astonishing. His attitude serves as an invitation to examine the biases of traditional historiography, which stresses the Jews' passivity, their silence, their desire to protect their own situation, to be forgotten. At the time of the Dreyfus affair and for many long centuries before, Jews had supposedly scraped and bowed, kept their defenses up, and waited for things to calm down. In republican France, Jews, whether they were shopkeepers or state Jews, are said to have pursued successful social integration, trusting in the values of 1789,[10] and to have been hostile toward any form of specific solidarity, confident in the institutions come what may. Does the audacity of Rabbi Taubmann—which is particularly astonishing in that, as an agent of the state like any minister of a religious faith, he was obliged to exercise reserve—contradict a dominant thesis that reinforces prejudice?

That accusation of passivity was formulated by Léon Blum and Hannah Arendt. The Dreyfusard Blum argued that "the Jews had accepted Dreyfus's conviction as definitive and just. They did not speak of the affair among themselves . . . A great misfortune had befallen Israel. It was endured without a word . . . The Jews of Dreyfus's age, those who belonged to the same social stratum, and who like him had passed difficult exams and had been introduced into the officers' staff or the most sought-out administrative corps, were irritated at the idea that a negative prejudice should come to limit their irreproachable careers." Hannah Arendt concurred that "Dreyfus found few open defenders among the French Jews . . . The publicity inspired an unhealthy terror, and they relied on subterranean maneuvers."[11] No judgment could have been more harsh. Out of fear of transforming the affair into a Jewish question and cutting themselves off from their fellow citizens, the Jews of France supposedly rejected any specific involvement. That view constitutes a radical condemnation of French Judaism, which supposedly sacrificed its personality to maintain its integration.

But the thesis does not hold. The Republic did not necessarily destroy either the capacity to protest as a citizen and as a Jew or the consciousness of a common destiny.[12] L'Univers Israélite argued in 1906 that "from the top of the social ladder to the bottom rung, the Israelites have not been afraid to expose themselves to their enemies' blows to hasten the deliverance of their unfortunate brother . . . The rehabilitation of Alfred Dreyfus is thus also the rehabilitation of the Jews."[13] A great deal of evidence attests to the courage of many unknown Jews who were not afraid of "publicity," of speaking in a public voice. Throughout France in these early months of 1898, as the anti-Semitic tide was spreading, constantly swelling in the large cities but also in midsized cities and even towns,[14] countless Jews adopted Taubmann's "arrogant" attitude. In Bar-le-Duc itself, in addition to the rabbi, several Jews were bold enough to register their disapproval. They were far from alone, as we can easily see if we look randomly through the archives.

In Rouen on January 18, 1898, Alexandre Bloch wrote directly to the prefect: "I have the honor of bringing to your attention the fact that young people, about fifty of them, came last night and struck my storefront . . . That disturbance lasted several minutes, and no officer appeared, even though there is a station on the same street, a hundred meters away. I dare hope, Mr. Prefect, that you will be kind enough to give orders that such events will not be repeated."[15] In Marseilles Léon Blum, also a shopkeeper, wrote to the prefect on January 17, 1898:

> Last night, at about eight o'clock, a group of approximately two hundred young people gathered outside my haberdashery shop to demonstrate noisily and then engaged in assaults, breaking my windows and thereby causing major damage. In view of that danger, I immediately sent my clerks out to request the police's help. But their actions were of no use; they did not encounter any officers in the neighboring streets . . . Fearing that similar scenes might manifest themselves in an even more serious manner, I have come to place myself under your protection so that you may be kind enough to take the necessary measures to prevent the recurrence of such deeds.[16]

On the nineteenth the owner of Simon and Company sent the mayor of Marseilles the following, forwarding a copy to the district attorney: "We feel that, as licensed French citizens, we have the right to the protection of the public authorities in the free exercise of our profession.

We have thus come to alert you, Mr. Mayor, that we will no longer close our doors in the face of demonstrations, and we beg you to take note, as municipal chief of police, that we leave the responsibility to you for all the consequences that could result from further demonstrations."[17] In Nantes "the Jewish merchants announced that they would defend themselves."[18] In Chalon-sur-Saône "the director of *Paris-Chalon* had his store guarded at night by five armed men."[19] In Avignon and many other cities, shopkeepers did not agree to close their stores: J. Roos, owner of Le Petit Paris, "firmly but politely refused to comply with that unofficial injunction, warning that he would close up at the usual time, adding that, having never provoked anyone, he intended to remain the master in his house and would take his own precautions to command respect."[20] In Grenoble the merchant David lodged a complaint to protest the anti-Semitic signs that were posted on the walls of the Jewish stores.[21] In Bordeaux "the rioters demolished the windows of the Nouvelles Galeries belonging to a co-religionist. The director of the store believed it appropriate to defend himself, since there was a risk that his bazaar would be invaded and looted. He thus had the faucets of his establishment's water mains turned on, and his private firefighting staff unleashed torrents of water on the demonstrators."[22]

The shopkeepers were not the only ones to defend themselves, even in the east, where the nationalist tendency was particularly keen. In Nancy, for example, when anti-Semitic riots erupted, a law student named Salmon came upon an officer who was shouting, "Down with the Jews!" Salmon asked him to stop; slaps were exchanged, and a duel was arranged. Officers of the Fifth Hussars refused to set up the duel, however, because the student was still a minor.[23] In the same city, a duel pitted a certain Netter against a pharmacist, who was wounded during the fight.[24] On January 20, 1898, two hundred students launched a noisy anti-Semitic demonstration, in the course of which "an Israelite student . . . went at one of the demonstrators tooth and nail and overcame him by kicking him. The latter naturally responded in kind; his comrades were about to defend him when the officers intervened . . . It is said that more than a hundred revolvers have been purchased by Israelites, as well as several old weapons that deserve instead to appear in gun collections."[25] The next day, again in the capital of Lorraine, "M. Rosenthal Junior was taking a walk with a friend when they heard the shouts 'Death to the Jews! Let's charge into them! Forward.' One demonstrator jumped them, shouting, 'Death to the Jews!' He received a punch that knocked him flat. At that moment three revolver shots were fired by demonstrators."[26] In the same city, the shoemaker Spire, the shopkeeper Salmon, the industrialist Lévy, and the attorney Kahn, among others, held a private meeting with the Protestants in an attempt to respond to the anti-Semitic demonstrations.[27] Also in Nancy, Professor of Medicine Bernheim lodged a complaint against one of his colleagues, who was running for the legislature under the label "anti-Semitic candidate," maintaining that, in so proceeding, he was insulting his Jewish colleagues. The university council declared itself unqualified to make a ruling. Not far from Nancy, in Lunéville, the anti-Semites were exasperated by "the mocking attitude and arrogance of certain Jews."[28] In Neufchâteau, when Jews were denied the right to put up horses for sale, David Birgé protested—and was assaulted by officers: "M. Picard, chairman of the Israelite community of Neufchâteau, as soon as he became aware of the incident, took up his cousin's defense. He said this morning in the middle of his coffee that he was sorry he was not present, that he would have taken care to put the president of the purchasing commission and the officers in their place. He added that he had sent an article on that subject to a newspaper in Paris and that, if need be, he would call for a challenge in the Chamber of Deputies."[29] Throughout the east, when copies of *L'Univers Israélite* were sent through the mails, the bands around them were systematically covered with anti-Semitic remarks. Certain subscribers lodged complaints: an employee in the central post office in Paris was found guilty and fired.[30]

In Tournon an anti-Semitic demonstration took place outside the home of Ratisbonne, a teacher at the high school. He described the events to the police superintendent: "Last night individuals came to my home and loudly shouted 'Down with Zola, down with the Jews, down with the Kikes and Yids.' They threw a dozen large stones against the main door. Before acting they had taken care to put out the gaslight not far from my home. After opening a casement window, I first threw a pail of water at them; then, seeing that they were not leaving, I went to the gendarmerie to lodge a complaint against them. The gendarmerie was located only 150 meters away."[31] In Arras, according to a police report, on August 21, 1898, as an officer from the ministry was tearing up a Dreyfusard poster, "M. Kohn, the editor of *Le Siècle*, intervened, and an altercation took place while many persons assembled demonstrated against Kohn."[32] In Orléans on January 24, 1898, as about a hundred high school students were demonstrating outside Lévy-Keiser's house to shouts of "Down with the Jews! Out with the Kikes!" "a few officers who happened to be there, aided by M. Lévy and his son, collared a few demonstrators and took them to the station."[33] In Montbéliard the Jews did not conceal their Dreyfusard feelings and, according to a police report, were "anticipating Dreyfus's acquittal."[34]

In Nantes a crowd formed around an unknown passerby, who was pointed out to be a Jew. The man tried to stand up to the young people and called them cowards. People rushed at him and struck him, and had the police not arrived, the assault would have continued. In that same city, on December 12, 1898, "M. Lévy, son-in-law of M. Ikelheimer, who owns the store Au Soldeur, wishing to enter the room where the anti-Semites were holding a meeting, was struck by canes by about twenty young people."[35] Shortly thereafter Benjamin Dreyfus, a business employee, gave a lecture on anti-Semitism within the context of the socialist-revolutionary committee, explaining that the Jews were true patriots: "Mangin, a member of the socialist federation, energetically protested the defense of the Jews given by Dreyfus, declaring that socialists in every country had no worse enemies than the Jews. He was very astonished that the militants of the Socialist Party had allowed Dreyfus to come defend his entire co-religionist clique and maintained that that did not advance the cause of the workers."[36] Also in Nantes Abraham Dreyfus, the chief postmaster, "loudly expressed his satisfaction with the idea of a review of his nephew's case. He was then violently taken to task by MM. Suzer and Colonel Parfait. M. Dreyfus, at the invitation of these gentlemen, left their society and finished his drink at a neighboring table. It seems this was not the first time that M. Dreyfus had gotten a scolding."[37] Also in the same city, Maurice Schwob, the editor of the newspaper *Le Phare de la Loire*, was the only one to defend Captain Dreyfus in his columns, and demonstrators protested under his windows. In Nantes Jews constituted a very small minority of two to three hundred people, but they faced the onslaught. According to the police superintendent's report, a young man

> had the habit, while passing the shop of the jeweler Diedishzeim, of insulting the shopkeeper's daughter. The young lady complained to her brother, who intervened to put down the anti-Semite's insolence. M. Diedishzeim Junior reproached him for his attitude toward a woman and summoned him to come by in twenty-four hours to apologize to her or risk a deserved punishment. The next day the young man came back, but he was escorted by two hundred Catholic, anti-Semitic individuals who noisily demonstrated outside the store. With two of his acolytes, the young man even managed to enter the store. But the three had to retreat, given the emphatic attitude of M. Diedishzeim Junior. As students, surrounded by about three hundred people, were shouting, "Apologize! Apologize! Death to the Jews!" Guyamard, a socialist bookkeeper from the Crémieux company, came out onto the sidewalk in front of the store, shouting, "Long live the socialist Republic!" The crowd prepared to attack him. A socialist leader then arrived on the scene and was astonished to find workers among the anti-Semitic reactionaries. Some then shouted, "Long live the socialist Republic," while others responded with vigorous shouts of "Down with the Jews! Down with the Republic! Down with the socialist Republic!"[38]

In Marseilles while Pierre Voinot, the mayor of Algiers, was having an aperitif at an outdoor café with several members of the Ligue des Patriotes, who were sporting cornflowers in their lapels, a newspaper vendor offered *L'Antijuif* to anyone within earshot. At that moment, a police superintendent noted, "because that newspaper was perhaps not to the taste of a certain Lévy, a customs clerk, the latter punched him in the face, which gave him a slight wound to the upper lip. An argument immediately ensued between the members of the league and the assailant, during which the latter was slapped by one of them, a business employee named de l'Eglise. A little later, I learned that a certain Léon Benchinol, an employee at that store, had come to have a drink on the terrace of the café on the place du Grand-Théâtre and had been caught by leaguists and hit in the face with a cane."[39] In Nice, after Camille Haumann shouted, "Long live Dreyfus!" he found himself "assaulted by an annoyed crowd, who manhandled him." Officers intervened. In Dijon, when Lucien Weil wished to hold a Dreyfusard lecture, "part of the population protested against that Israelite's anarchist schemes. The listeners, who were very overexcited, intended to do Weil some harm."[40] In Montpellier on January 19, 1898, as anti-Semitic demonstrations erupted, "a certain Phalippon was observed, accompanied by his fiancée, Hélène Strouzert, a native of Odessa, at the head of a few Jews and Russian students, who shouted, 'Long live Zola!' and 'Down with the priests!' "[41] Also in Montpellier, on December 11, 1898, "the friends of M. Lisbonne—who is Jewish—decided to boo an anti-Semitic professor and even to assault students who might accompany the professor in the street."[42] Again in that same city, according to the newspaper L'Eclair,

a few Jews were rash enough to slip in among the anti-Semitic demonstrators and learn of their intentions. One of them was recognized by the crowd, which booed him. The Jew was obliged to take refuge in a neighboring establishment . . . Several Jews followed the young people, who asked only to demonstrate peaceably, and provoked them with repeated cries of "Long live Zola! Down with the priests!" The demonstrators responded with shouts of "Out with Zola! Down with the Jews! Long live the army!" A few annoyed demonstrators responded as well with vigorous punches and blows with canes. One cane hit the head of an individual shouting, "Long live Zola!" who, bloodied, was immediately taken to the pharmacy.[43]

In Toulouse on January 20 and 21, 1898, Molina, a money changer, and Lévy, a shopkeeper, went to the central police station and filed a complaint against the damage done to their stores: "These plaintiffs want to be compensated," wrote the police officer. "I advised them to go to the organizers of the demonstration, but they claimed to want nothing to do with them and chose to seek the responsibility for this damage elsewhere." In that same city, Rauch, a professor of philosophy at the university, expressed solidarity with Pressensé, the president of the Ligue des Droits de l'Homme, who was there giving a very animated lecture. A group of students "expressed their discontent and hissed M. Rauch, to prevent him from conducting his class, because he was Jewish . . . The students accompanied M. Rauch to his home on the rue Saint-Bernard, hissing and booing him. There were about two hundred of them at the time. From there they came back to the university shouting, 'Long live the army, down with the Jews!' " A little later Cahen wrote to the prefect to get the anti-Semitic posters removed from the walls of the city—and was successful.[44]

In Paris several unknown Jews publicly demonstrated great courage. On November 14, 1898, anti-Semitic posters were put up on the walls of the Trousseau hospital. "When M. Lévy, a nonresident medical student attached to the hospital, learned about the sign, he tore it up, which led to the protest of several people," the police superintendent reported. "After a discussion M. Lévy invited them to come with him to the police station; they did not follow him. He presented himself alone and begged me to take note of his condemnation of what he called an incitement for citizens to hate one another and a call for murder."[45] In *L'Antijuif* Jules Guérin complained several times of the audacity of the Jews. He did not understand how "the Jew Laskar, a hippo of a Kike, backed by a band of ruffians of his own kind, whom he calls, in his Judische jargon, 'seferal yung mens,' had dared assault him . . . I advised the Jew Laskar that, at the first attack against me, from him or his gang, I would execute him first, without the slightest hesitation." On another occasion Guérin went to a show at the Folies-Bergère. During the intermission, as he was walking through the lobby, "a group of Jews insulted him under their breath," *L'Antijuif* reported. "One of these Kikes stuck out his tongue at him, like an ape grimacing to amuse himself. Jules Guérin, who is quick with his hands, caught the Jew's tongue and pulled it out of his ugly face. The Jew screamed an obscenity, which earned him a vigorous slap that knocked him against a seat . . . If the Jews make insults, they know what they will be exposing themselves to." Eugène Silberberg was not afraid to testify against Guérin and his anti-Semitic rants.[46] Many Jewish shopkeepers—for example, the owners of the Bloch store, the Houppe store, and the Godchaux store—wrote to the prefect to demand police protection, threatening to close their businesses otherwise and to leave a great number of employees and laborers out of work, which, a police report said, would cause "keen emotion in the working class." The prefect committed himself to protecting these stores.[47] Bernheim, after his factory was attacked with stones by a band of demonstrators, went to the deputy of his ward, who introduced him at the Palais-Bourbon to Barthou, the interior minister. Bernheim declared to the minister that, if he did not take measures to assure his protection, he would leave "for Nice or elsewhere—for a region, in any case, where French citizens of Israelite origin are safer than in the City of Light. I informed him as well," Bernheim wrote, "that I would send him the two thousand workers who would be left without means to survive if my establishment were to close. M. Barthou assured me of his profound regret and said that I would henceforth be protected. Since yesterday the number of officers has increased in my street and in the stations."[48] In September 1899, the young Benhaïm, a high school student in Oran who was admitted to the Ecole Centrale, hit someone with brass knuckles during the anti-Semitic demonstrations near Fort Chabrol. When arrested, he placidly explained that "in Algeria people never go out without them."[49] Also in September a group of Jewish workers called the Prolétariat Juif de France decided that the anti-Semites "would no longer encounter timid and irresolute people, as in the Middle Ages, but rather firm and organized men resolved to respond to force with force." On October 9, 1899, as the train from Raincy was entering the Gare de l'Est, a brawl erupted between travelers quarreling about the Dreyfus affair. Officers and Jews slapped and punched one another and hit one another with canes. Soon close to four hundred people were doing battle on the platforms; the police finally separated the adversaries.[50] In 1902 a brawl erupted on the rue Saint-Antoine in which several young Jews received knife wounds; many Parisian Jews did not hesitate to respond in kind.[51] In Algeria, of course, the violence was even greater, and a number of Jews were wounded or even killed. In Constantine, for example, on January 22, 1898, three hundred Jews confronted anti-Semitic gangs driven to act by Drumont and Max Régis. In Oran and other cities, brawls also led to loss of life.[52] There pogroms replaced verbal violence and the destruction of property more than they did in the metropolis.

Anonymous Jews clearly rejected anti-Semitic violence and expressed their desire to be acknowledged as full-fledged citizens and to enjoy the public protection of the law and the police. Many did not retreat from physical confrontations. Far from taking refuge in silence and passivity or resignation, they insisted on defending their dignity. Those who belonged to the highest strata of society often do not correspond at all to the contemptuous portraits drawn by Léon Blum and Hannah Arendt. In Bordeaux, for example, on February 20, 1898, Chief Rabbi Lévy wrote to the prefect asking to have anti-Semitic posters removed.[53] In Marseilles, Chief Rabbi Jones Weyl met with a journalist from *Le Soleil du Midi* to publicly denounce "the worst excesses in this city, which was once the home of law, justice, and freedom . . . Was it out of patriotism that individuals showed up outside the synagogue day before yesterday?" At that precise moment in the interview, demonstrators outside the house broke lamps; the rabbi added, "Even in my home, sir, vagrants are causing a ruckus."[54]

At the very highest level, however, the religious leaders do seem to have hesitated. Their silence elicited the exasperation of the *Archives Israélites*, which itself decried "those good little young people raised at the Church's knee, whose souls were molded by educators in cassocks, and who, without being provoked by anyone, destroyed the windows of the synagogue on the rue de Tournelle and attacked commercial establishments belonging to Israelites, screaming things like 'Death to the Jews.' "[55] The *Archives*, a very moderate newspaper, gave a dramatic account of events that

take us back several centuries, to the reign of good Philip the Fair [King of France 1285–1314] . . . The heinous riot, mounting an assault on houses inhabited by Israelite citizens, breaking into stores, looting merchandise, setting fire to whatever they could not carry away, and for three days, under the noses of the soldiers and the police, having almost a free hand to do anything they wanted and holding the forces of law and order in check! Then these Vandals, tired of raids, their pockets quite full, transformed themselves into Huns and hunted down the Jews they encountered and, two thousand to one, satisfied their insane bloodlust on two or three of these poor souls, one of whom even perished under their madmen's blows . . . The law's protection assured to every citizen has been a lie! Ask the Jewish shopkeepers in Marseilles, Lyons,

Nantes, Bordeaux, and especially Algiers! . . . Oh, the philosophy
of the events we have just endured is very bitter, and we find in it
only subjects of sadness concerning the injustice of men and the
perversity of a kind of press that, instead of enlightening public
opinion, seeks to lead it astray, and concerning Catholic intolerance, which, like a new phoenix, rises from the ashes of the pyres
it lit in the past![56]

The *Archives* clearly identified the adversary: "In France, for the first time
in five centuries, heinous shouts of 'Down with the Jews! Death to the
Jews!' have come to fill the atmosphere . . . Who were the organizers of
these medieval processions, if not the leaders of the clerical faction?
What screaming troops brought the cities to the boiling point with savage cries from another time? The youth of the Catholic clubs and the
Catholic university. And finally, to what monuments did those self-
righteous hordes, after breaking the windows of Jewish stores, go to
stage a bellicose demonstration? To the synagogues."[57] In February
1898 the newspaper bitterly observed, "They jump on us, they assail us
with insults and threats . . . The central consistory, our natural, legal organization, our intermediary with the government, is speechless. We are,
to use the biblical expression, like a flock without a shepherd, wandering
aimlessly." In that same issue, F. Uhry, former councilor general, wrote:

When, in France, from north to south and from east to west, this
shout from the Middle Ages reverberates: "Down with the Jews!";
when people loot and pillage their stores, until the time when they
will attack their persons; then indifference and impassiveness become a crime . . . It is time to react. If the central consistory, our
legal representative, does not wish, through a manifesto to France,
to dispel the dangerous misunderstandings that our enemies pro-
mote, let committees be formed in Paris, let them make known
our patriotic feelings for France, but let them demand equal justice
for Jews by protesting energetically . . . Let us act quickly—there is
no time to lose.[58]

L'Univers Israélite, whose editor, Isaïe Levaillant, was a former prefect and
general secretary of the Paris prefecture, also protested in writing

"against the ignoble passions, all the absurd prejudices, all the stupid and odious hatred of Jews that are swarming and thrashing about deep within the popular masses . . . Anti-Semitism has invaded all parts of the country and has penetrated the deepest strata of the population . . . Hatred of the Jew is blinding the mob."[59] When the demonstrations were at their height, he added, "An absolutely extraordinary deployment of law forces was necessary to contain the hordes of anti-Semites and to avert true catastrophes. We see all the hatred, all the ferocious and blind passions, all the violence of the Middle Ages, coming back to life."[60] In the face of such urgent dangers, Levaillant thundered against the irresolution of French Jews and warned that "it is time for them to prepare for battle." And again: "In the face of the formidable outcry about to occur, what will the Israelites of France do? Are they in a position to stand up to the enemy and to repel the assault with which he threatens them? Have they armed themselves to defend their rights? Is the situation so desperate for the Jews that they can do nothing more than put down their weapons and hand themselves over, bound hand and foot, to their implacable adversaries? The time has come to prepare for battle. Have the Jews of France thought to unite, to come together, to organize?" That former prefect, once responsible for keeping the peace, suggested that they "arm themselves to defend their rights."[61] L'Univers Israélite tirelessly repeated the same message: "When the storm has passed, we will philosophize. In the meantime we must defend ourselves."[62]

Chief Rabbi Zadoc-Kahn maintained a stubborn silence for many long months of rioting. Only on May 25, 1898, did he finally speak up in support of the Jews of Algeria, who had endured the gravest attacks and had the most wounded and dead among their ranks.

> For several months I ought to have, I would have liked to have, sent you an urgent appeal in support of our Algerian co-religionists, whose moral and material suffering exceeds anything that can be imagined . . . Out of a feeling of reserve that you will appreciate, I have refrained until today . . . Today it is possible to believe that one can without disadvantage speak the language of pity and plead the cause of thousands of human creatures plunged into the most profound poverty . . . That will give evidence of charity and even patriotism; for it must not be said that, in the late nineteenth

century, in a region where the flag of France waves, men, women, and children are condemned to starve to death because distraught individuals contest their right to existence because of their origin and their religious beliefs.[63]

L'Univers Israélite protested the rabbi's moderation: "We have read the appeal that the chief rabbi of the central consistory sent to his co-religionists in support of the Jews of Algeria . . . I do not know whether M. Zadoc-Kahn sent his appeal to the president of the Republic and to the ministers, but I do not see why he would not do so . . . If the central consistory intervenes in support of the Jews of Algeria, he would do well to give his interventions a little publicity. Why keep a secret of steps taken that are only too justified?"[64] The newspaper openly disputed Zadoc-Kahn's overly discreet steps and urged him to lay the matter before the government, to engage in a public protest campaign. Others, too, thought that the highest authorities in the Jewish world ought to speak up and put aside their reserve, even if it meant countering their obligations as civil servants. Zadoc-Kahn found himself in a difficult situation, since his slightest word would immediately lead to a public protest. Hence on Friday, January 28, 1898, in the Chamber of Deputies, Le Hérissé, a Boulangist deputy, demanded, "The minister of justice [*garde des sceaux*] will kindly explain to the Chamber how it happened that he has neglected to call the chief rabbi of France to order and to remind him of his duty when he is a long way from the reserve that his high office imposes on him and has allowed himself to intervene publicly during the recent trials that have deeply moved public opinion (*very good, very good, from various benches*)."

In reality, unknown to almost everyone, the chief rabbi was far from inactive. In January 1898 the police observed that he "does not want in any way to appear to be mixed up in the Dreyfus affair, which he nevertheless follows attentively, induced by the militants in the Jewish camp."[65] Zadoc-Kahn was close to Captain Dreyfus's family and presided over the the captain's own marriage at the synagogue de la Victoire. He was an Alsatian patriot and a champion of Franco-Judaism and assimilation. He may have been discreet, but he proved to be a man of action. In December 1894 he approached deputies many times and personally met with the ministers of interior and of justice, who promised protection measures. He finally decided to combat anti-Semitism discreetly by gathering a core of resolute men around him. That Jewish defense committee, by its mere existence, contradicts the passivity thesis. Like the German Verein zur Abwehr des Antisemitismus, this semiclandestine group, which included Paris rabbi Jacques-Henri Dreyfus, Baron Edmond de Rothschild, Narcisse Leven (president of the Alliance Israélite Universelle), Salomon Reinach, and former prefect Isaïe Levaillant, maintained that, "in the face of the threats that continue to be heaped upon us, it would be inexcusable if we were to be caught napping." The group took on "a great number of permanent or occasional correspondents who would keep it informed, in due course, of all the events that might interest it. Thanks to the information and advice with which it could thereby surround itself, it would be less likely to be lacking in vigilance."[66] L'Univers Israélite later reported that "the need then appeared to a great number of Israelites of France to finally defend themselves against the incitements, which were as evil as they were criminal ... We, the Israelites, have made an appeal only for the limited participation of our co-religionists, the circumstances being such that our action, to be effective, had to remain discreet."[67] Other equally prudent initiatives pointed to a real sense for action. As a police report noted, Julien Cahen, Paul Fribourg, Léopold Lévy, and Bernheim, aka "Turco," set in place a perfected system of "covert surveillance" of Major Esterhazy, probably acting on behalf of one of Captain Dreyfus's lawyers.[68]

On the morning of Sunday, February 13, 1898, the central consistory of the Israelites of France and the Israelite consistory of Paris assembled to meet with Chief Rabbi Zadoc-Kahn. According to the minutes of the discussion, one of the participants, Auguste Michel-Lévy, an engineer and member of the Institut de France, worried that their protest would "disrupt the efforts of those who, like M. Jaurès, are taking up our defense. We have no base of support. It will be wasted effort." Invoking Jaurès's protection, oddly enough, he refused to support granting the consistory's ability to act publicly as the representative of the Jews as a whole. By contrast, Dr. Théodore Klein judged that "the central consistory is the guardian of all the communities. It must ask whether we, as French Jews, do not have the right to protest and occupy that ground." Baron Alphonse de Rothschild, who presided over the session, argued that the assembly did. According to the minutes, he maintained that " 'the situation is no longer the same today. There are criminal acts at issue. The consistories must now protest, demand the government's protection. We must compose a letter to the Ministry of Religion and transmit the letter to the prime minister's officer and to the minister of justice.' . . . The baron now believes that there is reason to act. There is an extraordinary emotion among our co-religionists, and something must be done for them." A letter to the government was composed:

> Mr. Minister, the Republic does not have any citizens more re-spectful of its institutions than we are. We embrace in all fondness the national army, which encapsulates in itself all the glories of the past, all the hopes for the future . . . Nevertheless, for the last few years, the most odious slander has been directed against the Is-raelite population of France . . . Scandalous scenes occurred in Paris itself and in several provincial cities; bands of looters pil-laged and bloodied an entire neighborhood in Algiers; and our religious buildings were not respected—yesterday one of our syn-agogues was attacked in Paris. We call for your serious attention to this troubled situation, and we have firm confidence that the gov-ernment will take the most emphatic measures to prevent their continuation or recurrence.

The *Archives Israélites* of February 24, 1898, reported, "The central con-sistory sent the government a statement of protest against the hostile demonstrations of which the Israelites, both in France and in Algeria, have recently been the victims."[69] The newspaper raised a true cry of alarm against "the religious war" that was unfolding there.[70] Although the consistory and the chief rabbi chose not to be too public in their in-terventions and demonstrated their complete loyalty, they were far from bowing down and letting the situation continue. The Alliance Israélite Universelle did not broadcast outside the organization its own delibera-tions linked to the Dreyfus affair and the anti-Semitic demonstrations. At most we may note that on February 16, 1898, a paragraph appeared in the registry of its deliberations that revealed its concerns: "A delega-tion of the Israelites of Algiers attended the session. The delegates of Algiers spoke to the central committee about the situation of Algerian

Judaism following the recent troubles. The committee gave the delegates the assurance that the alliance would lend all its assistance to the recovery of the Israelite population of Algeria."[71]

A few months later, during the May 1898 electoral campaign, the two large institutional newspapers kept close watch on the views expressed by each candidate and wondered how Jewish voters, whose protection was hardly assured, would cast their votes. Isaïe Levaillant was very pessimistic about the waffling of the Opportunists, who had "shelved the principles of tolerance and justice." He was "disillusioned" by the behavior of the radicals and remained extremely cautious toward the socialists. As a result, he proposed that Jews vote without regard for political labels, solely as a function of the positions the various candidates had taken on justice. It hardly mattered where they came from: "For us, there are no longer any parties. We no longer recognize either pro- or antigovernment candidates, and the words *moderate, radical,* and *socialist* are meaningless to us. We now distinguish only between the opponents of freedom of conscience and the friends of freedom of conscience. We will do battle with the former, regardless of the label they wear, and we will support the latter, whatever aversions we may have to overcome." He added, "Thus, for the first time, at these elections we will obey a common idea and we will plant a common flag: freedom of conscience."[72] Henri Prague, editor in chief of the *Archives Israélites,* observed on the eve of the elections that "you will find that note of insulting mistrust of the Israelite population of France, cavalierly called 'cosmopolitan Jewry,' in a number of the platform statements that spring up during electoral periods and plaster all the walls."[73]

These heads of the Jewish press, worried about the elections' possible outcome, were subsequently delighted with the results. A very vigilant Levaillant rejoiced in the defeat of Bernis in Gard, Giraudeau in Loire-Atlantique, Le Senne in Paris, and Thiébaud in Vaucluse; of Beauregard, of the comte d'Hughes, and others. Nevertheless, he noted with regret and concern the success of Denis in Dax, Gervaise in Nancy, Ferrette in Bar-le-Duc, Bernard in Bordeaux, Cassagnac in Gers, and Millevoye in Paris. He rightly observed: "Although the electorate has in general refused to associate itself with the ignominious doctrines that tend toward the despoiling and proscription of an entire category of French citizens . . . nevertheless, a shameful and masked anti-Semitism that, under the name of nationalism, has exploited a patriotism gone awry and for which the Dreyfus affair has been a powerful lever of propaganda, has indisputably achieved great success." Shortly thereafter he again lamented the formation of the anti-Semitic group in the Chamber of Deputies: "The new Chamber had hardly met when an anti-Jewish group constituted itself within it. The anti-Semitism in France will now rival that in Austria." This careful observer of the political scene made an essential comment, one that has been missing from most analyses, even very recent ones: "The incorrigible Panglosses who not long ago proclaimed that there is no anti-Semitism and who considered the formation of the anti-Jewish group within Parliament a purely fanciful possibility will no doubt find new reasons to rest easy and remain confident, based on the numerical weakness of that group. 'Nineteen members,' they will exclaim, 'it's ridiculous!' . . . They are forgetting that there are other anti-Semites in the Chamber besides those who have officially enrolled under Drumont's banner. Are not those impenitent Boulangists who make up the nationalist group anti-Semites as well? And are not the two groups ready to march hand in hand and unite with the clericals?"[74] In the face of "the inertia and listlessness" of the republican circles, everything remained to be feared. What a paradox that one could simultaneously celebrate the tricentennial of the Edict of Nantes* and the formation of an anti-Semitic parliamentary group in the Chamber! "This is not the time," the *Archives Israélites* added, "to strew flowers over the statue of Henry IV at the pont Neuf but rather to cover it up!"[75]

---

*Edict of Nantes: the proclamation by King Henry IV in 1598 that extended partial religious freedom to Protestants.—trans.

Conclusion

When Zola referred to the crowd that was loudly rejoicing at the announcement of his conviction, shouting, "Out with Zola!" and "Death to the Jews!" as "cannibals," he was speaking metaphorically. In France the era of political savagery was past: cruelty now stemmed solely from wars; it had been almost extirpated from social relationships. The twenty to twenty-five thousand French people who died in May 1871 were war dead: killed in the war with Germany, in the civil war, in the social war. There were no war dead in 1898. Yes, the threat of foreign war hung in the air, giving rise to a fear of the "Prussians" and an obsession with treason; yes, rumblings of social war, diverted onto the eternal scapegoats, the Jews, could be heard; and yes, certain ingredients of civil war even came into being at Tivoli Hall and on the avenue de Wagram. But none of it went very far. The police charged, but they did not fire; nationalist demonstrators and Dreyfusard counterdemonstrators—long the minority—did not murder each other. Even the worst moment of the Dreyfus affair did not fit the classic pattern of the Franco-French wars. Undoubtedly, the internal schism that supposedly occurred in the 1890s has been greatly overestimated: outside the world of ideas and polemics between intellectuals, confrontations that might have torn apart the social body were rare or nonexistent in France. In the end the war of the two Frances had no reality.

The Dreyfus affair was nevertheless open season on Jews, and the hunt attracted a large number of people, university and high school students, artisans and workers, shopkeepers and employees, lawyers and doctors, the wealthy and the unemployed, idle young people, and even a few civil servants. For the Jews of France, death—so frequently present in the shouts and insults—remained a virtual threat. So many angry crowds, so many out-of-control demonstrations, so many stirred-up populations, so many knives brandished, so many wounded, but except in Algeria, actual murder was absent. In the end death did not have its way.

The "cannibals" of Paris, Bordeaux, Angers, Marseilles, Caen, Nancy, Dijon, Dinan, Nantes, Bar-le-Duc, and Avignon, those who revealed themselves with such bloodthirsty volition in Normandy, in Lorraine, and in Provence, had nothing in common with the "cannibals" of Hautefaye: in that city, in August 1870, anti-Semites massacred one Alain de Monéys, taking extreme sadistic pleasure in the act.[1] The bonfires built in 1898 burned only effigies, not a horribly tortured half-dead man, as in Dordogne. It would not have taken much to change this fact, but it is irrefutable: no Jew lost his life, contrary to the fears expressed in many police reports. In the end the anti-Semitic moment in no way evokes the tragedies of Kishinev, Algiers, and Vienna. Dreamed of, impatiently anticipated, hoped for aloud by so many worked-up leaguists, the "Saint Bartholomew's Day massacre of the Jews" did not take place. Nowhere in France did the "monsters" succeed in carrying out their sinister task.

The authorities in Nontronnais, who could not or would not put an end to the violence, proved more vigilant this time and defended public order by severely scolding their citizens. Countless mayors, prefects, subprefects, and police superintendents, constantly present in the streets, checked, broke up, or diverted the anti-Semitic violence. The state, the central and local politico-administrative institutions, showed few signs of weakness. The ferocity declined partly because it came up against the resistance of the authorities and the police force, who were determined to defend if not the Jews, of whom they were not always fond, then at least public order, the collapse of which they feared. What might have happened otherwise?

The anti-Semitic moment occurred as France was changing its repertoire of collective action, when the recourse to boundless violence was subsiding, when acts of vigilante justice and peasant revolts were becoming more remote. As a general rule, disputes were now conducted more through electoral campaigns, ritualized demonstrations, and strikes.[2] Despite that undeniable change over the long term, associated with the centralization of the state and the expansion of the market, rows, local celebratory displays, and conscript lottery days that degenerated into riots persisted more than some believe as episodes in which dreams and hatred still found expression. Modes of action spurred by irrational impulses also persisted more than some believe, modes that endured in turn-of-the-century France, where the great political and unionist forces were set in place, a France marked more than any other country by religious conflicts, which the republican state's policy of secularization set in motion once more. At the time only the Italian workers, savagely attacked with shouts of "Death to the Catholics!" by de-Christianized French workers, their direct rivals on the labor market, met—despite police protection—a fate as tragic as that of the poor soul from Hautefaye: suddenly cruelty emerged again, intact.[3]

Reactionaries of all stripes and even certain republicans, badly in need of a rooted identity, sought to attack the abstract and universalist Republic.[4] It was the Jews, however, who suffered as a result of that grudge.

All the evidence supports this view. The Catholic world, alongside the populist movements or combined with them, was the force behind that anti-Semitic movement, which was part of its plan to reject the secular state. Though the Church and the bishops maintained great reserve, we need only return to each of the stops on our tour of France to be persuaded that many priests, students at Catholic high schools, and militants in the Union Nationale and in various movements were impelled to act by a national or local Catholic press gone awry. The combination of Catholic refusal and populist protest fed on the most diverse ideological sources, including the extreme left. It threatened to sweep away all political divisions, including the cleavage between republicans and monarchists. It reshuffled the political cards by facilitating unexpected connections between socialists and nationalists, between radicals and re-actionaries. It resurrected beliefs long thought relegated to the past. Ha-tred of Jews thus slowed the change of repertoire and opened the way to the great return to conspiracy theories,[5] to shared fears, to mytholo-gies that put off the advent of modernity, the constitution of an open society. The hatred relied on the newest technologies to invent forms of political mobilization that would win a following. It found such a for-midable reception among the public that it is strange that it can still be denied today.

The demonstrations, in the large cities and in the little towns at vari-ous times throughout 1898, probably attracted hundreds of thousands of people, some taking action, others serving as onlookers and joyfully accompanying the anti-Semitic protest. Those numbers were unprece-dented: a new kind of popular politicization took shape around a xeno-phobic vision of the world. In France and elsewhere, it will not soon be forgotten. The 1898 elections were a different kind of politicization: in addition to the deputies who openly declared themselves anti-Semites, how many hundreds of other elected officials were anti-Semitic? And how many losing candidates, too often overlooked, though each of them attracted thousands of votes? Whether they ran as monarchists, Bona-partists, *ralliés*, republicans of various allegiances, radicals, or even social-ists, together they may have attracted one or several million votes. We will never know whether they got them because of their enthusiasm or not. Let us at least observe that their solid prejudices, freely expressed, did not in any way outrage the electorate. Suddenly, in an incalculable number of wards, probably the majority of them, whether they joined enthusiastically or "went along," people at least tolerated that unre-served racism, with its vocabulary of battle and exclusion. The anti-Semitic moment had unsuspected depth. The existing overviews have trouble imagining just how widespread and open the prejudices were, at each of the stops on this perilous tour of France.

Chronology of Events in the

Dreyfus Affair

1894

October: Captain Alfred Dreyfus is accused of sending a letter, called the *bordereau*, to Captain Maximilien Ivon Schwarzkoppen, the German military attaché in Paris, announcing that he intends to send the German embassy military documents. He is arrested and imprisoned.

December: Based on a secret dossier composed of a number of counterfeit or improperly dated documents, which are not shown either to Dreyfus or to his attorney, the captain is charged with treason by the highest authorities in the army. He is tried at a military court-martial and is found guilty.

1895

January 5: Dreyfus is stripped of his rank in the main courtyard of the Ecole Militaire; he is sent to Devil's Island, off French Guiana.

1896

March: Captain Georges Picquart, the new head of the Statistical Section of the French General Staff, examines a document that would become known as *le petit bleu* (the little blue), which Captain Schwarzkoppen had intended to send to Count Major Ferdinand Esterhazy but that was intercepted by his agents. Picquart compares its handwriting to Dreyfus's and realizes that Dreyfus is innocent and that there has been a miscarriage of justice.

August: Picquart realizes the real spy is Esterhazy.

September: The existence of the secret dossier used during the trial is revealed in *L'Eclair*.

November: Bernard Lazare publishes *Une erreur judiciaire. La vérité* (A Miscarriage of Justice: The Truth) in an attempt to win a new trial for Dreyfus. Picquart shows his evidence to his superiors at the French General Staff.

November 1: Major Hubert Henry of the Statistical Section fabricates a letter supposedly sent from the Italian military attaché to Schwarzkoppen that includes this passage: "I have read that a deputy is going to ask about Dreyfus. If new explanations are required at Rome, I shall say I never had any relations with this Jew. You understand." This is the *faux Henry* (the Henry forgery).

November 14: Picquart, now an embarrassment to the French General Staff, is sent to Tunisia.

1897

June: Fearing for his life, Picquart, on leave in Paris, confides his discoveries to the attorney Louis Leblois.

July 13: Picquart's lawyer, Leblois, reveals to Auguste Scheurer-Kestner, respected vice president of the Senate, the secret of Dreyfus's innocence.

October: Scheurer-Kestner speaks of the matter to the president of the Republic, Félix Faure, and to War Minister General Billot. His information is leaked to the press, where he is harshly attacked. His actions lead nowhere.

November: Mathieu Dreyfus, the captain's brother who has defended him since the beginning and is convinced of his innocence, learns that Esterhazy is the true culprit and the author of the *bordereau*. He lodges a complaint against him with War Minister Billot. Emile Zola publishes an article in *Le Figaro* that ends, "Truth is on the march and nothing will stop it." An inquiry under the control of the army calls the accusations against Esterhazy "unproved."

December: Esterhazy demands a full court-martial to clear his name. War Minister Billot again asserts that Dreyfus is the only guilty party.

1898

January 10–11: The court-martial acquits Esterhazy. Picquart is arrested on charges of communicating confidential military information to Leblois and is imprisoned.

January 13: *L'Aurore* publishes "J'accuse," Zola's open letter to the president of the Republic, in which he denounces the army leaders and proclaims Captain Dreyfus's innocence. Scheurer-Kestner is not reelected to the Senate.

January 14: Demonstrations occur throughout France against Zola and the Jews; Algiers sees the worst anti-Semitic violence.

January 14–16: Writers and scholars commit themselves to support Dreyfus by writing a series of petitions calling for a retrial.

January 19: Socialists reject "both factions of the rival bourgeoisie." The socialist leader Jean Jaurès, at this point still an anti-Dreyfusard, denounces the "Jewish pirates" who stand behind Dreyfus.

January 20: Legal action is taken against Zola as the government charges him with libel for "J'accuse."

February 7: Zola's trial gets under way at the Palais de Justice in Paris. He is defended by the attorney Ferdinand Labori.

February 17: General Georges de Pellieux, testifying at Zola's trial, invokes the *faux Henry* as evidence against Zola, without knowing that it is a forgery.

February 18: General Raoul de Boisdeffre, Army Chief of Staff, testifies that the document is authentic.

February 23: Zola is found guilty, and the crowd demonstrates against him.

April 10: Zola is assaulted.

May 8–22: Nationwide elections to the Chamber of Deputies. The results are mixed. Several candidates who ran on anti-Semitic platforms are elected. They form an anti-Semitic group in the Chamber.

June 4: The Ligue des Droits de l'Homme (League of Human Rights), which was formed in February, holds a general meeting. Its president is Francis de Pressensé.

July 7: Godefroy Cavaignac, the new minister of war, convinced of Dreyfus's guilt, reads to the Chamber of Deputies the text of the secret and counterfeit documents that were used as evidence against Dreyfus. He insists they are authentic. Picquart writes to Premier Brisson that they are fakes; he is arrested and imprisoned.

July 18: Zola is again convicted of libel and the next day travels to London to live in exile.

August: Jaurès publishes a series of articles that support Dreyfus's innocence.

August 13: Captain Louis Cuignet, Cavaignac's subordinate, discovers that the document fabricated by Henry is indeed a forgery.

August 30: Henry acknowledges he is the text's author; he is arrested.

August 31: Henry commits suicide. General Cavaignac resigns.

September 1–2: Many newspapers demand an official review of the Dreyfus case.

September 4: Esterhazy flees to Belgium, then to England. Lucie Dreyfus, the captain's wife, demands a review of the trial.

September 27: The *garde des sceaux* (minister of justice) initiates a review of Dreyfus's 1894 conviction. The Dreyfus case is sent to the Cour de Cassation, France's highest court, for examination.

October 25: The Chamber of Deputies reconvenes for the first time since the Henry crisis. A large anti-Semitic demonstration takes place at the place de la Concorde, organized by the Ligue Antisémitique and the Ligue des Patriotes. A coup attempt by Jules Guérin and the Ligue Antisémitique is quashed.

October 29: The Cour de Cassation announces its finding, based on an examination of the evidence, that the Dreyfus case must be appealed and that it would consider the case.

December 14: *La Libre Parole*, Drumont's newspaper, establishes a fund in support of Captain Henry's widow. This fund is known as the "Henry monument."

December 31: The Ligue de la Patrie Française (League of the French Nation) is formed; its members include the anti-Dreyfusards Maurice Barrès, Frédérique Mistral, Vincent d'Indy, and others.

1899

February: President Félix Faure dies. At Faure's funeral, writer Paul Déroulède attempts to turn the funeral procession into an uprising and seize power in a coup d'état. The attempt is a resounding failure.

February 21: The case is moved from the criminal chamber of the Cour de Cassation to the three united chambers of the Cour de Cassation, a move advocated by the anti-Dreyfusards.

June 3: The Cour de Cassation, after hearing the Dreyfus case again, delivers its verdict: Dreyfus's conviction is annulled. It also accuses General Auguste Mercier of rigging the 1894 court-martial against Dreyfus.

June 9: Dreyfus leaves Devil's Island. Picquart is released from prison and the charges against him are dismissed.

June 12: Pierre Waldeck-Rousseau becomes prime minister.

August 7: The second court-martial of Alfred Dreyfus begins in the city of Rennes. Anti-Dreyfusard leaders such as Déroulède and Jules Guérin are arrested.

September: The military court finds Dreyfus guilty and sentences him to ten years in prison. He appeals, and the president of the Republic, Emile Loubet, issues a pardon. Dreyfus is freed.

November 19: A large republican parade occurs in place de la Republique, Paris.

1900

January: Déroulède and Guérin are sentenced to prison. The right wins in the nationwide municipal elections. The nationalists are victorious in Paris.

1902

September 28: Zola dies.

1906

July 12: The Cour de Cassation reverses Dreyfus's conviction and reinstates him, along with Picquart, in the army.

1935

July 11: Lieutenant-Colonel Alfred Dreyfus dies.

Notes

Introduction

1. Arlette Farge, *Le goût de l'archive* (Paris: Le Seuil, 1997), p. 87.
2. Stephen Wilson, *Ideology and Experience: Antisemitism in France at the Time of the Dreyfus Affair* (London: Associated University Presses, 1982). Conversely, the great localist theses, whether recent or not, that include that period within a longer time span are curiously silent about this anti-Semitic moment. The solid mastery of history in Jeanine Bevinetto's *Les manifestations anti-sémites à Paris et en province en 1898 et 1899* (Paris: Université Paris-X-Nanterre, 1982) also relies solely on the Paris archives yet says nothing about the very rich file boxes in the Paris police prefecture concerning the events in Paris. Janine Ponty's thesis, *La France devant l'affaire Dreyfus: Contribution à une étude sociale d'opinion publique* (Paris: Ecole Pratique des Hautes Etudes, 1972), consists of a content analysis of the press. That research, based especially on the Paris archives, omits too many of the perceptions of actors in the field.
3. Hence I will also engage in an indirect debate with Michael Burns, who maintains that the peasant world, in contrast to the cities, proved relatively indifferent to the Dreyfus affair; at most the peasants reinterpreted its episodes as a function of "its particularistic vocabulary" distinct from that of the urban world, where the anti-Semitic mobilization took place. See his *Rural Society and French Politics: Boulangism and the Dreyfus Affair, 1886–1900* (Princeton, N.J.: Princeton University

Press, 1984), pp. 136 and 171. On this point, see Nancy Fitch's pertinent comments in "Mass Culture, Mass Parliamentary Politics and Modern Anti-Semitism: The Dreyfus Affair in Rural France," *American Historical Review* 97 (February 1992): 55–95.

4. In plunging into the local archives, I deliberately ignored Algeria, where extremely violent unrest broke out in an altogether specific context, which it was impossible to take into account here. For the same reasons, I set aside the eastern provinces that had been annexed by Germany.

Chapter I: Is Paris Burning?

1. APP (Archives de la Préfecture de Police), Ba 1043 and Ba 1044.
2. All the newspaper quotations are from their editions of January 12, 1898.
3. APP, Ba 1044.
4. APP, Ba 1043 and Ba 1103. See also the press reports of these demonstrations in APP, Ba 1304. A few pieces of information can also be found in Ba 1107.
5. I have used both the police reports in APP, Ba 1044, and the press file assembled by the prefecture in APP, Ba 1304.
6. *La Libre Parole* and *Le Journal* (January 17, 1898). See also *L'Echo de Paris* and *Le Petit Journal* dated the same day. *Le Rappel* of the seventeenth denounced these demonstrations: "On rue du Cardinal-Lemoine," it wrote, "individuals of a superior intelligence acted on the pretext that no name was inscribed on the shop of an antiques dealer: therefore he's a Jew!" According to a police report, the antiquarian's name was Vançon. I have also referred to the police reports in APP, Ba 1304. See Eric Cahm, "Pour et contre Emile Zola: Les étudiants de Paris en janvier 1898," *Bulletin de la Société d'Etudes Jaurésiennes* (October–December 1978): 12–15.
7. APP, Ba 1054.
8. These arrest lists are in APP, Ba 1043.
9. *Dans quel siècle vivons-nous donc?*
   C'est Loyola qui ressuscite!
   On n'entend que le drelin din don
   De tous les donneurs d'eau bénite.
   Le peuple et le roi Million
   Vont-ils descendre dans la rue?
   Voici la France revenue
   Aux guerres de religion.

   Que nous importent les Dreyfus
   Les Esterhazys et les autres?
   C'est même loi, même typhus
   Et ceux-là ne sont pas les nôtres.

Galliffet à l'occasion,
Par haine de la populace,
Ils nous fusilleraient en masse,
Qu'importe leur religion,

Que nous importe, mes amis,
Le bon dieu des capitalistes.
Qu'ils soient plus ou moins circoncis,
Ils sont tous aussi panamistes.
Tous ont l'amour du million,
Que l'un soit juif ou catholique,
C'est bien la même arithmétique
Et la même religion . . .

10. *Et si jamais, brave'citoyens*
Noc miniss' y z'avaient la frousse,
C'est à nous qu'est pas des mannequins,
C'est à nous, d'remplacer la rousse,
On enverra Scheurer, Mathieu,
Reinach et l'père Zola qu'enrage,
Rejoindr' le cher et tendre fieu
Qui s'em . . . bête tout seul dans sa cage.

11. I am also using box APP, Ba 1304, composed uniquely of police reports, and the many file boxes that primarily contain very complete press files: APP, Ba 1302, Ba 1305, Ba 1306, Ba 1307, Ba 1308. See also AN (Archives Nationales), F7 12461 and especially 12474, a very rich file containing police reports, dispatches from officers in the provinces, and anonymous letters concerning the entire Zola trial.

12. Joseph Reinach, *Histoire de l'affaire Dreyfus* (Paris: Editions de la Revue Blanche, 1903), 3:350.

13. *Quand donc finiras-tu, dis?*
Zola, d'défendre les Youdis:
Si tu veux plus qu'on t'embotte,
Ferm' ta boîte! . . .

Comm' nous tu sais bien, mon vieux,
Qu'les Youtres sont d'mauvais fieux.
Ta lettre est trop maladroite,
Ferm' ta boîte! . . .

T'as pris tes Youpins odieux
Pour des michets trop sérieux.
Mais leur conscience est étroite,
Ferm' ta boîte!

Comm' ton affaire est jugée
Et comm' c'est toi qu'as perdu,
Ils vont t'dire: Gueule enragée:
T'as assez vendu.

De l'innocence de ton traître
Tu restes l'seul convaincu;
Au fond t'en rigol's peut-être;
T'as assez vendu!

Another song, "La gueule à Zola" (Zola's Mug), was performed to the tune of "La berceuse verte" (The Green Rocking Chair):

One day a Yid
Met Zola-the-Panfaced,
And told him: Evil One,
Come give us a hand;
We'll pay for it—
No need to fear.
At those words came
A smile from Zola's mug.

Zola responded
Right away: That's just what I need.
But, my old Yiddie,
You have to pay by noon:
The Yid paid,
Emile pocketed the fee,
Then you saw, Oh là là,
A laughing mug on Zola!

Right after that
Emile grabbed his pen,
In the name of progress.
Wanted to get a review;
In vain he bawled,
Like a dog howls at the moon,
Everyone after that
Laughed at Zola's mug!

Everything he's said
Is just jokes and imposture,
Dreyfus betrayed
And not Esterhazy;

All the renegades
Supporting his adventure
Already regret
What Zola's mug has done.

Un jour, un Youpin
Rencontra Zola-Pot-Bouille.
Et lui dit: Malin,
Viens nous donner un coup d'main;
Nous paierons pour ça,
Pas besoin d'avoir la trouille.
A ce discours-là
Sourit la gueule à Zola.

Zola répondit
Du coup: J'en fais mon affaire.
Mais, mon vieux Youdi,
Faut payer avant midi:
Le Youtre paya,
Emile empocha l'salaire,
On vit, Oh! là là!
Rire la gueule de Zola!

Aussitôt après
Emile saisit sa plume,
Au nom du progrès.
Voulant reviser l'procès:
En vain il gueula,
Comme un chien hurle à la lune,
Chacun après ça
Rit de la gueule à Zola!

Tout ce qu'il a dit
N'est que blague et qu'imposture,
Dreyfus a trahi
En non pas Esterhazy:
Tous les renégats
Soutenant son aventure
Regrettent déjà
Le coup
de gueule à Zola.

14. [Refrain]

Un! *(coups de canne)*
Le Juif marrone!
V'là les tapins!
Rrran! *(coups de canne)*
L'armée claironne
Le mot de Cambronne
Pour les Youpins!
Zing! *(coup de canne)*
Deux! Trois!
Conspuez Zola! (bis). Conspuez!

Il a juste répondu à L'aurore,
Ce gros oeuf dur qui l'isola;
C'est pas l'coq gaulois qui pérore.
Et l'peuple répond: Conspuez Zola!
Après les articles qu'il nous câcle
Y'a plus qu'à faire jouer l'fermoir!
Ah! mes amis, quelle débâcle!
Pour Zola, l'coup de l'assommoir!

Pour t'être payé la débauche
De cracher sur notr' cher drapeau,
Qué qu'tas donc sous la mamell' gauche?
I't'faudrait douz'ball's dans la peau! . . .

On peut chanter la nuit entière,
Et tout l'lendemain, sans se r'coucher:
Avec Zola n'y a d'la matière.
Plus qu'à la Compagni' Richer!

Mais ça suffit. Faut qu'on termine.

Ça dégoûte: restons-en là.
On croit écraser d'la vermine
Quand on pronounce le nom d'Zola.

15. The songs, tract, and lampoon are found in APP, Ba 1302.
16. L'élément du Juif, c'est la crotte,
    Il s'y complaît, il y barbote,
    Et, quiconque à lui s'est frotté,
    S'en est toujours tiré crotté . . .

    Du circoncis d'îlot du Diable
    Qu'ils voudraient bien fair'décamper:

Moi, j'dis qu's'il n'était pas coupable,
On n'aurait pas pu lui couper . . .
Les vivres. J'comprends la canaille
Et la raison d'ses défenseurs:
Il travaillait dans la mouscaille
Du Syndicat des vidangeurs. . . .

Une bande de misérables,
Payés par ces hideux crapauds,
Font rouler sur toutes les tables
L'argent prussien chez les bistrots,
La répugnance valetaille
Des Youddis a des impudeurs
Qui pue à quinz'pas la mouscaille
Du Syndicat des vidangeurs.

Ils avilissent notre armée,
Voulant nous imposer leur joug;
Mais notre patrie alarmée
Va rendre aux Youtres coup pour coup.
Au pays, l'ignoble racaille
A montré tous les déshonneurs;
Il faut noyer dans sa mouscaille
Le Syndicat des vidangeurs.

Like the police reports that recorded these days in February 1898, this song is found in APP, Ba 1304.

17. I am using information drawn from APP, Ba 1302.
18. AN, F7 12474.
19. See ibid. An echo of that general relief can be found in the departmental archives. See, for example, AD (Archives Départementales) Meurthe-et-Moselle, I M 657.
20. *On dit que d'Dreyfus l'syndicat,*
    Et sa fripouille
    T'ont mis dans un si fichu cas,
    Mon pauvr'Pot bouille,
    Que lorsque tu mets l'nez dehors
    Sans la police,
    On f'rait sur'ment un mauvais sort
    A ta jaunisse!

    On dit qu'tu t'es, pour épater
    Fait circoncire . . .
    Et puis aussi qu'tu peux t'vanter

Qu'Berlin t'admire.
Eh ben! tu sais, je n'te l'cache pas,
J'suis qu'une salope
Mais s'faire l'copin des Judas
J'trouv'ça malpropre . . .

C'est pas parc'que l'Youpin Reinach,
C'te face huileuse
Dont la fortune vient d'un brach
D'mémoir'fameuse,
A juré d'faire la révision
Ou bien d'la casse
Que tu n'sras pas, mon vieux cochon,
Dans la mélasse!

AN, F7 12474.

21. APP, Ba 1103.
22. APP, Ba 1104.
23. Ibid.
24. AN, F7 12459. I have made extensive use of this very rich file.
25. APP, Ba 1107. See also AN, F7 12459.
26. APP, Ba 1107.
27. AN, F7 12882. On the Ligue Antisémitique, the most systematic presentation is in Zeev Sternhell's *La Droite révolutionnaire, 1885–1914* (Paris: Le Seuil, 1978), chap. 5. But Sternhell does not dwell long on the year 1898. On the Jeunesse Antisémitique, see Bertrand Joly, "The Jeunesse antisémitique et national-iste, 1894–1904," in Robert Tombs, ed., *Nationhood and Nationalism in France from Boulangism to the Great War* (London: HarperCollins Academia, 1991), pp. 147–59.
28. AN, F7 12463.
29. AN, F7 12461.
30. This survey, which is certainly incomplete, was constructed on the basis of APP, Ba 1106, Ba 1104, and Ba 1107, and AN, F7 12461 and 12462.
31. These copies of *L'Oeuvre Electorale* and of the brochure *Les sept péchés capitaux en France* can be found in APP, Ba 654.
32. APP, Ba 1107.
33. AN, F7 12474.
34. AN, F7 12459. On the close links established during these elections between Abbé Garnier and the league, see Stephen Wilson, "Catholic Populism in France at the Time of the Dreyfus Affair, the Union Nationale," *Journal of Contemporary History* 4 (October 1975): 695.
35. APP, Ba 1107, and AN, F7 12459.
36. On Paris, the only comprehensive study is still Louis Girard's *Les élections à Paris sous*

la III *République* (Dakar: Faculté des Lettres et des Sciences Humaines de l'Université de Dakar, 1966–1968), but it does not deal specifically with the 1898 legislative elections, and the few pages devoted to it (pp. 107–11) deal with anti-Semitism only sparingly. Nevertheless, Girard rightly remarks that "one can already make out the foundation on which the agreement of the nationalists will come about. The articles in *L'Intransigeant*, *La Libre Parole*, and *L'Autorité* already sound alike in 1898. *La Libre Parole*, using the slogan 'France for the French' as its subtitle, classifies the candidates depending not on whether they were royalists, republicans, or socialists but on whether they were supporters of the government, the 'Syndicate of treason,' and Freemasonry, or rather of anti-Semites and 'patriots.' " In 1902 that criterion would become the line demarcating supporters and opponents of nationalism. A certain number of these "patriotic" candidates would receive an appreciable proportion of the votes. In his very complete study, *L'agitation nationaliste à Paris (1898–1900) et les élections municipales de 1900* (Paris: Ecole des Chartes, 1981), pp. 494–503, Bertrand Joly deals only cursorily with these elections, spending more time on the year 1899 and on the 1900 municipal elections. In his *Dictionnaire biographique et géographique du nationalisme français (1880–1900)* (Paris: Honoré Champion, 1998), Joly presents the nationalist organizations both by Paris neighborhood and by city. On the nationalist and anti-Semitic Paris of the 1902 legislative elections, see Pierre Birnbaum, *La France aux Français: Histoire des haines nationalistes* (Paris: Le Seuil, 1993).

37. APP, Ba 656.
38. AN, F7 12461.
39. See, for example, APP, Ba 1107.
40. APP, Ba 657.
41. APP, Ba 658.
42. Ibid.
43. APP, Ba 659.
44. Ibid.
45. Ibid.
46. APP, Ba 1107.
47. Ibid.
48. Ibid.
49. APP, Ba 659.
50. APP, Ba 660.
51. Ibid.
52. APP, Ba 1107.
53. APP, Ba 660.
54. APP, Ba 654.
55. APP, Ba 1107.
56. AN, F7 12459.
57. APP, Ba 1107.
58. This file is presented in Céline Braconnier, *Improbable cité: Paris et la transition démo-*

cratique au début de la IIIe *République,* doctoral thesis in political science, Université Paris-I, 1998, 3:680ff.

59. APP, Ba 1107.

60. AN, F7 12463.

61. AN, F7 12459.

62. APP, Ba 1104.

63. Ibid.

64. APP, Ba 1107.

65. AN, F7 12882.

66. AN, F7 12451.

67. The police report is quoted in Joly, *L'agitation nationaliste à Paris,* pp. 213 and 478. On Déroulède's "naïveté," see ibid., pp. 479ff.

68. APP, Ba 1105.

69. See Chapter 9.

70. APP, Ba 1053.

71. AN, F7 12461.

72. Ibid. and APP, Ba 1104. We shall return to this particularly important day in Chapter 9.

73. APP, Ba 1107.

74. AN, F7 12454.

75. AN, F7 12451.

76. AN, F7 12461.

77. The best study remains Wilson, *Ideology and Experience,* chap. 4. See also Pierre Pierrard, *Juifs et catholiques français* (Paris: Fayard, 1970); and Georges Bensoussan, *L'idéologie du rejet: Enquête sur le monument Henry* (Levallois-Perret: Manya, 1993).

78. AN, F7 12461.

79. AN, F7 12454.

80. AN, F7 12451.

81. APP, Ba 1107.

82. APP, Ba 659.

83. AN, F7 12461.

84. See Janie Cara-Juillet, *Les Républicains de Seine-et-Oise: Députés, forces politiques et organisations, 1881–1900,* doctoral thesis in history, Université Paris-X-Nanterre, 1996. This author maintains that "the proximity of the capital and the mention in the press of the different phases of the Dreyfus affair spread information, to the point of influencing the behavior of the voters . . . Since 1898 Seine-et-Oise had experienced a real upsurge in nationalism" (p. 422). See also Thierry Wolff, *Le nationalisme dans la banlieue ouest de 1989 à 1902,* master's thesis, Université Paris-X-Nanterre, 1992.

Chapter 2: Journey to the Center of France

1. *Le Patriote Orléanais*, January 27, 1898.
2. *Le Républicain Orléanais*, February 25, 1898.
3. Ibid., January 26, 1898.
4. Ibid., January 27, 1898.
5. *Le Patriote Orléanais*, January 16, 1898. See also, on January 31, an article on the new beret worn by the students protesting against Captain Dreyfus.
6. AN, F 195922. Quoted by Georges Joumas, *Les élections législatives dans l'arrondissement d'Orléans de 1889 à 1914*, Diplôme d'Etudes Supérieures in history, school of letters and human sciences in Tours, 1966, pp. 115–16.
7. AD Loiret, I V I.
8. *Le Patriote Orléanais*, May 17, 1898.
9. AD Loiret, 4 M 104.
10. AD Loiret, 2 M 104.
11. See Joumas's analysis in *Les élections législatives dans l'arrondissement d'Orléans*, pp. 32ff.
12. AD Loiret, 5 M 7. This box contains a file with numerous letters from the prefect regarding the refusal to let the military band of the Seventy-sixth Infantry Regiment participate in religious ceremonies or enter the cathedral.
13. *Le Patriote Orléanais*, May 26, 1898.
14. AD Loir-et-Cher, 4 M 44. In Vendôme, Dr. Monnet, who ran as a "liberal and patriotic republican," maintained that his rival, David, "was calling on the traitor Dreyfus to help him."
15. *Le Journal du Loiret*, August 1, 1898. See also ibid., July 28, 1898.
16. Ibid., August 3 and 8, 1898.
17. *Le Patriote Orléanais*, January 5, 1899.
18. *Le Journal du Loiret*, January 6, 1899.
19. Ibid., January 9, 1899. See also *Le Républicain Orléanais*, January 9, 1898.
20. *Le Patriote Orléanais*, January 9, 1898.
21. *L'Avenir Républicain*, March 9, 1901.
22. AD Loiret, 2 M 107, 5 M 7.
23. See K. Widroiajegodomitcher, *L'Affaire Dreyfus et la presse du Loir-et-Cher*, history thesis, Université de Tours, 1992.
24. AD Cher, 25 M 92.
25. *Le Journal du Cher*, January 26, 1898.
26. Ibid., June 29, 1889.
27. Ibid., July 2, 1889. See Geneviève Dindinaud, "Quand Dreyfus était à Bourges," *Cahiers d'Histoire et d'Archéologie du Berry* (1970): 54–59. See also Claude Maillet, "Le capitaine Dreyfus à l'ECP," *Le Journal DGA* (July 1994): 18–57.
28. Quoted by Paulin Gérald, *Les monarchistes et les nationalistes dans le Cher entre 1870 et 1914*, master's thesis, Tours, school of letters, 1986, pp. 168ff. That same newspaper, in its issue of September 17, 1899, wrote, "He is convicted, that is the essential thing. Yes, he is convicted, the wretch who did so much harm to France,

the traitor, that is, the Jew who handed over the secret of our national defense to Germany. Long live France!"

29. *Le Petit Berrichon*, January 23, 1898.

30. Ibid., January 16, 1898.

31. Ibid., September 25, 1898.

32. AD Cher, 20 M 38.

33. Ibid.

34. AN, F7 12463.

35. AD Cher, 20 M 38. See also Valérie Sadet, *Les princes d'Arenberg et leur domaine de Menetou-Salon, 1792–1914*, master's thesis in history, Tours, Université Rabelais, 1994.

36. AD Cher, 25 M 92.

37. "Les dimanches nationalistes: La conduite de Bourges," *L'Aurore*, February 26, 1900.

38. AD Cher, 20 M 39.

39. Gérald, *Les monarchistes et les nationalistes dans le Cher*, p. 197.

40. These texts by Baffier are quoted in Bertrand Tillier, "L'antisémitisme du sculpteur Jean Baffier," *Berry Magazine* (Fall 1997): 52–53. See also Christian Roth, "Jean Baffier et le régionalisme en Berry-Bourbonnais-Nivernais (1885–1911)," *Fédération des Sociétés Savantes du Centre de la France* (July–December 1990): 117–18; (January–June 1991): 159–77.

41. *Le Messager du Cher*, April 10, 1902.

42. Text published in "Pour les Boers," article printed in February 1900 in *Jean Baffier: L'homme, son caractère, ses idées, sa doctrine*, AD Cher, 23 F 3, Louis Marin collection.

43. *L'Occident*, March 1907.

44. Neil McWilliam, "Race, Remembrance, and 'Revanche': Commemorating the Franco-Prussian War in the Third Republic," *Art History* 19 (1996): 479ff.

45. Neil McWilliam, "Craft, Commerce, and the Contradictions of Anti-Capitalism: Reproducing the Applied Art of Jean Baffier," in Anthony Hughes and Erich Rarifft, eds., *Sculpture and Its Reproductions* (London: Reaktion Books, 1997), p. 108; see also pp. 104ff.

46. AD Cher, Louis Marin collection, 23 F 9.5, 11, and 18. A few notations taken from his thick notebook concerning the year 1900 are presented in this archive.

47. Ibid.

48. *La Libre Parole*, January 24, 1898.

49. André-Georges Manry, *Histoire de Clermont-Ferrand* (Clermont-Ferrand: La Française d'Edition et d'Imprimerie, 1990), p. 337. Similarly, a recent history of Riom does not devote a single word to the Dreyfus affair (Edouard Everat, *Histoire de la ville de Riom* [Riom: André Bonne, 1989]).

50. *L'Avenir du Puy-de-Dôme*, January 18, 1898.

51. Ibid., January 19, 1898.

52. Ibid., January 20, 1898.

53. Ibid., March 1, 1898.

54. Ibid., April 26, 27, and 30, 1898; May 1, 3, and 6, 1898.

55. AD Puy-de-Dôme, M 014, police report.

56. AD Puy-de-Dôme, M 04518 and M 014.

57. AD Puy-de-Dôme, M 01874.

58. André Parrain, *La presse dans le Puy-de-Dôme de 1870 à 1914* (Clermont-Ferrand: Institut d'Etudes du Massif Central, 1972), pp. 74 and 81.

59. *Alerte! les Français de France,*
    Alerte! on touche à nos soldats!
    Poursuivons d'un cri de vengeance
    Tous ces vendus, tous ces Judas!
    Crachons sur la bande flétrie
    Qui, dans les mains aux doigts crochus,
    Met sa main pour sauver Dreyfus.
    Au pilori les Sans Patrie!
    Vive la France. Au pilori
    Zola, Picquart, et Labori!
    Le Juif a fait à la patrie
    La blessure de trahison
    Et de peur de l'en voir guérie
    Zola l'inonde de poison!
    L'étranger en trépigne d'aise
    Mais voilà qu'il reste anxieux,
    Devant l'attentat monstrueux
    La France redevient française.
    La France crie: Au pilori Zola, Picquart et Labori!
    Nous vous joignons à cette liste,
    O cénacle intellectuel,
    Rhéteurs-experts, experts-dentistes
    Journaux reptiles d'Israël
    Sur nos soldats vaillants et probes
    L'étranger vient aussi vomir.
    Themis fait semblant de dormir.
    Allez, félons de toutes robes,
    Allez rejoindre au pilori
    Zola, Picquart et Labori.
    [Signé:] Patriote

    L'Avenir du Puy-de-Dôme, February 21, 1898.

60. *Le Courrier du Puy-de-Dôme*, August 14, 1898.

61. *Le Tocsin Populaire*, April 16 and June 29, 1898.

62. AN, F7 12467.

63. Fitch, "Mass Culture, Mass Parliamentary Politics," pp. 85ff.

64. Jean-François Viple, *Sociologie politique de l'Allier* (Paris: Librairie Générale de Droit et de Jurisprudence, 1967), pp. 52ff. and 211.

65. AD Rhône, 4 M 254; *Le Progrès de Lyon*, January 17, 1898.

66. *La Croix de Lyon et du Rhône*, January 13, 1898; *La France Libre*, January 16, 1898.

67. *Le Peuple*, January 17, 1898; *L'Express*, January 18, 1898.

68. AD Rhône, 4 M 254.

69. Ibid.

70. Ibid.

71. AD Rhône, 4 M 254.

72. *La France Libre*, January 19, 1898; *Le Nouvelliste de Lyon*, January 20, 1898; *L'Express*, January 19, 1898; *Lyon Républicain*, January 19, 1898; *Le Progrès de Lyon*, January 17 and 19, 1898; *Le Peuple*, January 25, 1898. See the remarkable, very complete file AD Rhône, 4 M 259, as well as AN, F7 12467. On *L'Express*, see S. Galliot, *"L'Express" de Lyon et l'affaire Dreyfus*, master's thesis in history, Université Lyon-III, 1979.

73. *La France Libre*, January 19 and 20, 1898; *Le Nouvelliste de Lyon*, January 20, 1898; *La Croix de Lyon et du Rhône*, January 23, 1898.

74. *La France Libre*, April 8, 1898; *Lyon Républicain*, April 8, 1898; *Le Peuple*, April 9, 1898.

75. *Le Progrès de Lyon*, January 22, 1898.

76. AD Rhône, 4 M 256.

77. *La Croix de Lyon et du Rhône*, January 23, February 27, and July 17, 1898; *La France Libre*, July 15, 1898.

78. *Le Peuple*, January 19, 1898.

79. AD Rhône, 4 M 254.

80. Ibid.

81. *La Croix de Lyon et du Rhône*, June 5, 1898. For a straightforward account of the results of the 1898 legislative elections, see Jean-François Martin and Marc du Pouget, *Les élections législatives dans le département du Rhône sous la IIIe République* (Lyon: Archives Départementales, 1991), pp. 68ff.

82. *C'était un lundi, jour d'orage,*
Dans une réunion,
Plein d'espoir, escomptant le gage
De son élection,
Il avait compté sans Bessières,
Ce hardi lutteur
Qui lui a fait mordre la poussière
Devant ses électeurs.

Bessières lui dit:
"Honteux dreyfusard,
C'est pas aux Yonnais qui faut la faire,
Ancien Communard.

Retourne à Paris, en Gascogne,
Retrouver Canivet,
Alons, file ou je cogne
Sur ton cotivet.

Va-t'en, rebut de Cochinchine,
Charlatan, pantin,
Chercher un siège que tu guignes
Chez les sales Youpins,
A nos front la colère monte
Ça devient écoeurant,
Car pour nous c'est vraiment la honte,
Plus un mot, va-t'en."

AD Rhône, 3 M 1354.

83. Ibid.

84. *Le Nouvelliste*, October 24, 1898.

85. AD Isère, 8 M 31. Farther to the east, in Saint-Jean-de-Maurienne, after a concert on February 22, 1898, the musicians ran through the city shouting, "Down with the Jews! Long live the army!" carrying one figure representing Zola and another, Judas: AN, F7 12461.

86. Pierre Barral, *Le département de l'Isère sous la Troisième République, 1870–1940* (Paris: Armand Colin, 1962), p. 403.

87. Bernard Joly, *Dictionnaire biographique et géographique du nationalisme français (1880–1900)* (Paris: Honoré Champion, 1998), pp. 621–22.

88. AN, F7 12467 and 12461.

89. AD Haute-Loire, 3 M 329.

90. Auguste Rivet, *La vie politique dans le département de la Haute-Loire de 1815 à 1974* (Le Puy: Editions des Cahiers de la Haute-Loire, 1978), p. 81.

91. *Le Républicain de la Haute-Loire*, January 25 and 27, and February 24, 1898.

92. *Le Journal d'Yssingeaux*, February 27, 1898.

93. *Le Moniteur de Brioude*, January 9 and February 27, 1898.

94. *Le Journal de Brioude*, January 15 and 21, 1898.

95. *La Haute-Loire*, May 9, 1898.

96. *Journal de l'Aveyron* and *L'Union Catholique*, January 28, 29, and 30, 1898; *L'Aveyron Républicain*, January 28, 1898; see also *Le Moniteur de l'Aveyron*, January 28, 1898.

97. *Journal de l'Aveyron*, January 14, 16, 18, and 25, 1898.

98. *L'Union Catholique*, January 4, 7, 8, 12, 15, and 26, 1898.

99. AD Aveyron, 1 M (not yet fully classified).

100. AD Aveyron, 3 M 447.

101. In January 1900 the police again observed "nationalist disturbances" in Millau, associated with the course of the Dreyfus affair: AD Aveyron, 4 M 104; *La Libre Parole*, January 24 and 29, 1898.

102. *Le Radical de la Corrèze*, January 27, 1898.

103. AD Corrèze, 3 M 186.

104. Ibid., May 1, 1898; see Denis Faugeras, *Recherches sur l'évolution politique de la Corrèze sous la IIIᵉ République, 1871–1940*, doctoral thesis in law, Université de Limoges, 1983.

105. *L'Avenir de la Dordogne*, January 24, 1898.

106. Ibid., January 25 and 26, 1898.

107. AD Dordogne, 3 M 427.

108. AD Dordogne, 1 M 81.

109. AD Dordogne, 3 M 72. See also 4 M 191 and AN, F7 12460.

110. *L'Union Nontronnaise*, January 13, 16, 27, and February 27, 1898.

111. AD Dordogne, 3 M 427.

112. AD Dordogne, 3 M 427.

113. *L'Avenir de la Dordogne*, December 9, 1898.

114. AD Dordogne, 4 M 28. Similarly, in Ribérac and Nontron in 1899, anti-Semitic posters were still found on the walls of the city: AD Dordogne, 4 M 23.

115. John M. Merriman, *The Red City: Limoges and the French Nineteenth Century* (New York: Oxford University Press, 1985), p. 191. See also Chapter 7.

116. AD Haute-Vienne, 1 M 201.

117. Ibid.

118. Ibid.

119. The Ligue Nationaliste de Limoges would nevertheless be created in January 1899, in association with the Ligue des Patriotes: AD Haute-Vienne, 3 M 168.

120. AD Haute-Vienne, 3 M 155.

121. *Le Messager du Limousin*, November 26, 1898.

122. *La France du Centre*, February 21, 1898.

123. Ibid., May 8, 1898.

124. In her master's thesis in history entitled *Le militantisme politique en Haute-Vienne sous la IIIᵉ République*, Annabelle Lemoine devotes not a single line to that very particular aspect of the political struggles (School of Letters of Limoges, 1995).

125. Pierre Vallin, *Paysans rouges du Limousin: Mentalités et comportements politiques à Compreignac et dans le nord de la Haute-Vienne, 1870–1914* (Paris: L'Harmattan, 1985), pp. 227–29.

126. AN, F7 12467.

127. Daniel Dayen, "L'affaire Dreyfus dans la Creuse, 1898–1899," *Mémoires de la Société des Sciences Naturelles et Archéologiques de la Creuse* 43 (1988): 336.

128. G. Dauger and D. Dayen, *Histoire du Limousin contemporain* (Limoges: Lucien Souny, 1988), pp. 102–4.

129. Daniel Dayen, "Un prêtre creusois dreyfusard: L'abbé Pichot," in Michel Cassan, Jean Boutier, and Nicole Lemaître, eds., *Croyances, pouvoir et sociétés: Des Limousins aux Français* (Treignac: Les Monédières, 1988).

130. Quoted by Dayen, "L'affaire Dreyfus dans la Creuse," pp. 326–30.

Chapter 3: In Barrésian Lorraine

1. *La Croix de l'Est*, February 24, 1898.
2. Ibid., January 21, 1898; *L'Est Républicain*, January 21, 1898: see AD Meurthe-et-Moselle, I M 657.
3. AN, F7 12461.
4. *Journal de la Meurthe et des Vosges*, January 18, 1898.
5. *La Croix de l'Est*, January 18, 1898.
6. *La Croix de l'Est*, January 20, 1898; *Journal de la Meurthe et des Vosges*, January 20, 1898.
7. AD Meurthe-et-Moselle, I M 657.
8. *La Croix de l'Est*, January 22, 1898.
9. Ibid., January 26, 1898; *Journal de la Meurthe et des Vosges*, January 25, 1898; *L'Est Républicain*, January 22, 1898.
10. AN, F7 12467. See also AD Meurthe-et-Moselle, I M 635. The superintendent emphasized in this report that the demonstration was led by "a reactionary" and maintained that "the crowd did not depart at any time from the strictest propriety."
11. *Journal de la Meurthe et des Vosges*, January 26, 1898.
12. *L'Est Républicain*, November 12, 1898.
13. AN, F7 12461.
14. Jean Hurstel, *La question religieuse en Meurthe-et-Moselle de 1898 à 1905*, Diplôme d'Etudes Supérieures, school of letters, Nancy, June 1960.
15. AD Meurthe-et-Moselle, 3 M 85.
16. Ibid.
17. Ibid.
18. Ibid.
19. See Chapter 10.
20. Ibid.
21. AD Meurthe-et-Moselle, 3 M 85.
22. Ibid.
23. *Mon gros Nicolas,*
    Il faut que j'te dise
    Des chos's qu'tu prendras
    P'têt' pour des bêtises . . .
    Mais, mon pauvre gâs,
    T'connais ma franchise;
    T'es bon avocat.
    Mais ça n'prendra pas.

    On dit, Nicolas,
    Qu'tu touch's la galette
    Du grand syndicat,
    Dam, c'est pas honnête,

Ou t'appell'Zola,
Juif, marchand des lorgnettes.
Tout ça, c'est pas clair:
T'es rousti, mon cher.

Vrai, mon vieux colon,
L'affair' n'est pas belle;
T'as versé, dit-on,
*Aux Juifs d'*L'Etincelle
Sept cents francs sonnants,
C'est une bagatelle.
Elev' député
T'as mal débuté.

24. AD Meurthe-et-Moselle, I M 648.
25. Ibid.
26. Ibid.
27. Ibid.
28. Ibid.
29. Ibid.
30. *La Croix de l'Est,* January 19, 1898. See also AN, F7 12461. According to the police report, the night of February 9, 1898, anti-Semitic signs were put up on different houses in the city of Toul, particularly on the houses of Blocq, Julien, Benoît, and others. See also AN, F7 12460.
31. AD Meurthe-et-Moselle, I M 635.
32. AD Meurthe-et-Moselle, 3 M 85.
33. *L'Est Républicain,* May 11, 1898.
34. Michel Gacon, *L'Affaire Dreyfus et l'opinion à Nancy,* Diplôme d'Etudes Supérieures, school of letters of Nancy, 1967, p. 65.
35. *Journal de la Meurthe et des Vosges,* May 5, 1898.
36. AD Meurthe-et-Moselle, I M 648.
37. AD Meurthe-et-Moselle, 3 M 86.
38. Ibid.
39. AD Meurthe-et-Moselle, I M 635.
40. AN, F7 12461.
41. AD Vosges, 8 M 8.
42. AD Vosges, I M 185, 8 M 185, and 13 M ELE 51.
43. Ibid., and 12474. On the fire in Neufchâteau, see *La Croix de l'Est,* February 26, 1898.
44. J.-A. Morizot, *Sociologie électorale du canton de Dompaire (Vosges) sous la Troisième République,* master's thesis in history, school of letters of Nancy, 1969, p. 41.
45. AD Meurthe-et-Moselle, I M 635.
46. AD Marne, 30 M 56 and 51 M 29. See also AN, F7 12460.

47. Michel Baroin, *Les Aubois et la politique sous les IIIe et IVe Républiques* (Paris: Esper, 1970), pp. 63ff.

48. AD Côte-d'Or, 20 M 188; AN, F7 12467 and 12462.

49. AN, F7 12463 and 12460.

50. AN, F7 12462.

51. AN, F7 12461.

52. AD Haute-Saône, 7 M 20. On this file, see Henri Carel, *Le département de la Haute-Saône, 1878–1901*, doctoral thesis, school of letters of Tours, 1970, 2:681ff.

53. AD Haute-Saône, 7 M 19.

54. Joseph Pinard, *Antisémitisme en Franche-Comté: De l'affaire Dreyfus à nos jours* (Besançon: Cêtre, 1997), pp. 72–74.

55. AD Doubs, I Z 9, and communal archives of Besançon, II28.

56. AD Doubs, M 7788.

57. AN, F7 12461.

Chapter 4: Storm on the Coast: Algerian Marseilles

1. AD Bouches-du-Rhône, 3 M 210.

2. AD Bouches-du-Rhône, I M 1460.

3. AD Bouches-du-Rhône, I M 1322.

4. *Le Petit Provençal*, January 16–24, 1898.

5. *Le Petit Marseillais*, January 17, 1898; *Le Soleil du Midi*, January 17 and 19, 1898; *La Voix de la France*, January 23, 1898.

6. AD Bouches-du-Rhône, I M 1415.

7. *Le Petit Provençal*, January 18, 1898.

8. AD Bouches-du-Rhône, I M 1415.

9. Florence Berceot, *La communauté juive de Marseille sous la IIIe République: Regards sur les femmes, assimilation, renaissance*, master's thesis in history, Université d'Aix-Marseille, 1990.

10. Ibid.

11. *Le Marseillais*, January 19, 1898.

12. *Le Petit Provençal*, January 19, 1898.

13. AD Bouches-du-Rhône, I M 1415 and AN, F7 12467.

14. Thierry Mudry, *Le mouvement nationaliste dans les Bouches-du-Rhône, de l'affaire Boulanger à la Grande Guerre, 1888–1914*, doctoral thesis in law, school of law and political science, Aix-Marseilles, 1990, 1:351. On Nice, see Vincent Pacchioni, "L'affaire Dreyfus et la presse niçoise," *Recherches Régionales* I (1991). In Draguignan during the May 1898 elections, Joseph Jourdan addressed his voters, "In 1893 you drove off the Panamaist. In 1898 you will reject the men of the Dreyfus syndicate. The nation is in danger. A formidable conspiracy organized by the German Jews, a conspiracy unprecedented in history, has been hatched against France. The nation above all. Down with the traitors. Long live the national army." Although he was

in the lead in the first round, he was defeated in the second by a socialist candidate. See Jocelyne George, "Provinciales: La France aux quatre coins," in Pierre Birnbaum, ed., *La France de l'affaire Dreyfus* (Paris: Gallimard, 1994), p. 135.

15. AD Bouches-du-Rhône, I M 1322.

16. *La Voix de la France*, March 6, 1898.

17. AN, F7 12460.

18. *La Voix de la France*, June 5, 1898.

19. *La Libre Parole*, May 30, 1898.

20. AN, F7 12460.

21. AD Bouches-du-Rhône, I M 415.

22. Ibid.

23. AD Bouches-du-Rhône, I M 1461.

24. AD Bouches-du-Rhône, I M 1423.

25. Ibid.

26. *Le Provençal*, December 8, 1898; see also *Le Marseillais*, December 8, 1898.

27. *La Croix de Provence*, January 10 and 16, 1898. That newspaper describes with satisfaction the anti-Semitic mobilizations in January (for example, on January 23, 1898). See Isabelle Consolin, *"La Croix de Provence" et les Juifs: Etude d'un discours*, master's thesis in history, Université d'Aix-Marseille, 1990.

28. Mudry, *Le mouvement nationaliste dans les Bouches-du-Rhône*, I:212.

29. AD Bouches-du-Rhône, 3 M 211.

30. Ibid.

31. Quoted in Mudry, *Le mouvement nationaliste dans les Bouches-du-Rhône*, I:239.

32. See AN, F7 12460.

33. Mudry, *Le mouvement nationaliste dans les Bouches-du-Rhône*, I:267ff.

34. *Allons, enfants de la patrie,*
    Le jour vengeur est arrivé.
    Contre nous de la Youtrerie
    L'étendard immonde est levé;
    Entendez-vous, dans leurs repaires,
    Hurler ces infâmes escrocs,
    Qui vont, jusque sur nos drapeaux,
    Verser leur bave de vipère!

    Tremblez, Youpins, et vous, perfides,
    L'opprobre de tous les partis:
    Tremblez! vos projects parricides
    Vont enfin recevoir leur prix.
    Tout est soldat pour vous combattre:
    S'ils tombent, nos jeunes héros,
    La terre en produit de nouveaux
    Tout prêts, gredins, à vous abattre.

Amour sacré de la patrie,
Conduis, soutiens nos bras vengeurs!
Liberté, liberté chérie,
Combats avec tes défenseurs!
Sous nos drapeaux que la victoire
Accoure à tes mâles accents!
Que tous les Youpins expirants
Voient ton triomphe et notre gloire.

Nous entrerons dans la carrière
Quand les Youpins seront pendus.

35. *La Semaine Religieuse de l'Archidiocèse d'Aix,* January 16, 1898, quoted in Céline Roudil, *L'église catholique et les Juifs à Aix-en-Provence et à Marseille, de 1870 à 1939: Discours et comportements,* master's thesis in history, Université d'Aix-Marseille, 1994, p. 288.

36. *Histoire d'Aix-en-Provence* (Aix-en-Provence: Edisud, 1983), p. 456.

37. Jean-Philippe Marcy, *L'affaire Dreyfus à Aix-en-Provence,* Diplôme d'Etudes Supérieures, school of letters of Aix-en-Provence, p. 51.

38. Mudry, *Le mouvement nationaliste dans les Bouches-du-Rhône,* I:282.

39. AD Bouches-du-Rhône, 3 M 212.

40. AD Bouches-du-Rhône, 3 M 210.

41. Elisabeth Seror, *Salon-de-Provence, 1881–1970,* research essay, Fondation Nationale des Sciences Politiques, Paris, 1970, p. 95.

42. AN, F7 12467.

43. AN, F7 12467 and 12461.

44. AD Hérault, I M 1099.

45. AN, F7 12460 and 12467; AD Hérault, 41 M 143.

46. AD Hérault, 41 M 145.

47. AD Hérault, 54 M 17.

48. *L'Eclair,* October 31, 1898.

49. AD Hérault, 3 M 1117.

50. AD Hérault, 39 M 286 and 54 M 17.

51. AD Aude, 5 M 92 and 2 M 67. See Rémy Cazals, *Grandes injustices devant l'opinion* (Rouffiac: Archives de l'Aude, 1993). See also Rémy Pech, *La vie politique dans l'Aude,* Diplôme des Etudes Supérieures, Sorbonne, 1967.

52. AD Pyrénées-Orientales, 66, I Mp 395.

53. AD Pyrénées-Orientales, 3 M 293.

54. Ibid.

55. AD Pyrénées-Orientales, 66 I Mp 395.

56. *Le Mont Ventoux,* June 5, 1898.

57. Ibid., September 11, 1898.

58. Linda Arroudj, *L'affaire Dreyfus à Carpentras,* master's thesis in history, Université de Provence, 1993, pp. 38 and 45.

59. AD Vaucluse, I M 809.
60. AD Vaucluse, 10 Per 26; *Le Mont Ventoux*, January 23, 1898.
61. *La Tribune Libre*, April 28, 1898.
62. AD Vaucluse, I M 809.
63. *La Libre Parole*, October 3, 1899; *La Patrie*, October 3, 1899. On Dreyfus's stay in Carpentras, see the file APP, Ba 1048.
64. Quoted in Arroudj, *L'affaire Dreyfus à Carpentras*, app. 3.
65. AD Vaucluse, I M 809.
66. Ibid.
67. AN, F7 12463.
68. AN, F7 12461.
69. AD Vaucluse, I M 815.
70. AD Vaucluse, I M 809.
71. *L'Eclair*, February 24 and 26, 1898.
72. AD Gard, 3 M 424.
73. AD Gard, 3 M 813 and 750. See also Valérie Lamotte, *L'opinion gardaise face à l'affaire Dreyfus*, master's thesis in history, Montpellier, Université Paul-Valéry, 1993, pp. 74ff.
74. *Le Journal du Midi*, March 16, 1899.
75. Ibid., March 25, 1899.
76. AD Gard, I M 635.
77. Ibid.
78. AN F7 12467 and 12463.
79. *L'Eclair*, September 29, 1908, AD Hérault, 54 M 153.

Chapter 5: Radical Toulouse, Nationalist Bordeaux

1. AD Haute-Garonne, 4 M 113.
2. In his platform statement, Paul de Cassagnac wrote, "The earth, once fecund, the earth, alma mater of our youth, seems to be cursed. Never has my department been so solicited by Jewish money, Jewish means, everywhere, in Mirande and in Condom, in Lectoure and in Auch . . . Prefect, candidates rallied to the republic, and Jews will learn this at their expense."
3. See Michael Burns, *Rural Society and French Politics: Boulangism and the Dreyfus Affair, 1886–1900* (Princeton, N.J.: Princeton University Press), pp. 143, 147–50. See also Nancy Fitch, "Mass Culture, Mass Parliamentary Politics and Modern Anti-Semitism: The Dreyfus Affair in Rural France," *American Historical Review* 97 (February 1992): 71ff.
4. AD Haute-Garonne, 4 M 107.
5. AD Haute-Garonne, 4 M 113.
6. Ibid. The police reports are numerous and very precise.

7. *Le Messager de Toulouse*, November 15, 1898.

8. Ibid. See also AN, F 12462.

9. AD Haute-Garonne, 2 M 47.

10. *L'Express du Midi*, December 23, 1898.

11. AD Haute-Garonne, 4 M 113.

12. Ibid.

13. I have been influenced here by Viviane Vroemen, *L'antisémitisme: Toulouse au moment de l'affaire Dreyfus (1894–1900)*, Université de Toulouse-Le Mirail, October 1989 See also Marc Bousquet, *L'Affaire Dreyfus et la presse de la Haute-Garonne*, Diplôme d'Etudes Supérieures, school of letters of Toulouse, 1958; and Suzanne Tougne, *L'opinion publique toulousaine face à l'antisémitisme des années 1898–1899*, master's thesis in history, Université de Toulouse–Le Mirail, June 1971.

14. Henri Sempéré, *La semaine catholique de Toulouse (1861–1908)*, doctoral thesis (3d cycle), Université de Toulouse–Le Mirail, 1971, vol. 3.

15. *L'Express du Midi*, December 2 and 10, 1897; January 28, February 1, August 12, 1898, et al. See Vroemen, *L'antisémitisme à Toulouse*, pp. 148ff.

16. Ibid., January 21, February 12 and 27, and December 27, 1898.

17. *Le Messager de Toulouse*, May 23, August 22, and October 30, 1898; and September 29, 1899.

18. *La Croix du Midi*, May 27, 1895; January 18, 1896; August 8, 1897; and February 19 and September 3, 1899.

19. *La Semaine Catholique*, January 6, 1895, and July 31, 1898.

20. Henri Lerner, *"La Dépêche," journal de la démocratie: Contribution à l'histoire du radicalisme en France sous la Troisième République* (Toulouse: Publications de l'Université de Toulouse–Le Mirail, 1978). See also Vroemen, *L'antisémitisme à Toulouse*; Bousquet, *L'affaire Dreyfus et la presse.*

21. See Pierre Birnbaum, *La France aux Français: Histoire des haines nationalistes* (Paris: Le Seuil, 1993), chap. 10.

22. *La Dépêche du Midi*, February 10 and March 5, 1898.

23. Ibid., March 5, 1898. See also the use of the expression "Jewry" [*juiverie*], for example, on May 19, 1898. In the same style, *Le Messager de Toulouse* wrote, "The Jew is of the Semitic race, the European of the Aryan race" (February 5, 1898).

24. AD Haute-Garonne, 4 M 113.

25. In addition, the newspaper *Le Petit Radical de la Haute-Garonne*, which belonged to the same sphere of influence, upheld anti-Semitism and put it to use throughout the Dreyfus affair, even attacking, in 1901, the "Yid or Huguenot communities of believers," and the "Yids of high underworld society whose homeland clings to the soles of their vagabond shoes." Thereafter it accused Jean Jaurès of having "been paid by the Jews" to force on *La Dépêche* "screeds that, from the first lines, have the stink of being made to order for the Jews." See Vroemen, *L'antisémitisme à Toulouse*, pp. 80 and 128.

26. AD Haute-Garonne, 4 M 113.

27. AN, F7 12467.

28. Jean Faury, *Cléricalisme et anticléricalisme dans le Tarn, 1848–1900* (Toulouse: Publications de l'Université de Toulouse–Le Mirail, 1980), pp. 212–20.

29. Louis Claeys, *Deux siècles de vie politique dans le département de l'Ariège, 1789–1989* (Pamiers: L. Claeys, 1994), pp. 129ff.

30. These events are reconstructed on the basis of *L'Ere Nouvelle, Journal Indépendant des Hautes-Pyrénées.*

31. *L'Echo de Lourdes*, AD Hautes-Pyrénées, 2 J B2.

32. *Un ferblantier disait au préfet de police:*
    Dreyfus! Le Congo seul pouvait le faire blanc.
    Très possible! en tout cas, riposta monsieur Blanc,
    C'est bien le seul savon qui fasse la peau lisse.

    L'Ere Nouvelle, February 17, 1898.

33. *La Croix des Hautes-Pyrénées*, January 30, 1898.

34. AD Hautes-Pyrénées, 3 M 79.

35. See Philippe Peltier, *Politique et psychologie rurales dans les Hautes-Pyrénées depuis 1871* (Paris: IEP, 1957), pp. 35ff; Charles Lapeyre, *Histoire locale de l'arrondissement de Bagnères-de-Bigorre, 1870–1969*, doctoral thesis in law, Université de Bordeaux, 1975, p. 261. AD Hautes-Pyrénées, F 151.

36. AD Hautes-Pyrénées, 3 M 81.

37. AD Hautes-Pyrénées, I M 233.

38. *Le Mémorial des Pyrénées*, January 22, 1898.

39. Jean Bousquet-Mélou, *Louis Barthou et la circonscription d'Oloron, 1899–1914* (Paris: Pedone, 1972), p. 115.

40. *Le Mémorial des Pyrénées*, March 31, 1898.

41. AD Pyrénées-Atlantiques, 3 M 53.

42. Yann Brachet, *L'affaire Dreyfus à Bayonne*, master's thesis in history, Université de Pau et des pays d'Adour, 1996.

43. See, for example, *Le Mémorial des Pyrénées*, May 5, 1898.

44. Jean Micheu-Puyou, *Histoire électorale du département des Basses-Pyrénées sous la IIIe et la IVe République* (Paris: Librairie Générale de Droit et de Jurisprudence, 1965), pp. 92ff.

45. Elisabeth Cazenave, "L'affaire Dreyfus et l'opinion bordelaise: Essai de méthodologie," *Annales du Midi* (1972): 63–78.

46. *Le Nouvelliste*, January 14, 1898.

47. AD Gironde, I M 431.

48. *Le Nouvelliste*, January 15 to 25, 1898, and AD Gironde, 4 M 125.

49. *La Gironde*, January 19 and 20, 1898.

50. AD Gironde, I M 431.

51. Ibid.

52. *Le Nouvelliste*, May 19, 1898; *La Petite Gironde*, March 31, 1898; *La Gironde*, May 23, 1898; *La Démocratie*, February 3, 1898; *Bordeaux-Journal*, May 20 and 22, 1898.

On *Le Nouvelliste*, see Jean-Denis Abdou-Morenne, *Le Nouvelliste de Bordeaux, témoin catholique et royaliste au tournant du siècle (1890–1906)*, thesis, Université Bordeaux-II, 1990.

53. *Bordeaux-Journal*, April 20 and May 22, 1898.
54. AD Gironde, 3 M 243.
55. Ibid.
56. *Le Nouvelliste*, May 13, 1898.
57. Let us emphasize that in his youth Chiché was a student of the Jesuits of Cristoli in Bordeaux and that Bernard attended the seminary of Saint-Caprais. See Joël Dubos, *Les députés élus en Gironde entre 1876 and 1902*, master's thesis in history, Université Bordeaux-III, 1985, p. 75.
58. *Le Nouvelliste*, May 4, 6, 7, 19, and 22, 1898.
59. *Braves gens de La Rousselle,*
    De Talence et d'autres lieux,
    Apprenez le crime odieux
    Qu'en son audace cruelle
    A commis un scélérat
    Plus criminel que Marat!

    Dans Bordeaux, la métropole,
    Vivait un homme de bien,
    Ami des Juifs, bon chrétien,
    Qui débitait du pétrole,
    Sans odeur et, paraît-il,
    Recommandé par Rothschild.

    Gruet était son vocable,
    Habillé come un milord
    Plus chouette que Félix Faur'!
    Sa barbe était délectable,
    Il savait, c'est ça l'écueil,
    Porter le monocle à l'oeil!

    L'autre soir, c'était dimanche
    Vingt-deux du mois de mai,
    Respirant l'air embaumé,
    Nez au vent, point sur la hanche.
    Par hygiène circulait
    L'excellent M. Gruet.

    Le hasard de la promenade
    L'amène par un temps sec
    Au coin de Mériadeck!

Ah! Seigneur, qu'il est malade
Car l'assassin aussitôt
Se présente incognito.

C'était un très petit homme,
Mais robuste et fort râblé,
Vaillant et bien découplé;
C'est Bernard qu'on le dénomme.
Abordant le promeneur,
Il lui dit: N'ayez pas peur!

Je ne suis pas un escarpe,
Je suis pharmacien au coin
Pour vous servir au besoin,
Je ne veux que votre écharpe
Et votre médaille aussi.
Cédez-les-moi sans souci!

Il faut que le populaire
Soit enfin représenté,
Je dois être député.

Pour dissimuler son crime,
Ce Bernard, être infernal,
Met le corps dans un bocal
Ainsi qu'un foetus infime,
Le bouche hermétiquement
Sans crainte du châtiment!

En dépit de son astuce,
Le coupable est arrêté.
Mais à la majorité,
Aux accents de l'hymne russe,
Le grand juge Populo
Rend un verdict rigolo.

Par huit mille voix cinquante,
Il condamne sans retard
L'accusé Charles Bernard,
Dont l'attitude est choquante,
A cinq ans de détention
En chambre au Palais-Bourbon.

Moralité:

Petits enfants de l'école,
Vous, parents, vous, gens d'ici,
Apprenez par ce récit
Que les marchands de pétrole
Doivent, selon les anciens
Se méfier des pharmaciens!

AD Gironde, 3 M 243.

60. AD Gironde, I M 431. See Pierre Birnbaum, *Destins juifs* (Paris: Calmann-Lévy, 1995), translated by Arthur Goldhammer as *Jewish Destinies: Citizenship, State, and Community in Modern France* (New York: Hill and Wang, 2000), chap. 4; and below, Chapter 10.

61. *La Citadelle Blayaise*, October 27, 1898.

62. AD Gironde, 3 M 244.

63. *Le Médocain*, May 8, 1898.

64. Alain Bentejac, "Opinion et vie politique dans l'arrondissement de Bazas, 1885–1904," *Les Cahiers du Bazadais* I (1979): 8 and 13.

65. See Jocelyne George, "Provinciales: La France aux quatre coins," in Pierre Birnbaum, ed., *La France de l'affaire Dreyfus* (Paris: Gallimard, 1994), p. 131. See also the large file on Libourne, AD Gironde, 3 M 344, where many prejudices against foreigners who "suck out the gold and blood of France" nevertheless surface.

Chapter 6: Take Arms, Citizens of Vendée!

1. AN, F7 12460.

2. AD Maine-et-Loire, 4 M 6/2. On Sarthe, see Jean Connier, "Le journal de Château-du-Loir: La Sarthe et l'affaire Dreyfus," *Cahiers Fléchois* 9 (1988). In Mayenne, Monsignor Geay praised "the people, who protest in enormous masses against the intrigues of the Sanhedrin and the insulters of the army; the people, who do not believe that torrents of gold can absolve a crime and cleanse a traitor." In his report the prefect wrote that "the vast majority of residents of this department consider the review of the case to be a measure directed against the army. From the beginning, the question has been distorted . . . The population was told that all those who asked for a review were Jews and opponents of the army. The population, which accepts simple ideas more easily, believed it." Quoted in Michel Denis, *L'Eglise et la République en Mayenne, 1896–1906* (Paris: Klincksieck, 1967), p. 59.

3. Loïc Beziau, *Les élections législatives de 1898 en Maine-et-Loire*, master's thesis in history, Tours, Université François-Rabelais, 1990, p. 134.

4. *La Vendée*, January 23, 1898.

5. *Le Patriote de l'Ouest*, April 22, 1898.

6. Ibid., January 29, 1898.

7. Renée Beyens, *Antijudaïsme et antisémitisme dans le Maine-et-Loire: L'affaire Dreyfus*, master's thesis in history, Université d'Angers, 1966, p. 41.

8. Manvelle Benuteau, *L'Affaire Dreyfus: La sensibilité des républicains analysée dans deux quotidiens angevins*, master's thesis in history, Angers, Université Catholique, 1996.

9. Thierry Coutant, *Une crise de la République au pays des Blancs: L'affaire Dreyfus dans le Maine-et-Loire, 1898–1902*, master's thesis in history, Université Paris I, 1995, pp. 50–51, 66.

10. AD Maine-et-Loire, I M 6/55.

11. AD Maine-et-Loire, 4 M 6 and 3 M 304.

12. AN, F7 12463.

13. AD Maine-et-Loire, 4 M 6.

14. AD Maine-et-Loire, 4 M 53. According to a superintendent's report dated April 15, 1898, "people are still preoccupied with the Zola-Dreyfus obsession; the public would like to be delivered of it, with a stroke of the pen or of the saber." AD Maine-et-Loire, 3 M 304.

15. Ibid.

16. AD Maine-et-Loire, 2 V 24.

17. *Le Journal du Maine-et-Loire*, May 8, 1898.

18. Ibid., January 23, 1898.

19. Beziau, *Les élections législatives de 1898 en Maine-et-Loire*, p. 135.

20. *La Croix Angevine*, May 4, 1898.

21. AD Maine-et-Loire, 3 M 304.

22. Ibid.

23. Ibid.

24. Ibid.

25. Ibid.

26. Ibid.

27. Beyens, *Antijudaïsme et antisémitisme dans le Maine-et-Loire*, pp. 115–16.

28. AD Maine-et-Loire, I M 6/55.

29. Alain Jacobzone, discussing Grandmaison's political career, wrote, strangely, "It was truly by insisting on his tolerant republican but not clerical platform, conservative of the order but not immobile, that Georges de Grandmaison installed himself and, with himself, the Republic. To be sure, he was from Saumur, and Saumur was not Cholet. For all sorts of reasons, which André Siegfried has already elucidated, the Republic found a favorable climate there, but on certain conditions . . . It was Georges de Grandmaison, therefore, who would definitively transform the experiment by getting elected as a republican, but in his own way. And his way was undoubtedly the right one. In Anjou acceptance of new ideas depended on respect for society's beliefs, modes of operation, and structure. There was always an adjustment to the mild climate of Anjou" ("Georges de

Grandmaison et la République dans le Saumurois, 1893–1914," *Annales de Bretagne* [1992]: 487–88).

30. AN, F7 12461. General Auguste Mercier was Minister of War. He was linked to the nationalist right.

31. I am influenced here by Jean-Jacques Tatin-Gourier, regarding the representations of the Dreyfus affair in the press in France and abroad: "L'affaire Dreyfus dans la presse d'Indre-et-Loire," *Littérature et Nation*, special issue (1997).

32. AN, F7 12460.

33. AN, F7 12467.

34. Ibid.

35. Jacques Bodineau, *L'Affaire Dreyfus et le sénateur Mercier à Nantes*, Diplôme d'Etudes Supérieures in history, school of letters and human sciences of Nantes, 1962, p. 76; AD Loire-Atlantique, 2679 AI 788.

36. *La Fronde*, January 29, 1898.

37. AD Loire-Inférieure, I M 604, and AN, F7 12467.

38. *L'Espérance du Peuple*, January 23, 1898.

39. *Le Soleil*, January 26, 1898.

40. AD Loire-Inférieure, I M 625, AN, F7 12460.

41. Bodineau, *L'Affaire Dreyfus et le sénateur Mercier à Nantes*, p. 31.

42. AD Loire-Inférieure, I M 604.

43. *Au général Mercier qui mit nos coeurs en fête,*
    Quand la France tremblante alla le supplier,
    Vous donnerez vos voix, Bretons que rien n'arrête,
    Bretons que rien ne dompte et rien ne fait plier!
    Vous jetterez nombreux dans l'urne vengeresse
    Cette arme de combat placée dans votre main,
    Et les fils de Judas, cette race traîtresse,
    Pâliront en voyant votre élu de demain.

44. *L'Espérance du Peuple*, January 28, 1900.

45. AN, F7 12460.

46. AD Loire-Inférieure, I M 625 and AN, F7 12460.

47. *L'Espérance du Peuple*, December 14, 1898.

48. AN, F7 12460.

49. *Capitaines vaseux, gentillâtres dévots,*
    Et les sous-offs et les vicaires aux pieds sales
    Devant Grimaux ferment leur salle.
    Et tous, avec transport, beuglent comme des veaux.
    Car la province, dont les moeurs sont étonnantes,
    Prise Judet, Boisdeffre et Pellieux aussi,
    Les miracles de Lourdes et l'ange Esterhazy
    Conjouissent le coeur imbécile de Nantes.
    C'est pourquoi les marchands de thon, les hobereaux
    Se rebiffent à la manière des taureaux,

Abominant le Juif sur la Loire et sur l'Erdre.
L'eau bénite leur est un "sortilège bu."
Ce qu'on leur voit d'esprit court en Drumont se perdre.
A ses causes, il sied de dire, tel Ubu,
Pour la rime et pour la raison: Vive l'armèrdre.

Le Nouvelliste de l'Ouest, June 5, 1898.

50. Ibid., August 5, 1898; *Le Petit Journal,* August 5, 1898.

51. As an anecdote, let me note, maliciously, that within that moralistic atmosphere the press reported the death of Abbé Loyer, a native of the region, who had participated in the restoration of the wayside cross of Pontchâteau, his birthplace. The young Mathiot "eluded the touch of that sodomist-in-a-cassock by shooting him with a revolver . . . One fine night Mathiot, the son of the sexton, distraught, panic-stricken, found himself in the bedroom of the ogre-in-a-cassock. The latter pursued him, finally flung himself upon him. Mathiot had an impulse of supreme revolt: he grabbed his revolver and struck down the priest" (*L'Aurore,* December 15, 1898).

52. *L'Antijuif Nantais,* October 1, 1898.

53. AD Loire-Inférieure, I M 625, I M 604, and AN, F7 12460; *L'Univers Israélite,* January 28, 1898.

54. *La Vendée,* February 27, 1898.

55. AD Vendée, 4 M 2.

56. AD Vendée, 4 M 158.

57. AD Vendée, I M 445 and 4 M 178.

58. *L'Etoile de la Vendée,* January 16 and 23, and February 3, 1898.

59. *La Vendée,* January 16 and 19, and February 23, 1898.

60. *L'Electeur Vendéen,* April 23, 1898.

61. "Un député face à son époque: Le marquis de Lespinay," *Recherches Vendéennes* I (1994).

62. AD Vendée, 4 M 182.

63. *La Vendée,* April 24 and 29, and May 4, 1898.

64. AN, F7 12461.

65. AD Charente-Maritime, 4 M 5 46.

66. AD Charente-Maritime, 2 M 423.

67. *L'Indépendance de la Charente,* February 4 and 26, 1898; *La Charente-Inférieure,* January 15, 1898.

Chapter 7: The Battle of Brest

1. AN, F7 12460.
2. See AD Finistère, 11 T 252.

3. *L'Express de Brest*, January 2, 1899.

4. AD Finistère, Dreyfus file, unnumbered.

5. *L'Express de Brest*, January 23, 1898.

6. *L'Etoile de la Mer*, January 23, 1898.

7. *Le Journal de Rennes*, January 31, 1898, and AN, F7 12467.

8. *L'Union Malouine et Dinannaise*, January 30, 1898.

9. *La Libre Parole*, January 27, 1898; see also AN, F7 12467.

10. *L'Union Malouine et Dinannaise*, January 31, 1898.

11. AN, F7 12460.

12. AN, F7 12474, January 30, 1898; see also *Le Journal de Rennes*, February 2, 1898.

13. *L'Union Malouine et Dinannaise*, February 6, 1898.

14. AD Ille-et-Vilaine, I M 145.

15. *Le Journal de Rennes*, January 18, 19, and 20, 1898; *Le Petit Rennais*, January 20 and 21, 1898; *Nouvelles Rennaises*, January 17, 18, and 19, 1898.

16. *Le Journal de Rennes*, January 22, 1898.

17. AD Ille-et-Vilaine, 11 T 252. My thanks to the curator of the archives of Ille-et-Villaine for being kind enough to point out to me the existence of this very rich and unclassified file.

18. Ibid.

19. André Hélard, "Un universitaire à Rennes au temps de l'affaire Dreyfus: Les lettres d'Henri Sée à André-Ferdinand Hérold," *Société d'Archéologie d'Ille-et-Villaine* 49 (1996).

20. *Le Patriote Breton*, July 26, 1899.

21. AD Ille-et-Vilaine, I M 145.

22. *L'Avenir Hebdomadaire*, July 16, 1899. On the Dreyfus trial in Rennes and the demonstrations during that period, see Prosper Jardin, "L'affaire Dreyfus à Rennes," *Bulletin et Mémoire de la Société Archéologique du Départment d'Ille-et-Vilaine* 81 (1979). As for the letter from Victor Basch, his wife is quoted in Françoise Basch, "Victor Basch, chef des dreyfusards de Rennes," in Michel Denis, Michel Lagrée, and Jean-Yves Veillard, eds., *L'Affaire Dreyfus et l'opinion publique* (Rennes: Presses Universitaires de Rennes, 1995), p. 84. The list of people arrested and convicted is in AD Ille-et-Vilaine, I M 145.

23. Ibid.

24. AN, F7 12460.

25. Marie-Thérèse Quéré, *L'élection de l'abbé Gayraud dans la 3ᵉ circonscription de Brest en 1897*, Diplôme d'Etudes Supérieures in history, school of letters of Paris, 1965, and AD Finistère, 3 M 295.

26. AD Ille-et-Vilaine, 3 M 399.

27. Ibid.

28. Maurice Lucas, *L'évolution politique de la Cornouaille maritime sous la IIIᵉ République*, doctoral thesis (3d cycle) in history, Brest, Université de Bretagne Occidentale, n.d., pp. 493–95.

29. AD Finistère, 3 M 294.
30. *La Résistance (Croix de Morlaix),* April 30 and May 14, 1898.
31. AD Ille-et-Vilaine, I M 182.

Chapter 8: In the Region of Normandy

1. AD Seine-Maritime, 4 M 2710.
2. Ibid.
3. Ibid.
4. *Le Patriote de Normandie,* January 20 and 21, 1898.
5. *La Semaine Religieuse du Diocèse de Rouen,* January 19, 22, and 29, 1898; AD Seine-Maritime, JPL 14/32.
6. *Le Patriote de Normandie,* January 22 and 28, 1898.
7. Ibid., February 9, 1898.
8. AD Seine-Maritime, 4 M 2710.
9. Ibid. See also AN, F7 12461.
10. *Le Petit Rouennais,* April 2, 1898.
11. *L'Antijuif Nantais,* September 15, 1898.
12. *Le Patriote de Normandie,* April 10, 1898.
13. *La Semaine Religieuse du Diocèse de Rouen,* May 7, 1898.
14. AD Seine-Maritime, 3 M 328.
15. AN, F7 12461.
16. AD Seine-Maritime, 4 M 2710.
17. AD Seine-Maritime, 4 M 2711.
18. AD Seine-Maritime, 4 M 2710; AN, F7 12461. See also *Le Patriote de Normandie,* March 2, 1898.
19. *L'Impartial de Dieppe,* February 26, 1898; *La Dieppoise,* February 27, 1898.
20. AD Seine-Maritime, 3 M 324.
21. AD Seine-Maritime, 3 M 329.
22. AD Seine-Maritime, 4 M 2710.
23. Ibid.
24. *L'Echo de Neufchâtel,* April 16, 1898; *Le Journal de Neufchâtel,* May 17, 1898.
25. AD Seine-Maritime, 4 M 2710; *Le Patriote de Normandie,* January 22, 1898.
26. Ibid.
27. Ibid.
28. *La Croix du Calvados,* January 17 and 23, 1898; *Le Moniteur du Calvados,* January 19 and 28, 1898; see also *Le Bonhomme Normand,* January 21 and 28, 1898.
29. AN, F7 12467; *La Croix du Calvados,* January 30, 1898.
30. Ibid., February 6, 1898, and AD Calvados, M 2979.
31. These details of daily life were gleaned at random from several local dailies and police reports. The biweekly report cited is dated March 4, 1898; AD Calvados, M 2979.

32. AD Calvados, M 2878.

33. Michelle Perrot, "Note sur le catholicisme dans le Calvados au début de la IIIᵉ République: Les cercles d'ouvriers; l'abbé Garnier," *Annales de Normandie* (October–December 1957).

34. *La Croix du Calvados*, February 6 and 12, 1898. It also describes, for example, on February 27, "the dark Jewish stores and their stinking back rooms."

35. *La Croix du Calvados*, March 16 and May 1, 1898.

36. Ibid., February 20 and March 27, 1898.

37. *L'Antijuif*, September 15, 1898.

38. AD Calvados, M 2979.

39. *Le Patriote de Normandie*, February 13, 1898; *La Croix du Calvados*, December 4, 1898.

40. *Le Bonhomme Normand*, February 25, 1898.

41. AD Calvados, M 2979.

Chapter 9: Good Superintendent Leproust: Peacekeeping and Prejudice Among the Police

1. AN, F7 12461. This incident occurred on November 15, 1898.

2. AN, F7 12460.

3. AN, F7 12463. This was November 1898.

4. AN, F7 12460. This report dates from February 1898.

5. AD Meurthe-et-Moselle, 3 M 85.

6. AN, F7 12474.

7. "Boulangisme et antisémitisme: Affaire Dreyfus," AN, F7 12459.

8. AN, F7 12451. Similarly, the police superintendent of Blamont, near Lunéville, observed that "despite the efforts of a few agitators, the population is not at all the dupe of the misunderstanding the reactionary leaders would like to create, by hiding behind the mask of anti-Semitism" (AD Meurthe-et-Moselle, 3 M 85).

9. *L'Express*, January 19, 1898.

10. AD Gard, 1 M 635.

11. AN, F7 12461.

12. APP, Ba 1107, and AN, F7 12459.

13. AN, F7 12461.

14. See the very complete press files in AN, F7 12461, and APP, Ba 1105.

15. APP, Ba 1104 and Ba 1105. These files also include police reports, the almost complete minutes of the November trial (103 pages), and press clippings dealing with the two Guérin trials.

16. AN, F7 12467.

17. See Chapter 7.

18. On Paris, see APP, Ba 1044; on Toulouse, AD Haute-Garonne, 4 M 113; on Dijon, AD Côte-d'Or, 20 M 188; on Avignon, AN, F7 12474.

19. Ibid.
20. APP, Ba 1103.
21. Ibid.
22. AN, F7 12461.
23. Ibid.
24. *La Fronde*, January 27, 1898.
25. See Chapter 10.
26. *L'Univers Israélite*, March 4, 1898. The cited excerpts from *Le Rappel* can be found there.
27. *La Croix*, January 18, 1898.
28. Joseph Reinach, *Histoire de l'Affaire Dreyfus* (Paris: Editions de la Revue Blanche, 1903), 3:349.
29. AN, F7 12461.
30. AD Ille-et-Vilaine, I M 145. See, for example, the reports of December 24, 1898, and July 30, 1899.
31. APP, Ba 1044.
32. AN, F7 12460.
33. APP, Ba 1043.
34. AN, F7 12461 and 12474.
35. AN, F7 12467.
36. AD Haute-Garonne, 4 M 113.
37. *Gil Blas*, February 12, 1898.
38. *Le Peuple*, January 20, 1898.
39. *Gil Blas*, February 11, 1898.
40. *Le Radical*, October 3, 1898; *Le Rappel*, October 5, 1898; *La Lanterne*, October 4, 1898; *La Petite République*, October 3, 1898; *L'Aurore*, October 3 and 4, 1898; *La Libre Parole*, October 3 and 10, 1898.

Chapter 10: The "Arrogance" of Rabbi Taubmann: Passivity and Resistance Among the Jews

1. AD Meuse, I I 36.
2. *Les Archives Israélites*, March 3, 1898.
3. AN, F7 12461.
4. *De la juiverie*
   Ce sont les millions
   Qui dans not'patrie
   Soutiennent les espions.
   France bien-aimée,
   Veux-tu revivre enfin?
   Chasse de l'armée
   Tout c'qu'est nez youpin.

Les Juifs sont les maîtres
Grâce à leur pognon,
Y a de ces traîtres,
Même au quai Bourbon.
Chez nous tout ça mange.
Nous, on meurt de faim.
Y a pas, faut que ça change.
Sans ça c'est la fin.

Y a pas d'erreur, Dreyfus est seul coupable.
Il a beau crier
Pleurer, supplier,
Il ne reviendra jamais de l'îlot du Diable,
Il y restera jusqu'à ce qu'il crève du choléra.

AD Meuse, I I 36 and AN, F7 12461. See Jocelyne George, "Provinciales: La France aux quatre coins," in Pierre Birnbaum, ed., *La France de l'affaire Dreyfus* (Paris: Gallimard, 1994), pp. 122ff.

5. *L'Impartial de Nancy*, March 9, 1898.
6. These quotations are all found in the same file, AN, F7 12461.
7. *L'Univers Israélite*, March 4, 1898.
8. AD Meuse, 33 M 32. See also *La Croix de l'Est*, February 26, 1898.
9. Michel Salviac, "La carrière politique des frères Develle," *Bulletin des Sociétés d'Histoire et d'Archéologie de la Meuse* 4 (1977).
10. Pierre Birnbaum, *Les fous de la République: Histoire des Juifs d'Etat, de Gambetta à Vichy* (Paris: Fayard, 1992), translated by Jane Marie Todd as *Jews of the Republic: A Political History of State Jews from Gambetta to Vichy* (Stanford: Stanford University Press, 1996).
11. Léon Blum, *Souvenirs sur l'Affaire* (Paris: Gallimard, 1981), p. 67; Hannah Arendt, *The Origins of Totalitarianism* (San Diego: Harcourt Brace Jovanovitch, 1979). Similarly, Michael Marrus writes, "The weight of evidence seems to lie with those who believed that the predominant Jewish response was a passive one, and that Jews tended to refrain from any involvement at all." (*The Politics of Assimilation: A Study of the French Jewish Community at the Time of the Dreyfus Affair* [Oxford: Clarendon Press, 1971], p. 205.)
12. See Pierre Birnbaum, "Les Juifs entre intégration et résistance," in Birnbaum, ed., *La France de l'affaire Dreyfus*.
13. *L'Univers Israélite*, July 20, 1906.
14. See Stephen Wilson, *Ideology and Experience: Antisemitism in France at the Time of the Dreyfus Affair* (London: Associated University Press, 1982). Let us note that, in the chapter entitled "Antisemitism and Jewish Response," Wilson presents none of the facts of the Jewish resistance, analyzed here on the basis of local and not national archives, and at the same time he underestimates the Jews' will to confront anti-Semitism.

15. AD Seine-Maritime, 4 M 2710.
16. AD Bouches-du-Rhône, I M 1415.
17. Ibid.
18. AN, F7 12467.
19. Ibid.
20. *Les Archives Israélites*, June 2, 1898.
21. AN, F7 12460.
22. *L'Univers Israélite*, January 27, 1898.
23. AD Meurthe-et-Moselle, I M 635.
24. Ibid.
25. *Le Journal de la Meurthe et des Vosges*, January 25, 1898.
26. *La Croix de l'Est*, January 21, 1898.
27. *L'Est Républicain*, November 28, 1898.
28. *La Croix de l'Est*, January 26, 1898.
29. AN, F7 12461.
30. *L'Univers Israélite*, July 22, 1898.
31. AN, F7 12467.
32. Ibid.
33. *Le Patriote Orléanais*, January 23 and 24, 1898.
34. AN Doubs, M 788.
35. AN, F7 12461.
36. AN, F7 12460.
37. AD Loire-Inférieure, I M 625.
38. AD Loire-Inférieure, I M 604.
39. AD Bouches-du-Rhône, I M 415.
40. AN, F7 12467.
41. Ibid.
42. AD Hérault, 39 M 286.
43. AN, F7 12467.
44. AD Haute-Garonne, 4 M 113.
45. AN, F7 12463.
46. APP, Ba 1105; *L'Antijuif*, October 16 and November 29, 1898; *Le Siècle*, April 12, 1898.
47. AN, F7 12474.
48. *L'Univers Israélite*, February 18, 1898.
49. APP, Ba 1052.
50. APP, Ba 1048.
51. APP, Ba 222.
52. Geneviève Dermenjian, *Juifs et Européans d'Algérie: L'antisémitisme oranais (1892–1905)* (Jerusalem: Institut Ben Zvi, 1983); Pierre Hebey, *Alger 1898: La grande vague antisémite* (Paris: NiL, 1996).
53. AN, F7 12463.
54. *L'Univers Israélite*, January 18, 1898.

55. *Les Archives Israélites*, February 17, 1898.

56. Ibid., February 3, 1898.

57. Ibid., January 27, 1898.

58. *Les Archives Israélites*, February 3, 1898. On January 20, 1898, Uhry wrote in *Les Archives Israélites*, "There are fanatical Catholic clubs, clubs of anti-Semites; why couldn't the Israelite youth of Paris form action groups composed of educated men of good will to combat the unhealthy doctrines of all those sectarians? For each attack, a counterattack . . . Be of good cheer! Activity, courage, action, devotion. Let us wage the good fight for the Kiddushe Hashem, the good name of Israel; and the beautiful sky of France, momentarily darkened for us, will recover its radiant brilliance."

59. *L'Univers Israélite*, January 7, 1898.

60. Ibid., January 28, 1898.

61. Ibid. Louis Lévy wrote in a similar vein, on January 21, 1898, "I like to believe that the Jews are resolved to demonstrate their virility" (ibid.).

62. Ibid., June 22, 1898. On July 1, 1898, the newspaper wrote, "Let us be strong and virile men."

63. Ibid., June 3, 1898.

64. Ibid., June 10, 1898.

65. APP, Ba 1301.

66. Minutes of the Consistory, I E 6, no. 5.

67. *L'Univers Israélite*, June 23, 1902.

68. APP, Ba 1044.

69. Archives of the consistory of Paris, file 66. Roger Kohn does a remarkable job of presenting these documents in a too-little-known article, "Les racines de l'émancipation: La communauté juive pendant le procès Zola," *Les Nouveaux Cahiers* 57 (Summer 1979): 17–18.

70. *Les Archives Israélites*, July 14, 1898.

71. Archives of the Alliance Israélite Universelle, France, XII-A-I.

72. *L'Univers Israélite*, April 8 and 22, and July 22, 1898.

73. *Les Archives Israélites*, May 5, 1898.

74. *L'Univers Israélite*, May 13 and 27, and June 10, 1898. See also the more optimistic observations of Henri Prague in *Les Archives Israélites*, May 12, 1898.

75. Ibid., June 9, 1898.

Conclusion

1. Alain Corbin, *The Village of Cannibals: Rage and Murder in France, 1870* (Cambridge: Harvard University Press, 1992), translated by Arthur Goldhammer.

2. Charles Tilly, *The Contentious French* (Cambridge, Mass.: Belknap Press, 1986), chap. 11.

3. Pierre Milza, *Voyage en Ritalie* (Paris: Plon, 1993), chap. 4; José Cubero, *Nationalistes et étrangers: Le massacre d'Aigues-Mortes* (Paris: Imago, 1996).

4. For a comparison of the fate of the Italians and Jews of the time, see Pierre Birnbaum, *Destins juifs* (Paris: Calmann-Lévy, 1995), translated by Arthur Goldhammer as *Jewish Destinies: Citizenship, State, and Community in Modern France* (New York: Hill and Wang, 2000), chap. 9.

5. Pierre Nora, "1898: Le thème du complot et la définition de l'identité juive," in Maurice Olender, ed., *Le racisme, mythes et sciences* (Bruxelles: Complexe, 1981).

Index